# Devī Māhātmya
The Crystallization of the Goddess Tradition

# Devī-Māhātmya

## The Crystallization of the Goddess Tradition

Thomas B. Coburn

*With a Foreword by*
Daniel H. H. Ingalls

MOTILAL BANARSIDASS
*Delhi Varanasi Patna*
*Bangalore Madras*

*First Edition: 1984*
*Reprinted: 1988*

MOTILAL BANARSIDASS
Bungalow Road, Jawahar Nagar, Delhi 110 007

*Branches*
Chowk, Varanasi 221 001
Ashok Rajpath, Patna 800 004
24 Race Course Road, Bangalore 560 001
120 Royapettah High Road, Mylapore, Madras 600 004



ISBN: 81-208-0557-7



PRINTED IN INDIA
BY JAINENDRA PRAKASH JAIN AT SHRI JAINENDRA PRESS, A-45 NARAINA INDUSTRIAL AREA, PHASE I, NEW DELHI 110 028 AND PUBLISHED BY NARENDRA PRAKASH JAIN FOR MOTILAL BANARSIDASS, DELHI 110 007

For Cynthia

# Foreword

Among the most puzzling questions in the study of Indian religion is that concerning the historical background of the Goddess. It is true of course that we can pursue no religion to its ultimate source, for the source of religion must be as old as the origin of man and the first men did not write books or leave archaeological records. But the history, let us say, of Viṣṇu worship, or Śiva worship, has been traced back through a series of texts to the oldest religious work of India, the Rigveda. The religion of Devī, on the other hand, while there is circumstantial evidence for supposing it to be equally old, has scarcely been traced textually back of the fifth century A.D.

This discrepancy has often been remarked on by scholars, both Indian and Western, who have generally agreed in their explanation. The worship of Devī, they say, or Ambā or Umā or Pārvatī, Gaurī, Kālī, Durgā—for she has as many names as her male counterparts—is a cultural gift from pre-Aryan India. Our oldest written texts, on the other hand, come from the Aryan invaders. The Aryans, to judge from the Vedic literature, directed their worship almost solely to male divinities. The dawn-goddess Uṣas, or such sacrificial abstractions as Ilā or Bhāratī, occupy a very subordinate position in the overall picture of Vedic religion. It is only after the two cultures, Aryan and non-Aryan, had intermingled that the Goddess becomes textually prominent, however prominent she may have been in popular, pre-literate culture before that time.

The explanation is sound enough, I dare say, so far as I have stated it. But it has sometimes served as a basis for inferences and judgments that are false. One must not identify the religion of Devī as it is found in modern India, or even as it is found in the vulgate text of the Mahābhārata, with non-Aryan India. The cultural intermingling that took place in India must have transformed the nature of pre-Aryan religion. The Devī that we find in her famous Māhātmya is enriched with all sorts of Vedic concepts and notions. She is no more identifiable with one half of the Indian community than is Viṣṇu or Śiva with the other. In all three cases borrowings and superimpositions have altered the older monoethnical character.

Professor Coburn's book sheds much light on this process of adaptation and growth. He has sought out the earliest occurrence of virtually every epithet and myth attributed to the Goddess in the famous *Devīmāhātmya*, the earliest literary work in which the character of the Goddess as she is still conceived and still worshipped stands fully revealed. How many of these epithets are drawn from India's Vedic heritage, how many of these myths are shared with other figures of the epic pantheon, will come as a surprise, I think, to most readers, as it did to me.

Our curiosity concerning Devī will probably never be satisfied by a textual account of Goddess worship in India from the period before the Christian era. Even if the Indus Valley seals are someday translated, in a translation that two people can agree on, how much would these brief inscriptions be likely to tell us? Meanwhile we may be thankful to Professor Coburn. To many corners of the Devī tradition he brings light for the first time. By the use of a carefully developed method of scriptural analysis he permits us to see in an earlier form many traits of the culturally composite Goddess who has been worshipped in India for the past millenium and a half. Her character begins to take on a historical dimension which has hitherto been reserved in India to the great masculine gods. This illumination is a notable scholarly achievement.

Cambridge, Mass.
May, 1982

Daniel H. H. Ingalls

# Acknowledgements

During the course of the decade in which this study has moved from conception to dissertation to book, many people have contributed to its accomplishment. It is my very real pleasure to express a word of appreciation to the foremost among them.

It was Professor Wilfred Cantwell Smith who first enabled me to see the convergence of professional and personal concerns in a way that indicated the appropriateness of graduate work in the field of comparative religion. Though I did not deliberately set out to incorporate his thinking into this study, I have found it exceedingly helpful at a number of points. Professor Daniel H. H. Ingalls initiated me into the study of Sanskrit and then guided this study. He has given bibliographic advice, improved translations, deleted infelicities and offered encouragement with both kindness and erudition. It is fitting that he write a Foreword to this volume, and I am grateful to him for doing so. Professors John B. Carman and J. L. Mehta read early portions of this study and offered helpful comments on the theoretical issues involved. The late Professor Benjamin M. Rowland, Jr. developed my sensitivity to the artistic expression of Indian religiousness and, by introducing me to the splendid Mahiṣāsuramardinī in the Boston Museum of Fine Arts, is responsible for the particular topic of this study. Various people at Harvard's Center for the Study of World Religions have offered stimulating commentary, and Professor Alaka Hejib, in particular, has kindly shared her expertise in Vedic Sanskrit.

The former and present Deans at St. Lawrence University, Drs. D. Kenneth Baker, Donald C. Peckham, and George H. Gibson, have been very generous with their encouragement and support, as has the chairman of the Department of Religious Studies and Classical Languages, Professor Daniel W. O'Connor, Jr. The Interlibrary Loan staff at St. Lawrence has shown a much appreciated tenacity and ingenuity. Maria Cedargren has typed with great skill and care.

I am indebted to Cambridge University Press for permission to include material from my "The Study of the Purāṇas and the Study of Religion," *Religious Studies* 16-3 (Sept.1980), and to Berkeley Religious Studies Series for permission to include material from my "Consort of None, *Śakti* of All: The Vision of the *Devī-Māhātmya*." The Museum of Fine Arts, Boston has kindly consented to the appearance on the cover of a photograph of the sculpture that first prompted my study of the Goddess. Most recently, it has been a pleasure to work with Messrs. N. P. Jain of Motilal Banarsidass and Dr. N. G. Barrier of South Asia Books.

Finally, my inadequacy in expressing my thanks to my parents, who have given counsel and support in many ways through the years, is matched only by my utter incompetence in acknowledging the role of my wife Cynthia. Even her knowledge of the extent of my indebtedness to her is only approximate.

Boston, Mass,
July, 1982

Thomas B, Coburn

# Contents

# Abbreviations

| | | |
|---|---|---|
| AiA | — | *Aitareya Āraṇyaka* |
| AiB | — | *Aitareya Brāhmaṇa* |
| AiU | — | *Aitareya Upaniṣad* |
| AV | — | *Atharva Veda*, Śaunaka recension |
| BDŚ | — | *Baudhāyana Dharma Śāstra* |
| BGS | — | *Baudhāyana Gṛhya Sūtra* |
| BU | — | *Bṛhadāraṇyaka Upaniṣad* |
| BṛDe | — | *Bṛhad Devatā* |
| CU | — | *Chāndogya Upaniṣad* |
| DM | — | *Devī-Māhātmya* |
| Gītā | — | *Bhagavad Gītā* |
| GoB | — | *Gopatha Brāhmaṇa* |
| HV | — | *Harivaṃśa* |
| HOS | — | Harvard Oriental Series |
| IHQ | — | *Indian Historical Quarterly* |
| Jag | — | Jagaddhitecchu edition of MarkP |
| JAOS | — | *Journal of the American Oriental Society* |
| JB | — | *Jaiminīya Brāhmaṇa* |
| JBORS | — | *Journal of the Bihar and Orissa Research Society* |
| JGS | — | *Jaiminīya Gṛhya Sūtra* |
| JUB | — | *Jaiminīya Upaniṣad Brāhmaṇa* |
| KāGS | — | *Kāṭhaka Gṛhya Sūtra* |
| KeU | — | *Kena Upaniṣad* |
| KU | — | *Kaṭha Upaniṣad* |
| MāGS | — | *Mānava Gṛhya Sūtra* |
| MaiU | — | *Maitri Upaniṣad* |
| MarkP | — | *Mārkaṇḍeya Purāṇa* |
| MB | — | *Mantra Brāhmaṇa* |
| Mbh | — | *Mahābhārata* |
| MU | — | *Māṇḍukya Upaniṣad* |
| MuU | — | *Muṇḍaka Upaniṣad* |

| | | |
|---|---|---|
| P | — | *Purāṇa* |
| PU | — | *Praśna Upanisad* |
| PW | — | ("Peterburg Wörtersbuch") Bohtlingk and Roth, *Sanskrit Wörterbuch* |
| Rām | — | *Rāmāyaṇa* |
| RV | — | *Ṛg Veda* |
| RVK | — | *Ṛg Veda Khila* |
| ŚāṅA | — | *Śāṅkhāyana Āraṇyaka* |
| ŚāṅB | — | *Śāṅkhāyana Brāhmaṇa* |
| ŚāṅGS | — | *Śāṅkhāyana Gṛhya Sūtra* |
| ŚB | — | *Śatapatha Brāhmaṇa* |
| SBE | — | Sacred Books of the East |
| ŚDS | — | *Śāṅkha-likhita Dharma Sūtra* |
| SK | — | *Sāṃkhya Kārikā* |
| ŚU | — | *Śvetāśvatara Upaniṣad* |
| TA | — | *Taittirīya Āraṇyaka* |
| TāṇB | — | *Tāṇḍya Brāhmaṇa* |
| TB | — | *Taittirīya Brāhmaṇa* |
| TU | — | *Taittirīya Upaniṣad* |
| VaiDS | — | *Vaikhānasa Dharma Sūtra* |
| VaiGS | — | *Vaikhānasa Gṛhya Sūtra* |
| VDS | — | *Viṣṇu Dharma Sūtra* |
| Veṅk | — | Veṅkateśvara edition of MarkP |
| Vid | — | Jīvānanda Vidyāsāgara edition of MarkP |
| VPK | — | *Vaidika-padānukrama-koṣa* |
| YV | — | *Yajur Veda* |
| YVKā | — | Kāṭhaka recension of the YV |
| YVKāṇ | — | Kāṇva recension of the YV |
| YVKap | — | Kapiṣṭhala-kaṭha recension of the YV |
| YVMā | — | Mādhyandina recension of the YV |
| YVMai | — | Maitrāyanīya recension of the YV |
| YVT | — | Taittirīya recension of the YV |
| ZDMG | — | *Zeitschrift der Deutschen Morgenländischen Gesellschaft* |

# Prolegomenon

## 1. *Introduction*

The central concern of this study is with a text from classical India. More specifically, it is with the vision of the ultimate reality in the universe that is articulated in the *Devī-Māhātmya* (DM). This text forms a portion of one of the early Sanskrit Purāṇas, the *Mārkaṇḍeya* (Mark P), probably dates from the fifth or sixth century C.E.[1], and yet has, to the present day, an independent liturgical life of its own. The outstanding feature of its vision is that the ultimate reality is understood as female, as the Goddess.

At first glance, the pertinence of such an investigation seems obvious, for the discussion of sexuality, conceptualizations of sexuality, and the interplay between sexuality and religiousness has been widespread in recent years, ranging far beyond academic circles. Such discussion will, presumably, continue, and this study has sought to contribute to it only obliquely, adopting instead a more narrow focus.

Yet even within that more narrow focus, namely, the religion of the Indian subcontinent, it is apparent that the study of the Goddess tradition, or, to apply an Indian designation, the

[1]We have found no conclusive evidence to controvert this assertion, first made, apparently, by D. R. Bhandarkar on epigraphic grounds ("Epigraphic Notes and Questions", *Journal of the Bombay Branch of the Royal Asiatic Society* XXIII [1909], pp. 73-74). We shall, however, present further literary and inscriptional evidence for its integrity, along with the occasional questioning of its validity (primarily, V.V. Mirashi's "A Lower Limit for the Date of the *Devī-Māhātmya*", *Purāṇa* VI 1 [Jan. 1964], pp. 181-184) in the course of our study.

study of Śāktism, has been somewhat in vogue of late. While an investigation of the history of this study might itself constitute an interesting contribution to the history of ideas, we may here offer a single remark : among major studies of Śāktism, that of Payne,[2] which stood virtually by itself for many years, has now been followed in rapid succession by those of Beane,[3] Bhattacharyya,[4] Kumar,[5] and others. Regardless of the factors to which we may attribute this phenomenon, it is apparent that, even within the more circumscribed arena of the study of Indian religion, there is a contemporaneïty to the concern with the feminine and its symbolization.[6]

[2]Payne, Ernest, *The Śāktas: An Introductory and Comparative Study*, YMCA Publishing House (Calcutta, 1933) and Oxford University Press (London, 1933).

[3]Beane, Wendell, *Myth, Cult and Symbols in Śākta Hinduism: A Study of the Indian Mother Goddess*, E. J. Brill (Leiden, 1977).

[4]Bhattacharyya, Narendra Nath, *History of the Śākta Religion*, Munshiram Manoharlal (New Delhi, 1973 [74]).

[5]Kumar, Pushpendra, *Śakti Cult in Ancient India* (*With Special reference to the Purāṇic literature*) [sic], Bhartiya Publishing House (Varanasi, 1974).

[6]Although we shall subsequently make occasional reference to these studies, it may be helpful to offer a preliminary remark on their respective concerns, particularly since our ensuing discussion distinguishes our approach from that of these studies. (1) Payne's primary interest is in the contemporary phenomenon of Śāktism, the worship of the Goddess as *śākti* or power, in Bengal. He provides a wide-ranging examination of the background of this cult, touching on the classical Sanskrit heritage, the Tantras, non-Aryan motifs, and philosophical developments (chapters IV-VII) as well as descriptive and historical material on Bengal (II, III, VIII, IX) and non-Indian parallels (X, XI). Much of this material is not available elsewhere and continues to be valuable in spite of the author's self-avowed distaste for his subject, evidenced especially in his concluding chapter, "The Impermanence of Śāktism". (2) Beane's elaborate phenomenological study is, by contrast with Payne's, rich in sympathy: his appreciation of the subtle nuances and multi-valent significance of the Goddess as a religious symbol is what we have come to expect of a student of Eliade. His long historical prologue (chap. II) to his phenomenological remarks (III, IV, V) presents a wealth of heterogenous material in convenient form, for he there reviews the archeological evidence from the Indus Valley and later sites, suggests several linguistic affinities between Sanskritic names for the Goddess and Dravidian languages, and provides a brief review of Sanskritic passages which contribute to the mature conceptualization of the Goddess. This latter review—which anticipates our more systematic review of the Sanskritic antecedents of DM motifs—is somewhat cursory, perhaps as a result of Beane's heavy reliance upon the

It is the very contemporaneity of this concern, however, that raises a preliminary question. What need is there of yet further examination of the subject matter ? Given the richness of the Indian religious tradition, ought one not to raise up for examination a dimension of that tradition that scholarship has tended to slight, rather than one that has been so much under discussion ?

To this question, we offer two answers, one general and philosophical, the other specific and pragmatic. The former answer is simply to call attention to one feature of the academic enter-

---

selections translated by J. Muir in his *Original Sanskrit Texts*, especially volume four (Trübner and Co. [London, second edition, revised, 1873]). This brevity is not necessarily a liability, for Beane's intent is rather different from ours (as we shall further elaborate below): he is concerned with the almost trans-historical understanding of an all-India religious archetype, rather than the historical, contextual understanding of a particular text which has played a role in the elaboration of that archetype. The difference between our approaches may be seen as a manifestation of the difference between the phenomenological and historical approaches among students of *Religionswissenschaft*, on which see Eliade, Mircea, *The Sacred and the Profane*, Willard R. Trask (tr.), Harcourt, Brace and World, Inc. (New York, 1957, 1959), p. 232, and Eliade, Mircea, *The Quest*, University of Chicago Press (Chicago and London, 1969), pp. 35-36. (3) Bhattacharyya brings a welcome sociological perspective to his study, evident in his own remark (p. xi) that "emphasis has been laid in this work upon the functional role of the Śākta religion in Indian society and life throughout the ages. . . . Here it has been shown how the role of Śāktism changed from time to time in accordance with the changing social demands, from the guiding principle . . . [of] primitive hunting rituals and agricultural magics to that of the movement of national awakening, from the esoteric cults and practices arising out of the former to a liberal universal religion which had left a deep impress upon the latter." Biases of the work may be found in its slighting of textual material and in its quasi-Marxist jargon, e.g., (*loc. cit.*) "throughout the ages the Female Principle stood for the oppressed peoples, symbolizing all the liberating potentialities in the class divided, patriarchal and authoritarian social set up in India, and this alone explains why attempts were made from different corners to blacken Śākta-Tāntric ideals." (4) The focus of Kumar's study may be discerned in its subtitle, for the bulk of his work is a series of paraphrases of Purāṇic and Tantric material pertaining to the names, rituals, and theologies of the Goddess. There is little, if any, explicit analysis of this material. The most balanced and insightful of these recent studies promises to be that of J.N. Tiwari, *Goddess Cults in Ancient India*, forthcoming from Agam Prakashan (Delhi). This is a revision of the author's doctoral dissertation under A. L. Basham, at The Australian National University (1971).

prise, viz., its cumulative and open-ended nature. Later scholarship draws upon earlier, and in conjunction, perhaps, with a consideration of new evidence, strives for a more adequate understanding of the subject matter. Yet that understanding may, in turn, be complemented, even superseded, by subsequent scholarship. Simply because the above-noted studies are recent, we need not assume that they are final.[7]

In spite of the legitimacy of further inquiry in principle, however, we must hasten to add that our study does not aspire to cover the same ground as the studies cited above. It is here that our second answer becomes germane. What all of those studies have in common is an effort to be comprehensive, to illuminate the conceptualization of the divine as feminine throughout the whole sweep of Indian history : they include, in varying balances, consideration of pre- or non-Aryan material, historical evidence (which is variously delimited, though obviously with some overlap between studies), and data that is more or less contemporary. Our scope is more modest. As C.M. Brown has recently demonstrated,[8] it is possible to examine one particular "moment" in Indian religious history, in his case, a particular text, with considerable precision, and with consequences for the illumination not only of that particular "moment" but of Indian religiousness as a whole. Our aspiration is similar and is based on the conviction that material "that scholarship has tended to slight"[9] may as often be familiar as unknown. However, whereas Brown's text, the *Brahmavaivarta Purāṇa*, may be dated at the fifteenth or sixteenth century C.E.,[10] ours is older by a millennium, and the problems attendant on its study are quite different. Consequently, while we share with

[7]W. C. Smith has put this point well and has also articulated the relationship between our study and these broad examinations of Śāktism (see our following paragraph), when he notes that "even the more refined propositions of careful students are always liable to rebuttal [or, in our case, at least modification] by new empirical awareness": "Mankind's Religiously Divided History Approaches Self-Consciousness", *Harvard Divinity Bulletin* Vol. 29 1 (Oct. 1964), p. 10.

[8]Brown, Cheever Mackenzie, *God as Mother: A Feminine Theology in India*, Claude Stark and Co. (Hartford, Vt., 1974).

[9]See our discussion two paragraphs above.

[10]*Ibid.*, p. 205.

Brown an emphasis upon one particular "moment" in the history of India's appreciation of the divine as feminine, the structure of our study, to which we now turn, is unique.

The starting point for the development of our structure is a distinction that has frequently been made in studies of the philosophies of India. It is a distinction between two strands in the Indian philosophical tradition, the Aryan and the non-Aryan, which, it is suggested, arose out of radically different cultural milieus, and which have intertwined in varying ways in the different philosophical schools. In his introductory remarks to the scholastic philosophy of India, Heinrich Zimmer[11] makes the point clearly :

> As we shall see in the following chapters, the history of Indian philosophy has been characterized by a series of crises of interaction between the invasive Vedic-Āryan and the non-Āryan, earlier, Dravidian styles of thought and spiritual experience. The Brāhmans were the principal representatives of the former, while the latter was preserved, and finally reasserted, by the surviving princely houses of the native Indian, dark-skinned, pre-Āryan population. ...[12]

While one might have misgivings about Zimmer's reification of this non-Aryan strand into what he calls the "Dravidian factor",[13] he has nonetheless made a case for the heuristic utility

[11]We cite Zimmer, and subsequently Hiriyanna, not because they originate this distinction, but because they argue cogently for its heuristic utility. The differentiation of Aryan and Dravidian is, of course, far older and, as we shall see below in section 2, can become a highly nuanced discrimination.

[12]Zimmer, Heinrich, *Philosophies of India*, Joseph Campbell (ed.), Princeton University Press (Princeton, 1951, 1969), Bollingen Series XXVI, pp. 218-219.

[13]See the index entries under this rubric and also Campbell's apparent misgivings about such a hypothesis, p. 60n. Prof. John B. Carman has suggested to us (personal communication, Feb. 2, 1976) a refinement of Zimmer's position, proposing "that there are *at least* three major strands in Hindu tradition. The Sāṁkhya-Yoga strand is neither 'Aryan' nor 'Dravidian' in origin, . . . though it has been well entangled with both for millenia." As we shall see (Part I, s. v. "*prakṛti*"), such a further distinction is, at times, exceedingly helpful. However, it need not affect the basic conceptualization—the contrast of Sanskritic, Aryan tradition and non-Sanskritic, non-Aryan tradition(s)—for, as our ensuing discussion will indicate, the focus of our study is to be

of such a formulation in trying to grasp the dynamics of the history of Indian philosophy, in seeing through the apparent homogeneity that has emerged from the mutual borrowing of conceptions by the two originally independent strands.[14]

A more guarded use of this same fundamental dualism is seen in the work of M. Hiriyanna. He takes as his starting-point a distinction between the two strands made, not in ethnic, cultural terms, but in terms of the role of the Veda; one strand originates within the Veda, the other independent of it.[15] He does go on to point out that this is not merely a formal distinction but one of far-reaching consequences, e.g., both advocate the goal of asceticism but for very different reasons.[16] Nonetheless, it is for his crisp summary of philosophical developments that Hiriyanna's work commands our attention :

> The history of Indian philosophy is the history of the ways in which the two traditions have acted and reacted upon each other, giving rise to divergent schools of thought. Their mutual influence...has led to a considerable overlapping of the two sets of doctrines. ...In the course of this progressive movement, now one school and now another was in the ascendant. ...But finally the Vedānta triumphed. It has naturally been transformed much in the process, although its inner character remains as it was already foreshadowed in the Upaniṣads.[17]

One might go so far as to say that, in the discussion of Indian philosophy, the distinction of the two strands, the Aryan and the non-Aryan, or the Vedic and the non-Vedic, has become something of a commonplace.

The second stage in the development of our structure is to generalize from this model, for there is evidence that it may be

---

exclusively on the former of these, and, as Carman has noted, (*loc. cit.*), "from the standpoint of the Aryan tradition there is always an awareness of two traditions: itself and everything other."

[14]Zimmer, *op. cit.*, p. 315.

[15]Hiriyanna, M., *Outlines of Indian Philosophy*, George Allen and Unwin (London, 1932), p. 16.

[16]*Ibid.*, pp. 20-21.

[17]*Ibid.*, p. 25.

applicable in realms beyond the history of Indian philosophy. In fact, in his Foreword to Brown's study, Ingalls uses language that seems to suggest the appropriateness of such a model for understanding the history of the worship of the Goddess. Having observed that the silence of the historical record of Goddess-worship, which ensues on the suggestive archeological testimony of the Indus Valley, is broken in the early centuries of the present era by "the hymns of the *Harivaṃśa* and the *Viṣṇu Purāṇa*, ...the descriptions of Kālidāsa,...and...the rituals of the early Tantras"[18]—to which we might add "by the DM"—he continues :

> [This evidence from the early centuries of the Common Era appears] at the conjunction of two historical processes. On the one hand Sanskrit by the third century A.D. had become the nearly universal language of letters in India. On the other hand, the pre-Aryan worship of the Indians had spread by that time very widely among the Aryans. From the third or fourth century, at any rate, the religion of the Goddess becomes as much a part of the Hindu written record as the religion of God.[19]

Finally, we may simply note that Ingalls' suggestion here—that the basic impulse behind the worship of the Goddess is of non-Aryan, non-Sanskritic, indigenous origin—is a matter on which the opinion of scholarship, both Indian and Western, is virtually unanimous.[20]

[18]Brown, C. M., *op. cit.*, p. xiv.

[19]*Ibid.*, p. xv.

[20]For a representative sample of this opinion, see, in addition to the general studies cited above, the following: (1) Basham, A. L., *The Wonder That Was India*, Grove Press (New York, 1959), p. 311; (2) Bhandarkar, R. G., *Vaiṣṇavism, Śaivism, and Minor Religious Systems*, Indological Book House (Varanasi, 1965), p. 142; (3) Bhattacharya, A. K., "A Non-aryan Aspect of the Devī" in *The Śakti Cult and Tārā*, D. C. Sircar (ed.), University of Calcutta (Calcutta, 1971), pp. 56-60; (4) Brown, W. Norman, "Mythology of India" in *Mythologies of the Ancient World*, Samuel Noah Kramer (ed.), Doubleday and Co., Inc. (Garden City, N. Y., 1961), pp. 309-312; (5) Chattopadhyaya, Sudhakar, *Evolution of Hindu Sects: Up to the Time of Śaṃkaracārya*, [sic] Munshiram Manoharlal (New Delhi, 1970), pp. 151-152; (6) Danielou, Alain, *Hindu Polytheism*, Bollingen Series LXXIII, Pantheon Books (New York, 1964), p. 256; (7) Sinha, B. P., "Evolution of Śakti Worship in India" in Sircar, D. C. (ed.), *op. cit.*, pp. 46-47.

The structure of our study, then, takes as its point of departure the affirmation that the heartbeat of Indian culture has been the on-going and continuous interplay of the indigenous culture with that of the invading Aryans : some aspects of the latter have become indigenized, in different ways, at different times, and in different places, while facets of the former have, with comparable diversity, gradually percolated up into the aristocracy, have become Sanskritized. In the same vein, it recognizes that the text at the center of our study, the DM, constitutes one of the moments of major consequence in this latter process, when a comprehensive statement about the significance of the Goddess, a wide-ranging effort to establish her identity, and a full-blown worship of her, first appear in Sanskrit. Our study takes as its central task the understanding of our text in this original Sanskritic context.[21]

In order to accomplish this task, the primary need is to establish the relationship between the DM and earlier Sanskritic literature.[22] Since the significance of the DM derives, in large part, from the way in which it has brought together previously sown Sanskritic seeds and nurtured them with such fruitful consequences, the critical question is : what are those seeds, and, to continue the metaphor, what was their previous state of gestation ? It is the examination of these seeds—understood[23] as epithets, myths, and hymns—that constitutes the core of our study. It will be seen, of course, that there are certain important aspects of the DM which have no antecedents in the earlier Sanskritic literature,[24] and it is here that the specific bearing of

[21]A fuller account of our understanding of the word "context" will be given in section 2 below.

[22]The thorny issue of dating in India makes it impossible to make a clear-cut distinction between Sanskrit material anterior and posterior to the DM. As will be seen below in section 5, however, it is possible to distinguish between material that is (1) "clearly anterior", e.g., most of the Vedic and *sūtra* literature, (2) "clearly posterior", e.g., the *Devībhāgavata* and *Brahmavaivarta Purāṇas*, and (3) "roughly contemporaneous", e.g., Bāṇa's *Caṇḍīśataka*, Kālidāsa's *Kumārasaṃbhava*, and such a distinction will be seen to suffice for our purposes.

[23]For reasons to be given in the ensuing sections of our Prolegomenon.

[24]To argue that an absolute distinction can be made between motifs which are Sanskritic and those which are not is, at one level, somewhat of an oversimplification. For example, one of the Vedic contributions to the

the "two strand" model on our study becomes relevant. Unlike broader studies, our inquiry into the movement of Goddess motifs from the shadowy non-Aryan realm into the light of Sanskrit is in terms of the changes wrought in only *one* of these strands, the Sanskritic one. In other words, it is our intent to examine neither the pre-DM non-Sanskritic evidence for Goddess-worship, nor the post-DM Sanskritic evidence. Rather, it is to examine the pre-DM Sanskritic material which seems to have had a bearing on the understanding of the Goddess that emerges in the DM. Our task is to understand how, when there is such a dearth of material devoted to the Goddess in the early Sanskrit tradition, our text uses that tradition in order to give life to this "new" (from the Sanskritic perspective) figure of the Goddess. The question of the development of a Sanskritized form of Goddess-worship cuts in two directions : how is the Sanskritic tradition made contemporary, and how is the worship of the Goddess made traditional ?

Before turning to the evidence itself, it is necessary to develop our methodology more precisely, by addressing several preliminary matters. To these we turn in the following four sections.

## 2. "*Sanskritization*"

Since the DM does seem to be the first comprehensive account of the Goddess to appear in Sanskrit, our first inquiry must be into the significance of this fact, i.e., what has it meant to compose something in Sanskrit ? More broadly, we may ask : what has been the status of the Sanskritic literary tradition in India ? What, in short, are we to make of the DM's appearance in this particular language ?

---

conceptualization of the Goddess, to which we shall refer occasionally, is the great hymn to the earth found at *Atharva Veda* (AV) 12.1. Yet, as Tucci has pointed out (Tucci, G., "Earth in India and Tibet," *Eranos Jahrbuch* XXII [1953], pp. 323-364), in the on-going development of the Indian notion of earth, the non-Aryan, as well as the Aryan, contribution must be taken into account because of the complexity of the archetype. Nevertheless, it will be seen below that, in setting the context of the DM, it is possible systematically to identify those motifs which have a history in Sanskrit prior to the DM, regardless of whether they also have, or subsequently receive, elaboration stemming from non-Sanskritic sources.

It is appropriate to begin with such an inquiry, for over the course of the past two decades there has been a fair amount of discussion, originating in anthropological circles, of "Sanskritization" as a process to be observed at work in Indian culture.[25] Any study that proposes that the Sanskritic dimension of a particular religious phenomenon is significant in our understanding of that phenomenon must take at least some cognizance of this discussion. However, since the discussion often ranges far afield from our particular concern, in the balance of this section we limit ourselves to considering some of the remarks of four participants in this discussion, and then adapting them specifically to our point of inquiry. A listing of the salient materials in the larger discussion appears in our bibliography.[26]

The figure who is responsible for precipitating the Sanskritization discussion, the Indian sociologist M. N. Srinivas, provides a convenient starting point for our analysis. He proposed the concept in his *Religion and Society among the Coorgs of South India*,[27] and much of the ensuing discussion can be seen as deriving from the fact that he there employs the term in at least two different ways without clearly distinguishing them. At the outset, he proposes it as a concept for the analysis of society, defining it as one of the critical mechanisms of caste mobility :

> The caste system is far from a rigid system in which the position of each component caste is fixed for all time. Movement has always been possible, and especially so in the middle regions of the hierarchy. A low caste was able, in a generation or two, to rise to a higher position in the hierarchy by adopting vegetarianism and teetotalism, and by

[25]This discussion can be seen as a subset of the endeavor, throughout the past century or two, to locate the essence of Indian identity, the heart of her culture. We shall encounter several contributions to this quest in the course of this section. Two others may be mentioned here: Chatterji, S. K., "The Indian Synthesis, and Racial and Cultural Intermixture in India," Presidential Address, All-India Oriental Conference (Poona, 1953); Tagore, Rabindranath, *A Vision of India's History*, Pulinbari Sen ' (Calcutta, 1951).

[26]See the entries for the names W. N. Brown, David, Marriott, Morrison, Northrop, Raghavan, Redfield, Singer, Srinivas, Staal, Toynbee, van Buitenen, and Wright.

[27]Clarendon Press (Oxford, 1952).

> Sanskritizing its ritual and pantheon. In short, it took over, as far as possible, the customs, rites, and beliefs of the Brahmins, and the adoption of the Brahmanic way of life by a low caste seems to have been frequent, though theoretically forbidden. This process has been called "Sanskritization" in this book. . . .[28]

In addition to this usage, there is another nuance to the term that emerges toward the end of his study where it begins to take on cultural, rather than social, overtones. Here Srinivas suggests that Sanskritization can be seen as providing links between villages and regions, that those features of Hinduism which are most heavily Sanskritized are also those which are most universally found in India :

> Sanskritic Hinduism gives. . . certain common values to all Hindus, and the possession of common values knits people together into a community. The spread of Sanskritic rites, and the increasing Sanskritization of non-Sanskritic rites, tend to weld the hundred of sub-castes, sects, and tribes all over India into a single community. The lower castes have a tendency to take over the customs and rites of the higher castes, and this ensures the spread of Sanskritic cultural and ritual forms at the expense of others.[29]

Regardless of whether Sanskritization here be understood as a phenomenon facilitating social mobility, or as a process of cultural integration, two things are clear : first, the Sanskritic tradition possesses enormous symbolic appeal, representing a norm of socio-cultural excellence, and possessing virtually a proselytizing quality; second, the Sanskritic tradition is not a monolithic entity but is involved in symbiotic interplay with myriad local traditions, so that Sanskritization is a very complex, two-directional process, drawing from, as well as feeding into, non-Sanskritic culture.[30]

The second participant in the Sanskritization discussion whose contribution we may note here is also a social scientist, the American McKim Marriott. Marriott acknowledges his

[28] *Ibid.*, p. 30.
[29] *Ibid.*, p. 208.
[30] *Ibid.*, pp. 214, 222.

indebtedness to Srinivas's formulation[31] and, in general, his views are congruent with those of Srinivas. Two points, however, in his now famous study of the village of Kishan Garhi bear mention. The first is his striking documentation of the way in which Sanskritic and non-Sanskritic motifs intertwine at the popular level. Noting that fifteen of the nineteen festivals in Kishan Garhi are known "by one or more universal Sanskrit texts," he goes on to caution against ascribing undue significance to this fact and to argue for the vitality of "the little tradition":[32]

> First, there are four festivals which have no evident Sanskritic rationales. . . .
>
> Second, those festivals of Kishan Garhi which do have Sanskritic rationales represent only a small selection out of the total annual cycle of festivals which finds sanction in the great tradition. . . .
>
> Third, between the festivals of Kishan Garhi and those sanctioned by the great tradition, connections are often loosened, confused, or mistaken because of a multiplicity of competing meanings for each special day within the great tradition itself. . . . Accustomed to an interminable variety of overlapping Sanskritic mythology, villagers have ceased to be much concerned with distinguishing the "right" great-traditional explanation of a festival from such Sanskritic sounding and possibly newly invented ones as may be convenient.
>
> Fourth, behind their Sanskritic names and multiple great-traditional rationales, the festivals of Kishan Garhi contain much ritual which has no evident connection with the great tradition.[33]

[31]Marriott, McKim, "Little Communities in an Indigenous Civilization" in *Village India: Studies in the Little Community*, McKim Marriott (ed.), The American Anthropological Association, Vol. 57, No. 3, Part 2, Memoir No. 83 (June 1955), Comparative Studies of Cultures and Civilizations, No. 6, Robert Redfield and Milton Singer (edd.), p. 215. "This volume is also published in a trade edition by the University of Chicago Press."

[32]Our use of this phrase, and Marriott's of "the great tradition" in the following quotation, reflect the conceptualization of Robert Redfield.

[33]*Ibid.*, pp. 193, 194-195.

He then proceeds to maintain that it is not the "upward" process of Sanskritization but "the [downward] process of parochialization [that] constitutes the characteristic creative work of little communities within India's indigenous civilization."[34]

Nevertheless—and this is the second point of note—Marriott does find Sanskritization to be operative in a highly significant, symbolic manner, but in a rather more subtle way than Srinivas allowed. As is evident in our above quotation, the process by which local and Sanskritic motifs are identified is very unsystematic and, argues Marriott,[35] if this is true within a single village, how much more is it the case when distant villages or regions are considered. This fluidity in the identification process renders Srinivas's claim that Sanskritization enhances communal and all-India solidarity rather dubious. The process, however, is nonetheless significant, for

> although Sanskritic identifications do not necessarily bring adjacent little communities closer to each other, they do bring the great community closer to all little communities. To each little tradition, Sanskritic identifications lend the sense of derivative participation in the great tradition which is authoritative, not only because it is indigenous, but also because it is refined, learned, and ecumenical. Sanskritization thus heightens and dignifies the sphere of communication for each little community; it does not necessarily widen that sphere.[36]

Clearly, one of the problems besetting the anthropological inquiry into the Sanskritization process is the difficulty of specifying the "content' of the Sanskritic tradition, and it is on precisely this matter that the remarks of our third participant, the Sanskritist J. F. Staal, become germane. He maintains that it is fallacious to equate the Sanskritic and great cultural traditions, and this for two reasons. First, "the oldest and apparently most pivotal forms of the great tradition are often of a type which many anthropologists would tend to describe as 'non-Sanskritic', and which are in fact based upon

[34] *Ibid.*, p. 200.
[35] *Ibid.*, p. 217.
[36] *Ibid.*, pp. 217-218.

little traditions,"[37] viz., those of the Indus Valley. In a similar vein, "many so called non-Sanskritic forms (e.g., the cult of mother goddesses) have an all-India spread."[38] Second, the great tradition itself is no solid, homogenous entity. Rather, "the origins of the great tradition lie in numerous little traditions, widespread throughout Indian history and geography." Consequently, "whatever tradition one studies in the classical Sanskrit sources, almost always there are indications of popular cults, local usages and little traditions,"[39] and it is obvious that even the oldest Sanskritic literature originated "among relatively few families in a limited number of clans" in north-west India.[40] In sum, Staal may be seen as drawing on his knowledge of textual particularities to counteract the anthropological tendency to reify the Sanskritic tradition, to see it as having a life independent of its constituent parts :[41]

> ...any non-Sanskritic element incorporated in the great tradition must have been incorporated in a given region to start with. The great tradition is considered an all-India phenomenon [merely] because of lack of familiarity with what the great tradition consists of and because of the lack of geographical specifications in many works on classical Indology.[42]

The last figure whose remarks we may note is another Sanskritist, J. A. B. van Buitenen, for although he is a late

[37]Staal, J. F., "Sanskrit and Sanskritization," *The Journal of Asian Studies* XXII 3 (May 1963), pp. 266-267.

[38]*Ibid.*, p. 270.

[39]*Ibid.*, pp. 267, 268.

[40]*Ibid.*, p. 270. On the particularity of even so revered a document as the *Ṛg Veda* (RV), see Lanman's remark: "To the student of the Veda it is a source of perhaps contemptuous surprise, and to the teacher a source of some little embarrassment, that this venerable document smells so strong of the cow-pen and the byre;" Lanman, Charles R., "Sanskrit Diction as Affected by the Interests of Herdsman, Priest, and Gambler," JAOS XX 1 (1899), p. 12.

[41]The imputation of this tendency to anthropologists in general should perhaps be limited to non-Indian anthropologists, for there is some evidence that there is a basic difference in perception between Indian and non-Indian scholars: cf. the remarks of van Buitenen noted immediately below.

[42]Staal, *op. cit.*, pp. 269-270.

contributor to the Sanskritization discussion,[43] he has a number of shrewd insights and raises some issues that will be with us in the balance of our Prolegomenon. Van Buitenen comes at this discussion obliquely and offers his salient remarks only in conclusion to his examination of a more particular problem, viz., "why did the author or authors of the final version of the *Bhāgavata* [*Purāṇa*] want the book to sound Vedic?"[44] From that conclusion, we may excerpt three comments.

The first pertains to the Indian intuition regarding the chronological locus of truth:

> Central to Indian thinking through the ages is a concept of knowledge which, though known to Platonism and Gnosticism, is foreign to the modern West. Whereas for us, to put it briefly, knowledge is something to be *discovered*, for the Indian knowledge is to be *recovered*. Although doubtless a great many other factors have contributed to the reputed traditionalism of the Indian civilization, one particular preconception, related to this concept of knowledge concerning the past and its relation to the present, is probably of central significance: that at its very origin the absolute truth stands revealed; that this truth—which is simultaneously a way of life—has been lost, but not irrecoverably; that somehow it is still available through ancient life lines that stretch back to the original revelation; and that the present can be restored only when this original past has been recovered.[45]

The second comment pertains to the various means that have been employed to maintain contact with the primordial

[43]His critical article is "On the Archaism of the *Bhāgavata Purāṇa*," published in 1966 in *Krishna: Myths, Rites and Attitudes,* Milton Singer (ed.), East-West Center (Honolulu), pp. 23-40. Singer, however, seems to have known the article two years earlier: see his "The Social Organization of Indian Civilization," *Diogenes* 45 (1964), p. 102. Singer's article is reprinted in his *When a Great Tradition Modernizes: An Anthropological Approach to Indian Civilization,* Praeger Publishers (New York, Washington, London, 1972), pp. 250-271, but without the helpful and rather thorough topical bibliography which appears in the original.

[44]van Buitenen, *op. cit.*, p. 24.

[45]*Ibid.*, pp. 35-36.

deposit of truth, viz., "Sanskrit is felt to be one of the lifelines [sic], and Sanskritization in its literal sense, the rendering into Sanskrit, is one of the prime methods of restating a tradition in relation to a sacral past."[46]

Finally, we may note that, although Sanskritization is here understood primarily as a literary phenomenon, it has overtones that extend far beyond the realm of literature, a point that van Buitenen makes by referring to the cultural background of the originator of the whole Sanskritization discussion.

> Srinivas is an Indian[[47]]; for him Sanskrit is more than the name of a language, it is the summation of a way of life. His use, and that of others, of "Sanskrit" and "Sanskritic" has reference to a rather complex notion of normative self-culture, of which it is more or less consciously felt that the Sanskrit language was its original vehicle. It carries with it associations of a sacral character. One is *saṃskārya* (to be perfected or "sacralized" by appropriate ceremonies), one observes *saṃskāras* (sacramentals)—words derived from the same root *kṛ*—with the prefixed verb *sam*. In such words a meaning of "refining or perfecting one's nature and conduct by ritual means" becomes central. Other characteristic connotations help to widen the comprehension of the concept. "Sanskritic" is that which is the most ancient, therefore the most pure, and therefore hierarchically the most elevated; it thus provides a norm for exclusive personal or group conduct—exclusive for its purity and elevation—that most effectively proves itself in securing correct descent, backward by relating oneself to an ancient lineage or an ancient myth and forward by safeguarding the purity of future offspring.[48]

These various interpretations of the Sanskritization phenomenon ramify for our study in a number of ways. Clearly the most desirable approach for us would be to take our

[46]*Ibid.*, p. 36.

[47]The force of van Buitenen's remarks here is increased by the fact that Srinivas is a Brāhmaṇa as well: Prof. J. B. Carman, personal communication, Feb. 2, 1976.

[48]van Buitenen, *op. cit.*, p. 34.

cue from Staal and to treat the DM as a little tradition that has become Sanskritized : we would examine that local tradition in its original context and reconstruct the literary, social, and cultural history that the DM represents. The problem with such an approach, however, is obvious : the material for such an historical reconstruction is simply not available. We have seen that Staal himself comments on the lack of geographical information in many Indian texts and Morrison, too, has commented on the "extreme difficulty" scholars have had in extracting historically reliable information from textual material : the best Indological minds have wrestled with the *Mahābhārata* (Mbh) to try "to locate and date the war of Kurukshetra or to discount the historicity of the events," but the definitive answer has not been forthcoming.[49] If that is the case with the critically edited Mbh, how much more is it the case with our Purāṇic text for which no critical edition exists. There are, to be sure, various clues as to the geographic provenience of our text, and Pargiter has gone so far as to postulate Western India as the origin for the whole of the MarkP, and the Narmadā River valley, probably at Mandhāta, as the source of the DM.[50] We shall find little hard evidence to dispute this contention, though the inscriptions which we shall cite at the relevant junctures originate rather more to the north, with a few far to the east. But, as noted, the detailed reconstruction of our text's context, at the remove of a millennium and a half, is beyond the capacity of contemporary scholarship. Moreover, while we shall find little reason to challenge Pargiter's conclusion as to the origin of the DM, the method by which he arrives at it may be questioned. He relies heavily on the Śaiva associations of the Goddess, particularly the joint worship of Śiva and his spouse, to identify the text's origin, but, as we shall see, the Goddess has other associations in our text, most notably with Viṣṇu and Kṛṣṇa Gopāla, and of these various associations, the Śaiva is certainly not the predominant one.

[49]Morrison, Barrie M., "Sources, Methods, and Concepts in Early Indian History," *Pacific Affairs* XLI 1 (Spring 1968), p. 76.

[50]See the introduction to his translation of the MarkP: The Asiatic Society (Calcutta, 1904 [1888-1904]), Bibliotheca Indica, New Series No. 700, 706, 810, 872, 890, 947, 1058, 1076, and 1104, pp. viii-xiii.

In light of this, our use of the word "Sanskritize" will be far narrower, and therefore less complex, than the varying anthropological usages. As we use it, it will mean simply "to write about in Sanskrit." We shall use it to describe a literary phenomenon, while not denying that that phenomenon has larger social and cultural connotations. We are simply bracketing the latter in the interest of simplicity. As is evident from the remarks of van Buitenen, and as will be seen in detail in sections 4 and 5 below, this does not mean that we are ruling out treatment of the *religious* significance of our text. But before we can establish that connection, we must first consider that genre of literature in which the DM appears, viz., the Purāṇas.

As a bridge between the current section and that discussion, we may glance briefly at the role of Sanskrit, purely as a language, in Indian culture. To reconstruct that role historically is no easier than the reconstruction of an anthropological setting, but it is instructive to note the variety of ways in which that role has been construed. In a stimulating discussion many years ago, the leading English Indologists of the day—including E. J. Rapson, T. W. Rhys Davids, F. W. Thomas, G. A. Grierson, and J. F. Fleet—pondered the question, "In What Degree was Sanskrit a Spoken Language ?"[51] The variety of answers is extraordinary, ranging from Rapson's :

> At first the dialect of a district, then the language of a caste and a religion, it [Sanskrit] ultimately became the language of religion, politics, and culture throughout India. It became a great national language, and ceased to be so only when Hindu nationality was destroyed by the Muhammadan conquests.

to Grierson's :

> . . . I do not believe that Classical Sanskrit was anyone's vernacular at the time of Pāṇini or afterwards. The language was unsuited to be a vernacular; and all the evidence which we possess shows that the only vernacular

[51]This is the title of a paper by E. J. Rapson, *Journal of the Royal Asiatic Society*, 1904, pp. 435-456. It is followed in the *Journal* by an account of the discussion it precipitated among the Indologists cited, under the rubric "Notes of the Quarter," pp. 457-487.

> in existence, at the time, was in that stage of development which is commonly and conveniently called Pāli. At the same time, from Pāṇini to the present day, it has always been a second language, a polite language like Latin in the middle ages, learnt and spoken as an accomplishment by people the number of whom varied from century to century according to the extent of public education in India.[52]

We need not follow the nuances of this discussion, for on the one point that is critical for our study, there is virtual unanimity among these scholars : Sanskrit was the language of culture and respectability, a mark of dignity, piety, and tradition—might we even say of eternity (*apauruṣeyatva*)?—regardless of whether it was a spoken (vernacular) language or "merely" a literary tradition. This judgment is of a piece with the above-noted remarks of Marriott and van Buitenen on the "dignifying" consequences of Sanskritization. Together they point out the boundaries of the term "Sanskritization" in our study by conveying the symbolic significance of this process : "to Sanskritize" is "to write about in Sanskrit," and that, in turn, is to affirm the respectability, dignity, sanctity, antiquity, even the eternality, of what is written about.[53]

### 3. *The Purāṇas : Their Nature and Study*

As noted earlier, the DM constitutes a portion of one of the early Purāṇas. Having in the previous section investigated some of the significances of the DM's being written in Sanskrit, we turn now to the DM's occurrence in a Purāṇa, to see how that fact ramifies for our understanding of the text.

[52]*Ibid.*, pp. 456, 481.

[53]One wonders whether, in India where so many of even the illiterate are bilingual or multilingual, the discussion of the vernacular or literary existence of Sanskrit is not, in fact, something of a red herring. Is not the user's intent, the relative symbolic significances of the languages employed, of rather greater consequence ? For a discussion of this matter, where none of the languages involved is Sanskrit, see Shanmugan Pillai, M. "Code Switching in a Tamil Novel," in *Structural Approaches to South India Studies*, Harry M. Buck and Glenn E. Yocum (edd.), Wilson Books (Chambersburg, Pa., 1974), pp. 81-95.

Since many of the participants in the Sanskritization discussion developed an appreciation of the role of the Purāṇas in the Hindu religious tradition, we may introduce this topic by letting Srinivas be explicit :

> The *purāṇas* are religious stories in which figure deities, and many semi-divine characters, and the public reading of the *purāṇas* and epics is even now popular. The *purāṇas* have played a great part in the spread of Hinduism as ordinary people became familiar with deities and ideas of Sanskritic Hinduism through them. Even more important is the fact that the *purāṇas* facilitated the absorption of local myths and legends.... The *purāṇas* have been continually expanding, absorbing local myths and legends, and also weaving myths round great historical figures and events.... Thus, through the *purāṇas*, a local community becomes acquainted with the mythology of All-India Hinduism, and also its myths and legends are Sanskritized and made the property of Hindus all over India.[54]

What, then, are these Purāṇas ?

Initially one's answer to this question will depend on whether one accepts the prima facie evidence or the traditional Indian understanding, i.e., on whether one accepts those eighteen[55]

[54]Srinivas, *Coorgs,* pp. 220-221. On the contemporary recitation of the Purāṇas, see Raghavan, V., "Methods of Popular Religious Instruction in South India" in *The Cultural Heritage of India,* Haridas Bhattacharyya (ed.), The Ramakrishna Mission Institute of Culture (Calcutta, second edition, revised and enlarged, 1956), vol. IV, pp. 503-514, reprinted in *Traditional India: Structure and Change,* Milton Singer (ed.), pp. 130-138.

[55]We simply accept the Purāṇas as eighteen in number without comment, though that number, and which Purāṇas constitute it, has been the subject of some debate. For the generally accepted list of eighteen, see Hazra, R. C., "The Purāṇas," in *The Cultural Heritage of India,* vol. II (second edition, 1962), p. 240, and Winternitz, M., *A History of Indian Literature,* vol. I: Introduction, Veda, National Epics, Purāṇas, and Tantras, Mrs. S. Ketkar (tr.), Russell and Russell (New York, 1971), p. 531. See *ibid.*, pp. 553-554, 553n; Kane, P. V., *History of Dharmaśāstra,* Bhandarkar Oriental Research Institute (Poona, 1962), Government Oriental Series Class B, vol. V, part 2, pp. 829-831; and Hazra, R. C., "The Problems Relating to the Śiva Purāṇa," *Our Heritage* I 1 (1953), pp. 46-68, especially pp. 46-51, regarding the debate, which has largely centered around whether the *Śiva* or *Vāyu Purāṇa* should

texts as they appear to the contemporary investigator, or alternatively, as one inquires into the texts' classical self-understanding. The first readily datable formulation of the traditional understanding is found in the fifth century lexicon *Amarakośa* which defines "*purāṇa*" as "that which has five characteristics (*pañcalakṣaṇa*)." Several of the Purāṇas use this term[56] and enumerate the five characteristics as : *sarga* (creation or evolution of the universe), *pratisarga* (re-creation of the universe after its periodic dissolution), *vaṁśa* (genealogies of gods, patriarchs, sages, and kings), *manvantara* ("Manu-intervals," cosmic cycles, each of which is presided over by a Manu, the father of mankind), *vaṁśānucarita* (accounts of royal dynasties). In turning to the contemporary texts, however, not only do we find these five topics treated rather irregularly, but we also find extensive additions, such as :

> glorifications of one or more of the sectarian deities like Brahmā, Viṣṇu, and Śiva,...numerous chapters on new myths, and legends, and multifarious topics concerning religion and society, for instance, duties of the different castes and orders of life, sacraments, customs in general, eatables and non-eatables, duties of women, funeral rites and ceremonies, impurity on birth and death, sins, penances and expiations, purifications of things, names and descriptions of hells, results of good and bad deeds..., pacification of unfavorable planets, donations of various types, dedication of wells, tanks, and gardens, worship, devotional vows..., places of pilgrimage, consecration of temples and images of gods, initiation, and various mystic rites and practices.[57]

If we can reconcile these two understandings of the Purāṇas, we shall have come a long way toward understanding how we should approach our particular text.

---

be on the list. For the significance of the number eighteen (eighteen days of the Bhārata war, eighteen *parvans* of the Mbh, eighteen chapters of the *Bhagavad Gītā*, etc.), see Kane, *op. cit.*, vol. V, part 2, p. 842, 842n.

[56]See Kane, *op. cit.*, vol. V, part 2, p. 839 for a collation of the Purāṇic passages touching on *pañcalakṣaṇa*.

[57]Hazra, "The Purāṇas," pp. 246-247.

While the academic study of the Purāṇas dates back to the early nineteenth century,[58] it was not until the work of F. Eden Pargiter that the problem, as we have posed it, was addressed. Pargiter's concern was not the Purāṇas *per se*, but the reconstruction of early Indian history, particularly political history. Though many of his conclusions, both general and particular, have been widely disputed, while working through the Purāṇas to extract the historical material, he did perceive the dynamics of their growth, the general pattern of which has been subsequently confirmed.

> It is highly probable that they [the Purāṇas] consisted at first mainly of ancient stories, genealogies, &c, which formed the popular side of ancient literature, and were quite probably in Prakrit originally. In fact, it seems to me that they were largely in an old literary Prakrit used by the higher classes but that, as the spoken languages diverged in time more and more from Sanskrit through political vicissitudes, that literary Prakrit became unintelligible, while Sanskrit remained the only polished language of brahmanic Hinduism. Hence it was natural that this literature should be Sanskritized.... It was the brahmans probably who saved and improved the status of those old compositions by converting them into Sanskrit, and afterwards, perceiving what an excellent means they provided for reaching popular thought, made use of them to propagate their own views and doctrines by freely augmenting them with brahmanical fables, philosophical discussions, and ceremonial expositions.[59]

[58]Mention must be made here of the pioneering work of Horace Hayman Wilson. Wilson was clearly aware of the discrepancy between the Purāṇas' self-image and the extant texts [see the introduction to his translation of the *Viṣṇu Purāṇa*, Punthi Pustak (Calcutta, 1972), pp. iv-vii], but his tendency throughout his work [*ibid.*; also, "A Sketch of the Religious Sects of the Hindus," *Asiatick Researches* XVI (1828), pp. 1-136, XVII (1832), pp. 169-313, and "Analysis of the Purāṇas," comprising vol. III of his *Works*, Reinhold Rost (collector and ed.), Trübner and Co. (London, 1864), pp. 1-155.] was simply to infer the late date of the extant Purāṇas from this discrepancy and to focus on the nature of the individual Purāṇas, rather than inquiring into how the Purāṇas assumed their present form. This bias makes his work of only tangential relevance to our study.

[59]Pargiter, F. Eden (ed.), *The Purāṇa Text of the Dynasties of the Kali Age*, Oxford University Press (London, 1913), Introduction p. xvii note.

Pargiter's claim that the Purāṇic kernel existed originally in Prakrit has come in for crisp criticism,[60] as has his later assertion[61] that this kernel, along with other tales now in the Purāṇas was of clearly distinguishable *kṣatriya*, as opposed to *brāhmaṇa*, origin. But his general intuition of the organic quality of the Purāṇas has been largely substantiated and was given much support by the less speculative, more quantitative work of Willibald Kirfel. In his *Das Purāṇa Pañcalakṣaṇa*,[62] Kirfel examines the extant texts of the Purāṇas to see to what extent the five traditional characteristics can be applied to them. His conclusion is that, out of about 400,000 verses in the Purāṇas, only about 10,000, or less than three per-cent of the total, are concerned with *pañcalakṣaṇa* material.[63]

The decisiveness of this judgment has prompted further inquiry into the Purāṇas, and other literature, in search of clarity on the origin and development of the Purāṇas.[64] While general agreement has been reached on the process of development, the texts themselves attest to two traditions regarding

[60]E.g., Pusalker, A. D., "Were the Purāṇas Originally in Prakrit?", in his *Studies in the Epics and Purāṇas*, Bharatiya Vidya Bhavan (Bombay, 1963), Bhavan's Book University 36, pp. 63-67.

[61]Pargiter, F. E., *Ancient Indian Historical Tradition* (*AIHT*), Oxford University Press (London, 1922), *passim.*

[62]Kurt Schroeder (Bonn, 1927). Kirfel's introduction, in which he interprets the evidence he has assembled, has been translated into English by P. V. Ramanujaswami in *Journal of Śri Veṅkateśvara Oriental Institute* VII 2 (July-Dec. 1946), pp. 81-101, VIII 1 (Jan.-June 1947), pp. 9-33. Kirfel's conclusions have been summarized by Kane, *op. cit.*, vol. V, part 2, pp. 852-853.

[63]Haraprasad Shastri, M., "The Maha-Puranas," JBORS XIV 3 (Sept. 1928), p. 326.

[64]This "further inquiry" which we are about to review may be set in a helpful context by noting Kane's reflections on why the *Amarakośa* chose to characterize the Purāṇas as *pañcalakṣaṇa*. He maintains (*op. cit.*, vol. V, part 2, pp. 840-841) that the five characteristics were proposed, not as exhaustively circumscribing Purāṇic material, but as indicating the unique features of the Purāṇas in comparison with other classes of literature. Thus, it is suggested that there was a certain overlap between Purāṇas, Itihāsas, Ākhyānas, etc. (cf. *infra*, n. 70), but only the Purāṇas dealt with the material suggested by *pañcalakṣaṇa*. For a provocative reinterpretation of *pañcalakṣaṇa*, see Levitt, Stephan Hillyer, "A Note on the Compound *Pañcalakṣaṇa* in Amarasiṇha's *Nāmaliṅgānuśasana*", *Purāṇa* XVIII 1 (Jan. 1976), pp. 5-38.

their origin, one proclaiming a divine origin, the other a human.[65] An important point is at stake here, so let us look at these traditions in more detail.

The argument for the divine origin of the Purāṇas[66] draws on a number of early extra-Purāṇic texts. In the RV the word *purāṇa* occurs only as an adjective, meaning simply "ancient, old,"[67] but as early as the AV it appears as a singular noun, in a context where its sanctity is clear : AV 11. 7. 24, speaking of the remnant (*ucchiṣṭa*) of the sacrificial offering, reads : "The verses, the chants, the meters, the ancient [*purāṇam*], together with the formula : from the remnant were born all the gods in heaven, heaven-resorters."[68] The word is used again in a sacrificial context in the *Śatapatha Brāhmaṇa* (ŚB), though now in apposition with a singular pronoun : ŚB. 13.4.3.13 states that the Adhvaryu should instruct those who have assembled, saying, "The Purāṇa is the Veda; this is it," and should then "recite some Purāṇa."[69] This parity of the Purāṇa with the Veda is maintained by BU 2.4.10 where the *Ṛg*, *Yajur*, and *Sāma Vedas*, *atharvāṅgirasa*, *itihāsa*,[70] *purāṇa*, etc. are envisioned as the breath

[65]Gupta, Anand Swarup, "Purāṇas and their Referencing," *Purāṇa* VII 2 (July 1965), pp. 323-326.

[66]The data summarized here are drawn largely from *ibid.*, supplemented by Kane's more exhaustive collection of relevant passages (*op. cit.*, vol. V, part 2, pp. 815ff.) and other material as noted.

[67]Gupta, Anand Swarup, "Purāṇa, Itihāsa and Ākhyāna," *Purāṇa* VI 2 (July 1964), p. 454: Kane, *op. cit.*, vol. V, part 2, p. 855. See also the full study of Ludo Rocher, "The Meaning of *purāṇá* in the Ṛgveda", *Wiener Zeitschrift für die Kunde Südasiens* XXI (1977), pp. 5-24.

[68]*ṛcaḥ sāmāni chandānsi purāṇam yajuṣā saha/*
*ucchiṣṭāj jajñire sarve divi devā diviśritāḥ//*

Text given by Kane, *op. cit.*, vol. V, part 2, p. 816, n. 1325. The translation given is from *Atharva-Veda Saṁhitā*, translated with a critical and exegetical commentary by William Dwight Whitney, revised and brought nearer to completion and edited by Charles Rockwell Lanman, Harvard University (Cambridge, 1905), Harvard Oriental Series Vol. VIII, p. 646.

[69]*tān upadiśati purāṇam vedaḥ soyam iti kiṃcitpurāṇam ācakṣita.*

[70]The distinction between *itihāsa*, "history" (usually analyzed as *iti ha āsa*, "thus it truly was"), and *purāṇa* is not always clear. For an extended discussion of these terms, see Gupta, "Purāṇa, Itihāsa, and Ākhyāna." For a discussion of these and other terms in the larger context of Indian historiography, see Majumdar, R. C., "Ideas of History in Sanskrit Literature," in *Historians of India, Pakistan, and Ceylon*, C. H. Phillips (ed.), Oxford University Press (London, 1961), pp. 13-28.

of the Great Being (*mahad bhūtam*). At CU 7.1.2 the Purāṇa is cited, in a singular compound with *itihāsa*, as constituting the fifth Veda. Mazumdar builds on this Purāṇic connection with the sacrifice and the Veda to espouse a formal theory :

> ... it is clear that, at the time of the performance of the *yajñas*, recitation of the history of the mantras was an inseparable part of the ceremony, and that the knowledge of the Purāṇa or the origin of the *mantra*, was essential with the Vedic priests. ... There cannot be any doubt that this story-literature, absolutely necessary for the performance of the *yajñas*, was designated as Purāṇa or Purāṇetihāsa.[71]

This inclination to ascribe divine status to the Purāṇa is reinforced by a parallel tendency to argue from the fact that "in most of the earlier references, the word *Purāṇa* occurs in [the] singular and not in [the] plural as is the case at a subsequent period" to the conclusion that "Purāṇa was originally one but at a later stage it assumed its multifarious form."[72]

The early suggestion of the Purāṇas' divine origin is made more explicit in the Purāṇas themselves. The claim is made in several Purāṇas,[73] with some variation in detail, that originally Purāṇa was one and was first thought of by Brahmā, emanating from his fifth mouth to the extent of a hundred crores of *ślokas*. This original Purāṇa continues to exist in the world of the gods, but is abridged by Vyāsa, "The Arranger," in each *dvāpara yuga* into an essence of four *lakhs* of *ślokas*, and this essence is then divided by Vyāsa into the eighteen Purāṇas existing in this mortal world. The divinity of the Purāṇic origin

[71]Mazumdar, B. C., "The Origin and Character of the Purāṇa Literature" in *Sir Asutosh Mookerjee Silver Jubilee Volumes*, Orientalia, Calcutta University Press (Calcutta, 1925), Vol. III, part 2, p. 9.

[72]Gyani, Siva Datt, "The Date of the Purāṇas", *Purāṇa* I 2 (Feb. 1960), p. 219. The alleged original unity of the Purāṇa is, of course, compatible with either the divinity or the humanity of its origin. That it inclines toward the former, however, will be seen in the sequel, particularly in the next paragraph.

[73]Gupta ("Purāṇas and their Referencing," p. 324) cites *BhaviṣyaP* I.2.56f.; *NāradaP* I.92.22ff., I.109.30f.; *MatsyaP* 53.4.10; 57-58; *SkandaP* VII.2.8f. Kane (*op. cit.*, vol. V, part 2, p. 829) cites *MatsyaP* 53.3-11; *VāyuP* I.60-61; *BrahmāṇḍaP* I.1.40-41; *LiṅgaP* I.2.2; *NāradīyaP* I.92.22-26; *PadmaP* V.1.45-52; *ViṣṇuP* III.4 and 6.

is sometimes further asserted by affirming Vyāsa, to whom tradition also ascribes the authorship of the Mbh, to be an incarnation of the transcendent Viṣṇu himself, for, says the ViṣṇuP, "who else could have composed the Mahābhārata ?"[74]

The tradition that the Purāṇas are of human origin also draws on early, extra-Purāṇic material. We have already seen that *purāṇa* is used, at an early date, in the singular and in compound. At *Yājñavalkya Smṛti* 3.189 *purāṇa* and *itihāsa* are used in compound in the plural, at TA 2.9, both are used individually in the plural, and at *Manu Smṛti* 3.232 *purāṇa* occurs alone in the plural.[75] Such usages, this tradition would argue, seem to refer to separate classes of works and such usage may, in fact, be implicit even where *purāṇa* occurs in the singular : those instances are referring, not to the one, eternal Purāṇa, but are simply a continuation of the RV's adjectival use of the word, i.e., *purāṇa* in the singular is simply a generic reference to "an old story." What these instances of *purāṇa* in the plural then represent is the gradual emergence of a class of texts called Purāṇas. That this is the case is further shown by the fact that the *Āpastamba Dharma Sūtra* twice (1.6.19.13; 2.9.23.3-6) seems to quote from "Purāṇa" and, most conclusively, it specifically quotes (2.9.24.6.)[76] from a *Bhaviṣyatpurāṇa* : taken adjectivally, this is a contradiction in terms—"a future ancient" —and therefore can only be taken to mean "The Purāṇa which deals with the future."

The Purāṇic tradition of the human origin of the Purāṇas is based on seeing Vyāsa not as the editor of a divine Purāṇa, but, as his name implies, as the arranger of already existing material : "He [Vyāsa] who understands the true meaning of Purāṇic lore composed the *purāṇa-saṃhitā* out of tales, episodes, verses, and descriptions of the ages."[77] It is then affirmed that

[74]Winternitz quotes this passage from the ViṣṇuP without specific reference (*op. cit.*, p. 527n). Some Purāṇas see Vyāsa as an incarnation of Brahmā or of Śiva: see Kane, *op. cit.*, vol. V, part 2, p. 857 and 857, n. 1390.

[75]Hazra, R. C., *Studies in the Purāṇic Records on Hindu Rites and Customs*, The University of Dacca, Bulletin No. XX (Dacca [1940]), p. 2.

[76]*punaḥsarge bījārthā bhavantīti bhaviṣyatpurāṇe*
Text given by Kane, *op. cit.*, vol. V, part 2, p. 817, n. 1328.

[77]*ākhyānaiś cāpyupākhyānair gāthābhiḥ kalpajoktibhiḥ/*
*purāṇasaṃhitāṃ cakre purāṇārthaviśāradaḥ//*

Vyāsa taught this *saṃhitā* to his disciple Sūta Lomaharṣaṇa (or Romaharṣaṇa)who, in turn, taught it in six versions to six of his disciples. Three of these composed their own *saṃhitās*; these three, together with Lomaharṣaṇa's, comprise the basic compilation (*mūla saṃhitā*), from which the later eighteen Purāṇas were derived.[78]

It is important to note that, despite their disagreement on the critical issue of origins, the two traditions agree on certain matters. Both affirm that the extant Purāṇas are not identical with the original Purāṇa, whether that original be the utterance of Brahmā or the arrangement of Vyāsa. The transmission of Vyāsa's version to a succession of human disciples who revised that version is agreed upon, whether Vyāsa himself be seen as a divine *avatāra* or as a mere mortal. From our perspective, the most significant agreement of these two traditions is on the applicability of a phrase that has become the virtual motto of Purāṇic study: *itihāsapurāṇābhyāṃ vedaṃ samupabṛṁhayet.* R.C. Hazra translates this in its fuller context as follows :

> That twice-born (Brāhmaṇa), who knows the four Vedas with the Aṅgas (supplementary sciences) and the Upaniṣads, should not be (regarded as) proficient unless he thoroughly knows the Purāṇas. He should reinforce the Vedas with the Itihāsa and the Purāṇa. The Vedas is [ sic ] afraid of him who is deficient in traditional knowledge (thinking) "He will hurt me."[79]

---

*BrahmāṇḍaP* II.34.21; *VāyuP* I.60.21 (*varia lectio: kulakarmabhiḥ*); *ViṣṇuP* III.6.15 (v. 1.: *kalpaśuddhibhiḥ*). Text given *ibid.*, p. 858, n. 1392; also by Gupta, "Purāṇas and their Referencing," p. 325n, and by Hazra, *Purāṇic Records*, p. 5n.

[78]Gupta, "Purāṇas and their Referencing," p. 325; Hazra, "The Purāṇas," p. 244; Agrawala, V. S., "Original Purāṇa Saṃhitā," *Purāṇa* VIII 2 (July 1966), pp. 235-239; Ramchandra Dikshitar, V. R., "The Purāṇas: A Study," IHQ VIII 4 (Dec. 1932), pp. 753-755; Pargiter, *AIHT*, pp. 22-23.

[79]*Yo vidyāc caturo vedān sāṅgopaniṣado dvijaḥ|*
*Na cet purāṇaṃ samvidyān naiva sa syād vicakṣaṇaḥ||*
*Itihāsa-purāṇabhyāṃ vedaṃ samupabṛṁhayet|*
*Bibhety alpa-śrutād vedo māṃ ayaṃ prahariṣyati||*

Hazra, "The Purāṇas, " p. 268. Hazra gives no reference for this passage. Winternitz (*op. cit.*, p. 527n) notes that Rāmānuja cites it as "a Purāṇa text" in his commentary on the *Vedānta Sūtras* and that the text occurs at *VāyuP*

V. S. Agrawala interpretatively translates the critical line: ". . . the metaphysical truth of the Veda is intended to be demonstrated in the Itihāsa-Purāṇa manner."[80] Both traditions would agree that the Purāṇas are intimately related to the Vedas, with the former explicating, interpreting, adapting the truth of the latter; they agree on the Purāṇas' function, while disagreeing on their origin.

Before investigating the nature of the Purāṇas and their study any further, we may pause to counteract any reifying tendencies in the above discussion : in fact, while the two traditions are formally distinguishable, no effort is made in the texts themselves to establish one as logically superior. We seem to have here another instance of the widespread Indian intuition of the many-faced nature of truth, and perhaps the most authentically Hindu statement we could make would be that the Purāṇas are of *both* human and divine origin : if we insist on the correctness of only one tradition, we have missed the spirit in which either tradition is affirmed, let alone both together. Thus a single Purāṇa can affirm both that Vyāsa is the author of all eighteen Purāṇas and that the different Purāṇas have separate authors.[81] This fluidity, or admission of a variety

---

I.201, Mbh (Vulgate) I.1.267, and *Vāsiṣṭha Dharmasūtra* 27.6. Agrawala (see our following note) repeatedly cites this phrase, and it occurs very frequently in the editorials of *Purāṇa* journal, of which Agrawala was editor for some years: in virtually none of these instances does it carry a specific reference. The only additional documented use of this passage that we have seen occurs in Gupta, A. S., "The Problem of Interpretation of the Purāṇas," *Purāṇa* VI 1 (Jan. 1964), p. 54n, where it is identified simply as "Vayu-P., 2.181; etc." Ingalls has identified the two verses for us as Mbh (critical edition) 1.2.235 and 1.1.204, respectively.

[80]Agrawala, V. S., "Editorial," *Purāṇa* I 2 (Feb. 1960), p. 118. We shall have more to say of Agrawala's particular approach below.

[81]*BhaviṣyaP* I.1.58 and III.iii.28.10-15, cited in Gupta, "Purāṇas and their Referencing," pp. 333-334. This, of course, is not to say that the same individual composed both passages, for, as Hazra has shown (*Purāṇic Records, passim*) most of the Purāṇas have been subjected to multiple recastings. What is significant is that the final redactor did not see fit to smooth over the apparent logical incompatibility of these two traditions by editing out one of them: each is affirmed as a different facet of, or perspective on, the ultimate truth. For further reflections on this "Purāṇic spirit," see Brown, C. M., *op. cit.*, pp. 17-19.

of perspectives, is, in fact, pervasive of the Purāṇas and of scholarship thereon. Thus, it is admitted that the Purāṇas may be classified in a number of ways—(1) according to which of the three qualities, *sattva*, *rajas*, *tamas*, they embody; (2) according to the deity they glorify; (3) according to whether they are encyclopedic, sectarian, historical, concerned with *tīrthas*, or (4) twice-revised, or revised out of existence; (5) according to their apparent age[82]—without insisting on any one possibility alone. Similarly, while Vyāsa is almost always assigned a critical role in the arrangement of the Purāṇas, the next link in the chain of transmission, viz., Sūta Lomaharṣaṇa, has been variously interpreted : Mazumdar goes so far as to argue that Lomaharṣaṇa is not a proper name at all, but "a class-name to represent those persons, who by reciting some wonderful and thrilling stories to the people, made the hair to stand on the persons in the audience."[83] A comparable diversity of opinion has been expressed regarding the identity of the *sūta* who appears so often as an interlocutor in the Purāṇas.[84] The point here is simply that the Purāṇic spirit is one of "looking at a thing from several points of view and interpreting it accordingly,"[85] not of pursuing one exclusive train of thought.

Despite this spirit of tolerance and multiformity that pervades the Purāṇas, it is important that we try to reconcile the two

[82]For all five possibilities, see Gupta, "Purāṇas and their Referencing," pp. 340-344; for the second, see also Ramchandra Dikshitar, *op. cit.*, pp. 766-767; for the fifth, see O'Flaherty, Wendy Doniger, *Sexuality and Asceticism in the Mythology of Śiva in the Sanskrit Purāṇas*, Ph.D. Dissertation (Harvard University, 1967), Appendix IV: The Age of the Purāṇas (pp. 799-808); the bulk of this study has been published, in somewhat revised form, as *Asceticism and Eroticism in the Mythology of Śiva*, Oxford University Press (London, 1973), but the relevant Appendix has been omitted.

[83]Mazumdar, *op. cit.*, pp. 28-29: *loma*, "hair"; *harṣaṇa*, "causing delight".

[84]For this discussion, which revolves around the relationship between the meaning of *sūta* as "bard, charioteer" and its meaning as "a person of mixed *pratiloma* caste born of the union of a *brāhmaṇa* woman with a *kṣatriya* male," see Kane, *op. cit.*, vol. V, part 2, pp. 862-864; Hazra, "The Purāṇas," pp. 243-244; Pargiter, *AIHT*, pp. 16-17; Ramchandra Dikshitar, *op. cit.*, pp. 759-760; Ghoshal, U. N., *Studies in Indian History and Culture*, Orient Longmans (Bombay, 1957), chapter I ("The Beginnings of Historiography in the Vedas").

[85]Gupta, "The Problem of Interpretation of the Purāṇas," p. 56.

traditions regarding their origin, for they underlie what has been the major contemporary debate over the interpretation of the Purāṇas. That very question, of how we shall read a Purāṇa, is precisely our current concern. The debate has been carried on in the pages of *Purāṇa* journal and, rather than follow its chronological evolution, we may summarize the critical issues as follows.[86] The crux of the discussion has been the possibility, and the significance, of critical editions of *smṛti* literature. We have seen that both traditions of the Purāṇas' origin allow for human elaborations on the *purāṇa-saṃhitā* of Vyāsa. The central questions then are : if we edit a Purāṇic text along the lines laid down by V. S. Sukthankar for the critical edition of the Mbh,[87] have we violated "the Purāṇic spirit"?; and what is the significance of the constituted text at which we thus arrive, particularly in its relationship to Vyāsa who, according to one tradition at least, is the divine editor of the eternal Purāṇa ? We can identify three stances that have been assumed with regard to these questions : (1) a critique of Sukthankar's method, especially when applied to the Purāṇas, and the suggestion of a radically alternative approach to the Purāṇas; (2) a defense, in principle, of Sukthankar's method; (3) an adaptation of Sukthankar's method to the Purāṇic material.

[86]For the sake of simplicity, we may cite the relevant articles here at the outset, in chronological order: the three previously cited articles of A. S. Gupta, "The Problem of Interpretation of the Purāṇas" (Jan. 1964), "Purāṇa, Itihāsa, and Ākhyāna" (July 1964), "Purāṇas and their Referencing" (July 1965); Gupta, A. S., "Constitution of the Vāmana-Purāṇa Text" *Purāṇa* IX 1 (Jan. 1967), pp. 141-194; Biardeau, Madeleine, "Some More Considerations about Textual Criticism," *Purāṇa* X 2 (July 1968), pp. 115-123; Bedekar, V. M., "Principles of Mahābhārata Textual Criticism: The Need for a Restatement," *Purāṇa* XI 2 (July 1969), pp. 210-228; Biardeau, Madeleine, "Letter to the editor" subtitled "Dr. Madeleine Biardeau's rejoinder to Shri V. M. Bedekar's article written in reply to her article on the critical editions of the Mahābhārata and the Purāṇas," *Purāṇa* XII 1 (Jan. 1970), pp. 180-181; Biardeau, Madeleine, "The Story of Arjuna Kārtavīrya without Reconstruction," *Purāṇa* XII 2 (July 1970), pp. 286-303; Gupta, Anand Swarup, "A Problem of Purāṇic Text Reconstruction," *Purāṇa* XII 2 (July 1970), pp. 304-321.

[87]See Sukthankar's "Prolegomenon" to *The Mahābhārata*, for the first time critically edited by Vishnu S. Sukthankar, et al. Bhandarkar Oriental Research Institute (Poona), vol. I (Ādiparvan, 1933).

First, Madeleine Biardeau draws on Sylvain Lévi's critique of Sukthankar to point out the tension between Western text-historical methods and the traditional Indian ascription of an original version of a text to Vyāsa : "He [Sukthankar] cannot help thinking that Vyāsa and Vaiśampāyana are historical characters, and he holds the idea of an old organic poem, which is the basis of all alterations; but he also says about this poem that it 'practically never existed.' "[88] Part of the problem, she feels, is the application of methods of textual criticism to what is basically oral tradition that has been subsequently written down. More important, however, are the very different connotations of "oral tradition" in the West and in India. Whereas the West has tended to revere the written word more highly than the spoken, India reverses this evalution. Moreover, India makes a further distinction between *śruti*, revealed ("heard") truth, which is passed down in immutable form, and *smṛti*, "that which is remembered," which is of human composition[89] and acquires normative value through acceptance by the learned Brahmans (*śrutāḥ*) in a particular locale. It is this locus of authority on the local level—"any epic or purāṇic story is true if the local brahmins recognize it as part of their beliefs"[90]—which Biardeau feels Sukthankar and company have betrayed by trying to establish the earliest text and then treating *it* as authoritative by virtue of its greater chronological proximity to Vyāsa. To do this, she claims, is to introduce "the historical dimension into the realm of myth where it cannot exist."[91] Though she intends these remarks to be pri-

[88]Lévi, Sylvain, "Review of *The Mahā-Bhārata*, for the first time critically edited by Vishnu S. Sukthankar," *Journal Asiatique* CCXXV 2 (Oct.-Dec. 1934), p. 282, quoted in English translation in Biardeau, "Textual Criticism," p. 116. This passage occurs in Lévi's review of the seventh fascicule of the Mbh's critical edition. His review of fasc. I-III occurs in *Journal Asiatique* CCXV 2 (Oct.-Dec. 1929), pp. 345-348.

[89]Biardeau overlooks the tradition of the divine origin of the Purāṇas.

[90]Biardeau, "Textual Criticism," p. 121.

[91]*Ibid.*, p. 122. Biardeau points out ("Arjuna Kārtavīrya," p. 302n) what she thinks is a contradiction in Sukthankar's own attitude to this matter of authority: in his lectures on the Mbh (given in 1942, but not published until 1957 as *On the Meaning of the Mahābhārata*, The Asiatic Society of Bombay), he relied on the Vulgate rather than on the critical edition of the text. Ingalls

marily restrictive, rather than proposing a positive alternative,[92] she does suggest a new tack by proposing that the unity of any particular text "is to be found in the meaning of the stories and not in their particular contents or historical bearing."[93] When she gives substance to this concern through exemplification,[94] her position becomes clear : she maintains that the "meaning" of a particular story in a particular culture can only be discerned by examining as many variants of that story as possible. The problem with critical editions, she feels, is that there are many instances of irreconcilable conflicts between texts, and no decisive criteria for choosing between versions. Rather than arbitrarily constructing a constituted text, we should recognize that these conflicts are pointing to the critical issues of meaning for Hindus. Consequently, "what appears to many people as an unmanageable overgrowth of myths and *purāṇas* is actually an invaluable source of information for a better understanding of each of them."[95] Finally, we may note that Biardeau's stance here puts her in good company : her ahistorical approach, her feeling that story conflicts are not mere ineptitudes nor corruptions but are telling us something important, her focus on issues of meaning rather than on plot, her concern to trace a story through as many variants as possible in order to shed the maximum amount of light on its underlying structure, all this she shares with the anthropologist Claude Lévi-Strauss.[96] Consequently, she has much in common with Wendy O'Flaherty,

---

has pointed out to us that there is, in fact, no contradiction here, for the critical edition simply had not progressed far enough by 1942 (it was not completed until 1959) to allow Sukthankar to use it.

[92]Biardeau, "Letter to the Editor," p. 181.

[93]Biardeau, "Textual Criticism," p. 123.

[94]Which is the purport of Biardeau, "Arjuna Kārtavīrya."

[95]*Ibid.*, p. 293.

[96]These features of Lévi-Strauss's approach are apparent even in his most elementary writings. (Some would say they are blessedly apparent there, as they get lost in the luxuriance of his major works.) E.g., see Lévi-Strauss, C., "The Structural Study of Myth," in *Reader in Comparative Religion: An Anthropological Approach*, William A. Lessa and Evon Z. Vogt (edd.), Harper and Row (New York, Evanston, and London, second edition, 1965), pp. 562-574 (first published in *Journal of American Folklore* LXVII (1955), pp. 428-444, and frequently reprinted); also, the Overture (pp. 1-32) to his *The Raw and the Cooked: Introduction to a Science of Mythology:* I, John and Doreen

who employs many Lévi-Straussian insights in her analysis of Indian mythology.[97] Except for the fact that Eliade examines myths on a global scale, rather than limiting himself to a particular culture, we can detect a certain affinity with his phenomenological approach.

The second stance adopted in this discussion, the defense of Sukthankar's method against Biardeau's critique, is taken by V. M. Bedekar. While some of his arguments border on the *ad hominem*, he does shed light on the aims of critical editing. He first argues that the distinction between written and oral tradition, and between Western and Indian understandings of the latter, is beside the point: once a tradition is committed to writing, it becomes liable to textual criticism, regardless of its origin.[98] Bedekar does not deny that the traditional locus of authority was local Brahmans (whom he sees as expressing their "subjective preferences"), but he argues that this, too, is beside the point in trying to arrive at the earliest manuscript tradition: the text so constituted is simply a text, which may or may not have been sometime, someplace accepted as authoritative. "Sukthankar never claimed that the critical edition would be authoritative from the traditional point of view."[99] Bedekar is at his best when he allows his mentor to speak for himself, as follows:[100]

---

Weightman (trans.), Harper and Row (New York and Evanston, 1969). It should be mentioned that Biardeau does not seem concerned with the matter that lies at the heart of Lévi-Strauss's method, viz., the identification of oppositions or polarities, and the ways in which they are mediated.

[97]See *supra*, n. 82. For further identification of the methodological affinities of Biardeau's work, and exploration of the structuralist-historicist debate, see my "The Study of the Purāṇas and the Study of Religion", *Religious Studies* 16 3 (Sept. 1980), pp. 341-352, esp. p. 349 and 349n.

[98]Bedekar, "Principles," p. 219. This is a very tricky matter, by no means as straightforward as Bedekar implies. To it we shall return in the next two sections.

[99]*Ibid.*, p. 221.

[100]Bedekar's quotation of Sukthankar occurs *ibid.*, p. 225. Because Bedekar's quotation has a number of errors in transcription, our quotation follows Sukthankar's original ("Prolegomenon," p. cii) and is a bit fuller than Bedekar's.

> [The] essential fact in Mahābhārata textual criticism [is] that the Mahābhārata is not and never was a fixed rigid text, but is fluctuating epic tradition. . ., not unlike a popular Indian melody. Our objective should consequently not be to arrive at an archetype (which practically never existed), but to represent, view and explain the epic tradition in all its variety, in all its fullness, in all its ramifications. *Ours is a problem in textual dynamics, rather than in textual statics.*
>
> To put it in other words, the Mahābhārata is the whole of the epic tradition: the *entire* Critical Apparatus. Its separation into the constituted text and the critical notes is only a static representation of a constantly changing epic text—a representation made for the purpose of visualizing, studying and analyzing the panorama of the more grand and less grand thought-movements that have crystallized in the shape of the text, handed down to us in our Mahābhārata manuscripts.

The third stance, endeavoring to adapt this method to the unique features of the Purāṇas, is that of A. S. Gupta. It merits particular attention since Gupta is also the chief editor of the recently completed critical editions of the *Vāmana* and *Kūrma Purāṇas.*[101] Gupta is aware of several major issues raised by critical editing of the Purāṇas, e.g., the historicity of Vyāsa (he is clearly responding to Biardeau when he writes : "We Indians . . . are not used to regard [ing] all our ancient sages and heroes as mythical figures"[102]), the legitimacy of reducing the various extant versions of a text to a single universal version, the feasibility of arriving at the manuscript tradition which is oldest and therefore closest to the inferred original or to the lost archetype. However, he brackets these questions and instead

[101] *The Vāmana Purāṇa,* text critically edited by A. S. Gupta and others, All-India Kashiraj Trust (Varanasi, 1968); *The Kūrma Purāṇa,* text critically edited by A.S. Gupta and others, All-India Kashiraj Trust (Varanasi, 1972). The constituted texts of these Purāṇas, with an English translation thereof, have been published separately (with the same publisher and respective dates of publication). While publication of only the constituted text may seem to be a violation of Sukthankar's claim that the whole critical apparatus constitutes a particular textual tradition, this is consistent with Gupta's view of Purāṇic critical editing, as we shall see.

[102] Gupta, "Text-Reconstruction," p. 305.

addresses a practical matter: how shall a text-editor deal with material that is clearly an addition to earlier material but is nonetheless significantly attested ?[103] The answer he proposes ingeniously tries to strike a balance between the rigor of Sukthankar and the scepticism of Lévi.[104] It is based on seeing the entire Purāṇic literature as a whole, which started with the kernel of Vyāsa and grew organically to its current extent. The individual Purāṇas represent different parts or limbs of that organism, and it is possible to characterize each of those limbs according to its sectarian preference (presumably according to the kind of criteria Hazra has used in ascertaining the different sectarian recasts that individual Purāṇas have undergone, but Gupta is not explicit about this). It is then possible for an editor to constitute a text and to allow later additions to be incorporated into that text, though set off from the core of the constituted text by some means of annotation, provided that those additions are in accord with the over-all sectarian bias of that particular Purāṇa. Additions that do not accord with that bias are deemed "spurious" and relegated to the notes and appendices. There are obvious difficulties with this method. Brown has pointed out the danger of calling anything "spurious" in a culture that so profoundly appreciates the many-faced nature of truth.[105] Moreover, it presupposes that each Purāṇa, throughout its extant manuscript tradition, shows one clear-cut sectarian preference, and it is not explicit about

[103]This practical orientation is characteristic of Gupta's work. In his remarks on textual criticism as an aid to Purāṇic interpretation ("Interpretation," pp. 66-69), he is concerned solely with the establishment of an intelligible text, not with any of the larger issues. It may be that the difference between Gupta and Bedekar, on the one hand, and Biardeau, on the other, corresponds to the difference between lower and higher criticism.

[104]This and the following three sentences are a précis of Gupta, "Text-Reconstruction," pp. 310-321.

[105]Brown, C. M., *op. cit.*, pp. 17ff. The force of Brown's criticism is mitigated somewhat by the fact that Gupta provides all the "spurious" items in the notes anyway. A critical distinction may be: in light of the general Indian and particularly Purāṇic spirit it seems out of place to call any individual's perception of reality spurious, but in a particular manuscript tradition, if that tradition can be given a specific sectarian characterization as Gupta maintains (which, of course, is itself debatable), then discordant variations on that tradition may fairly be called spurious.

what criteria should be used in ascertaining what it is.[106] Finally, as Hazra has shown, many of the Purāṇas have undergone multiple recastings, by different sectarian groups. It is presumably the most recent recast that would be the standard of non-spuriousness in Gupta's method, and all evidence for former recastings would become mired in the critical apparatus. For all these weaknesses, however, given the extraordinary complexity of the Purāṇic material, Gupta's method has much to commend it: he himself is aware that the indication of strata in the constituted text may appear uncritical, but, on the other hand, he notes that it "may perhaps conform more to [the very nature of] our Purāṇa-tradition."[107]

This debate over the desirability and significance of critical editions of the Purāṇas may be seen as a particular instance of the more global discussion of the relationship between western notions of academic scholarship and sacred literature. The matter, obviously, is enormous, and complex. It is also very contemporary,[108] so that it is preposterous to attempt any sort of closure at the present time. Nonetheless, it is important that we identify some of the critical issues in the interpretation of the Purāṇas, for they affect our development of an appropriate approach to the DM.

First, then, there is the traditional Hindu understanding of the Purāṇas, an understanding which seems to be congruent with at least some of the historical evidence. That evidence, as we have seen, is that the Purāṇic tradition, like the Sanskritic, is not static, but dynamic. It may even be legitimate to postulate a process of "Purāṇicization" as a particular variety of Sanskritization: there is a clear parallel between the Sanskritic tradition growing around the Ṛg Vedic nucleus and the

[106]It will be interesting to see how the MarkP is critically edited according to these principles, for, apart from the devotion to the Goddess that the thirteen chapters of the DM evince, the Purāṇa shows no particular sectarian zeal at all.

[107]Gupta, "Text-Reconstruction," p. 314.

[108]Consequently, it is exceedingly difficult even to decide what the salient phenomena are, let alone to discern a pattern in those phenomena. Suffice it to say that the assumption that Western academic inquiry has a universal legitimacy is increasingly, perhaps, being shown to be hasty, if not facile: see Deshpande's remarks at the end of this section.

Purāṇic tradition growing around the nucleus of material that the early literature simply calls *purāṇa*, though we may not know what the nature of that material was. But it is imperative, in this regard, that we see this growth as Hindus do, i.e., against its Vedic background. We have already noted the widespread agreement that the Purāṇas are a confirming elaboration (*upabṛṁhaṇa*) upon the Vedas, and it is worth remarking that such a judgment is of two-fold significance : not only do the Purāṇas avoid innovation and the proclamation of new truths, but, in a positive sense, they also make the original Vedic truth available in a contemporarily relevant way. C. M. Brown has pithily expressed the relationship here by referring to the Veda as revealed truth, and the "Purāṇa as revealing truth."[109] His remarks convey the dynamic, but retrospective, quality of Purāṇic life incisively :

> Truth was fully revealed ["heard," as *śruti*] in the past. ...The Vedas are revealed truth, and even the perfect expression of that truth. But ... they are reserved for the twice-born classes and are not to be recited in public. Śūdras and women are prohibited from even hearing the Vedas. The Purāṇas, on the other hand, may be heard by all, especially in the *kali yuga* when *dharma* is in universal decline. The Purāṇas are an "easier" form of truth, adapted to the conditions of class and world age. . . . It is assumed that the [ Purāṇic] revisions are made in complete harmony with the truth contained in *śruti*. The Purāṇas represent, then, an interpretation or clarification of the *śruti*, revealing the eternal, immutable truth in a comprehensible form to all mankind in his changing, historical situation. The process of revealing truth by its very nature is never-ending. The truth, once revealed in *śruti*, must ever be newly interpreted or explained in *smṛti*.[110]

[109]The phrase in quotation marks is the title of Brown, C. M., *op. cit.*, chapter 1. See van Buitenen's remarks (cited in section 2, *supra*) on Sanskrit as one of the "life-lines" to the sacral past.

[110]*Ibid.*, pp. 18-19. Cf. Banerjea-Sastri's similar remark— ". . . literary tradition in India dies hard. The power of memory of people in India is overwhelming; it might almost be defined as the incapacity to forget" —in "Ancient Indian Historical Tradition," JBORS XIII part I (March 1927), pp. 78-79.

Clearly there is room for some divergence of opinion as to precisely how the Purāṇas are a harmonious revision of the Vedas, but in their recognition of some sort of change as a fact, the academic and Hindu perspectives are in agreement.

Second, there is the particular type of historical study proposed by Sukthankar, Bedekar, and Gupta, viz., the text-critical examination of particular scriptures. It should be noted that, although there may be religious implications to this type of study (as we shall see below), in and of itself it can lay claim to being value-neutral, i.e., to simply bracketing the question of the religious significance of a particular text. We have seen that the text editors themselves distinguish between the kind of authority that inheres in a text from the traditional point of view and that which inheres in a text by virtue of its constitution according to the principles of textual criticism. We may, perhaps, go one step further by clarifying one possible relationship between academic inquiry and personal faith. Let us take the two Purāṇic traditions regarding their origin, one affirming its divinity, the other its humanity. That the Purāṇas have developed from an early nucleus to their present extent is historically verifiable, according to academic criteria. Whether that nucleus was of human or divine origin is obviously beyond the range of these criteria. It is a matter on which, to use the Buddha's formulation, the question does not fit the situation. It is a matter of personal faith. Before it, academic inquiry must remain silent. Only the individual can respond, and that response is not of the intellect, but of one's whole being: it is faith, *śraddhā*, the "putting of one's heart." Similarly, the historicity of Vyāsa is a matter which present scholarship can neither affirm nor deny: given the nature of the evidence, it appears unlikely that an unequivocal judgment will ever be possible. That the Purāṇic material was, at some stage, "arranged" seems clear.[111] Whether we ascribe that work

[111]Though our remarks here address the issue of Vyāsa as arranger of the Purāṇic material, they clearly apply to him in his role as Veda-Vyāsa as well. In this regard, note Kane's critique (*op. cit.*, vol. V, part 2, pp. 858-861) of Pargiter: the latter had maintained (*AIHT*, p. 10) that the Vedas' silence on Vyāsa was due to a Brahmanical conspiracy to portray the Vedas as eternal. Kane points out that it is only the Vedic hymns or *mantras* themselves that are claimed to be eternal, *not* their arrangement. The post-Vedic

to an individual called Vyāsa, "The Arranger," and whether we regard him as a divine incarnation or as a human sage are matters of personal, individual faith. As noted earlier, the most typically Hindu affirmation may be that the Purāṇas are of both human and divine origin. But the Purāṇic spirit which delights in such apparently paradoxical formulations should not blind us to a critical discrimination: if a Hindu affirms one or the other Purāṇic tradition of origin, he has not necessarily, by that very affirmation, also cast his vote for or against the academic enterprise. These can be seen as distinct, though related matters. For Hindus, as for others, the life of critical inquiry may be compatible with the life of faith.[112]

However—and this is one of the reasons for the enormous importance of the issue of the relationship between critical

---

effort to glorify Vyāsa led to his being designated Veda-Vyāsa: this in no way affects the eternality of the Veda. Consequently, when we here suggest the possibility of understanding the historicity and role of Vyāsa as matters of faith, that does not affect the eternality of the Veda any more than it predetermines whether the Purāṇas shall be affirmed as of human or divine origin.

[112]There is an implication to Biardeau's comments on the matter of authority which should be noted in light of our remarks here. She felt, it will be recalled, that Sukthankar, et al. placed authority in that text which was chronologically closest to Vyāsa, rather than in the opinion of local Brahmans, and Bedekar replied that Sukthankar had never claimed authoritativeness, in traditional terms, for his text. Biardeau's point may then be reformulated: what Sukthankar has done is to place authority for interpretation of the Mbh in the principles of textual criticism, of academic inquiry, rather than in the opinion of local Brahmans. A corroboration of this might be seen in Bedekar's capitalization of the words "Western Scientific" when discussing the matter of authority ("Textual Criticism," pp. 218, 219). If this is the case, then there is an element of truth in Lévi's calling the critical edition of the Mbh "the recension of Poona" (*op. cit.*, p. 347): it is one recension, along side of many others, and they are differentiated from each other simply by the respective authorities to which (or to whom) they turn for the constitution of their individual texts. It should be noted, however, that even if the critical edition is thus seen as simply one of many recensions, it still retains one unique feature: it is also useful for a critical historical inquiry into the growth of the Mbh text tradition as a whole, and of Indian religion as reflected therein. Moreover, when commitment to text-historical inquiry is thus seen as being a matter of authority for the constitution of a text, it is even more clear that this commitment can be quite distinct from the commitment that is faith. In Indian terms, this is simply saying that the concerns of the *pramāṇas* overlap, but are not identical, with the concerns of *śraddhā*.

inquiry and religious faith—it is also clear that "some personal faith is conceived by those who hold it (or are held by it) to be closely linked either to historical facts or to ontological facts, or to both."[113] To the extent that critical inquiry calls certain of those facts into question, a *rapprochement* between inquiry and faith seems less readily made. And there are abundant examples of contemporary Hindus wrestling with precisely this issue. We have already seen the briskness with which Gupta replies to Biardeau's suggestion that ancient Hindu sages and heroes are "mythical figures."[114] Similarly, that some Hindus would be unwilling to follow Mazumdar's lead in reducing Lomaharṣaṇa from a proper- to a class-name by doing the same with Vyāsa is suggested by the fact that as recently as 1960 the All-India Kashiraj Trust sponsored an essay competition on "The Life and Works of Maharshi Vyāsa."[115] A final example may be seen in a recent journalistic account wherein one Ramakrishna Rao contends that S. K. Chatterji's recently publicized view "that Rama was not an 'avatar' of Vishnu..., taken together with Dr. Chatterji's statement that the Ramayana is fiction, has wounded religious susceptibilities of orthodox Hindus and overturned accepted ideas and traditional beliefs set out in several Hindu religious works."[116] Consequently, we must proceed with care, for while critical historical study is not intrinsically antipathetic to the concerns of faith, the point at which the former begins to encroach upon the latter may vary from individual to individual.[117]

Third, there is another kind of academic inquiry which; like the historical approach of Sukthankar and company, originates

[113]Prof. J. B. Carman, personal communication, Feb. 2, 1976.

[114]See the passage identified at n. 102.

[115]*Purāṇa* II 1-2 (July 1960), back cover.

[116]This quotation comes from an unidentified article sent to us by a colleague in India. We have been unable to locate its specific source and may simply note that it is entitled "Delhi scholar rebuts new Ramayana theory" and comes from a Delhi newspaper in late January 1976.

[117]W. C. Smith has offered a similar remark in a similar context. After discussing various challenges to any scholarly inquiry into religion, he comments, "Where only angels tread, he [one] would be a fool to rush in; though perhaps the wise may preserve their dignity if, aware of their presumption, they enter cautiously": *The Meaning and End of Religion*, Mentor Books, New American Library (New York, 1964), p. 13.

in the West, but which proceeds rather differently : this is the approach exemplified by Biardeau. Like the structuralists and phenomenologists, with whom we have suggested she has certain affinities, her focus is not upon historical developments, but upon the ahistorical, underlying "meaning" of textual material. Others[118] have demonstrated the virtues of such an approach, and in a culture, such as India's, that is not particularly self-conscious about historical factors,[119] those virtues may be considerable. We have, however, already distinguished our position from that of the phenomenologists;[120] but even if we had not, there seem to us to be certain difficulties with Biardeau's position.[121] Two of these may be mentioned without elaboration: she does seem to have offended the religious sensitivities of at least one of the people she is trying to understand (Gupta) ; and whatever the value of her approach for understanding Purāṇic stories, she says nothing about the rest of the Purāṇic topics, and the implication that those topics are less significant for understanding the Purāṇic genre seems to us to be unwarranted. There is one difficulty, however, that is more major: we articulate it at some length, drawing explicitly upon the insights of W. C. Smith, for it seems to us that his understanding of how one ought to conceptualize the religious life in general has a direct bearing on how we, as academics, should read a Purāṇa.

The difficulty we see with Biardeau's stance is her assumption that the alternative to a text-historical approach is to postulate, and then divine, the ahistorical, even transhistorical, "meaning" of the myths.[122] In other words, though she expresses concern for examining a literary tradition's relation to the "actual beliefs of the people,"[123] her way of doing this is

[118]E.g., those cited in our earlier exegesis of Biardeau: Lévi-Strauss, O'Flaherty, Eliade.

[119]We return to this matter below.

[120]*Supra*, section 1, esp. n. 6.

[121]Cf. also C. M. Brown's critique of Biardeau, *op. cit.*, pp. 12-15.

[122]Although our criticism here is primarily directed at Biardeau, it indirectly applies to Eliade when he implies (see the refs. given *supra*, n. 6) that historical study is almost necessarily historicism, trapped in a two-dimensional sequence of events, unable to discern issues of meaning.

[123]Biardeau, "Textual Criticism," p. 120.

not to examine the different historical contexts which gave rise to the corresponding textual variants of a story. Rather, it is to examine different versions of a particular story in search of its underlying "meaning," regardless of the historical relationship between those different versions. This strikes us as a premature flight from history. Is it not possible to bracket the question of the historicity of Vyāsa,[124] but to insist that it is still meaningful to speak of historical layers of textual and thematic accretion and development? From the Hindu perspective, this is simply acknowledging that *upabṛṁhaṇa* does, in fact, take place, that each generation and individual must make the Vedic truth his own, in his own way. From the standpoint of the historian of religion, this means being sufficiently detached from our contemporary conceptualizations, reifications, and categories of "meaning" so that we can appreciate the wholeness that characterizes each *individual's* religious orientation at every historical stage. For instance, we now have neat categories with which to order our knowledge of Hinduism, e.g., Śākta, Śaiva, Vaiṣṇava, Kṛṣṇa-ite. The problem is that if we treat each of these categories as a distinct entity and trace each of them backwards in history, we find (as we shall see in the body of our study) that they all overlap at at least one point : in the terminology, motifs, and symbols of the DM. This overlap does not, to be sure, include all that those individual concepts have subsequently come to connote, but we must somehow remain open to both the richness and the cohesiveness of the vision of the DM. If we prize our conceptual categories, we may say that that vision is conceptually eclectic,[125] but insofar as that vision is the vision of an individual,[126] it *ipso facto* has a certain coherence, viz., at the personal level. From this we can conclude either that we need a new concept to express the religiousness of the DM, or that a healthy scepticism toward our contemporary conceptual-

[124]Perhaps in the fashion we have suggested three paragraphs above.

[125]As many have, in fact, said: cf. our following section.

[126]We here simply assume, for the sake of continuity with Smith's affirmation (*Meaning and End, passim*; as particularly vivid passages, see pp. 138, 141, 165-168) that religious truth has to do primarily with religious *persons*, that the DM is the work of a single hand. There is, in fact, no evidence that this is not the case. Nonetheless, see our remarks two paragraphs below on the problem of applying Smith's personalist approach to an anonymous text.

izations is necessary if we are to fathom both features of human religiousness: it has an obvious variety of forms, and yet [equally obviously, but often overlooked] it is the individual person who provides the locus of integration, unity, and meaning. Since history is the context of every individual life, the sum of the circumstances into which mankind has been thrown, to use existentialist language, surely Biardeau et al. need not, indeed cannot, deny history in order to arrive at "meaning."

In specifying how it is possible, and in fact necessary, to take history seriously when studying human religiousness, it may be helpful to refer to the central distinction that Smith makes in his earliest major theoretical work. There he summarizes his position:

> The proposal that I am putting forward can, at one level, be formulated quite simply. It is that what men have tended to conceive as religion and especially as a religion, can more rewardingly, more truly, be conceived in terms of two factors, different in kind, both dynamic: an historical "cumulative tradition," and the personal faith of men and women.[127]

Given this framework, it then becomes possible to propose the role of the academic historian, for since "the cumulative tradition is wholly historical," it is clear that "the objective data of a tradition exist in this world and are observable by an historian."[128] But it is also clear that this is not to reduce human religiousness to its history, first, because of the presence, in varying degrees and ways, of the vivifying factor of personal faith,[129] and, second, because "history is not a closed system,

[127] *Ibid.*, p. 175.

[128] *Ibid.*, pp. 144, 145.

[129] Cf., *ibid.*, p. 143: "A man's faith is what his tradition means to him. Yet it is, further, what the universe means to him, in the light of that tradition." Though admitting the "unfathomability" of faith (p. 154), Smith does go on (p. 169) to affirm that it is possible, through "delicate procedures," to come to an apprehension, though not a comprehension, of another's faith. He is careful to indicate, however, that this is a far more subtle matter than the historical investigation of cumulative tradition: "By the exercise of imaginative sympathy, disciplined by intellectual rigour and checked by elaborate procedures, cross-checked by vigorous criticism, it is not impossible to infer what goes on in another's mind and heart."

since as agent within it stands man, his spirit in some degree open to the transcendent."[130] To examine the cumulative tradition at any given point in history, then, is to examine the "raw material" which is integrated—in which a pattern is "faithfully" apprehended[131]—by religious persons.

Let us return now to the Purāṇas and the DM. It may be noted, first, that there is a certain similarity between Smith's appreciation of cumulative tradition as dynamic, and the Hindu appreciation of the Purāṇic tradition as dynamic. But, it may be immediately remarked, is there not a personal component to Smith's formulation that is simply inaccessible when dealing with an anonymous text ? Can one speak of the faith attested in the DM if one knows nothing of its author(s) beyond what is presented in this particular version of the cumulative tradition ? The question here is an important one, for a certain adaptation of Smith's approach is clearly necessary when dealing with a Purāṇic text. Given the previously noted absence of knowledge about our text's context, it is impossible to engage in the rigorous cross-checking that apprehension of another's faith requires.[132] We may, in fact, come to some appreciation of that faith, but our only direct evidence is the text itself. Yet the anonymity of the text need not pose an insurmountable problem, for Smith himself has shown how it is possible to view such a text (the *Puruṣa Sūkta*).[133] It originally constitutes an expression of one individual's faith, but subsequently becomes a part of the cumulative tradition that later Hindus inherit. As we shall see in our next section, it is particularly appropriate to view the DM in a similar light. It is with regard to the question of whether the DM is the work of a single hand that we must modify Smith's personalist emphasis somewhat. No strong case can be made against the existence of a single author,

[130] *Ibid.*, p. 145.

[131] "Faith is not a factor in a man's life, one alongside others .... It is not one element in the total pattern of that person's life; rather, it *is* the pattern that the other elements form": Smith, W. C., "Traditional Religions and Modern Culture," Address presented at the XIth Congress, International Association for the History of Religions, Claremont, Calif., Sept. 9, 1965, mimeo., p. 26.

[132] Cf. Smith's remarks quoted *supra*, n. 129.

[133] Smith, *Meaning and End*, pp. 142-143.

but we have no way of knowing who he was, which branch (*śākhā*) of the Vedic tradition he may have been familiar with, etc. Consequently, when we have identified the appropriate "units" for our investigation of the cumulative (Sanskritic) tradition,[134] it will be necessary to examine them across the various recensions and *śākhās*. This does, to be sure, de-emphasize the personalist quality of the faith that is reflected in the DM. On the other hand, it does allow for a more thorough appraisal of the original impact of the DM, an impact which, if we are to judge by later events,[135] was rather widespread.

The conclusion emerging from this investigation is that our approach to the Purāṇas, while historical, need not (if carefully employed) violate the Purāṇic spirit, nor be destructive of individual faith. On the contrary, it may be seen as respecting that spirit, by indicating the diversity of the strands that have fed into the unitive vision of the DM, and it aspires to respect that faith, while examining in some detail an early expression of faith which has become a part of the Hindu cumulative tradition. Moreover, our use of critical editions in setting the context of the DM will be seen to be not only justifiable, but highly illuminating. The consensus of academic opinion is that both the Mbh and its supplement (*khila*), the *Harivaṁśa* (HV), antedate the DM and thus can be used to set the DM in its (literary) context. The critical editions of these texts[136] suggest some preliminary stages in the crystallization process with which we are concerned, e. g., two of the three myths about the Goddess in the DM appear in the constituted text of the Mbh, but in conjunction with other deities, while the two hymns to her in the Virāṭa and Bhīṣma Parvans have been relegated to the appendices as later additions. Both constituted text and appendices clearly feed into the understanding of the Goddess found in the DM. In addition to the utility of critical editions for the reconstruction of history, the value of close comparative analysis when dealing with Purāṇic

[134]See section 5 below.

[135]See section 4 below.

[136]For the Mbh, see *supra*, nn. 87, 91, a total of nineteen volumes. *The Harivaṃśa, Being the Khila or Supplement to the Mahābhārata*, for the first time critically edited by Parashuram Lakshman Vaidya, Bhandarkar Oriental Research Institute (Poona, 1969, 1971), two vols.

material has been demonstrated by Hazra,[137] and Hacker has shown how word-studies can be used to perceive an historical dimension in material that does not self-consciously attend to matters of chronology.[138] The specific bearing of these editions and approaches will be made explicit in section 5 below.

That we have to devise various schemes for introducing an historical element into the Indian material is, of course, itself significant. It is a reflection of the often-noticed feature of Indian life on which a recent study of Hinduism, by a Hindu, remarks in its opening sentence : "One of the characteristics of ancient Hindu thought is its indifference to history."[139] A host of reasons for this indifference has been suggested—ranging from alleged psychological peculiarities of Indians, absence of national sentiment, lack of scientific attitude of mind, inclination to mythologize, and lack of horizons beyond one's caste, to climactic determinism[140]—but they are not of concern to us here. What is important is that whatever insight we gain through various methodological ingenuities not be gained at the expense of the integrity of what it is we are trying to understand, viz., the vision of the Goddess in the DM, or, more precisely, the reality which is reflected in the vision of that text. We have tried in the above discussion to suggest the potential distinctiveness of matters of faith from matters of academic inquiry. That, however, was primarily a process of setting boundaries to the academic task, of suggesting what academic inquiry

[137]This method, employed throughout his work, is particularly evident in his *Purāṇic Records*. For an appraisal of the value of this method, see Morrison, *op. cit.*, p. 76.

[138]Hacker, Paul, "Eigentümlichkeiten der Lehre und Terminologie Śaṅkaras: Avidyā, Nāmarūpa, Māyā, Īśvara," ZDMG, C, pp. 246-286; Hacker, Paul, *Untersuchungen über Texte des frühen Advaitavāda, I. Die Schüler Śaṅkaras*, Franz Steiner Verlag (Wiesbaden, 1951), Akademie der Wissenschaften und der Literatur in Mainz, Abhandlungen der Geistes–und Sozialwissenschaftlichen Klasse, Jahrgang 1950, Nr. 26.

[139]Sarma, D. S. *Hinduism through the Ages*, Bharatiya Vidya Bhavan (Bombay, 4th ed., 1973) Bhavan's Book University 37, p. 1.

[140]The first three reasons are cited, and criticized, in Majumdar, R. C., "Ideas of History in Sanskrit Literature" (cf. *supra*, n. 70), pp. 26-27. The next two are subscribed to in von Fürer-Haimendorf, C. "The Historical Value of Indian Bardic Literature," *ibid.*, pp. 92-93. The final one is mentioned, without approval, in Basham, *op. cit.*, p. 3.

cannot do vis-à-vis religious matters. It also has a positive, constructive obligation. As Pathak has remarked, "there is a marked difference between the attitude of the modern historian with his exuberance of historical consciousness and of the ancient writer living in an ideal world and steeped in the tradition of the Vedico-agamic culture, based upon the intrinsic authority of the revealed word."[141] If the history that the "modern historian" writes does not adequately convey the attitude of that "ancient writer," then it is, in fact, no history at all. It is merely an intellectual autobiography of the "modern historian." To avoid such conceptual imperialism, and to delineate constructive alternatives is, of course, the central task of hermeneutics. Pathak has suggested that the particular problem with which we are faced is a function, not of India's lack of historical concern, but of her different understanding of history : "To the writers of *itihasa* [and, we might add, *purāṇa*] tradition, history was not just a meaningless succession of events [but mundane events] below which lay the fascinating drama of man's fulfilment of the sovereign purpose of human existence. *Itihasa* [and *purāṇa*] tried to grasp this inner story...," and, therefore, "what is needed [for the modern historian to accomplish his task] is to grasp the idea of the author which gave meaning to the whole narrative."[142] We have identified several of the "idealising agents"[143] operative in our material. Sanskritization is one of them. As another we have suggested a process of "Purāṇicization," where "the only [salient] characteristic of a Purāṇa is that it should be old. Anything old may be the subject of a Purāṇa, and it covers all the aspects of life."[144] In a subsequent section, we shall examine the role of epithets in our text's portrayal of this ideal. And, of course, all of these

[141] Pathak, V. S., "Ancient Historical Biographies and Reconstruction of History," in *Problems of Historical Writing in India*, Proceedings of the Seminar held at the India International Center, New Delhi, Jan. 21-25, 1963, pp. 15-16.

[142] *Ibid.*, pp. 13-14, 15. Cf. Huizinga, Johan, "A Definition of the Concept of History," D. R. Cousin (tr.), in *Philosophy and History*, R. Klibansky and H. J. Patton (edd.), Clarendon Press (Oxford, 1936), p. 9: "History is the intellectual form in which a civilization renders account to itself of its past."

[143] Pathak, *op. cit.*, p. 21.

[144] Haraprasad Shastri, M., *op. cit.*, p. 329.

media have as their backdrop the Veda, which is viewed as both primordial, and orderly. As Pathak puts it, "to an ancient man in India, the world and the overflowing stream of events were intelligible only with reference to this [Vedic] system, and therefore they understood historical changes in terms of the rearrangement of the ideas within the same system."[145] This "rearrangement" of existing motifs will be seen to constitute one of the major features of the DM.

Our reading of the Purāṇas, therefore, should be appreciative of their dynamic quality, for they are a process[146] which we are trying to arrest, or at least to examine, at one particular moment. It should be especially attuned to the Vedic resonance of the Purāṇic material. And in order to set our text in its original context, it should be historical, i.e., sensitive to the relationship between the DM's unitive vision and its literary antecedents and contemporaries. This multi-dimensional approach might appear eclectic, were it not for the fact that it is the very nature of myths and symbols to refract the light

[145]Pathak, *op. cit.*, p. 17.

[146]It has not been necessary for us to trace the details of this process, i.e., the growth of the early Purāṇic kernel to its present extent. Others have distinguished various stages in this process. E.g., Gyani ("The Date of the Purāṇas," *Purāṇa* I 2 (Feb. 1960), pp. 213-219, II 1-2 (July 1960), pp. 68-75 identifies four: an "Ākhyāna-Vaṁśa Stage," a "Bifurcation Stage," a "Pañca-Lakshana Stage," and a "Sectarian or Encyclopaedic Stage." Kane (*op. cit.*, vol. V, part 2, pp. 853-855) identifies (1) a Purāṇic kernel of unknown content, which (2) eventually came to constitute a class of works; (3) the addition to these of *gāthās*, *ślokas*, and *anuvaṁśaślokas*, with much *smṛti* material; (4) composition of the extent Mahāpurāṇas; (5) composition of the Upapurāṇas. Hazra ("The Purāṇas," pp. 246-253; *Purāṇic Records*, pp. 193-264) maintains that (1) a nucleus of *pañcalakṣaṇa* material was supplemented (2) by sectarian material authored by Smārta Brahmans in response to new non-Brahmanical sectarian movements, and (3) by Tantric material, of the same authorship, in response to popular Tantricism and to the disruptiveness of foreign invasions. Dimmitt and van Buitenen (edd. and tr., *Classical Hindu Mythology: A Reader in the Sanskrit Purāṇas*, Temple University Press (Philadelphia, 1978), pp. 5-8, maintain that "the Purāṇas represent an amalgam of two somewhat different but never entirely separate oral literatures", viz., a brahmin tradition and a bardic *kṣatriya* tradition, which were collected and edited in two different eras, in the wake of the *Mahābhārata* war about 1000 B.C.E., and again during the reign of the Guptas during the fourth to sixth centuries C.E.

of inquiry across such a spectrum. As Gupta has observed,[147] the Purāṇic spirit is crushed if one allows only one angle of vision.

It is, for the very same reasons, obviously false to insist that ours is the only responsible approach to the Purāṇas, even if only academic criteria are involved. Two alternative ways of construing the Purāṇic encounter with academic study, which have recently been articulated by Indians, may be mentioned briefly. The first is that of V.S. Agrawala and can be labeled a "symbolic" approach to Purāṇic material. We have earlier noted Agrawala's close linkage of the Vedas and Purāṇas,[148] and it is his contention that they both teach, in different ways, *sṛṣṭi vidyā*, or cosmic knowledge. This, however, is "no mere system of dialectic philosophy, but a discipline of metaphysics" and it is "symbols [that] are the language of metaphysics as words are of philosophy." Therefore, "the key to the Purāṇas lies in the unravelling of the Vedic symbolism, and *vice versa* the Vedic symbols find clarity of explanation in the Purāṇic legends."[149] The mood of this kind of interpretation may be felt in Agrawala's remarks on our text :

> The plot of the Saptaśatī [DM] has been conceived in three parts with a purpose, namely, the *pūrvacaritra* corresponds to the plane of *sattva* or *manas*, the *madhyamacaritra* to the plane of *rajas* or *prāṇa*, and the *uttaracaritra* to the plane of *tamas* or *Bhūtas*. The Āsuric darkness exists in the Psychic Man, the Vital Man and the Physical Man. The conflict with Madhu-Kaiṭabha refers to the first, that with Mahiṣa to the second, and that with Śumbha-niśumbha etc. to the third.[150]

[147]See Gupta, "The Problem of Interpretation of the Purāṇas," pp. 74-78 where he cites three different interpretations ("historical," "symbolical," and "spiritual or ādhyātmika") of the same Purāṇic topic.

[148]*Supra*, n. 79.

[149]Agrawala, V.S., "Purāṇa Vidyā," *Purāṇa* I 1 (July 1959), pp. 89, 100.

[150]Agrawala, V. S., "The Glorification of the Great Goddess," *Purāṇa* V 1 (Jan. 1963), p. 82. This article was reprinted as the Introduction to Agrawala's translation of the DM: *Devī-māhātmya: The Glorification of the Great Goddess*, [Text with English translation and annotations] by Vasudeva S. Agrawala, All-India Kashiraj Trust (Varanasi, 1963). The annotations

The second proposal is that of V. V. Deshpande.[151] It suggests an intriguing reversal that may prove significant in the ongoing interplay of East and West, for rather than asking how academic historians should approach the Purāṇas, it first asks how academic historians have, in the past, approached the writing of academic history.[152] Deshpande does, to be sure, cover the classical Indian significance of the Purāṇas, as we have, but that coverage has a long prologue,[153] in which he surveys and categorizes the various aims, methods, and assumptions of Western historical thinking during the past 2500 years, and particularly since the Renaissance. While an occasional apologetic note does creep in, his reading of Western historians and historiography is clearly more balanced, more academic, than the reading that those historians first gave the Purāṇas. Though Deshpande has not (yet?) tried to reconcile the Western historical and traditional Indian approaches to the Purāṇas, he has challenged, in an original way, the right of the former to occupy an Archimedean point, beyond the process of change, employing universally valid analytical tools. To that extent, he is making the same point we made above: any approach to the multi-dimensional Purāṇic tradition must itself be multi-dimensional.[154]

---

convey the same mood as the passage cited. This approach, called "almost new" by A. S. Gupta ("In Memoriam: Dr. Vasudeva S. Agrawala," *Purāṇa* IX 1 [Jan. 1967], p. 197), bears a strong resemblance to that which Winternitz (*op. cit.*, p. 529) sees Manilal N. Dvivedi to have taken in 1889. We may legitimately trace this kind of approach back at least to Śrī Aurobindo and his "symbolic" interpretation of the Veda, on which see Renou, Louis, *Religions of Ancient India*, Schocken Books (New York, 1953, 1968), p. 17.

[151]The proposal is set forth in Deshpande, V. V., "Nature and Significance of Itihāsa and Purāṇa in Vedic Puruṣārtha Vidyās," *Purāṇa* XVI 1 (Jan. 1974), pp. 47-66, XVI 2 (July 1974), pp. 245-260, XVIII 2 (July 1976), pp. 197-211.

[152]Our play on the word "history" is deliberate and is not intended to blur the formal distinction between history, the narration of history, and historiography. See Huizinga, *op. cit., passim.*

[153]Comprising roughly half of the whole article.

[154]We might make this a more authentically Hindu statement by saying: any approach to reality, which is patently multi-dimensional, must itself be multi-dimensional. Also, cf. Lévi-Strauss's remark (*The Raw and the Cooked*, p. 12) on the fact that his obviously scientific, academic study of myth is itself a myth.

### 4. *The Devī-Māhātmya : A Purāṇa, a Portion of a Purāṇa, or "purāṇa"?*

Having now established some necessary guidelines for an approach to the Purāṇas in general, we must ask whether they are sufficient for an approach to the DM in particular. This further question must be asked inasmuch as the DM does not constitute a whole Purāṇa, nor an Upapurāṇa, but consists of chapters 81-93 in the MarkP,[155] one of the generally recognized eighteen Mahāpurāṇas.

That this fact is significant may not be immediately apparent: why, it might be asked, does the approach to the genus not suffice for the species ? The reason that the DM's constituting only a portion of a Purāṇa is of consequence is that, as a self-contained text, it has had an independent life of its own. It has been approached, by both Hindus and Westerners, as scripture in and of itself, where its significance is intrinsic, not derivative from its Purāṇic context. In these approaches, the fact that the DM *also* occurs as a portion of the MarkP is practically irrelevant. The extent of the independent life that the DM has led is suggested by the fact that, in his compilation of the editions and translations of the MarkP, Chakravarti has identified a total of sixteen. Of the DM, he says simply, without

[155]There is an important exception to this enumeration of the chapters which we have seen noticed only once in the secondary literature (by Kane, *op. cit.*, vol. V, part 1 [1958], p. 155). The above enumeration is followed by two of the MarkP editions we have consulted: *Mārkaṇḍeya-purāṇa*, edited by Śrīdharātmajatryambaka Gondhalekara, Jagaddhihecchu Press (Poona [?], 1867) [abbr.: Jag], and *Mārkaṇḍeyapurāṇa*, edited by Jīvānanda Vidyāsāgara, Sarasvatī Press (Calcutta, 1879) [abbr.: Vid]. However the third edition we have consulted—*Mārkaṇḍeyapurāṇa*, Veṅkateśvara Press (Bombay, 1910) [abbr.: Veṅk]—has the DM in chapters 78-90. The reason for the discrepancy is that Veṅk collapses three Jag-Vid chapters (16, 17, 18) into one (16), then two Jag-Vid chapters (25, 26), into one (23). Veṅk continues to be three chapter numbers out of agreement with Jag and Vid to the end of the Purāṇa. All subsequent references, unless indicated to the contrary, will be to Vid since it is the briefest, and presumably the earliest, textual tradition: it contains 573 verses; Jag contains all of these, with the expected *variae lectiones*, and adds another *śloka* and a half; Veṅk contains all of the Vid verses and adds seventeen *ślokas*. One consistent alteration we make in Vid's text is the reading of a single, rather than double, consonant after "r".

A word may be added on the frequently encountered title of the DM *Saptaśatī*. The enumeration of its verses as seven hundred is probably based

elaboration, that it occurs in "numerous editions,"[156] while Winternitz observes that, "as an independent work,... it occurs in [virtually] innumerable MSS."[157] There is a suggestion of its independent life even when it occurs in the full edition of the MarkP : it is the only portion of the Veṅk edition that has a commentary on it. The perception of the intrinsic significance of the DM is also indicated by the early dates at which it was translated into European languages: in Riviere's list of European translations of Purāṇic texts[158] which is admittedly incomplete,[159] the 1823 English translation of the DM is the earliest entry.[160] This was followed by an analysis with excerpts in French in 1824,[161] a translation into Latin in 1831,[162] a translation into Greek in 1853,[163] and another translation into English in 1885.[164]

---

on the model of the *Bhagavad-Gītā* with its seven hundred verses. The higher figure is arrived at by counting phrases like *ṛṣir uvāca* as full verses. For an example of this enumeration, see *The Devī-Māhātmyam or Śrī Durgā-saptaśatī*, Swāmī Jagadīśvarānanda (trans.), Śrī Ramakrishna Math (Madras, 1969).

[156]Chakravarti, Chintaharan, "The Mārkaṇḍeya Purāṇa: Editions and Translations," *Purāṇa* III 1 (Jan. 1961), pp. 39-40.

[157]Winternitz, *op. cit.*, p. 565n.

[158]Riviere, Juan Roger, "European Translations of Purāṇic Texts," *Purāṇa* V 2 (July 1963), pp. 243-250.

[159]Riviere's list gives none of the items cited in our next sentence; also see our next note.

[160]*Saptaśatī or Chaṇdi-Pāṭha (Devīmāhātmya)*, translated from the Sanscrit into English by Cavali Vaṅkata Ramasswami, Columbian Press (Calcutta, 1823). Srivatsa Goswami has pointed out to us that there is, in fact, an earlier translation from the Purāṇas, viz., of the Bhāgavata Purāṇa into French: *Bagavadam ou Doctrine Divine, Ouvrage Indien, canonique; sur l'Être Supreme, les Dieux, les Géans, les hommes, les diverses parties de l'Univers*, &c., [traduit du Sanskrit d'après une version tamoule, par Meridas Poullé, un Malabare Chrétien, ] Paris: [Publié par Foucher d'Obsonville, ] 1788.

[161]Burnouf, Eugène, "Analyse et extrait du *Dévi Mahatmyam* fragmens du Markandéya Pourana," *Journal Asiatique*, Ier série, IV (1824), pp. 24-32.

[162]*Devimahatmyam*, Markandeyi purani sectio edidit latinam interpretationem annotationesque adiecit Ludovicus Poley, Impensis F. Duemmleri (Berolini, 1831).

[163]Δουργα, μεταφρασθεισα εκ του βραχμανικου παρα Δημητριου Γαλανου, Γ. Χαρτοφυλακος (Αθηναισ, 1853).

[164]Wortham, B. Hale, "Translation of Books 81-93 of the Mārkaṇḍeya Purāṇa," *Journal of the Royal Asiatic Society*, new series, XVII part 1 (Jan. 1885), pp. 221-274.

Our task in this section is to see how this independent life that the DM has led ramifies for our reading of the text. Having previously examined the significance of the DM's being in Sanskrit, and of its occurrence in a Purāṇa, we now turn to that of its being a scriptural entity in its own right. In this task, it will be convenient to consider first the *content* of the DM, and then to examine its *function*.

With only a few exceptions, scholarship has tended to view the DM as significant primarily because of its subject matter, viz., the Goddess and her worship. When the DM is cited in secondary sources, it is usually in the context of discussing the historical development of the worship of the Goddess, and the DM is seen as representing a critical stage in this process. There is some difference of opinion, however, as to why this stage is critical. One trend is toward viewing the DM as the integration of fragmented evidence for Goddess-worship in archeological remains and in Vedic and epic literature: it is the culmination of a long, earlier process. Another trend is toward viewing it as a statement, in nascent form, of the basic principles which were later made explicit in Śākta and Tantric philosophy and practice : it is the threshold of a long, subsequent process. Part of the DM's significance obviously lies in the fact that it stands at the juncture of these two processes. Therefore, let us look at the accounts of them in greater detail.

The studies which see the DM as the culmination of an earlier process tend to refer to a common body of evidence.[165] A starting-point is frequently taken in the Indus Valley civilization and its apparent respect for the powers of sexuality and

[165]Since the burden of the next three Parts of this study is the thorough presentation of the Sanskritic antecedents of the DM, here we shall mention only those antecedents which the secondary literature commonly cites. There will obviously be some overlap, but it is not extensive, and the structure of our approach to those antecedents is quite different from those in the studies here reviewed, for reasons which will become clear in the next section. Our review here is not intended to be exhaustive, but only to identify the "common body of evidence." For a more thorough review, particularly of archeology and the role of Dravidian linguistics, see Beane, *op. cit.*, chapter II. Mention may also be made of Kinsley's more thematic, less historical study of the DM: "The Portrait of the Goddess in the *Devī-māhātmya*", *Journal of the American Academy of Religion* XLVI 4 (Dec. 1978), pp. 489-506.

fertility.[166] Aniconically, the "ring-stones" found there can be seen as representations of the *yoni* particularly since there are corresponding representations of male sexuality in numerous phallic objects. Iconically, there are the myriad terra-cotta female figures, wide-hipped, full-breasted, scantily clad. Of the famous seals, two seem especially relevant : one which portrays a nude female upside-down, legs apart, with a plant issuing from her womb (on the reverse of which seal appears the suggestion of an animal sacrifice), and another which shows a woman standing among the branches of a (pipal ?) tree. Virtually all of these studies then draw on the RV. While there is general agreement with Ingalls' statement that "such goddesses as we meet [here] . . . are goddesses with a small 'g' rather than the singular embodiment that we might write with a capital,"[167] attention is drawn to the score of hymns to Uṣas, Dawn, who is called "mother of the gods" (*devānāṃ mātā*) at 1.113.19, to the hymns to Vāc, Speech (10.125), and Rātrī, Night (10.127), which became so consequential for later Goddess-worship, and to various lesser goddesses: Aditi, Sarasvatī, Pṛthivī, Ilā, etc.[168] Sometimes the focus is not on specific goddesses, but on the fact of gods having consorts and on the gradual emergence of the latter into a principle of divine power, as is evidenced in the terms *śakti*, *śacī* and *jñā*.[169] The passages in later Vedic texts which these studies frequently cite include:[170] the *Vājasaneyī Saṃhitā* (YV) reference (3.57) to Ambikā as the sister of Rudra, and the TA reference (10.18) to her as his consort; the AV hymn (12.1) to Earth; the KeU's introduction of Umā Haimavatī

[166]Banerjea, J. N., "Some Aspects of Śakti Worship in Ancient India," *Prabuddha Bharata* 59 (March 1954), pp. 227-228; Bhattacharyya, N. N., *op. cit.*, pp. 11-17; Chattopadhyaya, *op. cit.*, pp. 151-152; Kumar, *op. cit.*, pp. 6-9; Sinha, *op. cit.*, pp. 46-47.

[167]Foreword to Brown, C. M., *op. cit.*, p. xiii.

[168]Banerjea, *op. cit.*, p. 228; Bhattacharyya, *op. cit.*, pp. 26-29; Chattopadhyaya, *op. cit.*, p. 151; Payne, *op. cit.*, pp. 33-34; Kumar, *op. cit.*, pp. 9-17; Sinha, *op. cit.*, pp. 47-48; Dasgupta, Shashi Bhushan, *Aspects of Indian Religious Thought*, A. Mukherjee and Co. (Calcutta, 1957), pp. 46-64. The hymns to Vāc and Rātrī will be quoted in full in Part III.

[169]Sastri, G., "The Cult of Śakti," in *The Śakti Cult and Tārā*, D. C. Sircar (ed.), pp. 10-13; Sinha, *op. cit.*, pp. 48-50.

[170]The referencing conventions which these studies employ are various. We have cited the editions which we will use in Part I.

as the personified knowledge of Brahman (3.12); and the MuU's enumeration of two of Agni's seven tongues as Kālī and Karālī (1.2.4). A popular quotation is from the Greek source, *Periplus of the Erythraean Sea,* allegedly identifying the goddess Kanyā-Kumārī :

> Beyond this . . . there is another place called Comari at which are the Cape of Comari and a harbour; hither come those men who wish to consecrate themselves for the rest of their lives, and bathe and dwell in celibacy and women also do the same; for it is told that a goddess once dwelt here and bathed.[171]

Most of these studies, proceeding chronologically, then refer to the hymns in the Mbh, though none has used the critical edition to note their absence from the constituted text. Frequently, reference is made to the HV material.[172]

As noted earlier, these studies are agreed upon the integrative role of the DM, given this historical background. Sastri's judgment is that the Goddess here in the DM "appears as the centre of the great Śakti cult," while Sinha sees the DM as "the culmination of the Śakti conception."[173] Some, however, have detected a particular bias in the vision of the DM. Banerjea, while recognizing the unique importance of the DM, phrases this negatively by noting that the author "seems to have almost completely eschewed any explicit reference to the non-Aryan elements in the composite goddess so frequently and unblushingly mentioned in the [Mbh] Stotras."[174] This assessment is lent further credence by the fact that neither of the studies by Bhattacharya and Mazumdar,[175] which are explicitly

[171]Quoted in Chattopadhyaya, *op. cit.*, p. 154; Sinha, *op. cit.*, p. 53.

[172]The Mbh is cited by Banerjea, *op. cit.*, p. 154; Bhattacharyya, *op. cit.*, pp. 53-54; Chattopadhyaya, *op. cit.*, pp. 161-163; Dasgupta, *op. cit.*, pp.68-69; Kumar, *op. cit.*, pp. 30-37; Payne, *op. cit.*, pp. 38-39; Sastri, *op. cit.*, p. 15; and Majumdar, R. C. (ed.), *The History and Culture of the Indian People* (HCIP), Bharatiya Vidya Bhavan (Bombay), vol. II, p. 467. The HV is cited immediately thereafter by Banerjea, Bhattacharyya, Chattopadhyaya, Dasgupta, Kumar, Payne, and Mazumdar (ed.). The Mbh and HV hymns also will be quoted in full in Part III.

[173]Sastri, *op. cit.*, p. 15; Sinha, *op. cit.*, p. 54.

[174]Banerjea, *op. cit.*, p. 229.

[175]Bhattacharya, *op. cit.* (cf. *supra*, n. 20); Mazumdar, B. C., "Durgā: Her Origin and History," *Journal of the Royal Asiatic Society* 1906, pp. 355-362.

concerned with the non-Aryan character of the Goddess, makes any mention of the DM. Payne expresses this bias rather more positively by noting that although "there are many traces of magical beliefs, and descriptions of the terrifying appearance of the goddess [in the DM], . . . appeals are also made to her tenderer aspects, and a deep faith in her power is evidenced. ... In this fierce framework there are passages breathing deep religious feeling and enthusiastic adoration."[176] Two recent Indian studies are particularly impressed by the martial character of the vision of the Goddess that emerges in the DM, for Bhattacharyya claims that "in the *Mārkaṇḍeya Purāṇa*, the Devī is primarily conceived as the war goddess . . ."[177] while Kumar notes that, in our text, "in her perfect nature, she [the Goddess] has been described as the most beneficient; but her fierceness as a martial goddess dominates in the main episodes and we always find her killing the demons."[178]

Those studies that are impressed by the DM as the watershed of subsequent developments do not agree so readily upon what constitutes the relevant evidence: they concur that the DM has been consequential, but they cite quite different consequences. Brown, for instance, notes that many of the legends of Durgā in the *Brahmavaivarta Purāṇa*, to which he assigns a fifteenth or sixteenth century date, go back at least to the DM and that, in its tendency to identify one goddess with as many other goddesses as possible, the DM "foreshadows" many ideas of this Purāṇa.[179] Farquhar differs from the opinion of Banerjea, noted above, in that he is impressed by the "terrific" and "ghastly" qualities of the Goddess in the DM and of the ensuing Tantric cult.[180] He is joined in this assessment by Kirfel who

[176]Payne, *op. cit.*, p. 40.

[177]Bhattacharyya, *op. cit.*, p. 78.

[178]Kumar, *op. cit.*, p. 46.

[179]Brown, C. M., *op. cit.*, pp. 33, 149, 187, 190. That the DM "foreshadows" the ideas of many later Purāṇas seems clear. A few of these connections will be indicated at appropriate points below. In addition to Brown's treatment, we may mention one other examination of the DM's foreshadowing role: Sharma, Dasharatha, "Verbal Similarities between the Durgā-Saptaśatī and the Devī-Bhāgavata-Purāṇa and Other Considerations bearing on their Date," *Purāṇa* V 1 (Jan. 1963), pp. 90-113.

[180]Farquhar, J. N., *An Outline of the Religious Literature of India*, Oxford University Press (London, 1920), pp. 150-151.

sees the DM as describing "den Ursprung dieser Form des grimmigen Aspekts der Śakti."[181] Bhandarkar views the Tantras as the most significant items in the wake of the DM, for after summarizing the Mbh and HV hymns and the DM, he turns to the Tantras as "inculcating the worship of the goddess in these various forms" and briefly describes the metaphysics and practices of one Tantric school.[182] Sinha's study of the mature Śākta cult likewise gives the DM merely a preliminary glance, for its "account of the nature of the Devī,"[183] and then turns to a detailed discussion of the philosophy, psychology, and methods of Kuṇḍalinī Yoga, drawing almost exclusively on Tantric material.

The most comprehensive effort to assess the content of the DM in historical relation to the ongoing religious life of India, that of S. B. Dasgupta, calls for separate mention. As noted above, he does consider the Vedic goddesses, but that is basically an introduction to his lucid discussion of the principle of *śakti*.[184] It is Dasgupta's contention that, while it is possible to philosophize systematically about *śakti*, as has been done in the Trika school of Kāśmir Śaivism and the Pañcarātra school of Vaiṣṇavism, the basic intuition is far simpler. It is based on the empirical observation of the necessity of male and female for any kind of creation, and the speculative realization that, for anything to exist, the power (*śakti*) to exist is necessary. In the Purāṇas, the possessor of power, construed as male, is seen to exist in varying relationships to his power, personified as female. What we have in the DM is not only the identification of many local goddesses with the supreme Goddess, but also the recognition of the paramountcy of that Goddess as *śakti*. It is not "right to consider this Power as a mere spiritual entity ; she is

[181]Kirfel, Willibald, *Der Hinduismus*, A. Deichert (Leipzig, 1934), *Bilderatlas zur Religionsgeschichte*, H. Haas (ed.), p. xxiii. See also Kirfel, Willibald, *Symbolik des Hinduismus und des Jinismus*, Anton Hiersemann (Stuttgart, 1959), *Symbolik der Religionen*, Ferdinand Hermann (ed.), IV, p. 50.

[182]Bhandarkar, R. G., *op. cit.*, pp. 144-147.

[183]Sinha, Jadunath, *Śakta Monism: The Cult of Shakti*, Sinha Publishing House Pvt. Ltd. (Calcutta, 1966), p. 3.

[184]The next eight sentences are a précis of the third section of Dasgupta's article, i.e., pp. 73-100. The article is "Evolution of Mother Worship in India," comprising pp. 42-106 of his *Aspects of Indian Religious Thought*.

the power—spiritual, moral and mental, the Power—biological and physiological as well as grossly physical. Whatever there is, is due to her; whatever works, works because of her."[185] "What, then, is the significance of Mother worship to a real *sādhaka*? To feel that he and his universe are nothing but media for the manifestation of one all-pervading Power—the Power of God, that Power that is one with God."[186] The many battles that the Goddess wages against Asuras in the DM are simply allegories for the battle in which every individual participates between true power and ubiquitous proud pretenders. To realize the one true power, it is only natural that certain practical methods should arise, and that is what the Tantras provide. For Dasgupta, then, the DM represents the summation of earlier motifs, but also the ideal which subsequent Hinduism has sought to realize, and this quest is evident in figures as recent as Rāmprasād, Śrī Rāmakṛṣṇa, and Śrī Aurobindo.

What all of these studies have in common, regardless of whether they are impressed by the DM as an integrative, or as a generative, phenomenon, is a focus on the content of the text. This is quite natural and unextraordinary. We are accustomed to reading scripture for its content, for what it tells us about the beliefs of those who regard it as scripture.

Yet it is becoming increasingly clear to historians of religion, and especially, perhaps, to Indologists, that there is another approach to the phenomenon of scripture, one which asks not about content, but about function: what role has a particular text played in the lives of people? How and why do they approach, revere, transmit, employ a text, independent of what its subject matter may be?

Some of these questions can be answered for the DM on the basis of its comprising a portion of a Purāṇa. It is *smṛti*, the ever-new adaptation of the eternal truth of *śruti*. Yet this is not enough. The DM has not been regarded by Hindus as simply a portion of a Purāṇa, more or less on a par with all other *smṛti* material. As H.H. Wilson has observed, "In the present state of Hindu belief the Purāṇas exercise a very general

[185]*Ibid.*, p. 93.
[186]*Ibid.*, pp. 94-95.

influence. . . .Most Brahmans who pretend to scholarship are acquainted with two or more of them, and particular sections, as the Devī Māhātmya, are amongst the most popular works in the Sanskrit language."[187] Farquhar and Winternitz both remark on the employment of the DM in the contemporary liturgy of the Goddess,[188] and the DM itself points toward its use in a cultic context. While the passage occurs at the end of the DM and may therefore be an addition to the original core,[189] it is nonetheless attested in all versions of the DM that we have seen. The Goddess is speaking :

> He who shall, with composed demeanor, praise me constantly with these hymns,
> All his affliction I shall certainly put to an end.
>
> ..............................................................
>
> And those who, with singleness of mind, on the eighth, fourteenth, and ninth (days of the lunar fortnight)
> Shall listen with devotion (*bhakti*) to (this) supreme *māhātmya* of mine,
> To them nothing bad will happen, nor misfortunes arising from wrong-doings,
> Nor will there be poverty, nor separation from loved-ones[190] (for them).
>
> . . . . . . . . . . . . . . . . . . . . . . . . . . . . . . . . . . . . .
>
> That place where (this *māhātmya*) is constantly (and) properly recited in my sanctuary (*āyatana*),
> I will never abandon; my presence is established (*sthitam*) there.
> At the oblation-offering, at worship, at the fire-ritual (*agnikārya*), at the great festival (*mahotsava*),

[187]Wilson, Horace Hayman, "Two Lectures on the Religious Practices and Opinions of the Hindus," delivered at Oxford, Feb. 27-28, 1840, reprinted in vol. I of Wilson's *Works*, Reinhold Rost (collector and ed.), Trübner and Co. (London, 1862), p. 68.

[188]Farquhar, *op. cit.*, p. 357; Winternitz, *op. cit.*, p. 565.

[189]Hazra ("The Purāṇas," p. 251; *Purāṇic Records*, pp. 6-7) mentions the addition of new chapters as one of three methods employed in re-editing Purāṇic material; the other two are substitution of new material for old, and writing new works bearing old titles.

[190]Or "deprivation of desires," *iṣṭaviyojana*.

All these doings of mine are to be proclaimed and heard.
. . . . . . . . . . . . . . . . . . . . . . . . . . . . . .
A man who is filled with devotion, having heard this my *māhātmya*,
At the great annual (*vārsikī*) worship which is performed during the autumn (*śaratkāla*),
Becomes released from all afflictions, endowed with wealth, grain, and children,
Through my grace; (of this) there is no doubt.[191]

The mere mention of sanctuaries and rituals in conjunction with the Goddess is itself noteworthy. Particularly significant, however, is the time assigned to her worship, for it coincides with the great contemporary autumnal celebration of Durgā-pūjā, otherwise known as Durgotsava or Navarātra,[192] the climax of which is on the eighth and ninth days of the bright fortnight.[193] In the descriptions of this great festival, it is clear that the images used are based on the descriptions of the Goddess in the DM, though with obvious later embellishments.[194] But it is also clear that the text itself has a function in the liturgy, for on several occasions its recitation is provided for,[195] with explicit instructions: "The reading should not be too loud nor so low as not to be audible from a hundred yards. It should not be read fast nor so slow as to impair the sense of what is read. The book in the pothi form should be placed upon a raised table and the cloth round the waist should be slightly loosened."[196] Kane quotes the liturgical rubrics on the general advantages of such recitation :

"When some great danger threatens, one should recite (Devīmāhātmya) seven times; if repeated twelve times one secures fulfilment of one's desires and the destruction of enmity; if repeated 14 times, an enemy would be subdued and

[191]MarkP 92.1, 3-4, 8-9, 11-12.

[192]Kane, *op. cit.*, vol. V, part 1, p. 154.

[193]Ghosha, Pratāpachandra, *Durga Puja: With Notes and Illustrations*, "originally published in the 'Hindoo Patriot' for the 23rd October 1871," Printed at the Hindoo Patriot Press (Calcutta, 1871), p. xx.

[194]*Ibid.*, pp. 5ff.

[195]*Ibid.*, pp. 20, 39.

[196]*Ibid.*, notes p. xlii.

a woman would be brought under one's control; repeating a hundred times results in increase of one's kingdom; if repeated a thousand times Lakṣmī comes to a man of her own accord. As Aśvamedha is the prince among sacrifices, as Hari (is superior) among gods, so the laud called Saptaśatī is the highest among all lauds."[197]

That the DM is so thoroughly enmeshed in cultic life should not, of course, surprise us. Kees Bolle, in a study of a Purāṇic passage ostensibly dealing with cosmogony, has found that "ritualistic influences are apparently capable of *pervading* mythical accounts. Whatever may be that entity which we have vaguely referred to as the 'spirit' creating the great *purāṇas*, ritualism must have been an integral part of it."[198] Similarly, Alex Wayman has used the connection between the nuances of the Vedic goddess Uṣas and the structure of the DM to justify his thesis that "The peoples of the Indian subcontinent..., whether or not consciously aware of it, made regular correspondences between the crucial points of the day, the year, and man's life, and...important Indian mythology and many religious observances exemplify these correspondences."[199] At a more general level, an effort has been made to see an intricate mutual interdependence between myth and ritual arising as a consequence of their having the same function: "the gratification (most often in the negative form of anxiety reduction) of a large proportion of the individuals in a society."[200]

Nor, on the other hand, should we overlook the fact that the determination of the function of the DM is part of the larger question of the role of scripture in the Indian tradition. That question is enormous. A full answer is beyond the capacity of

[197]The *Tithitattva*, quoted in Kane, *op. cit.*, vol. V, part 1, p. 172. The *Tithitattva* is itself quoting the *Vārāhītantra*.

[198]Bolle, Kees, "Reflections on a Purāṇic Passage," *History of Religions* II 2 (Winter 1963), p. 291.

[199]Wayman, Alex, "Climactic Times in Indian Mythology and Religion," *History of Religions* IV 2 (Winter 1965), pp. 295, 296.

[200]See Kluckhohn, Clyde, "Myths and Rituals: A General Theory," *Harvard Theological Review* XXXV (1942), pp. 45-79, reprinted in *Reader in Comparative Religion: An Anthropological Approach*, William A. Lessa and Evon Z. Vogt (edd.), Harper and Row (New York, Evanston, London, 2nd ed., 1965), pp. 145-158: passage here cited, p. 149.

current scholarship. We may, however, note some of the subsidiary questions that have emerged in the course of our study. First, a matter touched on in the preceding section, what is the relationship between the extant Purāṇas and their classical antecedents? We have already seen that *smṛti* is traditionally understood as the adaptation and elaboration of *śruti*, and that a dynamic quality therefore inheres in the Purāṇic material. But what are we to make of the fact that the *Bhaviṣyat Purāṇa*, mentioned by Āpastamba and included in the traditional list of eighteen Purāṇas, in one of its current editions contains a summary of Biblical history from Adam to Abraham and "prophecies" which extend to the nineteenth century ?[201] In other words, does the notion of a closed canon have any applicability to *smṛti* material ? Second, does even *śruti* have the immutability that we would expect on the basis of the Hindu understanding noted earlier ? The Upaniṣads, for instance, traditionally enumerated at 108, fall clearly into the category of *śruti* and are therefore part of the primordial revelation, seen or heard at the beginning of this historical cycle, but essentially eternal (*apauruṣeya*). Yet in the index of words appearing in Vedic material,[202] no fewer than 206 Upaniṣads are indexed. Some are clearly of fairly recent origin. What is the status of these ? While it is tempting here to follow Biardeau when she argues for the authoritativeness of local Brahmanic opinion in the acceptance of new *smṛti* material,[203] can one even apply the notion of newness to *śruti* ? Is it not a contradiction in terms to speak of "an addition to *śruti*", and, if not, how do Hindus understand this matter? Third, another form of the preceding

[201]Pargiter, *Purāṇa Text*, pp. xvii note, xxviii.

[202]Which we have used for the location in *smṛti* and *śruti* material of the epithets in Part I: *Vaidika-padānukramakoṣa*, Viśveśvarānanda Vedic Research Institute (Lahore, 1935-1965), five volumes in sixteen parts, abbr.: VPK.

[203]See the ref. given *supra*, n. 90. Cp. David Snellgrove's observations on the dynamics of Buddhist "orthodoxy": "From some quarters there would always be opposition to new ideas, but the test of whether they were eventually Buddhist or not always consists in their receiving or not receiving sufficient acceptance for their absorption within the body of teaching and practice of any group who called themselves Buddhists"; *The Hevajra Tantra: A Critical Study*, by David L. Snellgrove, Oxford University Press (London, 1959), vol. I, p. 6.

question, what is the scriptural status of the *khilas* to the RV ? It is a common-place for the later Vedic literature to be viewed as inspired commentary on the RV, whether that commentary be liturgical or philosophical. But have we not moved virtually to another, rarely noticed dimension in the *khilas*? They can be seen as another form of commentary on the Vedic hymns, but a commentary which itself consists of hymns. Yet are the *khilas* *śruti* in the same sense that the RV itself is ?[204]

While a fully adequate understanding of the function of the DM must await the resolution of these and other questions, it is possible to propose an analogy for heuristic purposes, while recognizing that that analogy may have to be subsequently refined or abandoned. That analogy is between the function of the DM and the function of the RV. The preliminary basis for this comparison is that the DM, while capable of being recited and expounded upon just as any portion of any Purāṇa is, also admits of recitation in Vedic fashion, i.e., with the realization that "the correct repetition of the holy words in Sanskrit is as

[204]This question is of more than passing relevance to our study, for the following reason. The one piece of "hard evidence" used in the dating of the DM is a dedicatory inscription in Jodhpur state, which has one verse in common with the DM (91.9), and the date of which Bhandarkar reads as corresponding to 608 C. E. (Bhandarkar, D. R., *op. cit.*, pp. 73-74). While the direction of borrowing is by no means clear, the correspondence is frequently cited in order to indicate the contemporaneity of the DM with this inscription (e.g., Farquhar, *op. cit.*, p. 150; Winternitz, *op. cit.*, p. 565n). While V. V. Mirashi has argued (*op. cit.*, pp. 181-186), primarily on grounds of orthography, that the inscriptional date should be read as corresponding to 813 C.E. the existence of this common verse is, nonetheless, noteworthy. (We may note in passing that although Mirashi questions Bhandarkar's dating of the inscription, he is inclined to agree with him on the dating of the DM: cf. p. 186.). It is all the more intriguing, then, to find that this same verse occurs at RV *khila* 2.6.30, in the *khila* known as the *Śrī Sūkta* (*Die Apokryphen des Ṛgveda*, J. Scheftelowitz [ed.], M. and H. Marcus [Breslau, 1906], p. 79). While the verse is not stridently sectarian and therefore potentially applicable to any feminine diety, there are a number of distinctive epithets employed:

*sarvamaṅgalamaṅgalye śive sarvārthasādhike|*
*śaraṇye* [*khila: śaradhaye*] *tryambake gauri nārāyaṇi namo 'stu te||*

Why this one verse, which in the DM occurs in the middle of a long hymn (the whole of which will be given in Part III, as will the *Śrī Sūkta*), should appear in isolation, i.e., with none of the rest of the hymn, not once, but twice, is a puzzling matter. The determination of the scriptural status of the *khilas* would, no doubt, be a preliminary step toward resolving the issue.

important as understanding their meaning."[205] There are still more explicit grounds for comparison : as Kane has noted, "the *saptaśatī* is treated [in the cultic context] as if it were a Vedic hymn or verse with *ṛṣi*, metres *pradhānadevatā*, and *viniyoga* (for *japa*)."[206] Ghosha dramatically corroborates this observation by providing all of these Vedic liturgical rubrics for each of the three sections, or episodes (*caritas*), of the DM.[207]

As we shall see subsequently, this imputation of Vedic significance to the DM is not solely the work of later devotees of the Goddess, but seems to have been of concern to the author(s) of the DM as well. Therefore,. let us grant the provisional validity of a parallel between the DM and RV and see what the implications of this are for our reading of the text. Foremost among these is the loss of the dynamic, expanding quality which we have seen to be characteristic of the "Purāṇic spirit." Bogatyrev and Jakobson have chosen the RV and its fate to exemplify the process whereby material which has been created by oral poets becomes "oral" only in the sense that it is passed down by word of mouth : "wo die Rolle der Gemeinschaft allein in der Aufbewahrung eines zu einem unantastbaren Kanon erhobenen dichterischen Werkes besteht, gibt es keine schöpferische Zensur, keine Improvisation, kein kollektives Schaffen mehr."[208] To the extent that the DM has undergone such "elevation," such a characterization also applies to it.[209] To study

[205]Singer, "The Cultural Pattern of Indian Civilization," p. 33. Singer is here comparing certain forms of *Rāmāyaṇa* reading with Vedic recitation and chanting.

[206]Kane, *op. cit.*, vol. V, part 1, p. 155n; cf. also, p. 172.

[207]Ghosha, *op. cit.*, notes p. xlii.

[208]Bogatyrev, P. and Jakobson, R., "Die Folklore als eine besondere Form des Schaffens," *Donum Natalicium Schrijnen*, N.v. Dekker and van de Vegt (Nijmegen-Utrecht, 1929), p. 912.

[209]We do not mean to imply without equivocation that the DM, like the RV, was originally an oral composition. While we shall allude to the Parry-Lord theory of bardic composition (as articulated in Lord, Albert B., *The Singer of Tales*, Harvard University Press [Cambridge, 1960]) in the next section, Purāṇic material in general is not readily determinable as being of either oral or literary origin. In the current context, it may be helpful to note Renou's suggestion that "the division between *Śruti* and *Smṛti* also marks the frontier between orality and editing": Renou, Louis, *The Destiny of the Veda in India*, Motilal Banarsidass (Delhi, 1965), notes, p. 84. Our central point here is that the DM, while qua Purāṇa being *smṛti*, has nonetheless

a text transmitted in such a fashion and in such a context would no longer entail a text-historical approach, for, as Biardeau has remarked, "even the most staunch supporters of Western textual criticism in India would never dream of 'critically editing' the Vedas . . ., since they are absolutely authoritative as they are."[210] Rather, it would resemble Staal's approach to the recitation of the RV,[211] where the critical variable is not so much which words are recited as how the same words may be variously intoned. From the perspective of the reciter (*śrotriya*), a discrimination that we have made disappears, for here "there is no sharp distinction between word and meaning and between form and contents."[212] Given the uniformity of content, and the virtual irrelevance of a word's signification, the focus of inquiry is necessarily on the form of the words, i.e., on matters of intonation and pronunciation. In this context, "the *śrotriya* who recites without understanding should not be compared with a clergyman preaching from the pulpit, but rather with a medieval monk copying and illuminating manuscripts, and to some extent with all those who are connected with book production in modern society."[213] Renou remarks that this preoccupation with form rather than meaning is "over and above everything, quite Indian,"[214] but that there have been additional factors at work in leading the Veda to its present curious position of being widely revered as constituting an indivisible whole, yet being interpreted only piecemeal, by specialists with narrow,

---

frequently been treated in Vedic fashion, i.e., as *śruti*. If Renou is correct, then the DM has the unusual status of being a literary creation that has (usually) been transmitted orally. Furthermore, under these circumstances, it is possible to regard the additional verses in some editions of the DM (see *supra*, n. 155) in two ways: as typical Purāṇic (*smṛti*) elaborations in keeping with local or individual sentiment, or as *khilas* upon the original, revealed (*śruti*) *mantras* of the DM.

[210] Biardeau, "Textual Criticism," p. 117.

[211] Staal, J. F., *Nambudiri Veda Recitation,* Mouton and Co. ('s-Gravenhage, 1961), Disputationes Rheno-Trajectinae V.

[212] *Ibid.*, p. 16.

[213] *Ibid.*, p. 17.

[214] Renou, *Destiny*, p. 25.

particular biases.[215] One of those factors, Renou maintains, was the gradual eclipse of ritualistic religion by devotional religion, and the corresponding relativizing of all worldly activity. In this process, the Veda "has become the instrument, the intermediary of *bhakti*."[216] Another factor has been the very nature of the text and of the response it elicited from Hindus, for, Renou ruminates, "Can an oral text be really understood If the Veda had been read like the Bible, and not only understood, if it had been (like the latter) translated into vulgar languages (nay, into classical Sanskrit), the result would have been different."[217] We may conclude our brief excursus on the Indian approach to the Veda, and, by extension, to the DM in its cultic context, as Renou does, with a remark on the Veda's role in both Indian and global perspective:

> [By classical times] the Vedic world, whose very essential had passed, while transforming itself, into the very flesh of Hindu practices and speculation, was no more than a distant object, exposed to the hazards of an adoration stripped of its textual substance.
>
> This, however, is the oft-repeated fate of great texts, the founders of religions ("sacred, they are . . ."); what one can say is that the tendency where it arises has, as with so many others, been pushed in India, further perhaps, than elsewhere.[218]

On the basis of this review, it is clear that a comprehensive account of the independent life that the DM has led as a self-contained scripture should be sensitive to matters of both content and function. On the one hand, the DM is one "moment,"

[215]See *ibid.*, pp. 16, 23, 52-53. One of the tasks of Renou's brief but very important work is to indicate the partial nature, at least until the time of Sāyaṇa (fourteenth century), of the traditional approaches to the Veda: by etymologists, by Vedāntins, by the Karma-Mīmāṁsā, by *vedapāṭhakas*, etc.

[216]*Ibid.*, p. 40. The quoted phrase applies rather nicely to the cultic recitation of the DM.

[217]*Ibid.*, notes, p. 100. On the issue of translation, the comparison of the DM with the RV begins to break down, for the former has known vernacular translations, e.g., into Bengālī, Punjābī, Malayālam (Farquhar, *op. cit.*, p. 388), Maithili, and Assamese (Bhattacharyya, *op. cit.*, pp. 147, 149).

[218]*Ibid.*, p. 53. The irregular punctuation in our quotation follows the original.

an unusually significant one, in the historical unfolding of the Indian religious tradition. On the other hand, that moment has been frozen, reified, and the text has been addressed as an eternal, immutable entity. Considerations of content indicate that the DM is clearly *smṛti*. Considerations of function suggest an analogy with the function of *śruti*.

In order to make these insights operational for our study, three further remarks are necessary. The first is that a full examination of the function of the DM in the Hindu religious tradition is clearly beyond the scope of this study. As indicated previously, our aspiration is the more modest one of understanding the text in its original context. That the DM has had an important function in later contexts is clear. That that function is related to its original one may be a legitimate hypothesis, though as Renou's remark on the RV suggest, that relationship may be extraordinarily complex and subtle. To investigate it will constitute an interesting sequel to the present study.[219]

Secondly, however, it is also clear that by the very fact of isolating the DM as a phenomenon worthy of investigation, we have tacitly recognized that it has an on-going function, that it is, in fact, scripture. In one of the few extant treatments of scripture as a religious phenomenon, W.C. Smith has made this very point, for, he maintains, "the analysis [of the origins] of a thing is interesting, and can be highly significant, but only subsidiarily; strictly, the history of that thing *begins* once its parts are synthesized."[220] Thus it would seem that it is the ensuing history of the DM, the fact that it has had an important function in Hindu religiousness, that leads us to deem it a "thing," worthy of examination in its original context.

Nonetheless—and this is the third remark—Smith's central concern in his remarks on scripture is not to sanction the study

[219]It is our intention to produce such a study, tentatively entitled *Interpreting the Goddess*. It will involve, among other things, a study of the subsidiary texts, liturgical rubrics, and some of the commentaries that have gathered around the DM since the time of its composition.

[220]Smith, Wilfred Cantwell, "The Study of Religion and the Study of the Bible," *Journal of the American Academy of Religion*, XXXIX 2 (June 1971), p. 133.

of scriptural origins, but to call attention to certain biases in the prevailing academic study of scripture, specifically of the Bible. His primary point is simply that such study has focused almost exclusively upon the origins of scripture.[221] What he proposes as a complement to this is nothing less than a phenomenology of scripture, which will inquire into how a text, written at a given time, continues to function in the religious life of people in subsequent centuries or millenia.[222] There is clearly a certain similarity between Smith's distinction between the study of the origins of scripture and the study of its on-going role, and our distinction between the content and function of the DM. Taken together, they present us with the following problem: is it possible to study the content of a scripture in a way that does at least partial justice to its function ? Specifically, can the content of the DM be studied in relation to its original context in a way that will at least take cognizance of, and perhaps illuminate, its on-going role in Hindu religiousness ?

It is our hypothesis that such a study may, in fact, be possible and that the previously suggested analogy between the DM and the RV provides us with the critical link. We have previously seen that, because the DM appears in a Purāṇa, we ought to be especially attuned to its Vedic resonance. It now appears that this is doubly important, for having (as *smṛti*) re-presented certain features of the Vedic (*śruti*) tradition, our text itself has, in subsequent times, frequently been treated as *śruti*. It is this same analogy between the DM and the RV that will prove

[221] "They [Biblicists] have assumed that the Bible has the status and the importance that the Reformation gave to it. . . and therein fail to see, even to-day, that for the subsequent [i.e., post-Reformation] West, it is the Bible that has made ancient Palestine significant, not vice versa."; *ibid.*, p. 136.

[222] Such a study would ask such questions as, "What is involved [psychologically, sociologically, historically] in taking a certain body of literature, separating it off from all other, and giving it sacrosanct status ?. . . How and where did it first come about ? How did the Christian Church [or any other group] happen to take up this practice ? What attitudes, magical or otherwise, towards writing are involved ? And—once this is done—what consequences follow?": *ibid.*, p. 132. Smith is clearly aware of the enormity of the task he is proposing, for he concludes by asking, "Where could I find a man with doctoral training equipping him in this field ?": *ibid.*, p. 140.

of assistance in addressing the final methodological question, which arises from the present discussion: what specific features of those texts are worthy paying attention to ? That is, both texts have been *transmitted* verbatim for centuries, but if we are to understand one of them, the DM, in its original context, what are the critical issues in the *composition* of such a text ? It is to this matter that we now turn in our final section.

### 5. *The Dynamics of Composition and the Structure of this Study*

In the two preceding sections, we have sought assistance in our reading of the DM by considering, first, the significance of its occurrence in a Purāṇa and, second, the significance of its independent scriptural life. The former has suggested the importance of seeing it as part of a process which we are to view historically, against its Vedic background. The latter has indicated the need for an awareness of its ensuing resonance in the Indian tradition, wherein it was transmitted verbatim, mastered by rote, recited for devotional purposes. In the present section, we must look more closely at the particular mechanics of its original composition. That is, we must address the matter of oral and literary composition in its Indian context.

We have already encountered several awarenesses of there being an important issue here. Biardeau emphasizes the distinction between oral and literary traditions,[223] though she does not seem to appreciate how tempting it is to apply the canons of literary criticism to material, now written, that was originally transmitted orally. Bedekar, too, allows that the epics and Purāṇas were originally transmitted orally.[224] But he argues that their current existence in writing qualifies them for text-critical analysis, apparently without realizing that, in order to appreciate the characteristics of oral composition and transmission that are evident in the current textual material, a rather different set of criteria[225] is necessary. We have seen

[223]Biardeau, "Textual Criticism," pp. 116-118.

[224]Bedekar, *op. cit.*, p. 219.

[225]Such as Parry and Lord propose. See our discussion which begins in the next paragraph.

Renou suggest that the boundary between *śruti* and *smṛti* also marks the frontier between orality and editing.[226] Clearly these two modes of composition and transmission call for further examination.

In at least one respect, there is a similarity between the Purāṇic compilers and the bardic poets whose technique has recently begun to be studied, viz., in their self-avowed fidelity to tradition and in the fact that their work nonetheless does not literally reproduce that tradition. We have seen that, in India, this is a function of *smṛti*'s relationship to *śruti*. In oral epic poetry, this is a function of the nature of the creative process. Lord concisely conveys a sense of that material and that process :

> Stated briefly, oral epic song is narrative poetry composed in a manner evolved over many generations by singers of tales who did not know how to write; it consists of the building of metrical lines and half-lines by means of formulas and formulaic expressions and of the building of songs by the use of themes....By formula I mean "a group of words which is regularly employed under the same metrical conditions to express a given essential idea"....Formulas are not... ossified cliches ... but ... are capable of change and are indeed frequently highly productive of other and new formulas....The singer of tales is at once the tradition and an individual creator. His manner of composition differs from that used by a writer in that the oral poet makes no conscious effort to break the traditional phrases and incidents....His art consists...in the ability to compose and recompose the phrases for the idea of the moment on the pattern established by the basic formulas. He is not a conscious iconoclast, but a traditional creative artist.[227]

What is unique here is the possibility of variants of a story emerging, not through willful change, nor through forgetfulness, but unselfconsciously, in the course of the poet's artful, versified retelling of a familiar story. This unselfconsciousness is indicated by the fact that when Parry "asked a poet to recite the same

[226] *Supra*, n. 209.
[227] Lord, *op. cit.*, pp. 4-5.

poem in the same words as on a previous occasion, the poet agreed to do so but produced in fact something different."[228] Lord's summation of the bard's role suggests a striking similarity with that of the Paurāṇika, or of the *smṛti* writer in general. "The picture that emerges is not really one of conflict between preserver of tradition and creative artist; it is rather one of the preservation of tradition by the constant re-creation of it. The ideal is a true story well and truly retold."[229]

Because of this similarity of attitude, it is tempting to adopt the methods of oral epic study and to subject the DM to the kind of formulaic analysis that Lord has performed on the Homeric epics. Ingalls has remarked[230] that such analysis does seem applicable to portions of the Mbh, primarily those dealing with traditional epic themes, such as battle, and since most of the DM recounts the Goddess's battles with various Asuras, one could argue for the applicability of these methods to our text. However, in addition to the fact that the DM's brevity renders the identification of formulae rather difficult,[231] and in addition to the objection of Stith Thompson that the clear distinction between oral and written tradition is not only impossible, but even unnecessary, to make,[232] there are two more specific problems attend nt on hypothesizing the DM to be an oral composition and applying the Parry-Lord theory to it. Since these problems raise issues which our methodology has been designed to resolve, they are worth exploring in some detail.

[228]Bowra, C. Maurice, *Heroic Poetry*, Macmillan and Co. Ltd. (London, 1961), p. 217. Cf. Lord, *op. cit.*, p. 28.

[229]Lord, *op. cit.*, p. 29. This ideal may also be seen to underlie myth and its need ever to be retold anew; cf. O'Flaherty, *Asceticism and Eroticism*, p. 318. Also, cf. Lévi-Strauss, "The Structural Study of Myth," p. 574: "Repetition [of mythical sequences] has as its function to make the structure of the myth apparent."

[230]In a conversation with us, January 24, 1975.

[231]The 573 verses, or roughly (allowing for extra-and half-verses) 1150 lines, of the DM are meagre in comparison with the 27,000 lines of the Homeric epics (Lord, *op. cit.*, p. 158), and the 30,000 lines available for the singer whose work is used by Lord as the primary exemplification of formulaic construction (*ibid.*, pp. 45ff.).

[232]Thompson, Stith, *The Folktale*, The Dryden Press (New York, 1946), p. 5.

The first problem with treating the DM as an oral epic composition is that, in terms of content, it is far more than oral epic. While, in terms of quantity of verses, the Goddess's martial exploits are predominant, in terms of quality, these are surpassed by verses of another genre, viz., the hymns to the Goddess. Much of the power of the DM derives from the way in which the hymnic material is held in counterpoint to the discursive account of her salvific activity in the world, but to the reader-hearer it is clear that the devotional fervor of the text, and the synthetic work it is performing, emerge most intensely in the hymns. That this is the understanding of devotees of the Goddess, as well as our own, is suggested by Jagadīśvarānanda's prefatory remarks to his translation of the DM: "The hymns to the Devī in the cantos I, IV, V & XI are so sweet and sublime that they should, if possible, be chanted in the original."[233] The central importance of hymns in the emergence of the worship of the Goddess is also indicated by the fact that it is hymns that are the primary evidence for this emergence in the Mbh and HV. However, from our perspective, which is concerned to see this emergence as part of an historical process, there is a major problem attached to this centrality of hymnic material, and that is that it is exceedingly difficult to use such material for historical studies. Hymns are notoriously impervious to historical analysis. To cite but one example: if one were to try to understand contemporary Episcopalians on the basis of their hymnbook, one would be faced with an extraordinary heterogeneity of material, ranging from a Greek composition dated at c. 110 C. E. to an English one written in 1941.[234] Much of the significance of hymns derives, of course, from their transcendent, ahistorical quality. But it is that same quality that renders them problematical for an analysis that tends to matters of chronology. The first objection to analyzing the DM as an oral epic phenomenon then is that it would be a misplaced emphasis on what is most significant about the DM. The hymns are

[233] *Op. cit.*, p. v.

[234] *The Hymnal of the Protestant Episcopal Church in the United States of America*, The Seabury Press (Greenwich, Conn., 1940), hymns 195 and 504, respectively. For a convenient survey of Indian hymnic material, see Bhattacharyya, Sivaprasad, "Indian Hymnology", in *The Cultural Heritage of India*, vol. IV, pp. 464-478.

what should command our primary attention. An analysis of the discursive, mythical portions of the DM, not in terms of their oral vs. literary composition, but in terms of their literary antecedents, can help set the historical context for understanding the hymns, but some further historical leverage on our text is clearly desirable.

The means for obtaining that leverage is suggested by the second problem attendant on applying the Parry-Lord theory of bardic composition, without refinement, to Indian material. It will be seen in our above quotation from Lord that formulae comprise the basic tool of oral poets, and the cornerstone of the Parry-Lord theory is that diction in oral composition is, to a great extent, determined by considerations of metre. The creative work of the poet consists in fitting his narrative material to his traditional stock of formulae. The applicability of this understanding of the creative process to Indian verse, however, has been questioned by two Indologists.

The first is Louis Renou. He does not formally speak to the Parry-Lord theory, but his studies clearly have implications for its viability in the Indian context. While the focus of his concern has been Ṛg Vedic composition, his remarks appear to be of more general relevance, and since we have seen in the preceding section that there are grounds for understanding the DM on the analogy of the RV, his conclusions bear brief mention. There are two that are of particular relevance. The first is that there is a distinctive self-consciousness about the fact of utterance, an appreciation of the power of the spoken word, in the RV, and words, therefore, are important for their form, not just for their content or signification. This, of course, is simply stating that the *mantras* are viewed as eternal (*apauruṣeya*). It has prompted Renou, however, to examine how *vāc*, speech, and related words function in the RV as precursors of the subsequently identified substratum of reality as *ātman-brahman*.[235] This intrinsic significance of words is enlarged by the fact that the Vedic poet is

[235]This is the burden of "Les Pouvoirs de la Parole dans le Ṛgveda," in Renou, Louis, *Études Védiques et Pāṇinéennes*, E. de Boccard (Paris), Publications de l'Institut de Civilisation Indienne, vol. I (1955), pp. 1-27. In the course of this investigation, Renou calls attention (p. 8) to the fact that the Vedic hymns themselves are referred to as feminine and are seen as fecund in their own right, or by virtue of being fertilized by a male diety, or as a reflection

almost never telling a story, but is using expressions that are reflections of ritual formulae, praise of the gods, and liturgical descriptions: there is a multi-valence to the language, and one continually slides from one register to another.[236] Consequently, there is an intentionality, a deliberateness, in the diction that becomes characteristic of Indian verbal expression:

> Que la réflexion sur l'oeuvre se confonde avec le contenu même de cette oeuvre, le fait ne saurait trop nous surprendre dans l'Inde sanskrite où nous voyons si souvent—notamment en grammaire, mais point seulement dans ce domaine—que la manière dont les choses sont dites comporte une valeur didactique presque au même degré que le fond.[237]

Renou's second noteworthy conclusion emerges from his study of Ṛg Vedic refrains.[238] For each *maṇḍala*, he examines various phenomena: repetition between hymns, repetition within one hymn, and phrases in the "family books" that are characteristic of that family. He summarizes the evidence thus presented:

> Tous les faits ici étudiés se distinguent donc par des traits bien marqués d'avec l'ensemble des répétitions védique: contrairement à ces dernières, ils sont soumis à des tendances assez nettes et accentuent l'unité, soit du poeme, soit de la strophe, soit du maṇḍala, unité que mettait sans cesse en péril le foisonnement des emprunts et des répétitions inorganiques.[239]

In other words, Vedic composition is concerned not merely with meeting metrical requirements and establishing continuity

---

of the transcendent neuter abstraction (*brahman akṣara*). From this construal of hymns as feminine, it is a small step to the construal of an individual verse as feminine, and as we shall see in Part I, many of the epithets of the Goddess in the DM have a previous usage in characterizing a verse, e.g., *ṛc vaiṣṇavī*. While the primary thrust of such instances is toward recognition of the male diety, e.g., Viṣṇu, it should not be overlooked that, by extension from the Vedic understanding of the word, the verse and its efficacy, its fecundity, have feminine connotations.

[236] *Ibid.*, p. 26. Cf. also, Renou, *Religions of Ancient India*, pp. 10-11.

[237] *Ibid.*, p. 27. This complexity of Vedic composition is also dealt with in "L'Hypercaractérisation dans le Ṛgveda," *ibid.*, pp. 45-69.

[238] "Les Refrains dans le Ṛgveda," *ibid.*, vol. II (1956), pp. 31-54.

[239] *Ibid.*, p. 51.

through the use of formulae. It is also aware of various "units" of composition and is concerned with the integrity of these units. As in Renou's first conclusion, it is suggested that there is a greater self-consciousness, a greater deliberateness, than in the oral poet's composition in the course of performance.

The second Indologist to speak to these matters is J. Gonda. While he, too, is primarily concerned with Vedic composition, he explicitly speaks to larger issues, and he deals directly with the Parry-Lord theory. Gonda is clearly appreciative of the insights that the studies of Bowra, Parry, and others have yielded, for he observes that "oral heroic poetry...could hardly exist without formulae,"[240] since these formulae make it easier both for the bard to compose and for the audience to listen. However, it is not so much the applicability of these studies in general that interests Gonda as it is a particular variety of formulaic construction, viz., epithets. While this stylistic device may lend itself to abuse in certain genres, its virtues, he maintains, should not be overlooked:

> ...it may have the effect of increasing the author's vocabulary and enriching his power of expression. A well-chosen epithet often constitutes a picture by itself, adding an element of vividness to the context, rubbing up a vague and worn noun and throwing light upon those of its connotations which should attract the attention of the audience. An epithet may typify and express an opinion, beautify and add to the intelligibility of a passage, without interrupting the course of the narrative or the movement of the poem by a long parenthesis or burdening them by a cumbersome description. It often is the best way to secure brightness, beauty, distinction and sublimity to the style.[241]

It is this function of epithets that Gonda feels is slighted by undue emphasis on the role of versification in the composition process, and he notes that Parry's theory has not remained uncontradicted. Hinterlechner's unpublished thesis "argues that the main—and so far as we know oldest—function of many true epic

[240]Gonda, J., *Epithets in the Ṛgveda*, Mouton and Co. ('s-Gravenhage, 1959), Disputationes Rheno-Trajectinae IV, p. 28.

[241]*Ibid.*, p. 7.

epithets was a distinctive one: they served, first and foremost, to distinguish definite persons or objects from similar entities, referring to their characteristic features and properties."[242]

Whatever may be the implications of this epithetical function in the larger context of oral epic theory, its significance in Indian literature, both epic and non-epic, is felt by Gonda to be major, and he has lavished much attention on the role of epithets and proper names in that literature. He is aware that it is not always possible to draw a hard and fast distinction between epithets and descriptive adjectives,[243] but he shares Renou's appreciation of the fact that, in at least the Ṛg Vedic context, "words [themselves]...were regarded as being instinct with power."[244] Consequently our inability to make such a firm distinction is not a serious liability. On the basis of his survey of the ways in which such words are used in the RV, Gonda concludes that the unity of form and content in that text, on which we have seen Staal comment with regard to the perspective of the reciter,[245] makes "the expletive and merely versificatory character of the epithets...a priori improbable."[246] The Vedic poets' use of epithets is thus seen as answering two concurrent needs: "they succeeded in inserting these words in their verses so as to comply with, on the one hand, the function and character of these texts and the exigencies of the religious practice and on the other the rules and traditions of versification."[247] To the extent that our suggested parallel between the RV and the DM is valid, these remarks may be seen as qualifying the utility of the Parry-Lord theory for our study.

Beyond this delimiting role, however, Gonda's remarks suggest that the nomenclature applied to the divine is worthy of special attention in any religious context, in hymns, prayers, exorcisms,

[242]*Ibid.*, pp. 29-30.

[243]Gonda, J., *Notes on Names and the Name of God in Ancient India*, North Holland Publishing Co. (Amsterdam, London, 1970), Verhandelingen der Koninklijke Nederlandse Akademie van Wetenschappen, afd. Letterkunde, Nieuwe Reeks, Deel 75, No. 4, p. 15. Cf. also Gonda, *Epithets*, pp. 7-8.

[244]Gonda, J., "The Etymologies in the Ancient Indian Brāhmaṇas," *Lingua* V 1 (1955-56), p. 78.

[245]See the ref. given *supra*, n. 212.

[246]Gonda, *Epithets*, p. 255.

[247]*Ibid.*, p. 259.

etc.[248] Gonda is here forging a link with the phenomenological work of van der Leeuw, particularly where the latter, having noted that the notion of personality is not essential to the idea of a god, goes on to remark that "the man who must come to some understanding with a power, and who therein experiences a will, attempts by every possible means to give an outline to this experience, in order to delimit it from other similar experiences; and this he does by assigning to it a *Name*. For the Name is no mere specification, but rather an actuality expressed in a word."[249] In a monograph,[250] Gonda has examined the origins of this practice in India. His assessment of the material is that Indians did not sharply discriminate between personal and impersonal representations of power, and shifted their ground rather easily on this matter. Far from being exclusively characteristic of the Indian mind, however, the lack of this distinction is, Gonda maintains, pervasive of non-modern, pre-scientific, "primitive" modes of thought,[251] within which "an individual representing an 'idea'—whether it be the idea of a nationality, a family, a trade, technical skill, or religious conviction—can be indicated as its manifestation in flesh and blood, and conceived as having sprung from it."[252] More uniquely Indian, maintains Gonda,

[248]*Ibid.*, p. 32.

[249]Van der Leeuw, G., *Religion in Essence and Manifestation*, translated by J. E. Turner with Appendices to the Torchbook edition incorporating the additions to the second German edition by Hans H. Penner, Harper and Row (New York and Evanston, 1963), vol. I, p. 147. This passage is noted by Gonda, *Notes*, p. 5n, and quoted, *Epithets*, p. 32.

[250]Gonda, J., *Some Observations on the Relations between "Gods" and "Powers" in the Veda, a propos of the Phrase "Sūnaḥ Sahasaḥ"*, Mouton and Co. ('s-Gravenhage, 1957), Disputationes Rheno-Trajectinae I.

[251]*Ibid.*, pp. 5-6, 96, 101.

[252]*Ibid.*, p. 105. While Gonda may well be right in citing this fluidity regarding the impersonal or personal representations of power as a generic feature of "primitive" thought, we should not overlook the fact that disagreement over the appropriateness of these different representations has occasioned some brisk debate in later Hindu thought, in the different schools of Vedānta. For example, Parāśara Bhaṭṭar is clearly taking issue with Śaṁkara's notion of *nirguna brahman* when he maintains that the thousand names of Viṣṇu "are not names that have arisen by mere accident, because they are expressive of purposive and meaningful characteristics and are not conventional. . . . As these names are based on the qualities and actions of Bhagawan, those that recognize their greatness should not have anything to do with those who deny

are the later appreciations of the power of names in the popular *nāmastotras*.[253] Herein we find a plethora of names, which are designed to penetrate the esoterism of which the gods are fond, which often reflect historical, legendary or mythological events and "capture" their power, and the recitation of which gives the devotee a certain reciprocal power over the deity thus praised.[254] Gonda sees this devotional practice as essentially continuous with the Vedic intuition of the eternality of sound forms, but he also points out that, when we are involved in the hermeneutic enterprise, "to us these names and their choice, frequency and combinations are valuable means of understanding the ideas fostered by the worshippers and the qualities attributed by them to the object of their adoration."[255]

It is the intentionality and deliberateness of Sanskrit diction, upon which both Sanskritists have commented, and in particular the significance of the epithets that an author employs and that devotees recite, that provide us with the means of structuring our historical approach to the DM and of examining the content of our text in a way that also takes cognizance of its function. As noted above, the devotional fervor of our text reaches its greatest intensity in the hymnic material, but if we are to see this material in its historical context, some kind of chronological leverage is necessary. Some of this can be provided by examining the literary antecedents of the myths recounted in the DM. But still greater leverage is possible by tracing the epithets and descriptive adjectives which are applied to the Goddess in the DM in the earlier Sanskritic literature.

Part I of our study, therefore, consists of a series of word-studies.[256] Taking our cue from Gonda's remark in our last

---

qualities to Bhagawan": *Śrī Vishnu Sahasranāma Bhasya* (*Commentary by Śrī Parāsara Bhaṭṭarya*), L. Venkatarathnam Naidu (tr.), Tirumala Tirupati Devasthanams (Tirupati, 1965), pp. 31, 32.

[253] Gonda, *Notes*, pp. 67ff.

[254] *Ibid.*, pp. 81-82, 21, 95. On the power inherent in mythical events residing in namesakes of that event, cf. also Gonda, "Etymologies," p. 80.

[255] Gonda, *Notes*, p. 72.

[256] Methodologically, therefore, our study bears a certain resemblance to those of Hacker, cited *supra*, n. 138. One difference between our two approaches, however, may be that Hacker is focussing on words in order to separate different conceptual levels historically, i.e., to distinguish Śaṁkara's

quotation, we shall take the frequency with which particular epithets and descriptive adjectives have been applied to the Goddess in the DM as significant: starting with the most common appellation, Caṇḍikā, we shall proceed to examine, in the order of their frequency, those names and characterizations which are applied to her at least twice in the DM.[257] We have seen the importance of reading any Purāṇic text against its Vedic background, and consequently our primary concern will be to trace the usage of these designations in the Vedic literature that is "clearly anterior"[258] to the DM. In identifying the salient passages, our primary tool has been the Vedic word index alluded to earlier,[259] but where there is some doubt as to whether the texts there indexed are, in fact, anterior to our text, we have placed limits on the scope of our inquiry. Thus, for instance, while the VPK indexes 206 Upaniṣads,[260] we have limited our inquiry to the dozen or so that are clearly of an early date. Besides sketching this Vedic backdrop, we shall also allude to epic material, as well as to inscriptional evidence and secular literature of anterior or "roughly contemporaneous"[261] date when such allusions can shed light on a particular epithet or descriptive adjective.

Aside from considerations of utility, which put this inquiry into our text's diction first in our study in an effort to acquire historical leverage on our text, there are more compelling reasons for putting it first. We have seen that the very core of our task is to see how the DM has made the Sanskritic tradition contemporary and the worship of the Goddess traditional.[262] The primary means it has employed in this endeavor is, in fact, the use of ancient Sanskritic terminology to describe this "new" figure

---

thought from that of his followers, while we are using this focus to see how the author of the DM integrates diverse strands. The method can clearly be variously applied.

[257]In the course of this investigation, we shall note in passing a few of the appellations which are used only once, but which are of unusual interest or significance.

[258]See *supra*, n. 22.

[259]*Supra*, n. 202.

[260]See our rumination on this fact, *supra*, pp. 62-63.

[261]See *supra*, n. 22.

[262] *Supra*, p. 9. 13-14.

of the Goddess. Van Buitenen has shown how a similar technique was subsequently employed in the *Bhāgavata Purāṇa* : "There is a...reaching back to the most ancient sources—however imperfectly known—to make the old foundation support the new edifice," so that the *Bhāgavata* can proclaim, in effect: "I am not only orthodox in the Vedic tradition, I even sound like the Veda."[263] While the DM does not exhibit the *Bhāgavata's* inclination to use archaic word forms, many of the epithets and adjectives have clearly been chosen for their Vedic resonance.

That the theology of our text enables it to sow these seeds of antiquity and nurture them into an integrative vision of the Goddess is particularly evident at the very end of the final episode (*carita*). Up to this point, the Goddess has been assailed by various Asuras sent forth by the archvillain Śumbha, but each has been vanquished, occasionally by the Goddess herself, but more frequently by someone in her retinue: by one of the *śaktis* which came forth from the bodies of various male deities,[264] or, more confoundingly, by apparent *śaktis* of the Goddess herself.[265] This retinue is variously characterized, affording the text ample opportunity to draw on past characterizations and epithets. This having been done, the stage is set for the final dramatic encounter by reducing the combatants to the bare minimum. Śumbha accuses the Goddess of false pride and haughtiness, for in the foregoing battles she has relied, not on her own strength, but on that of others, whereupon the Goddess proclaims her relationship to the apparently heterogeneous forms:

[263]Van Buitenen, *op. cit.*, pp. 38, 31.

[264]MarkP 88.12ff.

[265]As we shall see, one facet of the Goddess's character is that of being the great deluder, or even illusion itself, and this confounding is therefore utterly appropriate. It is nonetheless startling to have one's conceptual categories—e.g., the common tendency to regard the female as an emanation or *śakti* of the male in Indian religion—frontally assaulted, such as occurs at (1) MarkP 85.38-40, where Śivā Kauśikī comes forth from Pārvatī's body in order to inform the latter that it was she who was being hymned by the gods, (2) MarkP 87.5ff., where Kālī emerges from the Goddess's furrowed brow in order to dispatch two of Śumbha's vassals, and (3) MarkP 88.22, where, most arrestingly, it is explicitly stated that the *śakti* of Caṇḍikā came forth from the body of the Goddess (... *devīśarīrāt* ... *viniṣkrāntā* ... *caṇḍikāśaktiḥ* ...). For further reflection on our text's (and, by implication, the Goddess's)

I alone exist here in the world; what second, other than I, is there ?
O wicked one, behold these my hierophanies[266] entering (back) into me.

Our text continues:

Thereupon, all the goddesses, led by Brahmāṇī,
Went to (their) resting-place, the breasts of the Goddess; then there was just Ambikā, alone.

And the Goddess throws down the gauntlet for the final combat:

When I was established here in many forms, it was by means of my extraordinary power.
That has (now) been withdrawn by me. I stand utterly alone. May you be resolute in combat.[267]

In tracing the earlier use of the words which are here applied to the hierophanies of the Goddess, before they are resumed into her, we have found that they do not always occur in conjunction with a specific goddess, but are often simply adjectives applied to nouns which are grammatically feminine, e.g., *ṛc vaiṣṇavī*, *dig aparājitā*. It is tempting not to cite such instances in Part I of our study, on the grounds that they are irrelevant to an understanding of the Goddess in the DM. Yet such a course of action, we have come to see, would, in fact, be a serious omission and would deprive us of a useful tool in the hermeneutic enterprise, i.e., of an important avenue into an understanding of our text's *Weltanschauung*. The understanding of diction at which we have arrived is that whenever a word is chosen, in any language, for either speaking or writing, it is chosen because of its particular

---

challenge to our contemporary conceptual categories, see *supra*, pp. 42-43. See also *infra*, Part I, s.v. "*śivadūtī*" and "*śakti*", and Appendix A.

[266]Or "extraordinary powers": *vibhūtayaḥ*.

[267]MarkP 90.3-5:

*ekaivāhaṃ jagaty atra dvitīyā kā mamāparā/*
*paśyaitā duṣṭa mayy eva viśantyo madvibhūtayaḥ//*
*tataḥ samastās tā devyo brahmāṇīpramukhā layam/*
*tasyā devyāḥ stanau jagmur ekaivāsīt tadāmbikā//*
*ahaṃ vibhūtyā bahubhir iha rūpair yad āsthitā/*
*tat saṃhṛtaṃ mayaikaiva tiṣṭāmy ājau sthiro bhava//*

appropriateness for expressing the user's intent. That appropriateness is determined primarily by the user's more or less deliberate reflection on the words available in his or her vocabulary.[268] The user's assessment of different words' adequacy is, in turn, determined to a great extent by their past associations for him or her. That is, each word carries with it a certain amount of subconscious or subliminal baggage, the nature of which is a function of the individual's previous encounters with that word. Consequently, in an effort to come as close as possible to our text's view of reality,[269] Part I of our study will examine the full range of the earlier usage of words which are applied to the Goddess in the DM. Thus we may uncover the associations, whether intentional on the part of our text or not, which these words had in their original Sanskrit context.[270] Moreover, by

[268]In terms of our earlier discussion, there is clearly greater opportunity for deliberate reflection if the composition is literary rather than oral, or if an individual is writing rather than speaking, but that words do, in fact, have subliminal connotations—see our next sentence—is true regardless of the medium of communication.

[269]We are aware that a shift has occurred in this sentence, from talking about the diction of a person to talking about the diction of a text, and that, in some cases, the distinction between the two is major. However, it seems to us that the previously noted remarks of Renou and Gonda suggest that, in this particular case, i.e., in India, in a religious text, and particularly in a text that resembles the RV, that distinction is far less consequential than might otherwise be the case. See also our remarks beginning three sentences below. Also, see our remarks on the matter of the DM's anonymity, *supra*, pp. 44-45.

[270]The value of the understanding of diction espoused here will finally be determined by the amount of light it sheds on the subject matter. We may mention simply in passing that this understanding dovetails with much contemporary discussion in the field of psycholinguistics. For a helpful introduction to the latter, see Izutsu, Toshihiko, *Ethico-Religious Concepts in the Qur'ān*, McGill University Press (Montreal, 1966), McGill Islamic Studies I, esp. the Introduction, entitled "Language and Culture." Izutsu there starts from the Bergsonian position that "our immediate experience of reality is in itself an undifferentiated whole" and goes on to maintain that, upon this "originally formless mass of existence, the human mind has drawn an infinite number of lines, and made divisions and segments, large and small; and the world of reality has in this way received the imprints of linguistic and conceptual formulation; and an order has been brought into the original chaos" (p. 10). What is significant, argues Izutsu, is that (1) each individual is so accustomed to having reality "filtered" through his culturally inherited linguistic-conceptual structure that he is usually not even aware of the existence of this filter; (2) there is an order which every filter provides, but

investigating the antecedents across the various recensions and *śākhās* of the Sanskritic heritage, we have a way of appreciating how it was received by contemporaries of varying Sanskritic backgrounds.[271] What we have in Part I, then, is the identification of the Sanskritic verbal associations of the DM's epithets, their associations for the text's author(s), hearers, reciters, at the time of its composition. No one individual, obviously, would have known all the associations, but taken together, they present the range of possibilities during that historical era.

Part II of our study will focus, not upon the Goddess herself, but upon her opponents in the three episodes (*caritas*) of the DM. It will examine the myths there associated with the Goddess both in their "clearly anterior" versions—in the various strata of the Mbh and HV—and in the Purāṇic material and secular literature that appears to be "roughly contemporaneous" with our text. Our approach in this Part therefore resembles the close comparative analysis employed by Hazra, the value of which we have already commented upon.[272]

Having laid this historical groundwork, we shall then turn finally, in Part III, to the hymns of the DM. There we shall assemble and translate the various hymns which devotees of the Goddess have prized: from the RV, RV Khila, Mbh, and HV, as well as from the DM itself. By annotating our translations so as to indicate both the relationships between the texts and the previously discussed historical material, the unique features of the hymns of the DM, which we have indicated to be the devotional heart of our text, will emerge more readily than would

---

(3) there is, in fact, a plurality of ways of filtering "raw" reality, i.e., reality is "capable of being divided up into as many segments as you like, in whatever way you like, and from whatever angle you prefer" (p. 11). In order to appreciate the nature of the Islamic "filter" in the realm of ethics, i.e., more technically, the semantic field of Islamic ethical discourse, he then examines the conditions in which the relevant words are used. By analogy with this venture, Part I of our study may be seen as investigating the semantic field of the DM's discourse on the Goddess, by examining the conditions in which the relevant characterizations have been used.

[271] See *supra*, pp. 44-45 where we discuss the need for investigation across the different recensions in order to compensate for our lack of knowledge about the identity of the DM's author(s).

[272] See *supra*, n. 137 and our textual remark occasioning this note.

be the case without the historical leverage provided by Parts I and II.

Such an approach might appear methodologically eclectic, so it has been the function of this Prolegomenon to demonstrate its non-arbitrary character and its appropriateness to the task before us. Because of the complexity of that demonstration, we may review its highlights in five steps, as follows. (1) Since the DM is the first comprehensive account of the Goddess to appear in Sanskrit, the first appearance of an originally non-Aryan vision of the divine to appear in that language, the significance of composition in that language has been examined. It has been seen that Sanskrit was the language of culture and respectability, and, by virtue of constituting one of the "life-lines" to the primordial revelation, was resonant with overtones of piety, tradition, and eternity. Because Sanskritic culture is a symbol, and therefore dynamic, it is not possible to circumscribe it, as some social scientists have hoped, but it remains feasible to speak of "Sanskritization" as a literary phenomenon that reflects appreciation of a social, cultural, religious norm. (2) Because the DM constitutes a portion of a Purāṇa, a species within the genus of Sanskrit literature, the nature of the Purāṇas has been investigated, along with the issues raised by the academic study of them. Hindus have been found to be in agreement that the Purāṇas are a "confirming elaboration" or "harmonious revision" of the Vedas, though there are different traditions regarding the divinity or humanity of their origin. Academic inquiry into the Purāṇic corpus has been seen to be a complex matter, on which the last word has not been said, and on which opinions are likely to continue to vary because of different ways of construing the academic enterprise and because of the varieties of religious faith. Nonetheless, following the lead of W. C. Smith, the possibility has been discerned of academically and historically investigating the cumulative (Vedic and Sanskritic) tradition in a way that illuminates one expression of faith, the DM, while respecting others. (3) Because the DM is not simply a portion of a Purāṇa but has also led an independent life of its own, the significance of this fact has been examined. In terms of its content, we have noted that the DM can be seen both as the culmination of a long preceding process and as the threshold of a long subsequent process. It both integrates earlier developments and precipitates later ones. In terms of its function, we have noted that it has had a liturgical involvement and devotional role which we have suggested resembles that of the RV. This, in turn, has suggested that, in addition to the general Purāṇic reference back to the Vedas, the DM may have a particularly vital rapport with the Vedic tradition. (4) This has necessitated an examination of how such works are composed. Here it has been seen, negatively, that bardic theories of oral composition require modification in the Indian context, and that they would lead us away from the devotional core of our text, viz., its hymns. But, positively, it appears that Indian authors' emphasis upon religious factors has led them to pay particular attention to different "units" of composition and that one of those units, viz., epithets, admits of historical investigation throughout the Vedic corpus. To investigate these epithets is to provide some historical leverage on the intrinsically ahistorical hymns. (5) The resulting structure thus builds toward an appreciation of the hymns in their original setting. First, it examines the Sanskrit resonance, in general, and the Vedic resonance, in particular, of the DM's epithets. Through examination of the earlier tradition, it identifies the various associations of these words at the time when the DM was composed. Second, the structure examines the epic and early Purāṇic material, frequently utilizing critical editions, to trace the previously discrete myths that the DM integratively associates with the Goddess. Third, it presents annotated translations of hymns that are frequently associated with the Goddess, beginning with the RV, including the epics, and culminating in the hymns of the DM itself.

The deliberateness with which this demonstration has been made has been necessary, for we are dealing with Indian material, and, as Morrison has remarked, "there are no established and tested approaches to the historical analysis of the Indian past" and each "scholar is forced to create his own concepts and methods. . . ."[273] More recently, W. C. Smith has argued on an even broader scale that "method should be developed

[273]Morrison, *op. cit.*, p. 85.

out of the particular problem that one is considering, not vice versa. . . ."[274] That our method was so developed has been indicated in the preceding pages. Its adequacy for the problem, viz., the understanding of the DM's view of reality in its original context, may be determined on the basis of the evidence presented in the following three Parts.

[274]Smith, Wilfred Cantwell, "Methodology and the Study of Religion: Some Misgivings," Iowa University School of Religion, Symposium on Methodology and World Religions, April 15, 1974, mimeo., p. 22.

# Part I

# The Epithets

# The Epithets

In the epithetical investigation that constitutes the first portion of this study, there are a number of strata to our inquiry. The first is simply that of our text itself. In light of Renou's and Gonda's remarks, cited at the end of our Prolegomenon, on the intentionality of Sanskrit diction, we shall ask: how does the DM deploy its language when speaking of the Goddess? What is the internal evidence offered for how our text understands, and associates, a particular epithet? Following Gonda's claim that the frequency with which an epithet is used is a clue to its importance, the over-all structure of Part I is to start with the most common epithet in the DM and to proceed in the order of decreasing frequency. For each epithet, the first stratum of inquiry is how that epithet is used in the DM itself.

The second stratum is determined by the fact that, as our Prolegomenon makes clear, any Purāṇic text should be read/heard against its Vedic background. If the Purāṇas are an *upabṛṁhaṇam*, or confirming elaboration, of the Vedas, then we must ask: when the DM uses a particular epithet, what is it in the Vedic tradition that is being confirmingly elaborated? This second stratum, therefore, is the Vedic. Starting with the earliest attested usage of an epithet, located through the VPK's localization of words, we examine its semantic associations, and development, if any, in the Vedic tradition.[1] We do not, for obvious

[1]We here understand that tradition to be comprised of: (1) the four Saṃhitās (*Ṛg-*, *Sāma-*, *Yajur-*, and *Atharva-Veda*), in their various recensions; (2) the corresponding Brāhmaṇas and Āraṇyakas; (3) the early Upaniṣads: *Īśa*, *Aitareya*, *Kaṭha*, *Kena*, *Kauṣītakī*, *Chāndogya*, *Taittirīya*, *Praśna*, *Bṛhadāraṇyaka*, *Māṇḍukya*, *Muṇḍaka*, *Maitri*, and *Śvetāśvatara*; (4) the Śrauta-, Dharma-, and Gṛhya-Sūtras, plus assorted Vedāṅgas. This understanding is adapted from the structure of the VPK which, in identifying where words occur, has broken the Vedic tradition down into its most precise form, viz., the different

reasons, cite all of the instances.[2] Rather, our endeavor is to convey a sense of the resonance that a particular epithet has in the heart of the Sanskritic tradition. At times, this will mean no more than identifying the grammatically feminine nouns with which a particular descriptive adjective has been associated,[3] while, at others, the epithet will be seen to itself designate a particular goddess, female figure, or abstract noun. This procedure of starting with an epithet's earliest occurrence(s) and noting if, and how, it develops within the tradition has certain other advantages. First, it provides us with a way of discriminating between epithets with the same number of occurrences in the DM. Since one of the endeavors of the DM is to link the worship of the Goddess to the Sanskrit tradition, the importance of any epithet in that endeavor is a function of its resonance in that tradition and that in turn, it seems, is a function of its antiquity in that tradition. Consequently, the second principle governing the structure of Part I is that, among epithets of equally

---

recensions. While we have found it useful to maintain the distinction between Saṃhitās and sometimes, primarily in the Black YV, between recensions, we modify the approach of the VPK by (1) usually citing only one occurrence of a passage which recurs across Saṃhitās and recensions, and throughout subsequent liturgical commentary, (2) considering only the early Upaniṣads identified above (cf. Proleg., p. 62 for the problem of later Upaniṣads), (3) selecting for consideration only those Vedāṅgas (in which the VPK includes the Sūtra literature), from the enormous range of the 118 texts indexed as such by the VPK, which seemed likely to illuminate a particular epithet, e.g., ruling out purely grammatical treatises. While our bibliography (to a lesser extent, our list of abbreviations) gives a rough indication of the scope of the Vedic tradition so understood, other texts consulted do not appear there if (1) their usage of the epithets has proven unilluminating; (2) parallels exist in other, more readily quotable texts—e.g., the *Sāma Veda* is not listed; or (3) a text has proven inaccessible—of the items that are indexed by the VPK, that contain instances of DM epithets, and that we selected for investigation, only the *Agniveśya Gṛhya Sūtra* and the *Vādūla Śrauta Sūtra* fall into this category. The only other limitation on our scope is that when an epithet is overwhelmingly attested, e.g., *śrī*, or a text has proven to shed little new light on an epithet, e.g., a Śrauta Sūtra, we have not persisted in examining every instance.

[2]To do so would be to make this study itself an index. For the principles of selectivity, see the preceding note.

[3]Which constitute the "subconscious or subliminal baggage" of that word, according to the theory of diction espoused at the end of our Prolegomenon.

frequent usage in the DM, the one with the longest Sanskritic history is treated first, and others are dealt with in order of their Sanskritic age.[4] The second advantage of proceeding from early to later instances of an epithet is that it bears a loose resemblance to the way the Indian scriptural tradition has itself operated, with layers of commentary building upon, and nourished by, an early scriptural deposit. It should be clear from the outset, however, that we are not concerned to present a *history* of each individual epithet: to do so would take us far beyond the boundaries of the Sanskritic material.[5] Our aim is the more modest one of identifying verbal associations: when a fifth-sixth century text, the DM, uses language that, among other things, seeks to capitalize on its Vedic reverberations, just what are those reverberations ? Put another (but historically unrealistic) way: if an individual knew only the Vedic tradition and then heard the DM recited, how would he understand its epithets?

There is a third stratum of material that requires consideration if we are to appraise adequately the resonance of the epithets at the time of the DM. That is the epic material. While it is true that, in the absence of a comprehensive index for epic studies that would be comparable to the VPK for Vedic, our inquiry via the extant indices[6] must be limited to proper names, that inquiry is of no mean significance. Much of the force of the DM derives not simply from its Vedic resonance, but also from its integration of theretofore heterogeneous figures and names, the primary example of which is the Goddess's dramatic concluding resumption of her various forms into herself.[7] Many of these

[4]Thus, in our Table of Contents' list of epithets, the epithets that are grouped together occur the same number of times in the DM. Within that group, the Sanskritically eldest comes first.

[5]I.e., into questions of archeology, ethnology, Dravidian languages, etc., as well as into the voluminous Vedic scholarship produced by the nineteenth-century Sanskritists. While this latter is often helpful, and is cited in the sequel when appropriate, the more biased focus of our study (see our next sentence) renders much of it only tangential to our study.

[6]Primarily, Sϕrensen, Sϕren, *An Index to the Names in the Mahābhārata*, Motilal Banarsidass (Delhi, 1963, reprint of 1904 ed.) and Rai, Ramkumar, *Vālmīki-Rāmāyaṇa Kosha* (*Descriptive Index to the Names and Subjects of Rāmāyaṇa*), Chowkhamba Sanskrit Series Office (Varanasi, 1965), Kashi Sanskrit Series 168 (in Hindi).

[7]MarkP 90.3-5, quoted at the conclusion of our Prolegomenon.

forms have names that are also found in the epics. This third stratum, then, seeks to add to the Vedic testimony whatever information the epics supply on the use of the epithets as proper names in the *Rāmāyaṇa* (Rām), Mbh, and HV.[8]

[8]The edition of the Rām we have used is Vālmīki, *Rāmāyaṇa*, Kāśīnāth Pāṇḍuraṅg Parab (ed.), Nirṇaya-Sāgara Press (Bombay, 1888), Two vols., since that appears to have been the edition used by Rai in compiling his index, and since the Rām does not figure prominently enough in our study to warrant the laborious cross-referencing to the critical edition.

For the Mbh, however, we have checked Sǿrensen's references against the critical edition cited *supra*, Proleg., nn. 87, 91, 136. Of course, there was no critical edition in his time, and, now that there is, two comments on the utility of his work (which is great) are in order. On the one hand, instances of epithets that he does not cite may have crept into the constituted text (which is probably not a terribly frequent occurrence, occurring only when an alternative reading to *both* the Bombay and Calcutta edd. has been preferred) or into the Appendices (which may be more frequent, in light of the enormous number of texts collated for the critical edition). Consequently, when we subsequently speak of the epic testimony regarding a particular epithet, that should be understood as qualified by the statement "insofar as we have access to it via Sǿrensen." On the other hand, this cross-checking means that not all of Sǿrensen's references are mentioned in our study, for many do not appear in the constituted text of the Mbh. In fact, as a generalization, we may say that the conclusion to be drawn from the relegation of the two Durgā hymns to the Mbh appendices (see Proleg., p. 45)—viz., that the Goddess is a relative newcomer to the Sanskritic tradition, and her worship only gradually became Sanskritized—is also borne out by an investigation of the epithets. For instance, taking the first epithet for which there is epic evidence, Sǿrensen cites four different characters with the name Ambikā: (1) the spouse of Śiva, (2) the sister of Ambā and Ambālikā, (3) an *apsaras* who sang and danced at Arjuna's birth, (4) a *mātṛ*. Neither of the latter two Ambikās appears in the constituted text, the *apsaras* being a *v. l.* on 1.114.51, and the *mātṛ* being a *v. l.* on 9.45.12, in one case, and part of an excised passage (Appendix I 18, line 60), in the other. While one could argue that, in any case, these two Ambikās are not to be identified with the Goddess, it would nonetheless appear that Sanskrit-using authors only gradually came to apply Goddess-like names to miscellaneous female figures. In order to appreciate this fact throughout Part I, we cite, as a rule, those epithet-usages that appear in the constituted text. Exceptions to this rule are made only for the very popular epithets in the DM, or for uncommonly significant usages in the Mbh and HV appendices. This also avoids double citation of those epithets that occur in Mbh and HV hymns to be presented in Part III (for most of those hymns appear in epic appendices), while providing a second stratum of background (the first being the Vedic) to our reading of those hymns.

For the HV we have used, as the only extant tools, the references of Böhtlingk and Roth (*Sanskrit-wörterbuch von der Kaiserlichen Akademie der Wissenschaften,*

On rare occasions, we add to these strata with miscellaneous material. Such occasions arise when an epithet has no Vedic or epic history, or when a particularly significant piece of evidence turns up in inscriptional, iconographic, secular literary, or Purāṇic sources, even though these sources may be more contemporary with, rather than prior to, the DM. We have eschewed, in particular, myriad references to Purāṇic parallels, first, because the DM itself seems to stand at a fairly early point in the Purāṇic process,[9] and, second, because to make them would involve us in the thorny matter of relative dating of Purāṇic texts.[10] A crucial corollary of this selectivity is that one may not justifiably infer that the DM is solely responsible for bridging any gaps between its own use of an epithet and that found in the Vedic and epic antecedents. There are simply too many other factors—other early Purāṇas, non-Sanskritic sources, unpreserved material—to allow such an inference. That the DM is responsible for bridging many of these gaps is, of course, entirely possible. Our task, however, is, as noted above, not to present a history of the epithets as culminating in the DM. It is, rather, by investigating material that may reasonably be assumed to be prior to our text, to indicate the resonance, perhaps only the minimum resonance, that the epithets had when employed by the DM. The fundamental question in our study is: how was the DM, as a Sanskritic phenomenon, understood in its original context ?

---

Buchdr. d. K. Akademie der Wissenschaften (St. Petersburg, 1855-75, 7 vols., abbr: PW) and the index to Langlois' translation (*Harivansa*; *ou, Histoire de la Famille de Hari*, Oriental Translation Fund of Great Britain and Ireland [Paris, 1834-35] Two vols.) and have endeavored (not always successfully) to cross-check these references with the critical edition cited Proleg., n. 136. While this is clearly the least satisfactory of the methods used for dealing with the three epic texts, it is our impression, based on familiarity with the HV itself, that not much that is of relevance in that text has escaped detection.

If, in our treatment of a particular epithet, one (or more) of these three epic texts is not mentioned, it may be assumed that it has no light to shed on the epithet under discussion.

[9]See O'Flaherty, *Sexuality and Asceticism*, Appendix IV: The Age of the Purāṇas.

[10]We shall, however, in our study of the DM's mythology in Part II, take account of the VāmanaP narrative of the Goddess's exploits, which may antedate the DM.

Turning to the epithets themselves, we may first recall Gonda's remarks on the difficulty of drawing a hard and fast distinction between epithets and descriptive adjectives, for this difficulty is compounded by the fact that various proper names of particular goddesses (with a small "g") are also applied to the Goddess (with a capital "g") and her forms in our text. In order not to prejudge the status of the various designations, we initially identify all of them in lower case and then subsequently capitalize a particular designation if the evidence so warrants. As we shall see, there are many reasons for indicating the deity, whose glories our text proclaims, to be the Goddess, written with a capital. As a preliminary indication of that, we may note that the most common designation for the Goddess in the DM is the generic Sanskrit word for "goddess," *devī*. It occurs in our text as a separate word, i.e., excluding its use in colophons and chapter titles, but including such phrases as *devy uvāca*, a total of 160 times. The word occurs in all three episodes and consequently shows no particular affinity with one specific myth. In fact, *devī* occurs at least three times in every chapter of the DM, but in none of these instances does it appear to be used in a particularly pregnant sense. Because of this almost casual usage of the word in our text, and because of the generic, non-specific usage of the word in Sanskrit, our study of epithets begins with the next most frequent, and far more specific, designation of the Goddess in our text.

*caṇḍikā*

The epithet *caṇḍikā* is applied to the Goddess a total of twenty-nine times in the DM. If we take the definition of the St. Petersburg dictionary as our starting-point,[11] this designation appears to be a true epithet, rather than a mere descriptive adjective, for it is there defined primarily as an "epithet of Durgā", derivative from the feminine adjective *caṇḍī*, "fierce, passionate,"

[11]For certain epithets whose signification is not immediately apparent, we may take the PW definition as an approximate, preliminary definition. It is, of course, only approximate, for it is based on the whole history of Sanskrit usage and not simply on pre-DM material. Our ensuing treatment of that material will permit refinement of the initial approximation, on the basis of the pre-DM material alone.

an adjective which is never used in the DM. Caṇḍikā, then, is "the violent and impetuous one."

This designation is not used at all in the first episode of our text, the episode involving Madhu and Kaiṭabha. It is employed six times in the Goddess's encounter with Mahiṣa, which constitutes the second episode, and twenty-three times in the third episode, wherein the Goddess vanquishes Śumbha, Niśumbha, and their entourage.[12]

The primacy of this epithet, in terms of the frequency of its occurrence, is reinforced by certain instances of its usage. The one to whom Kālī returns after slaying the Asuras Caṇḍa and Muṇḍa (87.22,24), from whom, by implication, Kālī had emerged (87.5), is called Caṇḍikā. At 88.12 it is round Caṇḍikā that the *śaktis* of the various male deities gather. It is Caṇḍikā who, at 88.52ff., solves the riddle of Raktabīja's apparent invincibility. It is Caṇḍikā against whom Śumbha turns (89.6) after skirmishing with lesser goddesses. And, most convincing, though the Goddess into whom the lesser goddesses are resumed (90.4)[13] is there called Ambikā, the name Caṇḍikā is subsequently applied to this supreme form of the Goddess (90.13ff.).

In light of the primacy of this designation of the Goddess, it is striking that the word *caṇḍikā* has virtually no earlier history in Sanskrit. There are no instances of its occurrence in the Vedic literature we have surveyed. The epics are similarly barren: neither the Rām nor the Mbh give evidence of this epithet, although in one of the hymns inserted in the latter, the adjectives *caṇḍā* and *caṇḍī* are applied to the deity there praised.[14] The

[12]The occurrences in the second episode are 82.48; 83.27, 33, 34; 84.3, 24; those in the third 87.22, 24; 88.7, 12, 21, 22, 52, 56; 89.6, 8, 13, 26, 28, 30, 31, 32; 90.13, 18, 19, 21; 91.26; 92.29; and 93.9. The significance of breaking down the usage of epithets according to episode will become clear after reviewing the mythological parallels of these episodes in Part II. We shall see that the myths associated with the Goddess in the DM come from rather different theological or sectarian backgrounds. Having the epithets broken down according to episode will then aid in identifying the sectarian resonance of each epithet. The evidence thus compiled, correlating the epithets with the respective myths, is summarized in Appendix B.

[13]See Proleg., n. 267 for the text, a translation of which is given at that point in our Proleg.

[14]See line 10 of the Durgā Stotra (Mbh Book 6, Appendix I 1), given below in Part III.

HV's testimony on this epithet is also limited to these adjectives, and these, too, occur not in the constituted text but in a later insertion.[15]

In the secular literature that is roughly contemporaneous with the DM, the works of the seventh-century[16] poet Bāṇa are virtually the only ones to shed light on this particular epithet. Foremost among these works, for our purposes, is his *Caṇḍīśataka*,[17] which is often cited as being based upon the DM.[18] While it is true that Bāṇa's poem "is rather a literary than a religious work, and its value as a source is thus rather limited,"[19] several features of the poem are worthy of note. First, while the author has indicated the primacy of the designation Caṇḍī for the goddess whose praises he sings by using it in the title of his work, "the name Caṇḍī, or Caṇḍikā, occurs in but five of the stanzas."[20] Moreover, an analysis of the twenty-eight appellatives applied to the goddess in the *Caṇḍīśataka* reveals that the horrific connotation of the word *caṇḍī* is not the primary characterization of the goddess here. Quackenbos has divided these epithets into four categories, with the following distribution pattern:[21]

(1) Epithets belonging to Caṇḍī as the daughter of Himālaya: seven epithets occurring a total of forty-two times.
(2) Epithets belonging to Caṇḍī as the wife of Śiva: six epithets occurring a total of twenty-five times.
(3) Epithets belonging to Caṇḍī in her horrific aspects: nine epithets, nineteen total occurrences. (Caṇḍī and Caṇḍikā are included here by Quackenbos.)

[15]See lines 7 and 31 of Aniruddha's hymn (HV Appendix I 35), given below in Part III.

[16]Basham, *op. cit.*, p. 390.

[17]*The Sanskrit Poems of Mayūra*, edited with a translation and Notes and an Introduction together with the text and translation of Bāṇa's *Caṇḍīsataka* [sic] by George Payn Quackenbos, AMS Press (New York, 1965). Hereafter cited as Quackenbos, *op. cit.*

[18]Chattopadhyaya, *op. cit.*, p. 168, Farquhar, *op. cit.*, p. 150, Winternitz, *op. cit.*, p. 565n.

[19]Farquhar, *op. cit.*, p. 200.

[20]Quackenbos, *op. cit.*, p. 258. Though the title implies that the poem contains a hundred stanzas, there actually are 102: *ibid.*, p. 245.

[21]*Ibid.*, pp. 258-259.

(4) Epithets belonging to Caṇḍī in her benign aspects: six epithets, twenty-seven total occurrences.

Clearly for Bāṇa the name Caṇḍī not only is at least as benign as it is horrific, but it also has a strongly Śaiva resonance to it. This is borne out as well by the mythological references. "All but four of the stanzas of the *Caṇḍīśataka* picture some detail of the prolonged struggle between the goddess Caṇḍī...and the buffalo-shaped demon Mahiṣa,"[22] and, as we shall see in Part II, the mythological antecedents of the Mahiṣa episode in the DM are intimately involved in the development of Śaivism. To the extent that the *Caṇḍīśataka* is a religious composition,[23] it is impressed by the graciousness, and even the physical beauty, of Caṇḍikā as the spouse of Śiva. The spirit of the whole is nicely conveyed by the first stanza:

"Spoil not thy coquetry, O brow; O lower lip, why this distress? O face, banish thy flushing;
O hand, this (Mahiṣa) is not indeed living; why dost thou brandish a trident, with desire for combat?"
While Devī (Caṇḍī) caused by these words, as it were, the parts of her body that displayed signs of rising anger to resume their normal state,
Her foot, which took away the life of (Mahiṣa), Foe of the Gods, was set down upon his head.
May the foot of Devī (Caṇḍī) destroy your sin![24]

[22]*Ibid.*, p. 247. It is worth noting that the umbha-Niśumbha episode wherein the DM most frequently uses the designation Caṇḍikā, receives no explicit mention from Bāṇa. However, in three of the stanzas where the Mahiṣa episode is not mentioned (25, 45, 54), reference is made to Kaṃsa's attempted slaying of the goddess and her frustration of that attempt. This is surely a reference to the Kṛṣṇa-Yoganidrā myth as that appears in the HV, ViṣṇuP, etc., for, as we shall see in Part II, it is in the context of *that* myth that the names of Śumbha and Niśumbha are first linked with the Goddess.

[23]Quackenbos has, in fact, suggested that the secular romantic quality of the poem predominates over the religious. Having noted that "in more than 60 of the stanzas . . . the killing of Mahiṣa is attributed to the power of the goddess's kick" (p. 247), and proposing that "it is the kick of the goddess, rather than the goddess herself, that is praised in a majority of the stanzas as the conqueror of Mahiṣa" (p. 251), he hazards "the suggestion that perhaps the Caṇḍīśataka was written by Bāṇa to propitiate the anger of his wife by praising the foot with which she had spurned him" (p. 247n).

[24]*Ibid.*, p. 267.

There is one other instance in Bāṇa's work[25] where he refers to a goddess by the name of Caṇḍikā: as part of a long description of Mātaṅga, the leader of the Śabaras, it is said that "he had mighty arms reaching to his knees, . . . and his shoulders were rough with scars from keen weapons often used to make an offering of blood to Caṇḍikā,"[26] but there is no further elaboration.

While the argument from silence is, at best, inconclusive, we have, in fact, found no further contemporary literature, nor any contemporary iconographic or inscriptional evidence, to illuminate the DM's use of the epithet Caṇḍikā. Though it may be frustrating to have such a dearth of Sanskritic material on this most preferred epithet, the evidence does suggest the appropriateness of Pargiter's judgment: "it seems reasonable . . . to conclude that . . . the form Caṇḍikā occur [s] apparently [for] the first time in this poem [the DM]."[27]

*ambikā*

If the most popular epithet in the DM highlights the Goddess's horrific nature, this second most common epithet, employed on

[25]Chattopadhyaya (*op. cit.*, pp. 167-168) presents a quotation from Cowell and Thomas's translation of Bāṇa's *Harṣa-carita* (Motilal Banarsidass [Delhi, 1961], pp. 135-136) as yet another instance of the worship of Caṇḍī, and the context does seem characteristic. The description here is of how various citizens, distraught at the illness of Harṣa's father, sought his cure through various practices, such as burning themselves to propitiate the Mothers, offering oblations of their own flesh, standing with upraised arms "to conciliate Caṇḍī," etc.. However, the two Sanskrit editions we have consulted (*Harṣa Carita* of Bāṇabhaṭṭa, ed. and published by Śūranāḍ Kunjan Piḷḷai [Trivandrum, 1958] University of Kerala Sanskrit Series 187, p. 226.; *The Harshacarita* of Bāṇabhaṭṭa, P. V. Kane [ed.], Motilal Banarsidass [Delhi, 1973] p. 21) both read the masculine *caṇḍikam* where Cowell and Thomas's either read, or was misread, as *caṇḍī*. Therefore, we have not included this passage in our above treatment of Bāṇa's works.

[26]*The Kādambarī* of Bāṇa, translated with occasional omissions by C. M. Ridding, Royal Asiatic Society (London, 1896), p. 28. Ridding's translation, in fact, reads ". . . an offering of blood to Kālī," yet it is clear that it is Ridding who is making the identification of Kālī and Caṇḍikā, for the original reads *caṇḍikārudhirabali-*. . . . (Bāṇa, *Kādambarī*, Peter Peterson [ed.], Government Central Book Depot [Bombay, 1883], p. 30). We have emended Ridding's translation accordingly.

[27]MarkP, Pargiter tr., Introduction, p. xii.

twenty-five occasions,[28] introduces a motif that is of at least equal importance, viz., her maternal character. Though there is good evidence, as we shall see, for treating Ambikā as a proper name, it can also mean simply "mother" or, more evocatively, "mother dear." At the most diffuse level, *ambikā* is simply "a good woman."[29]

Although this designation is applied to the Goddess only in the latter two episodes, there is little doubt that it is intended to apply to the supreme form of the Goddess in the DM. For instance, in the encounter with Mahiṣa, it is Ambikā's breaths that become transformed into fighting hordes (82.51), and in the gods' hymn celebrating her victory, it is the name Ambikā that is employed to invoke the Goddess in both the first and last stanzas (84.3,32). Similarly, it is from Ambikā's furrowed brow that Kālī emerges (87.4-5). Finally, we have already seen[30] that the deity into whom all heterogeneous forms are resumed before the final showdown with Śumbha is called Ambikā (90.4). The one juncture at which the applicability of this epithet to the supreme form of the Goddess might be questioned is at the outset of the third *carita* where the gods, seeking assistance against Śumbha and Niśumbha, proceed to the Himālayas and there hymn a goddess called Viṣṇumāya (85.6). At the conclusion of the hymn, this goddess, now called Pārvatī (85.37), does not know to whom the hymn is addressed, and it takes an auspicious emanation of herself to remind her, "This hymn is addressed to me...."[31] Since this auspicious (*śivā*) form named Kauṣikī,

[28]82.51, 66; 83.1, 11, 23, 29; 84.2, 23, 26, 32; 85.40, 42; 86.9, 10, 20; 87.4; 88.8, 16; 89.15, 22; 90.4, 8, 14, 20, 38.

[29]Though it anticipates our discussion below, Eggeling's comment on *Śatapatha Brāhamaṇa* (ŚB) 13.2.8.3 is worth noting here. The text contains the phrase " 'Ambā, Ambikā, Ambālikā' ", which, he observes, "are simply three variants used in addressing a mother (Mutter, Mütterchen, Mütterlein) or, indeed, . . . any woman (good lady! good woman!)": *The Śatapatha Brāhmaṇa*, according to the text of the Mādhyandiṇa School, Julius Eggeling (tr.), Clarendon Press (Oxford, 1882-1900), Five parts, SBE vols. 12, 26, 41, 43, 44. As we shall see, the Goddess is twice called Ambā in the DM, though she is never addressed as Ambālikā in our text. Cf. also *sūtra* 6.1.118 of Pāṇini's *Grammatik* [*Aṣṭādhyāyī*], hrsg., übers., erläutert . . . von Otto Böhtlingk, H. Haessel (Leipzig, 1887).

[30]See Proleg., p. 81.

[31]*śarīrakoṣataścāsyāḥ samudbhūtābravic chivā/*
*stotraṃ mamaitat kriyate . . . //*

arising from Pārvatī's sheath (*koṣa*), is subsequently called Ambikā (85.40), one could argue that Ambikā is, in some sense, derivative from, or secondary to, Pārvatī. Two considerations militate against such a conclusion, however. First, the text makes virtually nothing of the potential Pārvatī-Ambikā distinction, and, in fact, the three instances of Pārvatī that are clustered in the five verses 85.37-41 are the only three occurrences of the designation Pārvatī in the entire DM. Second, it should be noted that the auspicious emanation does not say, "This hymn is addressed to you," but, "This hymn is addressed to me," implying that, though apparently distinct, the two goddesses are essentially one. It is precisely this point—the essential homogeneity of apparently heterogeneous forms—that lies at the very heart of the DM. What we seem to have here, then, is the text's glorying in the metamorphic potential of the Goddess,[32] rather than its use of Ambikā as a secondary characterization.

The Vedic antecedents of this epithet begin, not with the RV, but with the *Yajur Veda* (YV). The usage is attested in all six recensions of the YV,[33] and since one passage, attested across the recensions, ramifies in a number of directions, it is worth quoting at length. The context is the liturgy of the Rājasūya sacrifice, at the juncture where a cake is offered to Rudra:

> ...This is thy portion, O Rudra, with thy sister
>     Ambikā; rejoice in it
> (Give) medicine for ox, for horse, for man,
> And medicine for us, medicine
> That it be rich in healing,
> Good...for ram and sheep.
> We have appeased, O lady [*ambā*], Rudra,

[32]For further reflection on this potential, see Proleg., n. 265. For further remark on the Pārvatī-Ambikā relationship, see *infra*, s. v. "*gaurī*," "*pārvatī*," "*kṛṣṇā-tāmasī*" and n. 70. Since the viability of this interpretation depends to an extent, on material to be presented hereafter, one need not be utterly persuaded by it at this juncture. We offer a more thorough, retrospective analysis of this episode, *infra*, Part II, note 125.

[33]Of the Black YV : the Kāṭhaka (YVKā), Kapiṣṭhala-Kaṭha (YVKap), Maitrāyaṇīya (YVMai), and Taittirīya (YVT) recensions. Of the White YV or Vājasaneyi Saṃhitā: the Mādhyandina (YVMā) and Kāṇva (YVKāṇ) recensions. Full bibliographic information on these appears in the notes as the respective texts are cited.

The god Tryambaka;
That he may make us prosperous,
That he may increase our wealth,
That he may make us rich in cattle,
That he may embolden us.
To Tryambaka we make offering,
The fragrant, the increaser of prosperity;
Like a cucumber from its stem,
From death may I be loosened not from immortality....[34]

This passage calls for a number of comments. First, and most obvious, is the fact that Ambikā is identified as the sister of Rudra and is addressed by the generic word for mother, *ambā*. More subtle is the fact that Rudra is here addressed by himself, in the singular, rather than as one of a class of Rudras or Maruts, storm-gods—i.e., Rudra is a proper-rather than class-name and he is addressed as Tryambaka, "a common epithet of Śiva is post-Vedic literature."[35] Without going into the complex matter of the relationship between the Vedic Rudra and the post Vedic Śiva, it is worth noting that the last four lines of the above passage are a quotation of RV 7.59.12, wherein occurs the sole Ṛg Vedic usage of the name Tryambaka.[36] This curious epithet is alternatively analyzed as "he who has three eyes" or "he who has three mothers."[37] While the former etymology points toward later iconographic representations of Śiva,[38] it is clearly the latter that suggests Ambikā's link with Rudra-Śiva;

[34]YVT 1.8.6, A. B. Keith tr.: Harvard University Press (Cambridge, 1914), Two vols., HOS 18, 19. For details of the Rājasūya, see Keith's introduction pp. cxi-cxiii and Keith, Arthur Berriedale, *The Religion and Philosophy of the Veda*, Harvard University Press (Cambridge, 1925) Two vols., HOS 31, 32, pp. 340-343.

[35]Macdonell, Arthur Anthony, *Vedic Mythology*, K. J. Trübner (Strassburg, 1897), p. 74.

[36]On the "complex matter, " see Bhandarkar, R. G., *op. cit.*, pp. 102-106; Danielou, *op. cit.*, chapters 15 and 16; O'Flaherty, *Asceticism and Eroticism*, chapter III. Vs. 12 of RV 7.59 seems clearly to be an addition to the original hymn: see Oldenberg, H., *Ṛgveda*: *Textkritische und exegetische Noten*, Weidmannsche Buchhandlung (Berlin, 1909-12), vol. 2, p. 47.

[37]*ambaḥ* or *ambakaḥ*, "eye". See O'Flaherty, *Asceticism and Eroticism*, pp. 206, 248. For further discussion of the word Tryambaka, see Keith, *op. cit.*, p. 149.

[38]See Danielou, *op. cit.*, pp. 214-215; also, Vidyākara, *Subhāṣitaratnakoṣa*, Daniel H. H. Ingalls (tr.), Harvard University Press (Cambridge, 1965), HOS 44, pp. 69-70.

in fact, the DM on one occasion applies the feminine Tryambakā to the Goddess.[39]

In the Brāhmaṇas on this YV passage, its teasingly brief allusion to Ambikā is elaborated upon and, in the process, her ambivalent character is suggested. On the one hand, the ŚB calls Ambikā "the dispenser of happiness" and prescribes the invocation of her brother Tryambaka for young maidens, for he is "the fragrant bestower of husbands."[40] On the other hand, the Brāhmaṇa portions of YVMai and YVKā suggest that the year (*saṃvatsaraḥ*) is Rudra's and the *Taittirīya Brāhmaṇa* (TB) agrees with them in the consequent identification of Rudra's sister Ambikā with the autumn (*śarad*).[41] Caland's translation of the relevant passage[42] suggests the implications of this identification: "Der Herbst ist Rudra's Geburtsstätte: seine Schwester Ambikā. Nach dieser dringt er in (das Vieh und die Menschen) ein (Krankheit und Fieber verursachend). Daher kommt es, dass er im Herbst am meisten tötet." In sum, the Vedic exegesis of this first YV passage draws attention to Ambikā's affiliation with Rudra, explicitly as his sister but with undertones of a maternal relationship, and it is aware of both the beneficent and the destructive aspects of this affiliation.

There is one other YV passage, recurring throughout the Vedic literature, where the word *ambikā* occurs. It is not clear that it is a proper name here, and the whole passage seems to

[39]91.9. This is the verse on whose curiously recurring usage we have commented Proleg., n. 204. When the Goddess arises from the *tejas* of the gods at the beginning of the second *carita*, her three eyes are said to have come from Agni. She is also called *trinetrā* (33 18) and her face (*vadanam*) is *trilocanabhūṣitam* at 91.23.

[40]ŚB 2.6.2.13-14, Eggeling tr.

[41]YVMai 1.1.20: *Maitrāyaṇī Saṃhitā*, Leopold von Schroeder (ed.), F. A. Brockhaus (Leipzig, 1881-86). YVKā 36.14: *Die Saṃhitā der Kaṭha-śākhā*, Leopold von Schroeder (ed.), F.A. Brockhaus Leipzig, 1900-1910, Three vols. TB 1.6.10.4: *Kṛṣṇayajurvedīyam taittirīyabrāhmaṇam*, Nārāyaṇa Śāstri (ed.), Apte (Poona, 1898), Three vols., Ānandāśrama Sanskrit Series 37. It is worth recalling in this context that autumn is the occasion for the festival of Durgāpūjā: cf. Proleg., pp. 59-60.

[42]YVMai 1.10.20, when it is quoted at *Āpastamba Śrautasūtra* 8.18.1: *Das Śrautasūtra des Apastamba*, W. Caland (tr.), vol. 1: Vandenhoeck und Ruprecht (Göttingen, 1921), vol. 2: Koninklijke Akademie van Wetenschappen te Amsterdam (Amsterdam, 1924).

have occasioned some embarrassment among the traditional exegetes. Yet, significantly, the word *ambikā* has received virtually no attention from them, while it is the ritual context that has been the focus of concern. Accordingly, we may glance briefly at that context, for the underlying issue is one that is central to the identity of the Goddess, viz., fertility. The passage in question occurs in the midst of the famous Aśvamedha sacrifice.[43] After the horse has returned from its year of wandering and has, together with other victims, been appropriately prepared, "the horse is covered with a garment and slain: the queens go round it from left to right thrice, and thrice *vice versa*: the chief queen goes near the horse: both are covered with a garment, and the queen unites with it: meanwhile the priest and the maidens and the other wives engage in ribald dialogue. Then the horse and the other victims are cut up."[44] It is as the queens approach the horse, before circumambulating it, that the *mantras* occur:

> O Ambā ! O Ambālī ! O Ambikā !
> No one leadest me.
> The wicked horse is sleeping.[45]

Precisely who utters these *mantras*, and the significance of the ensuing actions and dialogue, are matters on which there is no

[43]For a full discussion of which, see Keith, *op. cit.*, pp. 343-347, the introduction to YVT, Keith tr., pp. lxvii-lxviii and cxxxii-cxxxvii, and two works of Paul-Émile Dumont: *L'Aśvamedha: Description du sacrifice solennel du cheval dans le culte védique d'après les textes du Yajurveda Blanc*, P. Geuthner (Paris, 1927) and "The Horse Sacrifice in the Taittirīya Brāhmaṇa: The Eighth and Ninth Prapāṭhakas of the Third Kāṇḍa o. .he Taittirīya-Brāhmaṇa with Translation," *Proceedings of the American Philosophical Society* Vol. 92 (1948), No. 6, pp. 447-503.

[44]Keith, *op. cit.*, p. 345.

[45]YVT 7.4.19, Keith tr. All recensions include the word *ambikā*, though they have apparently inconsequential variations on other diminutives for the word "mother," e.g., *ambi*, *ambālikā*; cf. YVMai 3.12.20, YVMā 23.18: *The Vājasaneyi-Sanhitā in the Mādhyandina-* and the *Kāṇva-sakhā*, Dümmler's Verlagsbuchhandlung (Berlin, 1852), and Williams and Norgate (London, 1852), Part One of *The White Yajurveda*, ed. by Albrecht Weber in Three Parts. Why Keith should call the horse "wicked"is not clear, for the text (YVT 7.4.19.1) reads simply *sasasty aśvakaḥ*: *kṛṣṇayajurvedīya-taittirīya-saṃhitā*, Kaśīnāthaśāstrī Āgāśe (ed.) Āpte (Poona, 1900-1908), Nine vols., Ānandāśrama Sanskrit Series 42. We have already quoted Eggeling's understanding of the three names, *supra*, n. 29.

unanimity.[46] Nor is there any consensus among modern scholars as to the over-all meaning of the Aśvamedha.[47] Yet those scholars do concur that the ritual context, narrowly considered as the episode encompassing these few *mantras*, is a fertility rite, and the explicitness of the ritual would account for the commentators' difficulties. And this link of *ambikā* and fertility, tenuous though it may be, is virtually all that the evidence allows.

The only remaining Vedic evidence of note occurs at *Taittirīya Āraṇyaka* (TA) 10.18.1, where Rudra is hymned as "husband of Ambikā (*ambikā-pati*)," rather than as her brother, and, in the same breath, is called *hiraṇya-pati* and *umā-pati*, but there is no elaboration of any of these names.[48] For completeness on this important epithet, we may mention the occurrence of Ambikā in lists of deities in the litanies at *Baudhāyana Gṛhya Sūtra* (BGS) 2.8.9 and 3.7.17,[49] and her designation at *Yājñavalkya Smṛti* I.271ff., as the mother of Vināyaka,[50] but in none of these cases is there a means for assessing the significance of the epithet's occurrence.

Turning to the epic antecedents of this epithet, while the Mbh does confirm Śiva's identity as husband of Ambikā,[51] the primary legacy that the epics bequeath to our epithet is the Mbh's account of the three sisters Ambā, Ambikā and Ambālikā.[52] It may, of course, be true that epic characters are initially human or,

[46]For discussion of the speakers, see the notes on YVT 7.4.19, Keith tr. and on ŚB 13.2.8.3ff., Eggeling tr. For an example of a traditional symbolic exegesis (which Eggeling calls "far-fetched"), cf. ŚB 13.2.8.3-9.9 and 13.5.2.1-9.

[47]The different opinions are discussed in the references given at n. 43.

[48]*Taittirīya Āraṇyaka*, Rājendralāla Mitra (ed.), Asiatic Society of Bengal (Calcutta, 1872), Bibliotheca Indica NS 60, 74, 88, 97, 130, 144, 159, 169, 203, 226, and 263. In the ongoing elaboration upon the Goddess's character, the identification here of Ambikā and Umā is significant, but in light of the close association of these names in later times, it is all the more noteworthy that the DM itself never employs the name Umā.

[49]*The Bodhāyana Gṛihyasūtra*, R. Sama Sastri (ed.), University of Mysore (Mysore, 1920), Oriental Library Publications Sanskrit Series 32/55.

[50]Cited in Banerjea, Jitendra Nath, *The Development of Hindu Iconography*, University of Calcutta (Calcutta, 1956), p. 355.

[51]7.57.53.

[52]The similarity to YVT 7.4.19 is striking, though it may, of course, be purely coincidental, a function of the names being three pleasantly alliterative diminutives.

more true to the epic tradition, superhuman characters who have been swept up into a process of divinization and mythification.[53] Therefore Ambikā may be more likely to retain human qualities here than in, say, the Purāṇas. It may also be true that the women in the book of the Mbh in which the story of the three sisters occurs tend to be "self-effacing."[54] But since that story is so central to the identity of epic characters, and the name "Ambikā" is so inextricably bound up in it, we may recount it briefly.[55]

Bhīṣma, son of Śaṃtanu and the river goddess Ganges, and ruler of Kurukṣetra, was desirous of providing wives for his half-brother Vicitravīrya when the latter came of age. Hearing that the king of Kāśī was to hold a *svayaṃvara* for his three daughters, Ambā, Ambikā and Ambālikā, he proceeded thence and, putting forth the claim that "students of the Law hold that that bride is the best who is carried off by force," proceeded to abduct the three. Opposition was offered primarily by king Śālva, but he was vanquished by Bhīṣma and the entourage returned to Hāstinapura. Prior to the wedding, Ambā explained that she had previously promised herself to Śālva and was allowed to depart.[56] Ambikā and Ambālikā, however, described as "tall

[53]This euhemeristic theory, while not universally accepted, is implicitly affirmed by van Buitenen in his introductory remarks, vol. 1, pp. xix-xxi of *The Mahābhārata*, J.A. B. van Buitenen (ed. and tr.), University of Chicago Press (Chicago and London), vol. 1: The Book of the Beginning (1973), vol. 2: The Book of the Assembly Hall, and The Book of the Forest (1975).

[54]This is van Buitenen's phrase (*ibid.*, vol. 1, p. 15), though, as we shall see, it hardly applies to such a woman as Ambā. Moreover, since this is The Book of Origins, and since the Ambā-Ambikā-Ambālikā story occurs so close to what was probably the beginning of the original narrative (*ibid.*, vol. 1, p. xvi), the primary narrative concern here is, quite naturally, the establishment of genealogies, rather than full characterization.

[55]Our presentation here ignores the half dozen "bald" references to Ambikā in the Mbh, i.e., those references where she is simply noted as Ambā's sister, etc. The following paragraph is a précis of Mbh 1.96-100, with primary reliance upon the first and last of those chapters. In the interest of simplicity, we have not elaborated on the involuted genealogies involved, an involution which van Buitenen feels (*loc. cit.*) is deliberate. All quotations are from his translation.

[56]The Mbh returns to Ambā's story, which we shall resume under our treatment of the epithet "*ambā*," at 5.170ff.

and dark and with blue-black curling hair, red pointed nails, and buxom breasts and buttocks," were married to Vicitravīrya and remained thus until he died seven years later, childless. Subsequently, Bhīṣma's mother, Satyavatī, requested that he invoke the custom of levirate in order to continue the Bhārata line, but he refused. She then revealed that she had had a premarital son, Kṛṣṇa Dvaipāyana, and with the consent of Bhīṣma, Kṛṣṇa, and the widows, he sired two of the major figures of the Mbh, Dhṛtarāṣṭra by Ambikā and Pāṇḍu by Ambālikā. Through all of this,the only glimmer that we have of Ambikā's character occurs when Kṛṣṇa, of "matted orange hair...fiery eyes,... [and] reddish beard," seeks to sleep with her again. "...As she thought back on the appearance, and the smell, of the great seer, the woman, lovely as a Goddess, was from sheer fright incapable of doing [so]..." and sent a slave girl in her stead. Might we see here an uncommon fragility, or an acute sense of pique, or is it a healthy repugnance at the bohemian Kṛṣṇa ?

Except for passing references to Ambikā when the Mbh returns to the story of Ambā (5.170ff.), the only remaining testimony in the epics occurs in the appendices to the HV where the connection with Śiva is central. Ambikā is cited as *bhūtadhātrī* in Kṛṣṇa's hymn to Śiva, and on another occasion she seems to be identified with Umā.[57]

Finally, evidence that is roughly contemporaneous with the DM is equally meagre, the only reference being a simile in Bāṇa's *Kādambarī* that indicates Ambikā's trident to have been wet with the blood of Mahiṣa,[58] but in light of Bāṇa's attraction to the Goddess-Mahiṣa myth,[59] this association is not surprising.

### *nārāyaṇī*

Though the Goddess is called *nārāyaṇī* fifteen times in our text, this frequency is somewhat deceiving for the instances occur in consecutive *ślokas* at 91.7-21 as part of a hymnic refrain. There are additional verses to this hymn, both preceding and succeeding these *ślokas*, but the predominance

[57]Appendices I 29, line 1324 and I 29A, line 40, respectively.

[58]*Op. cit.*, p. 31: . . . *ambikātriśūlam iva mahiṣarudhirārdrakāyam* . . .

[59]See *supra*, s. v. "*caṇḍikā*."

of this particular epithet has led to the designation of the whole hymn as the Nārāyaṇī-stuti.[60] It will be presented *in toto* in Part III.

Although the St. Petersburg dictionary suggests that Nārāyaṇī is primarily an epithet of Lakṣmī, Viṣṇu's spouse, the source it cites is substantially later than the DM and, as we shall see, the prior evidence does not know such an identification under the name of Nārāyaṇī. As a preliminary approximation, then, we may simply take this designation in its literal sense as "she who is related to Nārāyaṇa." We might possibly go one step further and see it as the feminization of the etymological analysis of *nārāyaṇa* "the resting place or goal of men," or even "the resting place or goal of gods."[61] In any case, this is clearly a designation that is simultaneously epithet and descriptive adjective.

In light of the first of these senses, the primary question obviously is: who is this Nārāyaṇa, to whom the Goddess is related ? A full answer to this question lies beyond the scope of this study, but we may make reference to Bhandarkar's detailed analysis of the process by which the Vedic Viṣṇu, the Vāsudeva Kṛṣṇa of the Bhāgavatas, the Nārāyaṇa of late Vedic and epic times, and Kṛṣṇa Gopāla came to be identified.[62] The crucial features of Nārāyaṇa's identity seem to be that he is originally a priestly figure, appearing in the ŚB as performing a *pañcarātra* sacrifice, in the TA as endowed with the attributes of the one supreme deity, and in the Nārāyaṇīya section of the Mbh as one of the four forms of the supreme deity.[63] By the time of our text, however, "the names Nārāyaṇa, Hari, Vishnu, Vāsudeva, and Krishna were used interchangeably with reference to the Lord, Bhagavān, worshipped by the devotees called Bhāgavatas."[64]

[60]Banerjea, "Some Aspects . . . ," p. 229.

[61]Bhandarkar, R.G., *op. cit.*, p. 30.

[62]*Ibid.*, pp. 1-42. For Nārāyaṇa alone, see esp. pp. 4-8, 30-33. See also Das Gupta, Mrinal, "Early Viṣṇuism and Nārāyaṇīya Worship," IHQ VII (1931), pp. 93-116, 343-358, 735-759 (incorrectly paged as 655-679), VIII (1932), pp. 64-84.

[63]Bhandarkar, R. G., *op. cit.*, pp. 31, 5.

[64]Hopkins, T., *The Hindu Religious Tradition*, Dickenson Pub. Co. (Encino and Belmont, CA, 1971), p. 89. It is worth noting that the latest strand

The Sanskritic antecedents of this epithet can be dealt with briefly, for they are few, and it is not even definite that they are, in fact, antecedents. From the Vedic corpus, the sole occurrence of Nārāyaṇī is in the RV *khila* (RVK) known as the Śrī Sūkta, to which we shall turn in Part III.[65] From the Mbh, Sørensen's two quotations of it as referring to Indrasenā, daughter of Nārāyaṇa and wife of Mudgala, do not appear in the constituted text,[66] a fate which also befalls the HV's use of the epithet.[67]

*kālī*

Etymologically, *kālī* is simply a feminine adjective, "the dark or blue-black one," but to the extent that it has undertones of the masculine noun *kāla*, it shares that noun's meaning of "time," or "the fullness of time," and, by implication, time as "that which brings all things to an end, the destroyer." However, more so than perhaps any other designation in the DM, Kālī is clearly a proper name, a pure epithet for a particular goddess, with a particular character.[68]

---

feeding into this process is the Kṛṣṇa Gopāla strand, the initial vehicle of which is, of course, the HV. If we accept Ingalls' dating for the HV as the first three centuries C.E. (Ingalls, Daniel H. H., "The *Harivaṃśa* as a *Mahākāvya*," *Mélanges d'Indianisme*, à la mémoire de Louis Renou, Éditions E. de Boccard (Paris, 1968), Publications de l'Institute de Civilisation Indienne, fasc. 28, p. 394), or Vaidya's dating of the first 98 *adhyāyas* at 300 C.E. (Introduction to the HV critical edition, p. xxxix), then the chronological proximity to our text is rather great. As we shall see in Part II, the Śumbha-Niśumbha myth comes out of a Kṛṣṇa Gopāla background, and since the Nārāyaṇī-stuti occurs in the context of this myth, it is possible to see this third *carita* of the DM as making a contribution, albeit somewhat oblique, to the emerging identification of Nārāyaṇa and Kṛṣṇa Gopāla.

[65]RVK 2.6.30. This is, in fact, the mysteriously recurring verse on which we have commented *supra*, Proleg., n. 204, and I, n. 39.

[66]They are variants on 3.113.24 and 4.20.8.

[67]It does appear thrice in excised passages: once in the prologue to an embellishment of Viṣṇu's praise of Nidrā (591*), and twice in Aniruddha's hymn (App. I 35, lines 90, 93). See Part III for these hymns.

[68]While this statement is true as it stands, it is worth noting that, in the hymn of the first *carita*, which is clearly addressed to the supreme form of the Goddess, two names occur which, as we shall see, are closely related to

The name Kālī appears in our text fourteen times, all of the instances being in the third episode.[69] Several of these are of little consequence, however, and we may see her character being fully delineated in three particular episodes. The first of these is when the Goddess, seeing that Caṇḍa and Muṇḍa had returned to engage her in combat, bristled in anger: "Her face became black (*masīvarṇam*) with rage (and) from her furrowed brow sprang forth Kālī, of terrible countenance, with sword and snare in hand."[70] This emanation is then described as

> Carrying a many-colored skull-topped staff, wearing a garland of human (skulls),
> With a garment of tiger-skin, exceedingly frightening with (her) dried-out skin;
> With widely gaping mouth, terrifying with (her) lolling tongue,
> With sunken, reddened eyes, (and) a mouth that filled the directions with roars.[71]

In the ensuing combat, her special means of dispatching her enemies is by pulverizing them with her teeth.[72] The second episode occurs after Kālī has vanquished Caṇḍa and Muṇḍa. She presents their heads to the Goddess, who declares that because Kālī has overcome these two demons, she will become

---

the identity of Kālī, viz., "the night of destruction (*kālarātri*)" and "the great night (*mahārātri*)," to which the hymn then adds a motif that is characteristic of the first *carita*, "the night of delusion (*moharātri*)."

[69]87.5, 15, 18, 22, 24; 88.9, 10, 31, 52, 56; 89.20, 27, 35, 39. To these we might append the use of Mahākālī at 92.35, where it seems to apply to Kālī's cosmic role at the end of time (*mahākāle*), but which Pargiter thinks (MarkP, Pargiter tr., p. 521n.) applies to her worship at the Śaiva shrine of Mahākāla in Ujjain. It may, of course, be both of these.

[70]87.4cd-5. The similarity to the way in which the Goddess herself springs from the furrowed brows of the gods in the second *carita* (82.8ff.) is striking. Also, we have here further evidence of our author's glorying in the metamorphic character of the Goddess, for whereas earlier (85.37ff.; see *supra*, s. v. "*ambikā*") an auspicious emanation, named Kauṣikī had sprung from Pārvatī, who was subsequently described as black (*kṛṣṇā*) and consequently called Kālikā, "The Black One" (85.41, the sole instance of this epithet in our text), now the process is reversed with the dark goddess emanating from the (implied) auspicious source.

[71]87.6-7.

[72]Cf. Gītā 11.27.

renowned in the world under the name of Cāmuṇḍā.[73] We shall examine this particular epithet in its appropriate place, simply noting here that it is used as a virtual synonym for Kālī throughout the rest of our text. The final episode of note occurs in chapter 88 where Raktabīja has been baffling the Goddess's forces because of the fact that, as his name suggests, each drop of his blood turns into another Asura like himself. It is Kālī who is the instrument of his demise when, at the Goddess's behest, she drinks up his blood and offspring, while the Goddess herself dispatches Raktabīja.

In prior Sanskritic usage, although there is a suggestion of the personification of the masculine Kāla, Time, in the AV,[74] it is only later in the *Śāṅkhāyana Āraṇyaka* (ŚānA) that the feminine first appears, and this first instance gives evidence of the sinister connotation that the word is to retain in subsequent usage. The context is a discussion of what happens to "a man when he is to die before the year's end." At first, he "sees visions of the year. His shadow is crooked, or is not seen at all." Subsequently "follow the dream visions," among which is one of "a yellow-looking or black woman, with loosened hair or shaved," upon seeing which various rituals are prescribed.[75] Kālī first appears as a proper name in the *Kāṭhaka Gṛhya Sūtra* (KāGS) in a list of deities—including Agni, Soma, Indra, Skanda, Rudra, Ṣaṣṭhī, and Bhadrakālī—to be invoked with perfume offerings at the marriage ceremony, but there is no comment on her significance.[76] A frequently cited passage occurs at MuU 1.2.4

[73]This explicit identification of Kālī and Cāmuṇḍā is worthy of note, for Cāmuṇḍā is a common designation for one of the Seven Little Mothers (*sapta-mātṛkās*). In our text, however, Cāmuṇḍā is not conceived as one of the *mātṛkās* but as this more major figure of Kālī. For further remarks on the *sapta-mātṛkās* and on Kālī 's relationship to them in the DM, see Appendix A.

[74]19.53.54, cited by Macdonell, *Vedic Mythology*, p. 120.

[75]ŚānA 11.3.4: *Śāṇkhāyana Āraṇyaka*, Arthur Berriedale Keith (tr.), Royal Asiatic Society (London, 1908), Oriental Translation Fund, NS Vol. XVIII. The text of the heart of this passage is: *pāṇḍuradarśanām kālīṃ strīṃ muktakeśāṃ muṇḍāṃ*. For the text of ŚānA, see *Śāṅkāyana Āraṇyaka*, Ānandāśrama mudraṇālya (Poona, 1922), Ānandāśrama Sanskrit Series 90.

[76]KāGS 19.7: *Kāṭhaka Gṛyha Sūtra*, Willem Caland (ed.), Research Dept. Dayanand Anglo-Vedic College (Lahore, 1925), DAV Sanskrit Series Vol. 9.

where Kālī is named as one of the seven quivering tongues (*lelāyamānā saptajihvāḥ*) of Agni, along with Karālī, Manojavā, Sulohitā, Sudhūmravarṇā, Sphuliṅginī, and Viśvarūpī.[77] While it may be the case that these tongues are feminine simply because *jihvā* is, some have argued that we have here an early intuition of the *sapta-mātṛkās*.[78] Be that as it may, Kālī and fire eventually come to participate in the common matrix of Kālī as agent of the world's incineration, which is at least symbolically continuous with this passage.[79]

Turning to the epic testimony, in the Mbh there are several inconsequential occasions on which *kālī* is applied simply as a descriptive adjective to Satyavatī,[80] and the epithet is employed in each of the excised hymns.[81] It is, however, in the Sauptika Parvan that an episode occurs that represents a crucial stage in the growth of Kālī's identity. The context is Aśvatthāman's night attack on the Pāṇḍava camp. As he rushes about with his terrible sword, the action is initially described, not as the work of Aśvatthāman, but as follows:

> Kālī[82] of bloody mouth and eyes, smeared with blood (and) garlands,
> With reddened garment, alone, crested (and) noose in hand,
> The night of death (*kālarātri*), laughing derisively (and) standing firm, did the (Pāṇḍavas) see.

[77]Here, and in subsequent citations from the Upaniṣads, unless otherwise noted, we have followed the text given in *The Principal Upaniṣads*, S. Radhakrishnan (ed. and tr.), George Allen and Unwin Ltd. (London, 1968), emending it here by reading *karālī* for *karalī*.

[78]Chattopadhyaya, *op. cit.*, p. 155, Banerjea, *Development*, p. 491. Their case might appear to be fairly speculative, since of the seven names appearing here, only Kālī subsequently appears as the name of one of the *sapta-mātṛkās*, though she could surely be characterized as *karālī*. Nonetheless, a broader consideration of the evidence does tend to support the association of Agni and the Seven Little Mothers: cf. Appendix A.

[79]For the related elaboration of this matrix in terms of the interplay between Agni and Śiva, see O'Flaherty, *Asceticism and Eroticism*, pp. 90-110.

[80]Mbh 1.54.2; 1.99.21; 5.172.1; 5.145.29; 6.114.33. This is also true in the HV, e.g., at 23.119.

[81]Durgā Stava line 34, Durgā Stotra line 8.

[82]Or: "the black one." There are no contextual grounds for preferring either the proper noun or descriptive adjective. We opt for the former simply because of its subsequent applicability to the figure here described.

Binding men, horses, and elephants with terrible snares did she sally forth,
Carrying off various spirits who were bound with snares, their hair disheveled.
And, good sir, on other nights, in (their) dream(s), the leaders of the troops constantly saw her
Carrying off those who were asleep, (and) the sons of Droṇa (Aśvatthāman) slaying (them).
Ever since the battle between the Kuru and Pāṇḍava armies had broken out,
They had seen (her) activity and (that of) the son of Droṇa.

. . . . . . . . . . . . . . . . . . . . . . . .

Recalling this former vision, the (Pāṇḍava) heroes,
Tormented by fate, thought, "This is it !"[83]

This is, so far as we have been able to determine, the first discursive account of Kālī/Kālarātri in Sanskrit, and it is clearly impressed by the gruesomeness and violence of her activity, as well as by the mysterious premonitions of that activity. That she is somehow associated with the abnormal or unconventional, whether that be understood as a course of action or as a level of consciousness is suggested (1) by the controversy that Aśvatthāman's proposal of a night attack arouses,[84] (2) by the subsequent ascription of his success to, among other things, the delusive power of sleep.[85] Finally, we should note that there is

[83]Lit., "this is that"; loosely, "the jig is up!" The text (Mbh 10.8.64-67, 69) runs:

*kālīṃ raktāsyanayanāṃ raktamālyanulepanām/*
*raktāmbaradharām ekāṃ pāśahastāṃ śikhaṇḍinīm//*
*dadṛśuḥ kālarātriṃ te smayamānām avasthitām/*
*narāśvakuñjarān pāśair baddhvā ghoraiḥ pratasthuṣīm/*
*harantīm vividhān pretān pāśabaddhān vimūrdhajān//*
*svapne suptān nayantīm tāṃ rātriṣv anyāsu māriṣa/*
*dadṛśur yodhamukhyās te ghnantam drauṇim ca nityadā//*
*yataḥ pravṛttaḥ saṃgrāmaḥ kurupāṇḍavasenayoḥ/*
*tataḥ prabhṛti tāṃ kṛtyām apaśyan drauṇim eva ca//*

. . . . . . . . . . . . . . . .

*tad anusmṛtya te vīrā darśanaṃ paurvakālikam/*
*idam tad ity amanyanta daivenopanipīḍitāḥ//*

[84]Mbh 10.1-5.

[85]Mbh 10.8.139, 142, 148. We shall see this sleep motif elaborated below, primarily under the epithets "*viṣṇu-māyā*" and "*yoganidrā-nidrā*" and

an undertone of a relationship between Kālī and Śiva, for it is through invoking the latter that Aśvatthāman receives the sword of Śiva and his own personal invincibility.[86]

To this eloquent testimony, the HV adds explicit reference to Kālī only once, and that is in one of the excised hymns.[87] However, there are two occurrences of closely related epithets at one significant juncture in the constituted text. When Viṣṇu descends to the nether regions (*pātāla*) to arrange for the goddess Nidrā, Sleep, to be born of Yaśodā and to dispose the *ṣaḍgarbhas* as the foetuses of Devakī, he first sees those *ṣaḍgarbhas* "sleeping in the water in embryonic form, as if enveloped by Nidrā," who is said to have the form of death;[88] and at the very end of his subsequent hymn to Nidrā, in which an effort is made to understand her as *the* Goddess, the name Kālarātri is applied to her (47.54).[89]

Finally, in material contemporary with the DM, Kālī appears with the *mātṛkās* in the *Kumārasaṃbhava*,[90] but of even greater moment perhaps is the fact that the author of that work, the peerless Kālidāsa, should call himself "the slave of Kālī."

---

in conjunction with the Madhu-Kaiṭabha myth in Part II, but also in our next paragraph.

[86]Mbh 10.6-7.

[87]See Aniruddha's hymn in Part III, line 20.

[88]HV 47.24: *jale suptān . . . garbhasaṃsthitān nidrayā kālarūpiṇyā . . . antarhitān iva.*

[89]The manuscript tradition at this point is very complicated, for this verse lies at the "seam" between Viṣṇu's hymn in the constituted text and the embellishments which now appear in Appendix I 8. (We shall deal with both constituted text and Appendix in Part III.) Consequently, it would be unwise to place too much significance on this particular epithetical occurrence. Nonetheless, the context—Viṣṇu's solicitation of Nidrā—suggests that *some* hymnic material is utterly appropriate in the constituted text and that fact is of rather greater significance: it is the first—and only—time that a hymn employing numerous "Goddess motifs" appears in the constituted text of the critical edition of the epic.

[90]Kālidāsa, *Kumārasaṃbhava*, Nārāyana Rāma Āchārya (ed.), Nirṇaya Sāgara Press, 14th ed. (Bombay, 1955), VII. 39. We owe this reference to Bhattacharyya, N., *op.cit.*, p. 76n, where he also indicates that Kālī occurs at *Raghuvaṁśa* XI.15, a reference that is not borne out by the text: *Raghuvaṁśa*, with the comm. of Mallinātha, with Eng. tr. and nn. by Gopal Raghunath Nandargikar, Radhabai Atmaram Sagoon, third ed. Bombay, 1897). **For**

*bhagavatī*

This designation of the Goddess, applied on nine occasions throughout our text, is always applied to her supreme form and usually occurs in, or in close proximity to, hymnic material.[91] It does not seem to have a more pregnant sense than the ordinary adjectival use would suggest, viz., "blessed, venerable, fortunate" or, more analytically, "one who is possessed of *bhaga*, i.e., happiness or prosperity."[92]

Though the Vedic literature employs this word on a half-dozen or so occasions, most of these are repetitions of two original usages, one from the RV, the other from the Brāhmaṇas on the YV. The sole Ṛg Vedic usage occurs in a hymn to the *viśve devāḥ* and calls attention to the beneficent character of the cow. It runs, in Geldner's translation:

> So mögest du denn auf guter Weide grasend glücklich [ *bhagavatī*] sein und auch wir möchten glücklich sein. Friss allezeit Gras, o Kuh, trink reines Wasser, (zur Tränke) kommend ![93]

The other Vedic use of *bhagavatī*, while in the narrow sense simply predicating it of the *iḍā* benediction, presents an interesting mythology and attests strongly to the fecundity of whatever is *bhagavatī*. According to ŚB 1. 8. 6-7,[94] after the flood had swept away all creatures, Manu was left alone. Desirous of offspring, he offered a sacrifice, from which, after a year, a woman was produced.

---

a broader account and interpretation of Kālī, see Kinsley, David, *The Sword and the Flute*: *Kālī & Kṛṣṇa, Dark Visions of the Terrible and the Sublime in Hindu Mythology*, University of California Press (Berkeley, Los Angeles, London, 1975).

[91] 81.42, 53; 84.8, 9, 30; 85.66; 89.29; 92.29, 32.

[92] Though we might expect an implied relationship to Viṣṇu as Bhagavān—on which, see *supra*, s.v. "*nārāyaṇī*" and refs. given at n. 62—it will be seen that the Sanskritic antecedents do not suggest such a nuance.

[93] RV 1.164.40: *Der Rig-Veda*, Karl Friedrich Geldner (tr.), Harvard University Press (Cambridge, 1951-57), Four vols., HOS 33-36. For the text, see *Ṛg Veda Saṁhitā: The Sacred Hymns of the Brahmans*, Max Müller (ed.), W. H. Allen and Co. (London, 1849-74), six vols.

[94] And its parallel at YVMai 4.2.10.

> Manu said to her, "who art thou?" "Thy daughter," she replied. "How, illustrious one [*bhagavatī*], (art thou) my daughter?" he asked. She replied, "Those offerings ... which thou madest in the waters, with them hast thou begotten me. I am the blessing (benediction): make use of me at the sacrifice! If thou wilt make use of me at the sacrifice, thou wilt become rich in offspring and cattle. Whatever blessing thou shalt invoke through me, all that shall be granted to thee" .... With her he went on worshipping and performing austerities, wishing for offspring. Through her he generated this race, which is this race of Manu; and whatever blessing he invoked through her, all that was granted to him.[95]

At the risk of overinterpretation, we may draw the inference that she who is *bhagavatī*, in addition to being beneficent, is the creatrix of humanity or, more precisely, it is through her who is *bhagavatī* that Manu is creative. The anticipation of the god-*śakti* relationship, of which more below, is intriguing.

The only additional antecedents or contemporary occurrences that are worthy of note are the designation of Aditi, "mother of the Rudras, daughter of the Vasus," as *bhagavatī* at KāGS 24.19 and an invocation at *Mānava Gṛhya Sūtra* (MāGS)[96] 2.14.30: at the establishment of a new house, the *ācārya* is to invoke a series of non-specific feminine benefactors, "O one who possesses prosperity (*bhagavatī*), grant me prosperity (*bhaga*) O one who possesses color (*varṇavatī*), grant me color (*varṇa*)," etc. All further instances of this epithet are in hymnic material to be considered in Part III: in the Śrī and Rātrī Sūktas of the RVK and the Durgā Stotra of the Mbh.[97]

### *durgā*

This famous designation for the Goddess is used in our text on seven occasions,[98] and in all three episodes. It is clearly applied to her supreme form, for four of its appearances are in

[95] ŚB 1.8.1.9, 10, Eggeling tr.

[96] *Das Mānava-gṛihya-sūtra,* Friedrich Knauer (ed.), L'Academie Imperiale des Sciences (St. Petersburg, 1897).

[97] In verse 23, verse 3, and line 22 of the respective hymns.

[98] 84.10, 16; 85.10, 66; 89.29; 90.2; 91.22.

hymns, one is an epilogue to a hymn, and one characterizes the Goddess who resumes all goddesses into herself. Though, as we shall see, the word *durga/durgā* has a long history as an adjective or common noun, our text employs it as a true epithet and takes unusual care to explain the epithet, either etymologically or by an explicit phrase of characterization. To see how *durgā* is used in our text, we may therefore simply cite its own remarks on who Durgā is:

> You are Durgā, a vessel upon the ocean of life (that is so) hard to cross. ...[99]
> O Durgā, (when) called to mind (by the faithful), you take away fear (or danger) from every creature.[100]
> Hail to Durgā, the inaccessible further shore ...[101]
> Protect us from terrors, O Goddess; O Goddess Durgā, let there be praise to you.[102]

In our text's view, Durgā is thus the great protectress from worldly adversity (*durga*), and is at the same time herself inassailable and hard-to-approach (*durgā*).

Although, as is frequently remarked, the name Durgā does not appear in the RV, it does not follow that the RV has had no impact on the epithet's history. In fact, that history, particularly its later Vedic history, gives clear evidence of certain Ṛg Vedic motifs being operative as quite conscious models. The RV does employ *durga* as both a masculine and neuter adjective and substantive, carrying a general sense of "a place difficult of access" or "danger," but it is never employed in the feminine.[103] The first occurrence of a feminine is in the AV

[99]84.10: *durgāsi durgabhavasāgaranauḥ* ...

[100]84.16: *durge smṛtā harasi bhītim aśeṣajantoḥ.*

[101]85.10: *durgāyai durgapārāyai ... namaḥ.*

[102]91.22: *bhayebhyas trāhi no devi durge devi namo 'stu te.*

[103]Geldner's various translations may give a sense of its range: Bergfest (5.34.7), Engweg (7.25.2), Fährlichkeit (7.60.12), Gebirge (8.27.18). It is not immediately apparent from the VPK that there are no feminines in the RV, largely because of the Vedic usage of *durgā* as a neuter plural, e.g., 7.60.12. A review of all such possibly feminine forms reveals, however, that *durgā* is never applied to a feminine substantive nor used as a feminine epithet.

[104]AV 12.4.23, Bloomfield tr.: *Hymns from the Atharva Veda*, Clarendon Press (Oxford, 1897), SBE 42, p. 176. For the Sanskrit, see *Atharva Veda*

where it is predicated of the earth: the claim is made that the sterile cow rightfully belongs to the Brahmans and that "he that refuses the sterile cow to him that knoweth thus, and gives him to others, difficult to go upon [*durgā*] is for him the earth [*pṛthivī*] with her divinities."[104] It is, however, in texts that are probably somewhat later that the Ṛg Vedic role begins to become apparent.

The first hint of such a role is evident in that summary of Ṛg Vedic deities and myths, the *Bṛhad Devatā* (BṛDe), which may be dated between 500 and 400 B. C. E.[105] BṛDe 2.77, which is enumerating the middle forms of Vāc,[106] reads:

> [She on becoming Durgā (and) uttering a stanza may own a (whole) hymn]. Her (other) names are Yamī, Indrāṇī, Saramā, Romaśā, Urvasī; she first becomes Sinivalī and Rākā, Anumati, Kuhu;

The brackets in this passage are those of the critical editor, Macdonell, for which he offers the following justification: "There can be no doubt that this line is an interpolation, for Durgā, not being a Vedic goddess, is not to be found in the Naighaṇṭuka, as are all the other deities here enumerated; the line, moreover, interrupts the sense of the passage, besides giving half a śloka too much to the *varga*." While this fact may make this passage younger than the rest of the text, nonetheless, "it must . . . have been an early interpolation, as it occurs in MSS of both groups,[107] i.e., in the two basic recensions of the BṛDe.

---

*Sanhitā*, R. Roth and W. D. Whitney (edd.), Ferd. Dümmler's Verlagsbuchhandlung (Berlin, 1855). All further references are to this recension, the Śaunaka, unless indicated to the contrary.

105*The Bṛhad-Devatā*, Arthur Anthony Macdonell (ed. and tr.), Harvard University (Cambridge, 1904), Two vols., HOS 5, 6, Introduction, pp. xxii-xxiii.

106In our discussion of Kālī we have seen an epithetical affinity of the Goddess with Agni, an affinity that will also appear in our ensuing discussion of Durgā. One wonders to what extent such affinities have been encouraged by the fact that both Agni and Vāc are understood to have three forms, terrestrial, intermediate, and celestial: cf. BṛDe 1. 66-75.

107Macdonell's note on BṛDe 2.77. For details regarding "both groups," which basically represent a shorter and longer recension, see his Introduction pp. xi-xiii.

In fact, there is further evidence of the "Vedicization" of Durgā from about this time. Passing reference may be made to her appearance in the Rātri hymn in the RVK,[108] but it is TA 10.1, a passage dating from about the third century B.C.E.,[109] that is of major consequence. The first point of note is that there is a series of variations on the famous Gāyatrī *mantra* (RV 3.62.10), replacing Savitṛ, who is invoked in the Ṛg Vedic original,[110] with various other deities, such as Rudra, Naṇḍi and Garuda. Among those variations appears the following :

*kātyāyanāya vidmahe kanyākumāri dhīmahi |*
*tan no durgīḥ pracodayāt ||*

We have already met *kanyākumārī* ("the young virgin")[111] with whom Durgī is here identified, and we shall meet *kātyāyanī* below, as a separate epithet. Further comment as to who this Durgī is is presented shortly thereafter by the text (TA 10. 1) itself, though now using the more familiar Durgā. Having

[108]RVK 4.2.5, 12, 13, q. v. in Part III.

[109]According to the table of contents of TA, *prapāṭhakas* 7, 8, and 9 of that text constitute the TU, while *prapāṭhaka* 10 is called the *Yājñikī Upaniṣad.* Macdonell (*A History of Sanskrit Literature*, D. Appleton and Co. [New York and London, 1929], p. 211) remarks that this Upaniṣad is also known as the *Mahā-Nārāyaṇa Upaniṣad* and it is a text by this name that Farquhar (*op. cit.*, p. 49) dates as "probably not later than the third century B.C." It should, however, be noted that there are two different texts that go by the name *Mahā-Nārāyaṇa Upaniṣad*, the one noted above that belongs to the TA of the Black YV, and the one edited by Colonel Jacob (*The Mahānārāyaṇa Upanishad*, Government Central Book Depot [Bombay, 1888], Bombay Sanskrit Series XXXV), which he indicates on the title-page to belong to the AV. Jacob's edition is clearly the later of the two texts, for it "not only contains almost everything of this [epithetical and iconographic] nature found in the *Taittirīya Āraṇyaka* [which our present paragraph is about to examine], but has also some additional *mantras* . . ." (Banerjea, *Development*, p. 577). Consequently, no matter which *Mahā-Nārāyaṇa Upaniṣad* Farquhar is dating in the third century B.C.E., such a date may be taken as the *terminus ad quem* for the TA passage here under discussion.

[110]The text of which, for comparison with TA's variant is:
*tat savitur vareṇyam bhargo devasya dhīmahi|*
*dhiyo yo naḥ pracodayāt||*

[111]See the ref. given at Proleg., n. 171.

quoted RV 1.99.1— a one-verse hymn to Agni which Geldner translates as follows :

> Dem Jatavedas wollen wir Soma pressen; er soll das Besitztum des Missgünstigen niederbrennen. Er führe uns über all Schwierigkeiten [*durgāṇi*], Agni über die Fährlichkeiten wie mit dem Schiff über dem Strom.

—there is the following declaration :

> In her who has the color of Agni, flaming with ascetic power (*tapas*), the offspring of Virocana (*vairocanī*) who delights in the fruits of (one's) actions,
> In the goddess Durgā do I take refuge; O one of great speed, (well) do you navigate. Hail (to you) ![112]

The link that TA 10. 1 thus forges, between Durgā and Savitṛ on the one hand, between Durgā and Agni on the other, united by the conception of Durgā as the flaming one, is strengthened by several passages in the *sūtra* literature. Thus at *Baudhāyana Dharma Śāstra* (BDŚ) 4.3.8,[113] *Śaṅkha-likhita Dharma Sūtra* (ŚDS) 105,[114] and *Viṣṇu Dharma Sūtra* (VDS) 56.9,[115] the general topic is the expiation of sins and how it may be obtained. After certain actions are prescribed, a list of Vedic verses is given, recitation of which is deemed efficacious in this regard. One of these verses is called the *durgā-sāvitrī*, which is identified as RV 1.99.1, that is, the same verse we have seen commented upon in TA 10.1.

Turning to the epics, the only salient evidence is in hymnic material to be treated later: the two Mbh hymns, Pradyumna's

[112]*tām agnivarṇāṃ tapasā jvalantīṃ vairocanīṃ karmaphaleṣu juṣṭām/*
*durgāṃ devīṃ śaraṇam ahaṃ prapadye sutarasi tarase namaḥ/*
These lines recur verbatim in the RVK on the Rātrī Sūkta (RVK 4.2.13). This *khila* also quotes RV 1.99.1 piecemeal: cf. Part III.

[113]*Das Baudhāyana-dharma-śāstra,* E. Hultzsch (ed.), F. A. Brockhaus (Leipzig, 1884), Abhandlungen für die Kunde des Morgenlandes VII Band No. 4, and Bühler's English translation in *The Sacred Laws of the Āryas*, Part II, Clarendon Press (London, 1882), SBE 14.

[114]*Dharma-sūtra of Śaṅkha-likhita,* P. V. Kane (ed.), *Annals of the Bhandarkar Oriental Research Institute*, vol. VII Parts I and II (1926), pp. 101-128.

[115]Translated as *The Institutes of Vishnu,* Julius Jolly (tr.), Clarendon Press (Oxford, 1880), SBE 7.

hymn, and an addition to Viṣṇu's praise of Nidrā.[116] At this juncture, we might simply note that it is, in fact, with the name of Durgā that tradition has entitled the two hymns in the Mbh, viz., Durgā Stava and Durgā Stotra.

Although the literature contemporary with the DM is relatively silent on this epithet, there is much other evidence to suggest the existence of a flourishing cult of Durgā by this time. Bhattacharyya, for instance, documents the existence of a structural temple to Durgā at Aihole dating from the mid-sixth or-seventh century,[117] but even earlier than this there is the testimony of late Gupta seals showing a goddess whom Banerjea identifies as Durgā, mounted on a lion,[118] just as the Goddess appears in our text. As we shall see when we come to the Mahiṣa episode in Part II, there are sculptural representations of this episode dating from the first century B.C.E. or C.E., and iconographers have often called the goddess there represented Durgā.[119] Coins from the Gupta period suggest a further nuance to Durgā's identity, for she appears there in a curious iconographic interplay with the goddess Lakṣmī : while "generally Durgā and Lakṣmī are mentioned in contrast to each other..., the Gupta gold coins... [in fact] suggest the close affinity of the two goddesses."[120]

As a final example in this selective presentation of evidence for the existence of a Durgā cult at the time of our text, we may cite the famous, but not necessarily representative, experience of the seventh-century[121] Chinese Buddhist pilgrim Hsüan Tsang (Yuan Chwang):

[116]In the Durgā Stava, lines 2, 39, and 51. In the Durgā Stotra, lines 4 and 22. In Pradyumna's hymn, HV Appendix I 30, line 376. In Viṣṇu's praise, HV Appendix I 8, line 2.

[117]Bhattacharyya N., *op. cit.*, p. 82.

[118]Banerjea, *Development*, pp. 185-186.

[119]E.g., Sahai, Bhagwant, *Iconography of Minor Hindu and Buddhist Deities*, Abhinav Publications (New Delhi, 1975), pp. 183-184. Such statements may, of course, say more about the predilections of the iconographers than about the facts of the matter. As we have seen, there is no explicit connection of the epithet Durgā with Mahiṣa in the Sanskrit literature that is clearly anterior to our text. For further remarks on the Mahiṣa episode, see Part II.

[120]*Ibid.*, p. 174.

[121]Basham, *op. cit.*, p. 67.

When about 100 li on the way, in a wood of asoka trees, the boat was attacked by Thugs who robbed the party. When these Thugs saw that the Chinese pilgrim was an uncommonly fine-looking man they decided to sacrifice him to their cruel deity Durgā. From this terrible fate the pilgrim was preserved by a providential hurricane which put the wicked Thugs in fear, and made them release their doomed victim, treat him with awe and reverence, and under his teaching give up their wicked profession, and take the vow of lay-Buddhists.[122]

*vaiṣṇavī*

The derivative or relational sense of the word *vaiṣṇavī* "one who is related to Viṣṇu," is a sense that our text fully affirms, for our first meeting with *vaiṣṇavī* establishes that she is Vaiṣṇavī, a power or *śakti* of the supreme Goddess, but a power that has the characteristics of the god Viṣṇu. When the Goddess multiplies her forces, i.e., diversifies her own forms, in order to counter Śumbha's advancing hordes, our text describes (88.11-12) how the various *śaktis* of the Goddess, "endowed with excessive virility and strength, sprang forth from the bodies of Brahmā, Śiva, Skanda, Viṣṇu, and Indra, having the form of each (*tadrūpaiḥ*)." Since our text then actually goes on to describe a total of seven *śaktis* (among them, Vaiṣṇavī) who are subsequently called the Mothers (*mātāraḥ*, *mātṛgaṇa*: 88.38,44,49, etc.), part of our text's understanding of who Vaiṣṇavī is, is determined by who the Seven Little Mothers are, a matter we have dealt with independently in Appendix A.

[122]Watters, Thomas, *On Yuan Chwang's Travels in India*, T. W. Rhys Davids and S. W. Bushell (edd.), Royal Asiatic Society (London, 1904, 1905), Two vols.: vol. 1, p. 360. For more on the Thugs, in whom the West has often taken a rather prurient interest, see *The Encyclopedia of Religion and Ethics*, James Hastings (ed.), Charles Scribner's Sons (New York, 1908-27), T. and T. Clark (Edinburgh), 13 vols., art. "Thags" and references given there.

As a parting comment on Durgā, we might add that, while somewhat later Durgā appears as one of the *mātṛkās* (Sahai, *op. cit.*, p. 214), we have found no evidence for such a conception by the time of our text. The perhaps related motif of the nine-fold Durgā (*nava-durgā*: *ibid.*, pp. 191-192) also appears to be a later development.

In the context of this group identity, however, Vaiṣṇavī has her own uniqueness; for when she (*vaiṣṇavī śakti*) comes forth, she is described as "mounted upon Garuḍa, with a conch, discus, club, bow, and sword."[123] Such a description is, of course, very similar to the iconographic description of Viṣṇu,[124] and it is worth noting that in the remaining appearances of Vaiṣṇavī in our text the destructive power of her discus (*cakra*) is particularly emphasized.[125]

In the case of *vaiṣṇavi*, we are faced with a word whose entire history in the Vedic and epic literature is as a descriptive adjectives, characterizing objects as "belonging or dedicated to Viṣṇu."[126] Consequently, the most we can hope for here, in keeping with our understanding of diction, is a familiarity with the possible subliminal connotations of the word *vaiṣṇavī* at the time of our text. What other things have been called *vaiṣṇavī* prior to the DM's designation of *vaiṣṇavī śakti* as Vaiṣṇavī?

By far the most common usage of *vaiṣṇavī* is its use in a ritual context simply to characterize a verse to Viṣṇu (*ṛc vaiṣṇavi*). Such instances are frequent, and their logic obvious, but this should not blind us to a fact noted earlier,[127] viz., that there is implicit in the conceptualization of hymns and verses as feminine an appreciation of their fecundity. Other than verses, *vaiṣṇavī* has been used to characterize the following grammatically feminine words by the time of our text: certain bricks (*iṣṭakā*) in the fire altar,[128] the metre *anuṣṭubh*,[129] the

[123]88.177.

[124]Cf. Banerjea, *Development*, pp. 385-427, *passim*, esp. pp. 396n, 401-406; also, Danielou, *op. cit.*, pp. 152-163.

[125]Those appearances are at 88.33, 46, 47; 89.38; 91.4, 14. On the significance of Viṣṇu's *cakra*, see Danielou, *op. cit.*, p. 155.

[126]Virtually the only (and very minor) exceptions to this are the citations of Vaiṣṇavī as one of the *mātṛs* in excised passages of the Mbh, 271* and 272* which are inserted in Mbh 9.45, a chapter which lists the names of approximately two hundred other *mātṛs* in the constituted text.

[127]Proleg., n. 235.

[128]YVT 5.6.9.2-3.

[129]*Tāṇḍya Brāhmaṇa* (TāṇB) 9.6.9 and 13.5.4: *Tāṇḍya Mahābrāhmaṇa*, Ānandachandra Vedāntavāgīśa (ed.), Asiatic Society of Bengal (Calcutta, 1870, 1874), Two vols., Bibliotheca Indica NS (vol. 1) 170, 175, 177, 179, 182, 188, 190, 191, 199 and 206, (vol. 2) 207, 212, 217, 219, 221, 225, 254, 256 and 268.

earth (*kāśyapī, pṛthivī*),[130] an Upasad ceremony,[131] and, rather idiosyncratically, the polecat (*jahakā*).[132]

On other possible connotations of *vaiṣṇavī*/Vaiṣṇavī, the literature is silent.

*mahāmāyā*

Mahāmāyā which, depending upon how one analyzes the compound, means "she who possesses great deceptiveness" or she who *is* "the great illusion," is one of the more intriguing epithets in our text. It is clearly a proper name for the supreme form of the Goddess, yet it is one of the few epithets whose use is confined to a single *carita*, and it is the brief first *carita* at that.[133] Furthermore, it is the first epithet employed in our text and, in fact, it is used to introduce the sub-story, or the *upabṛṃhaṇam*, in the MarkP that is the DM. At MarkP 80.3 Mārkaṇḍeya, the chief interlocutor in this portion of the Purāṇa,[134] had prophesied that Sāvarṇī, son of Sūrya, would become the eighth Manu, and now in the first verse of the next chapter, where the DM begins, he picks up that thread:[135]

[130]Mbh 13.91.25. Cf. also *Vāsiṣṭha Dharma Śāstra* (VāDS) 28.16, in *The Sacred Laws of the Āryas*, Part II, Georg Bühler (tr.), Clarendon Press (Oxford, 1882), SBE 14. Though we might expect a wider association of "earth" and Viṣṇu, in light of his common association with the goddess Bhū (Banerjea, *Development*, pp. 30, 398), these are the only two such associations we have encountered.

[131]*Aitareya Brāhmaṇa* (AiB) 3.18: *Aitareyabrāhmaṇa*, Tukārām Tātya (Bombay, 1890), and A. B. Keith's translation in *Rigveda Brāhmaṇas*, Harvard University Press (Cambridge, 1920), HOS 25.

[132]YVMai 3.14.17. Though one might expect *vaiṣṇavī māyā* in the Mbh, Sørensen has not led us to any instances.

[133]The epithet is employed at 81.2, 40, 41, 42, 45, 58, 73; *paramā māyā* is used at 91.4, a verse that recapitulates many of the motifs of the first *carita*.

[134]See MarkP, Pargiter tr. Introduction, p. iv for a helpful breakdown of the interlocutors in the different parts of the Purāṇa.

[135]Dr. J. L. Mehta has pointed out to us what an excellent example of a *vyāsa's* or *paurāṇika's* craft the DM itself is: it starts from an existing cue, weaves an *upabṛṁhaṇam* upon it, and eventually returns to its starting point. The last verse of the DM (93.17) reads: "Thus, having received a boon from the Goddess, that best of *kṣatriyas*, Suratha, having obtained a birth from Sūrya, will become the Manu Sāvarṇi, " and in MarkP 94 Mārkaṇḍeya resumes his identification and enumeration of the different Manus, starting with the ninth.

Sāvarṇi, who is the son of Sūrya, is called the eighth Manu:
Listen while I tell you the details of his birth (and)
How, through the majesty (*anubhāva*) of Mahāmāyā, the illustrious Sāvarṇi
Became the son of the sun (and) lord of (this) Manu-interval.[136]

Our text then falls silent on the Goddess while it recounts the frame-story of the king Suratha and the *vaiśya* Samādhi, their disenchantment with their families and with the world in general, and their turning to the *ṛṣi* Medhas. The seer expatiates on the relativity of knowledge and the folly of sensual attachment (81.34-38), and then dramatically proclaims:

O best of men, human beings have a craving for offspring,
Out of greed expecting them to reciprocate; do you not see this ?
Just in this fashion do they fall into the pit of delusion, the maelstrom of egoism,
Giving (apparent) solidity to life in this world (*saṃsāra*) through the power of Mahāmāyā.
There should be no surprise in this, (for) the Yoganidrā of the lord of the worlds,
Hari, is (this same) Mahāmāyā, and through her is this world being deluded.
This blessed Goddess Mahāmāyā, having forcibly seized the minds
Even of men of knowledge, leads them to delusion.
Through her is created this whole universe, that which both does and does not move.
Just she is the gracious giver of boons to men, for the sake of (their) release (*mukti*).
She is the supreme eternal knowledge (*vidyā*) that becomes the cause of release
From bondage to mundane life; she indeed is the queen (governing) all who have power.[137]

Understandably, the auditors want to know more. What they are told comprises virtually the entire balance of the DM,

[136] 81.1-2.
[137] 81.39-44.

though we shall examine much of the immediate sequel to the above passage under the epithet *yoganidrā-nidrā* and in our treatment of the Madhu-Kaiṭabha myth in Part II. Here, however, we may simply note that it is Mahāmāyā's inducement in those two Asuras of delusions of grandeur (81.73), thinking that they can outwit Viṣṇu, that leads to their undoing. Taken together with the above passage, the implication is clear. As the Great Illusion, she it is who entices humans into taking themselves, i.e., their egos, seriously, thereby perpetuating the pain of life in *saṃsāra*. But it is also she who provides release therefrom, because she is also knowledge (*vidyā*), knowledge that this saṃsāric existence, this ego and sense-life, is, in fact, an illusion.[138]

There is not, apparently, any occurrence of the word *mahāmāyā* in either the Vedic or epic literature. However, an examination of its major element, *māyā*, yields several noteworthy points. First, the word itself is as old as the RV, where it means "wile" or "magic power," a power that belongs primarily to Varuṇa.[139] Second, there is some evidence of its connection with the Asuras, i.e., with those beings who, in all but the earliest strata of the Vedic literature, are understood as enemies of the gods.[140] If *māyā* is associated with the Asuras, then she who is Mahāmāyā should also be the supreme Asura, and this is precisely what our text affirms shortly after the passage quoted above, in Brahmā's hymn to Mahāmāyā, when it calls her *mahāsurī* (81. 58). Moreover, the reason that she has such power over the Asuras can then be seen to be because, in some sense, she *is* the Asuras.[141] Third, while it may be true

[138]A psychological and epistemological interpretation is offered here as being most consistent with the epithet Mahāmāyā and with the sense of the passage. It does not address, because the epithet and passage do not seem to raise, the further philosophical question: what is the ontological status of this illusion? We shall, however, touch on this matter under the more appropriate epithet of *prakṛti*, which is, in fact, used in close proximity to the passage discussed here, at 81.59. See also our discussion *infra*, s. v. "*mahāvidyā-vidyā*."

[139]Keith, *op. cit.*, pp. 247, 468; Macdonell, *Vedic Mythology*, p. 24.

[140]Keith, *op. cit.*, pp. 231-232; Macdonell, *Vedic Mythology*, pp. 156-157. There are, quite naturally, occasional exceptions in the later literature.

[141]The Deva-Asura conflict is, of course, a complex and far-reaching issue in Indian religiousness. For a single example of how it ramifies for literary

that, in the late Vedic search for the underlying substratum of the universe *māyā* failed to be sufficiently widely generalized,[142] now, in Purāṇic times, such a generalization has become possible. The DM itself is one of the major agents in that process. The reason that such a generalization has now become possible is, of course, because of the intervening philosophical creativity of the Upaniṣads. It is beyond the scope of this study to examine the enormous significance of the word *māyā* in philosophical discourse, both prior and subsequent to the date of our text.[143] There may, however, be justification for our noting the word's resonance in the way that the DM itself does: not in the philosophical context, but in the mythological, where language is not so much precise as suggestive.[144] The archetypal image in this regard, the metaphor standing behind

---

interpretation, see Brown, W. Norman, "Proselytizing the Asuras," JAOS XXXIX Part 2 (April 1919), pp. 100-103. For an intriguing effort to establish the historicity of the Asuras, see the following articles of A. Banerji-Sastri: "The Asuras in Indo-Iranian Literature," JBORS XII 1 (March 1926), pp. 110-139; "Asura Expansion in India," JBORS XII 2 (June 1926), pp. 243-285; "Asura Expansion by Sea," JBORS XII 3 (Sept. 1926), pp. 334-360; "Asura Institutions," JBORS XII 4 (Dec. 1926), pp. 503-539. For a similar study that includes other groups (Vrātyas, Belurs, etc.), see Chattopadhyay, K.P., "Ancient Indian Cultural Contacts and Migrations," *Our Heritage* 9 (1961), pp. 75-109. For consideration of the subject in the context of Indo-Iranian mythology, see von Bradke, Peter, *Dyaus Asura, Ahura Mazdā und die Asuras,* M. Niemeyer (Halle, 1885). Note also the recent major work of Hale, Wash E., *Asura—in Early Vedic Religion,* Ph.D. dissertation, Harvard University, 1980. While the central concern of our study is to examine the DM as a Sanskritic phenomenon, it is tempting to speculate that the reason for the Goddess's unique popularity in Indian culture is because she expresses non-Aryan, here "Asuric," motifs in unparalleled fashion.

[142]Keith, *op. cit.*, pp. 446-447.

[143]The sheer bulk of the philosophical literature is overwhelming. As basic material, suggesting the scope of the issues, we proffer, somewhat diffidently, the following: the two previously cited works of Hacker; Ghate, V. S., *The Vedānta: A Study of the Brahma-sūtras with the Bhāṣyas of Śaṃkara, Rāmānuja, Nimbārka, Madhva and Vallabha,* Bhandarkar Oriental Research Institute (Poona, 1960), Keith, *op. cit.*, pp. 489-600; Hiriyanna, *op. cit.* pp. 336-413; Ingalls, D. H. H., "Śaṁkara on the Question: Whose is Avidyā?", *Philosophy East and West* III 1 (April 1953), pp. 69-72.

[144]This is not to say that our text is *un*philosophical or *im*precise, but simply that its intent is not to establish a philosophically impregnable position, nor to convince the hearer-reader of its logical truth. It is aware that

so many devotional discussions of *māyā* is, of course, the "two birds in a tree" of ŚU 4.6-7. Having articulated that distinction between the Lord (*Īśa*) and the individual soul, that text proceeds to relate them to *māyā*:

> The Vedas, the sacrifices, the ceremonies, the acts of devotion, the past, the future, and what the Vedas declare—
> All this does the Lord (*māyin*: the possessor of *māyā*) pour forth out of this (Brahmā), and in it is the other (individual soul) confined by *māyā*.
> Know *māyā* to be *prakṛti* (the material stuff of the world), the possessor of *māyā* to be the great Lord.
> This whole world is pervaded by beings that are parts of him.[145]

It is this approach to illusion, an approach that is poetic rather than prosaic, mythologically suggestive rather than philosophically precise, that our text adopts in articulating its vision of the great deluder, the great illusion, Mahāmāyā.

*nityā*[146]

*Nityā* is used in our text simply as an adjective, rather than

---

religious faith is not (not merely? not at all?) a matter of rational demonstrability.

[145]The text of the critical lines (ŚU 4.9cd-10) reads:

*asmān māyi sṛjate viśvam etat tasmiṁs cānyo mayayā saṁniruddhaḥ||*
*māyāṁ tu prakṛtiṁ viddhi māyinaṁ tu maheśvaram|*
*tasyāvayavabhūtais tu vyāptaṁ sarvam idaṁ jagat||*

We follow Hume [*The Thirteen Principal Upanishads*, Robert E. Hume (tr.) Oxford University Press (Oxford, London, New York, 1971)] in taking *asmān* as implying Brahmā. The identification here of *māyā* and *prakṛti*, an identification at which our text only hints (see *supra*, n. 138 and *infra*, s. v. "*prakṛti*"), is a matter to which we shall return.

[146]If we were to include *all* designations of the Goddess in our account, *bhavatī* should properly come here, for it is applied to her on seven occasions which span all three episodes (81.58; 84.13, 14, 15, 18; 86.7; 91.31). However, since it is simply an honorific substitute for the second person pronoun and is used in our text in straightforward fashion, primarily as the subject of declarative sentences, with six of its occurrences coming in hymnic material, we here simply note its use in passing. Such innocent diction would hardly merit even this note were it not for the fact that *bhavatī* has one major verbal association inherited from earlier usage, viz., in Yājñavalkya's words to Maitreyī—"Beloved, indeed, have you (*bhavatī*) been to me; (now) your

as a name, but the way in which it is used, on a total of six occasions,[147] is noteworthy in that four of those instances are clustered in a single episode, within a few verses of one another. Since this cluster appears at the outset of the brief first episode, our text seems to be imputing a fair amount of significance, as well as dramatic power, to this epithet. It is first employed at the juncture between the frame story and the Madhu-Kaiṭabha myth. In response to his auditors' clamor to know more about Mahāmāyā, the seer replies:

> She is eternal (*nityā*), having the universe as her form; by her is all this spread out.
> Even so, her coming-into-being is manifold; hear (about this) from me.
> When she becomes manifest, for the sake of accomplishing the purposes of the gods,
> Then she is said to be born in the world, even though she is eternal (*nityā*).[148]

This is a bold proclamation of the basic theology of the Goddess: while eternal and, in some sense,[149] coextensive with the universe, she also, upon occasion, adopts a specific, tangible form that is operative within that universe, on earth.[150]

---

dearness has increased. Since this is the case, dear one (*bhavati*), I will explain it to you. . . ." '(BU 4.5.5, the only feminine singular use of this honorific we have uncovered in the Vedic literature)—which introduce his famous teachings on the nature of the *ātman*. There is, perhaps, a consequent subliminal connection of *bhavatī* with this core of Vedāntic teaching.

[147] 81.47, 48, 54, 55; 85.8; 92.32.

[148] 81.47-48:

> *nityaiva sā jaganmūrtis tayā sarvam idaṃ tatam/*
> *tathāpi tatsamutpattir bahudhā śrūyatāṃ mama//*
> *devānāṃ kāryasiddhyārtham āvirbhavati sā yadā/*
> *utpanneti tadā loke sā nityāpy abhidhīyate//*

[149] Primarily as *prakṛti*, q. v. *infra.*

[150] The similarity to the theology of the *Bhagavad Gītā*, particularly as it is articulated at 4.1-8, is striking. The occurrence of *nityā* at 92.32 of the DM makes this same theological point.

It is, of course, the burden of the rest of the DM to illustrate the dynamics and ramifications of this theology. Almost immediately, however, our text provides further evidence of its understanding of the *nityā* status of the Goddess. Directly after the verses cited above, the seer commences his narration of the Madhu-Kaiṭabha myth, the core of which is Brahmā's invocation of the Goddess,[151] asking her to allow Viṣṇu to awake, so that he may slay the Asuras. Brahmā begins his hymn as follows :

> You are Svāhā; you are Svadhā ; you are Vaṣaṭkāra; you have speech (*svara*) as your very soul.
> You are the nectar of the gods, O imperishable (*akṣare*), eternal (*nitye*) one; (you) abide, having the three-fold syllabic moment (*mātrā*) as your very being.
> You are the half-*mātrā*, steadfast, eternal (*nityā*), which cannot be uttered distinctly.[152]
> You are she; you are Sāvitrī (the Gāyatrī *mantra*) ; you are the Goddess, the supreme Mother.[153]

However one may understand the features of this passage that are open to varying interpretation,[154] its commencement with

[151]Here understood primarily as Mahāmāyā and Yoganidrā. See the hymn in Part III.

[152]We here emend the reading of Vid (the only edition to divide the text into words) *anuccāryāviśeṣataḥ* to *anuccāryā viśeṣataḥ*, for the point is clearly to emphasize the steadfastness and eternality of the Goddess as the spoken word, even though she is less than the normal minimum (a *mātra*) for syllabic quantification.

[153]81.54-55.

*tvaṃ svāhā tvaṃ svadhā tvaṃ hi vaṣaṭkāraḥ svarātmikā |*
*sudhā tvam akṣare nitye tridhāmātrātmikā sthitā ||*
*arddhamātrā sthitā nityā yānuccāryā viśeṣataḥ |*
*tvam eva sā tvaṃ sāvitrī tvaṃ devī jananī parā ||*

[154]The phrase giving rise to these variations is *akṣare nitye tridhāmātrātmikā*, on the meaning of which there is no unanimity among commentators and translators. Our reading of this as two vocatives and a nominative is based on considerations of simplicity: while the vocatives do interrupt the string of nominatives, this is not uncommon in the hymns of the DM, though it is rare in this particular hymn. The standard interpretation of *tridhāmātrātmikā*, which seems plausible to us, particularly since the word *mātrā* recurs in the following *śloka*, is that the reference is to the three *mātrās* in the *mantra aum*. Our text is surely subsequent to the MU's famous meditation on this

the three sacrificial formulae, drenched in Vedic significance, and the inclusion of the peerless Gāyatrī *mantra* make it clear: wherever the spoken word is operative, so is the Goddess. While the rest of the DM goes on to describe the mundane activity of the Goddess in splendid detail, the starting point here is with the more cosmic or ontological question of her identity apart from her redemptive activity. As the word, she is the basis for the whole sacrificial structure of the Vedas. Though the DM itself never addresses the Goddess as *vāc*, it is clearly the realm of *vāc*—eternal and efficacious—that is the primary association of *nityā* in our text.[155]

It would be tempting to see this association of the power of the conventionally spoken (primarily ritual) word and the eternal throughout the earlier literature as well, for in almost all of its Vedic usages, *nityā* modifies, or implies, a feminine word for "verse," usually *ṛc* or *pratipad*.[156] However, *nitya(ā)* is a word whose meaning has, through the centuries, undergone significant development, which we may summarize as follows. Originally, the word seems to have meant "found inside of," but by the time of the RV it has already undergone a semantic development that leads to three connotations in that text's usage: (1)

*mantra*, perhaps also to Gauḍapāda's *Kārikā* on that Upaniṣad, and reference to that meditation would be quite natural, even important. Others, however (see Pargiter's note), divide the word "*tridhāma trātmikā*, '[thou] hast the three mansions [i.e., the three worlds, the three Vedas, the three chief deities, etc.], [thou] hast the preserver [Vishṇu] for thy soul.'" Still another variation (see Agrawala's translation and note) follows our reading of *tridhāmātrātmikā*, but takes *akṣare nitye* as a neuter locative indicating the three-fold Goddess's existence within the imperishable Brahman. While this interpretation is perhaps supported by the ensuing description of the Goddess as *prakṛtiḥ . . . guṇatrayavibhāvinī* (81.59), it strikes us as a more philosophically precise statement on the Goddess's status than our text usually favors.

155On the role of *vāc* as a philosophical notion, see Proleg. p. 73 and n. 235. We may note here that the fifth use of *nityā* in the DM (85.8) is in a hymn and neither contravenes, nor further illuminates, its significance on these first four occasions; it appears there contiguous with *gaurī* and *dhātrī*, q.v.

156The following is typical of the dozen or so usages: ". . . he offers sacrifice with the usual (verse) [*nityayaiva*].": *Aitareya Āraṇyaka* (AiA) 5.32 (A. B. Keith [ed. and tr.], The Clarendon Press [Oxford, 1909], Anecdota Oxoniensia Aryan Series 9). Other instances of its occurrence are to modify *vāc* (RV 8. 75. 6), and *āśir*, "milk" (RV 8. 31. ) .

*svīya, sahaja*, "one's own," (2) *priya*, "dear," (3) *dhruva*, "constant, permanent."[157] Hara argues that the original meaning remains implicit in the Vedic usage and even, he ventures, under certain circumstances, in classical Sanskrit.[158] Nonetheless, it is clearly the third of these meanings that has come to predominate in classical Sanskrit, and we may note that Hara quotes with approval the following remarks of Müller and Brough on how the original developed into the classical meaning :

> "...what is inside, or in a thing or place, is its own, is peculiar to it, does not move or change, and hence the secondary meaning of *nitya*—, one's own, unchanging, eternal."

> "If an expression like *aranya—nitya*—began by meaning 'dwelling in the forest,' it could readily have acquired the additional connotation of 'constantly dwelling in the forest.' The usual later senses of *nitya*—"regular, constant, permanent" are easily derived from this type usage."[159]

Consequently, when the DM applies the word *nityā* to the Goddess, this is not simply an affirmation that she is eternal—no mean affirmation in itself—but also a suggestion that there is an interior, inward quality to her eternality. This manifests itself in our text's association of *nityā* with the power of words, and, as we shall see, that association is a specific instance of the general appreciation of the Goddess as power itself, as *śakti*.

[157] This sentence is a précis of Minoru Hara's argument, made on etymological grounds, and his summary of Venkatasubbiah's position (as it had been set forth in *Vedic Studies* 1 [Mysore, 1932], pp. 1-50) in his "Note on the Sanskrit Word *Ni-tya-*", JAOS 79 (1959), pp. 90-93.

[158] *Ibid.*, pp. 92-95. The "certain circumstances" he proposes are "when it stands as the last member of a compound" (p. 94). Even when the word is not in compound, it may be fruitfully understood as retaining nuances of the original meaning, as we shall suggest below.

[159] Respectively, M. Müller, *Vedic Hymns* (SBE 32, 1891), 1, p. 215, and J. Brough, "Audumbarāyaṇa's Theory of Language," *Bulletin of the School of Oriental and African Studies*, University of London 14 (1952), p. 77, both cited *ibid.*, p. 94.

*aindrī*

As in the case of Vaiṣṇavī, the DM is clearly aware of the derivative sense of *aindrī*, "the one who belongs or is related to Indra." That both emphasize the derivative character of the respective goddesses is not surprising, for this goddess is, in fact, Aindrī and she, like Vaiṣṇavī, is one of the Seven Little Mothers. All six of her appearances thus occur in the third episode.[160] As with the other *mātṛs*, there is a description (88.20) of her salient features—

> Then Aindrī, with thunderbolt [*vajra*] in hand, mounted upon the lord of elephants,
> Went forth; she had a thousand eyes, just like Indra.

—where the comparison with Indra seems justified by the iconography of the latter.[161] Furthermore, in the ensuing battle, the famous *vajra* lives up to its reputation. A final point of significance in the DM's conception of Aindrī is that she is explicitly called "the *śakti* of Indra (*indraśakti*:88.41)," a characterization whose implications we shall probe below.

In the case of *aindrī*, we have another word (in this regard again, like *vaiṣṇavī*) whose prior usage has been exclusively as a descriptive adjective, modifying feminine nouns. Once again the overwhelming majority of these instances is when it modifies, or implies, *ṛc*, a verse to Indra. There are, however, other occasions : sacrificial animals,[162] butter libations,[163] the *triṣṭubh*,[164] have all been considered as *aindrī*. Of somewhat more moment are the suggestions that the eastern direction (and therefore the sun?) is Indra's,[165] and that Indra is responsible for speech (*vāc*), both mythologically and etymologically :

> O Agni,...thou art speech, derived from Indra, destroying the foe ... ; do thou enter me with speech, with power (*indriyeṇa*).[166]

[160]88.20, 34, 41, 46; 89.38; 91.17. See Appendix A for the implications of Aindrī being one of the Seven Little Mothers.

[161]Banerjea, *Development*, pp. 522-524.

[162]YVT 2.1.2.4-5; 2.1.5.4.

[163]AiB 8.10.

[164]YVKā 20.5.

[165]ŚāṅA 4.8.

[166]YVT 1.6.2.2-3, Keith tr.

If this is the extent of the earlier verbal association of *aindrī*, in both Vedic and epic literature, what, one might ask, has happened to Indra's wife, a figure as old as the RV?[167] It is at this juncture that the DM seems to be making an interesting, though subtle, distinction. It is true that, since Ṛg Vedic times, Indra has been known to have a wife. At first she is simply called Indrāṇī, which seems to be purely a formal name,[168] but by late Vedic times she was given a name of her own, Śacī, probably on the basis of a misunderstanding of Indra's epithet *śacipati*, "lord of strength."[169] Throughout the subsequent literature, epic as well as Vedic, Indra's wife is referred to by these two names, Indrāṇī and Śacī, as well as by several others, but *never*, so far as we have found, by the name Aindrī. It is, therefore, significant that when the DM has to use a derivative of the word "Indra" in order to name the *śakti* of Indra, it chooses a word that explicitly *lacks* earlier mythological associations, viz., Aindrī. The text's point seems to be that this *indraśakti* is not simply his wife, but his power. She is far more similar, therefore, to the *indriya* or *vāc* in the YV passage cited above than to the spouse Indrāṇī-Śacī of popular repute. The latter is merely Indra's consort, while the former is his very essence. And that, on a broader scale, is very close to the central point of the entire DM.[170]

[167]The primary description of her occurs at RV 10.86, the famous Vṛṣākapi hymn.

[168]Keith, *op. cit.*, p. 218.

[169]*Ibid.*, p. 81.

[170]One might, of course, argue that this is over-interpreting matters, that all our text is doing is following a standard way of forming derivatives: take the *vṛddhi* of the initial vowel and change final "a" to "ī". That our text does this with most of the other *śaktis* is clear: Vaiṣṇavī, Māheśvarī, Kaumārī, Vārāhī, Nārasiṃhī. But that our text uses only this form of derivation is disproved by Brahmāṇī, whom it might have called Brāhmī. Brahmāṇī, however, as the *śakti* of Brahmā, does not run the risk of confusion with some other mythological figure, nor, for that matter, does any of the other *śaktis*, regardless of which method of derivation is employed. Of all the gods who have *śaktis* appear in MarkP 88, only Indra has a famous wife (as we shall see, Māheśvarī has not become a widespread designation for the wife of Śiva by the time of our text), so only in his case does the DM have to be careful in its diction, in order to exclude the misleading mythological associations.

*paramā*

The application of this straightforward superlative to the Goddess on six occasions[171] is not surprising, nor does the investigation of these instances shed light on any peculiarities in its usage : it means simply "supreme," and is always applied to the "supreme" form of the Goddess, with four of its occurrences coming in hymns. On one occasion, it is predicated of the Goddess as knowledge (*vidyā*), on another of her as *māyā*, and on still another of her as the primal matter of the universe (*prakṛtiḥ... ādyā*).[172] But, on balance, the innocence of its application to the Goddess in our text is conveyed by the half-verse—*parāparāṇāṃparamā tvam eva parameśvarī* (81.62cd) : "highest of all things high and low, you are the highest queen," i.e., you are the one that transcends the normal categories of comparison.

In light of this innocent usage in the DM, it may suffice to note that the Vedic usage of *paramā* is comparably innocent. This may be seen in a brief sampling of the evidence, for *paramā* has been applied to the uppermost of three levels of earth,[173] and of the three degrees of assistance.[174] It has also been predicated of the *anuṣṭubh*,[175] the furthest distance,[176] and a particular form of *vāc* : "the voice of the drum is the highest (form of) speech."[177] AiB 3.15 has gone so far as to equate the furthest distance, the *anuṣṭubh*, and speech, but in none of these cases is there anything extra-ordinary (except that the word *paramā* implies "extraordinary") to report.

*cāmuṇḍā*

In our study of the epithet Kālī, we have seen that our text understands Cāmuṇḍā to be a nickname of Kālī, given to her by

[171]81.44, 62; 84.6, 8, 13; 91.4; it also appears in the compound *parameśvarī*, q. v.

[172]Therefore, cf. these epithets or their kin (i.e., "*mahāmāvā*").

[173]RV 1.108.9-10.

[174]RV 6.25.1.

[175]YVT 5.4.12.1.

[176]RV 5.61.1; AV 3.4.5.

[177]YVT 7.5.9.2.

the Goddess for having vanquished the Asuras Caṇḍa and Muṇḍa.[178] Consequently, our remarks on the DM's conception of Kālī, her emanation in horrific form from the Goddess's furrowed brow, should be applied to the epithet Cāmuṇḍa as well. The other occurrences of Cāmuṇḍa[179] simply confirm that she is Kālī, and only one (91.19) provides any further description :

O one whose mouth is terrifying (*karāla*) with its teeth,
O one who is ornamented with a garland of heads,
O Cāmuṇḍā, O crusher of Muṇḍa(*muṇḍamathanā*),
O Nārāyanī, praise be to you !

This description does not differ substantially from the earlier one of Kālī. However, our text is here also substantiating its affirmation that Kālī and Cāmuṇḍā are interchangeable names by using "Kālī-like" words to describe Cāmuṇḍā. Thus its use of *karāla* is evocative of Kālī and Karālī, the tongues of Agni at MU 1.2.4, and *muṇḍamathanā*, which here simply means "the crusher of (the Asura) Muṇḍa," may also pick up the prior association of the words *kāli* and *muṇḍa*.[180] Since we have seen our text to be impressed by the destructiveness of Kālī's teeth, we might call Cāmuṇḍā simply "the head cruncher." Although she has often been conceived as one of the Seven Little Mothers, our text clearly distinguishes her from this group.[181]

In the case of Cāmuṇḍā, we seem to have the explicit assimilation of a non-Sanskritic goddess to the Goddess, for our investigation has not uncovered a single instance of this epithet in the Vedic or epic literature. We can, therefore, only affirm Pargiter's judgment [182] that the name

[178]MarkP 87.25.

[179]88.52, 58; 59, 60; 91.19.

[180]ŚāṅA 11.3.4. See *supra*, n. 75.

[181]On this point, see Appendix A. For a full study of the iconography of Cāmuṇḍā, see Sahai, *op. cit.*, pp. 197-205. Sahai notes (p. 198) the widespread distribution of Cāmuṇḍā images, as well as the fact that she appears sometimes by herself. None of these images, however, is clearly antecedent to the DM.

[182]MarkP, Pargiter tr., Introduction, p. xii. The only possible qualification of this judgment hinges on the dating of the VāmanaP account of the Śumbha-Niśumbha episode (which we shall consider in Part II), for Kālī,

appears in Sanskrit for the first time in the DM.[183]

who there, too, emerges from the Goddess's furrowed brow (29.56), is once called Cāmuṇḍā (29.85), after she has dispatched Caṇḍa and Muṇḍa.

[183]Because Bhavabhūti's *Mālatī-Mādhava* (editions of which are given at the end of this note) probably dates from the early eighth century (Basham, *op. cit.*, pp. 441-442), and thus postdates the DM by several centuries, its testimony cannot fairly be entered in an assessment of the literary context of the DM. However, in an effort to shed some further light on the identity of this Cāmuṇḍā, who so abruptly appears in the DM, passing mention may be made of this drama. While it is primarily a love story, two of the significant characters, Aghoraghaṇṭa and Kapālakuṇḍalā, are described as devotees of Cāmuṇḍā. In Act 5 there is an extraordinary description of the carrion and gore in the Cāmuṇḍā temple environs (so extraordinary that Wilson has seen fit to bowdlerize his translation at this juncture), in the course of which are a number of familiar motifs: Cāmuṇḍā herself is called Karālā (5.5), and the air is filled with the cries of howling jackals (5.19; see *infra*, s. v. "*śivadūtī*"). Subsequently, there is a hymn to Cāmuṇḍā, from which we may quote an excerpt (Wilson tr.):

Hail ! hail ! *Chāmuṇḍā*, mighty goddess, hail !
I glorify thy sport, when in the dance
That fills the court of *Śiva* with delight,
Thy foot descending spurns the earthly globe.
.........................................
The elephant hide that robes thee, to thy steps
Swings to and fro; the whirling talons rend
The crescent on thy brow;—and from the torn orb
The trickling nectar falls, and every skull
That gems thy necklace laughs with horrid life.

It is difficult, of course, to know how fair a description of the Cāmuṇḍā cult *Mālatī-Mādhava* provides, for Bhavabhūti was a Brahman (Macdonell, *History*, p. 362) and therefore might well caricature such a non-Vedic cult. In any case, at least for dramatic purposes, he has cast that cult in a bad light, as disruptive of the central romance, and including the suggestion that blood sacrifice can serve as a mask for revenge (8.8-9). Granting the possibility of some distortion, it is still worth noting that, as the above hymn indicates, Cāmuṇḍā is here clearly associated with Śiva, in fact, seems to be his consort, an association that is distinctly lacking in the Cāmuṇḍā of the DM. A closer study of the text than we can here provide might, however, indicate more precisely the continuities and discontinuities between this drama and the DM. For the text and very literal (and correspondingly wooden) translation, see Bhavabhūti, *Mālatīmādhava*, M. R. Kale (ed. and tr.), Motilal Banarsidass (Delhi, 1967); for a more readable, though edited, translation, see *Mālatī and Mādhava, or The Stolen Marriage*, in *Select Specimens of the Theatre of the Hindus*, Horace Hayman Wilson (tr.), Trübner and Co. (London, 1871), Third Ed., Vol. II, pp. 1-123. For the text alone, see *Mālatī-Mādhava*, R. G. Bhandarkar (ed.), Government Central Book Depot (Bombay, 1905).

*Śivadūtī*

Śivadūtī, too, appears in our text on six occasions,[184] and it is she who presents the great challenge to the conventional conceptualization that associates a female *śakti* with a male god, for she is the *śakti* of the Goddess herself.[185] She bears a close relationship to the Seven Little Mothers, though she is not one of them.[186] After the Seven Little Mothers have emerged from their respective gods, Śiva asks that they be sent forth into battle, whereupon our text proceeds :

> Then from the body of the Goddess came forth the very frightening
> *Śakti* of Caṇḍikā, gruesome (and) yelping (like) a hundred jackals (*śivāśataninādinī*).
> And she, the invincible one (*aparājitā*), spoke to Śiva, of smoky, matted locks :
> "O lord, become a messenger to Śumbha and Niśumbha[187] (saying),
>
> . . . . . . . . . . . . . . . . . . . . . .
>
> 'If you are desirous of battle, because of pride in (your) strength,
> Then come (and) let my jackals (*śivā*) become satiated with your flesh.' "
> Because Śiva himself was appointed as messenger[188] by (this) goddess,
> She has become famous throughout the world as Śivadūtī ("she who has Śiva as messenger").[189]

The only further characterization of this goddess is in the ensuing battle where emphasis is placed upon the destructive power of her fiendish laughter (88.37, 89. 21), while we may see a similarity to Cāmuṇḍā (Kālī) and the Seven Little Mothers in general in the fact that she devours her victims (88.37).

[184]88.27, 37; 89.21, 35, 39; 91.18.

[185]See Proleg., n. 265.

[186]See Appendix A for a discussion of this relationship.

[187]Lit., "Go to messengerhood towards Ś. and N.": *dūtatvaṃ gaccha pārśvaṃ śumbhaniśumbhayoḥ*.

[188]Vid erroneously reads *daityena* for *dūtyena* (Veṅk) or *dautyena* (Jag.).

[189]88.22-23, 26-27.

There is no evidence for Śivadūtī in the earlier literature, and even in the later literature she appears only occasionally,[190] though she does seem to have received some iconographic representation.[191] Lacking a sharp identity of her own in the DM, she serves to emphasize (1) the subordination of even Śiva to the Goddess,[192] (2) the paradox, conveyed here largely through a play on words, of the Goddess being associated with jackals (*śivā*) and also being auspicious (*śivā*),[193] and (3) the overwhelming mystery of the Goddess who can, in her supreme form, be addressed as *śakti* and yet who herself here produces a *śakti*, Śivadūtī, on analogy with other deities.[194]

*īśvarī*

Of the seven epithets that occur five times in the DM, *īśvarī* calls for our attention first because, in addition to these five occurrences,[195] it also forms one element of compounds which will receive consideration at the appropriate juncture: *māheśvarī*, *parameśvarī*, *viśveśvarī*. The internal evidence shows that *īśvarī* is always used of the supreme form of the Goddess in the DM, for all but one of these occurrences are in hymns, the sole exception (82.50) being its application to the Goddess in the midst of her engagement with Mahiṣa. She who is *īśvarī*, then, is "she who is powerful, competent, sovereign, the queen."

The antecedents of *īśvarī* are rather modest. Perhaps its earliest occurrence is in the Śrī Sūkta,[196] where it is applied to the goddess Śrī, an application that is confirmed, in identical

[190]The basis for this statement is the unpublished index of Purāṇic proper names compiled by the late Professor Walter Clark, to which we have been given access by D. H. H. Ingalls. Śivadūtī is indicated there to appear on only four other occasions in the Purāṇas.

[191]Banerjea, *Development*, p. 34.

[192]Compare the subordination of Viṣṇu to the Goddess in the Madhu-Kaiṭabha myth treated in Part II, on which also cf. *infra*, s. v. "*yoganidrā-nidrā*."

[193]Q. v., as an epithet in its own right, *infra*.

[194]This third point will become clearer below, s. v. "*śakti*."

[195]81.60; 82.50; 84.24; 85.35; 91.2. She is also called *sarveśvareśvarī* at 81.44, *akhileśvarī* at 91.35.

[196]RVK 2.6.9, q. v. in Part III.

words, at TA 10.1[197] when Śrī is called "queen of all creatures (*īśvari sarvabhūtānām*)." To these, the only instance we can add from either Vedic or epic sources occurs in a very interesting passage at MāGS 2.13.6. The passage is interesting, first, because its use of *īśvarī* is in its direct quotation of the verse appearing in the Śrī Sūkta and, second, because that quotation occurs in the description of a ceremony known as the Ṣaṣṭhī-kalpa (MāGS 2.13.1). The precise significance of the name Ṣaṣṭhī ("the Sixth") is not clear. It appears in the Mbh as an alternative name for Devasenā, spouse of Skanda (3.218.47), a name which van Buitenen argues is derivative from the fact that on the sixth day, the day after he was joined by Śrī (3.218.49), Skanda became successful.[198] However, there may be another association here in conjunction with the significance of the sixth face of Skanda to the band of Mothers.[199] In any case, both of these motifs are picked up in the description of the Ṣaṣṭhī-kalpa, for Ṣaṣṭhī is there "connected with new-born childern" and in the invocations "the author imperceptibly proceeds to commingle Ṣaṣṭhī's individuality with that of Śrī."[200] It is this association of *īśvarī* with maternity and prosperity that is bequeathed to the DM.[201]

*śivā*

In its five usages of *śivā*, the DM takes full advantage of the word's rich resonance and its potential for paradox, for it uses the word in quite different ways: when the Goddess crys-

[197]This is that curious passage in which a number of new names appear in Sanskrit, on which we have commented *supra*, s.v. "*durgā*." As suggested there, the passage includes a number of miscellaneous invocations, in which that of Śrī is included.

[198]Mbh, van Buitenen tr., vol. 2, p. 833n. on 3.218.45ff.

[199]Mbh 3.217.11-12. See our discussion of this passage in Appendix A.

[200]Gonda, Jan, *Aspects of Early Viṣṇuism*, N. V. A. Oosthoeck's Uitgever's Mij (Utrecht, 1954), p. 218.

[201]We shall subsequently see more of Śrī under that epithet. For more on Ṣaṣṭhī, and on the general relation of folk goddesses to our textual material, see Banerjea, J. N., "Some Folk Goddesses of Ancient and Mediaeval India," IHQ XIV (1938), pp. 101-109. Also, cf. C. M. Brown, *op. cit.*, pp. 39-40 for a later view.

tallizes out of the *tejas* of the different gods, the summary line describes her as *śivā* (82.17); she is twice hymned as *śivā* where the Śaiva association is emphasized, through the concurrent use of *mahādevī* in one case (85.7), and *tryambakā* in the other (91.9); when Pārvatī does not recognize herself to be the object of the gods' hymn, the figure who springs from her bodily sheath (*śarīrakoṣa*) to remind her, who is subsequently called Kauśikī (85.40), is called *śivā* (85.38); and, finally, one of the Seven Little Mothers, Vārāhī (here called *varāharūpiṇī*), is hymned as *śivā*(91.15). While it is true that, in all of these cases, the straightforward sense of "auspicious" would suffice, we have seen above[202] that our text does play on the word *śivā* as "jackal," and we would do well to recall that the name Śiva becomes applied to the Vedic Rudra largely as a euphemism.[203] What our text seems to appreciate is the enormous suggestive power of the word *śivā*. It hints at, but does not require, a relationship with Śiva, and it may be applicable in quite literal fashion, though its euphemistic application is not denied.

As a simply descriptive adjective, *śivā* has, of course, been used on hundreds of occasions in the Vedic literature, but if we limit our inquiry to its feminine singular occurrences, a sense of its various associations becomes readily apparent. Its Ṛg Vedic appearances are rather modest, being used as a modifier of *dhāsi* ("wholesome food," 5.41.17) and as a characterization of a woman: of the gambler's wife before his losses (10. 34.2), and of a caring, consoling mother (10.95.13). It is in the YV that we first encounter *śivā* in conjunction with *tanū*/*tanu*, "body" or "form," as a prime example of which we may take the following:

> The fire [*agni*] is Rudra; now two are his bodies [*tanuvau*], the dread [*ghorā*] the one, the auspicious [*śivā*] the other; in that he offers the Śatarudrīya, he soothes with it his dread form; in that he offers the stream of wealth, he delights with it his auspicious form.[204]

This notion that a deity has more than one *tanū*, one of which is

[202] S. v. "*śivadūtī*."
[203] O'Flaherty, *Asceticism and Eroticism*, p. 83.
[204] YVT 5.7.3.3, Keith tr.

*śivā*, occasions several invocations of this auspicious form, and while the deity so invoked is usually Rudra,[205] the imputation of a *śivā tanū* to Agni is also attested.[206] The most common juxtaposition of these two words occurs, however, in conjunction with the soothing quality of water, of which the following is a representative example :

> With propitious eye behold me, O waters [*āpaḥ*] ; with propitious body [*śivayā tanvā*] touch my skin ; they that are ghee-dripping, clean, purifying—let those waters be weal, pleasant to us.[207]

Other isolated applications of *śivā* are to Rudra's arrow (*iṣu*),[208] to Aditi,[209] to Sarasvatī,[210] to Śrī and Rātrī in their hymns in the RVK,[211] and in an unelaborated *namaskāra* to *vāc*.[212] But it is primarily, as we might expect, in the formulae of the AV that its occurrences are most frequent. There we find it applied to a favorable asterism,[213] to an ill omen (a twinning cow) whose influence one is trying to avert,[214] and there seems to be one instance of *śivā* as "jackal," ordinarily a bad omen which "in virtue of the spell of this verse... [has] a totally opposite influence."[215] In addition to such euphemistic usage, *śivā* is also used without the *double entendre*, to characterize the bride at a marriage ceremony.[216] Finally, *śivā* is used in con-

[205]YVT 4.5.1.1; 4.5.10.1.

[206]TB 1.1.7.2-3; *Śāṅkhāyana* (*Kauṣītaki*) *Brāhmaṇa* (ŚāṅB) 1.1: *Śāṅkhāyana Brāhmaṇa*, Gulābrai Vajeśamkar Chāyā (ed.), Ānandāśrama Mudraṇālaya (Poona, 1911), Ānandāśrama Sanskrit Series 65, and A. B. Keith's translation in *Rigveda Brāhmaṇas*, Harvard University Press (Cambridge, 1920), HOS 25.

[207]AV 1.33.4, Whitney-Lanman tr.; cf. also YVMā 4.2; YVT 5.6.1.2; AiB 8.6.

[208]YVT 4.5.1.2..

[209]YVT 4.4.12.5.

[210]TA 1.21.3; ŚāṅA 7.1; AV 7.68.3. These are all variations on the refrain *Śivā naḥ śaṃtamā bhava sumṛdīkā sarasvati.*

[211]RVK 2.6.3.30 and 4.2.4, the Śrī and Rātrī Sūktas, respectively, q. v. in Part III.

[212]TA 4.1.1.

[213]19.7.3.

[214]3.28.2-3.

[215]Whitney-Lanman's n. on 19.8.5.

[216]14.1.64; 14.2.13; 14.2.18.

junction with two of the major Indian symbols of the feminine: night (*rātri*)—

> Propitious to me [be] night and [the time] after sunrise; be the mother of cold (hima) easy of invocation for us; notice, O well-portioned one, this song of praise, with which I greet thee in all the quarters.[217]

and earth (*bhūmi*)—

> Upon the firm, broad earth, the all-begetting mother of the plants, that is supported by (divine) law, upon her, propitious and kind, may we ever pass our lives ! [218]

To these verbal associations of the word *śivā*, the epic adds several brief portraits of females named Śivā. The first of these is given mere passing mention at Mbh 1.60.24, where Śivā is cited as the wife of the Vasu Anila and mother of Purojava and Avijñātagati. The second Śivā appears in the familiar[219] story of Skanda's birth where she is the wife of one of the seven seers, Aṅgiras, and is described as "endowed with a fine character, beauty, and virtue."[220] In the multiple cohabitation of Agni and Svāhā from which, according to the first Mbh account, Skanda was born, it was Śivā's body (*rūpa*) that Svāhā first assumed in her lust for the fire-god.[221] Finally, the HV picks up on a very different sense of *śivā*, for when Andhaka is describing to Kaṃsa some of the evil omens that have occurred in anticipation of the latter's demise, he cites a fire-breathing jackal (*śivā*), which sallied forth from the cremation ground, "showering charcoals from her snorts, bellowing aplenty."[222]

It is this deep ambivalence about the nature of that which is called *śivā*—whether it be truly "auspicious," or whether one

[217] 19.49.5: all punctuation here is part of Whitney-Lanman's conjectural reading of a grammatically difficult verse.

[218] 12.1.17, Bloomfield tr.: this is part of the famous hymn to Earth that is AV 12.1.

[219] See Appendix A.

[220] Mbh 3.214.1, van Buitenen tr.

[221] Mbh 3.214. This is the first account of several that the Mbh gives of Skanda's birth and motherhood. For a discussion of its other accounts, see Appendix A.

[222] HV 66.26. Cf. Vidyākara, *op. cit.*, pp. 398, 400, 569.

hopes to make auspicious what is intrinsically hostile by calling it auspicious—that the DM itself so fully appreciates.

*sthitā*

While this past participle of *sthā* is sometimes used simply to describe the Goddess as "standing" somewhere (88.28; 90.5), there are five occasions on which it is used hymnically in a more pregnant sense.[223] On these, it may be taken as "steadfast, abiding," even approximating *nityā*, with which it is contextually linked on two occasions (81.54, 55). Typical is the declaration (91.3): "You alone have become the support of the world, since you abide in the form of earth (*mahīrūpeṇa sthitā*)."

The antecedents of this epithet are few in number and seem to carry little more than their intrinsic adjectival weight. The only noteworthy passages we have encountered are at *Gopatha Brāhmaṇa* 1.3.16 and *Ṣaḍviṃśa Brāhmaṇa* 4.7[224] where *sthitā* is conjoined with a personification of the sacrificial exclamation Svāhā in a lovely description of the latter. Even here, however, as in the DM itself, the line between *sthitā* as being physically descriptive and as being a cause for praise is not sharp.

*kaumārī*

The conception of Kaumārī in the DM's five applications of the name[225] is that she is one of the Seven Little Mothers, a fact whose implications are drawn out in Appendix A. Here we may note that the connection between Skanda (Kumāra) and the Mothers in the Mbh account is continued, even "systematized," in the DM by viewing Skanda as one of the gods, the third in order, from whom a *śakti* of the Goddess emerges:

> Ambikā, having the form of Guha (Skanda), (as) Kaumārī went forth to fight,

[223] 81.54, 55; 85.34; 91.3, 30.

[224] *Gopatha Brāhmaṇa* (GoB), Rājendralāla Mitra and Harachandra Vidyābhushana (edd.) Ganeśa Press (Calcutta, 1872), Bibliotheca Indica NS 215, 252. *Ṣaḍviṃśa Brāhmaṇa*, Willem Boudewijn Bollée (tr.), Drukkerij A. Storm (Utrecht, 1956).

[225] 88.16, 33, 48; 89.36; 91.13.

With spear (*śakti*) in hand, having the best of peacocks as her vehicle.[226]

In the ensuing battle, it is her *śakti* that stands her in good stead, and the concluding hymn (91.13) adds that she is surrounded by cocks (*kukkuṭa*), all of which legitimates her iconographic correspondence with Skanda.[227]

The only previous appearance of this word in the literature we have examined is at Mbh 9.45.36 where it is used in the plural, *kaumāryaḥ*, "those who are related to Kumāra," and characterizes the preceding list of roughly two hundred *mātṛs*. Although these Mothers are said to be "followers (*anucārāḥ*)" of Skanda (9.45.1), not all are said to be "related to" or "derivative from" him, for the same verse (36) also refers to those who are "related to Vāyu (*vāyavyāḥ*)" and "related to Brahmā (*brāhmyāḥ*)."

*māheśvarī*

Māheśvarī, too, in her five appearances[228] in the DM, is understood to be one of the Seven Little Mothers, the second in order of appearance, "the one who is related to Maheśvara" :

Māheśvarī sallied forth, mounted upon a bull, bearing the best of tridents [*triśūla*],
Having great serpents for bracelets, adorned with the moon's crescent.[229]

The only information added in subsequent instances of this epithet is that the *triśūla* is Māheśvarī's preferred implement in battle. Since Maheśvara is used throughout the Mbh as a name

[226]88.16.

[227]Cf. Banerjea, *Development*, pp. 364-367. For a full discussion of the iconography of Skanda, see Sahai, *op. cit.*,pp. 99-117. We might note in passing the occasional iconographic confusion of Kaumāri with Sarasvatī: *ibid.*, pp. 145, 152.

[228]88.15, 33, 48; 89.37; 91.12. We here rule out, for reasons given in Appendix A, n. 3, the occurrence of *Maheśvarī* at 84.31.

[229]88.15. The last phrase is, more literally, "adorned with streaks from the moon," *candrarekhāvibhuṣanā*; we prefer the less literal reading as closer to the iconography of Śiva as *candraśekhara*, on which cf. Banerjea, *Development*, pp. 464, 466-467.

of Śiva,[230] the probability is that our text understands Māheśvarī to be Śiva's *śakti*. This is, however, never explicitly stated, and given the enormous variety of ways in which Śiva has been represented,[231] there is less precise correspondence in iconography between god and *śakti* here than in other instances. In general terms, however—the bull, the trident, the moon—it is clear that the cognizances are Śaiva.[232]

In the Vedic literature, there are no uses of Māheśvarī, which, in light of the oft-noted non-Vedic character of Maheśvara, is not surprising. What is rather striking is how little the name Māheśvarī has come into currency by epic times as well. As noted, Śiva is well known throughout the Mbh under the name of Maheśvara, and it is also well known that he has a wife, for whom by far the most common name is Umā.[233] Sørensen cites only one instance of Māheśvarī, however, in a passage where she is also called Mahādevī and Pārvatī.[234] Maheśvarī, too, is attested but once in a passage of Śaiva resonance, where she is said to assume the form of Mahākālī in order to accompany Vīrabhadra, who had emerged from Śivā's wrath, in his destruction of Dakṣa's sacrifice.[235] Since the DM never uses the epithet Umā, we may make the same inference we made in the case of Aindrī : when our text speaks of the *śakti* of a god, it wishes to make it clear that the *śakti* is not merely the spouse of that god, and it does this by explicitly eschewing the then current names for the various spouses. We may even wonder whether our text intended the identification, often made subsequently, of the Goddess and Umā, the consort of Śiva. Be that as it may, the avowed preference of the DM is patent. When it speaks of Māheśvarī, it is speaking of a goddess who does not have only (at all ?) a formal, external relation-

[230] See Sørensen, *op. cit.*, s. v. "Śiva."

[231] The evidence of Banerjea, *Development*, pp. 446-488 suffices to legitimate this statement. That provided by Gopinatha Rao (*Elements of Hindu Iconography*, Law Printing House [Madras, 1914-16], Two vols.) makes any documentation seem obsequious.

[232] Cf. Vidyākara, *op. cit.*, pp. 69-70.

[233] See Sørensen, *op. cit.*, s. v. "Umā."

[234] Mbh 14.43.14-15.

[235] Mbh 12, Appendix I 28, line 74. The similarity between Vīrabhadra's emergence from Śiva's wrath here and that of Kālī from the Goddess's in the DM is marked.

ship to Maheśvara, but who is far more fundamental, more internal, to his very identity, who is, in fact, his power (*śakti*).

*brahmāṇī*

The last of the epithets of five occurrences,[236] Brahmāṇī, is also one of the Seven Little Mothers, "the one who is related to Brahmā" :

> In a heavenly conveyance drawn by swans, with rosary and water pot (*kamaṇḍalu*),
> Came forth the *śakti* of Brahmā; she is called Brahmāṇī.

Brahmāṇī is here (88.14) the first *śakti* to appear: hence, the phrase of explanation, the explicit correlation of her name with the fact of being the god's *śakti*. Brahmāṇī maintains this primacy both in our text—when the diverse forms of the Goddess are resumed into Ambikā (90.4), they are described as "led by Brahmāṇī"—and in most lists of the Seven Little Mothers. In battle, she is perhaps less horrific than her peers, for she is described as "slaying with water sprinkled from her *kamaṇḍalu*" (88.32), and elsewhere that destructive water is described as "purified by the *mantras* of Brahmāṇī" (89.36). This may, however, be simply a reflection of the fact that Brahmā carries no ordinary weapon, so Brahmāṇī takes his *kamaṇḍalu* and makes a weapon of that. In any case, what little iconographic representation of Brahmā there is,[237] indicates a clear correspondence with the *śakti* here operative.

We have found no instances of the word *brahmāṇī* in the Vedic or epic literature.

*śakti*

Although we come now to our treatment of *śakti* as the first, and therefore most important, epithet of four occurrences in our

[236]88.14, 32; 89.36; 90.4; 91.11. We may note here that while in some appearances of the Seven Little Mothers (cf. Sahai, *op. cit.*, p. 207, Bhattacharyya, N., *op. cit.*, p.102) Sarasvatī replaces Brahmāṇī, the DM shows no such tendency: Sarasvatī appears only once (91.22) and that is in a hymn where her name and identity are not elaborated upon.

[237]See Banerjea, *Development*, pp. 516-519.

text, it should be clear that we are here *not* considering those instances where *śakti* is associated with a particular god. Those latter instances are dealt with in Appendix A, in conjunction with the DM's conception of the Seven Little Mothers, and it would be redundant, as well as potentially confusing, to discuss them here as well.[238] We may therefore dismiss them here with a summary remark: our text does have an understanding of *śakti*, "power," as a plural phenomenon and it, in fact, uses the plural on several occasions (88.12, 21), associating each individual *śakti* with the deity, usually a god, from whom it emerges (88.13). Thus Brahmā (88.14), Viṣṇu (88.17), the Varāha form of Hari (88.18), Indra (88.41), and even Caṇḍikā herself (88.22) are explicitly said to have *śaktis*, but it is implied that at least the other gods mentioned in conjunction with the Seven Little Mothers, and probably those not mentioned there as well, also have *śaktis*.

In addition to this understanding of *śaktis* as plural and particular phenomena, the DM has an understanding of *śakti* as a singular and universal phenomenon. It is the four instances of this usage, where *śakti* is not something that a deity has, but something that the Goddess *is*, that concern us here. The basic conception, and the fact that it is predicated of the supreme form of the Goddess, are evident in its first occurrence (81.63):

> Whatever and wherever anything exists, whether it be real or unreal,[239] O you who have everything as your very soul,

[238]The distinction that we make here is largely a formal one, although it does correspond to a difference in the way the DM employs the word, a difference that helps structure our study. The text itself suggests how one moves from one sense of *śakti* to the other. At 84.2, the gods declare that they are bowed down to Ambikā, "by whom through her power (*śakti*) this world is stretched out, whose body is the aggregate of the power (*śakti*) of the multitude of gods (*devyā yayā tatam idam jagad ātmaśaktyā niḥśeṣadevagaṇa-śaktisamūhamūrtyā*)." Another "linking" usage is found at 91.22 where the Goddess is said to be *sarvaśaktisamanvitā*, "endowed with the power of all."

[239]The paradox here is a brilliant example of how the DM skirts the philosophical issues in the interest of devotion. Rather than inquiring into the ontological status of what is real and unreal (*sadasad*), it says that they both exist (*vastu*) and that the Goddess is the power of both. If we grant that and press on to inquire into the status of that which does not exist, then we are

Of all that, you are the power (*śakti*) ; how then can
you be (adequately) praised ?[240]

Subsequent instances confirm this view by affirming that she abides in the form of *śakti* (*śaktirūpeṇa*) in all beings (85.18), and that she is operative in cosmic processes: 91.8 sees her at work in the cessation (*uparati*) of all at *pralaya*, while 91.10 sees *śakti* as responsible for creation and maintenance, as well as destruction.

In turning to the antecedent usages of this epithet, it is astonishing to note, in light of the enormous significance that the word *śakti* has come to have in identifying the Goddess,[241] how modest its earlier occurrences are, in terms of both frequency and intensity. In the RV, the word *śakti*, "ability, power, capacity," appears on only a handful of occasions, though the precise number is not certain because of the existence of another word *śakti*, "help, service," whose usage is attested only in the RV.[242] Among those instances that are clearly of the

---

trapped by our translation, for the juxtaposition in the original (see the following note) of *vastu* and *sadasad* is deliberately and inherently paradoxical. The positive ontology implied in *vastu* is denied, or transcended, by *asad*, a formulation of which even Nagārjuna might be proud !

[240]*yac ca kiñcit kvacit vastu sadasad vākhilātmike/*
*tasya sarvasya yā śaktiḥ sā tvaṃ kiṃ stūyase tadā//*
Veṅk reads *mayā*, "by me," for *tadā*.

[241]Reflected, perhaps, in the ubiquity of the word *śakti* (or a derivative thereof) in the titles of studies devoted to the history of Goddess worship in India: see the titles of the previously cited works by Beane, Bhattacharyya, N., Kumar, Payne, and Sircar (ed.).

[242]The PW and VPK agree in making this distinction, with the former tracing it to different underlying verbal roots, *śak* and *śikṣ*, respectively. Both also agree on which RV instances belong to which of the two *śakti*-s. (In our ensuing discussion, we cite the four instances that they both give for *śakti*, "power.") While it is true that the two verbal roots are ultimately identical (an opinion that Böhtlingk and Roth themselves favor: Whitney, William Dwight, *The Roots, Verb-forms, and Primary Derivatives of the Sanskrit Language*, Breitkopf and Härtel (Leipzig, 1885) and Trübner and Co. (London), Bibliothek Indogermanischer Grammatiken Band II, Anhang II, reproduced by the American Oriental Society (New Haven, 1945), American Oriental Series Vol. 30, s. v. "śak"), it is worth maintaining the distinction between the two nouns, as a quotation of one of the instances of *śakti*, "help," may make clear:

Ich verlange nach deiner grossen Freundschaft [*sakhya*], nach deinen guten Diensten [*śakti*]. Dem Vṛtratöter gehen viele Gaben zu. Gross

former *śakti*, we may cite the prayer to Agni—"Erbaue dich an dieser Beschwörung, o Agni, die wir dir nach bestem Können [*śakti*] oder Wissen gemacht haben"[243]—and the simile regarding Indra—"Denn wie einen langen Haken trägst du die Kraft [*śakti*], o Ratreicher"[244]—as examples of its use in the singular. That we are still distant from the conceptualization of a deity's possessing one single power or energy, however, is evident from the occurrence of *śakti* in the plural: "Denn unter Preislied hatten die Götter im Himmel den Agni erzeugt, der mit seinen Kräften [*śaktibhiḥ*] die Welt erfüllt."[245]

This kind of usage, where *śakti* is understood as power or ability, which may be possessed by god or man in either single or diverse form, continues virtually without elaboration throughout the other Vedas and Brāhmaṇas.[246] This notion is not

---

ist das Loblied; wir sind in die Gunst des Herrn gekommen. Sei uns, du Gabenreicher, fein ein Beschützer [RV 3.31.12, Geldner tr.].

The whole tone of the passage is such as to make it clear that this is not an instance of *śakti*, "power." That the distinction between the two words is not always clear, however, is evident in the way Geldner has challenged the tidy division of instances, on which the PW and VPK agree, by moving between the two senses of the word (e.g., 2.39.7). In the absence of an ability to appraise the Vedic Sanskrit ourselves, we have remained content with the traditional division of instances. That *śakti*, "help," is attested only in the RV is suggested by the PW, and we may, perhaps, see evidence for the early date at which *śakti*, "power," became the predominant understanding of the word in the fact that as old a text as the *Nighaṇṭu* lists *śakti* in close proximity to another word for "power," viz., *śacī* (*Nighaṇṭu* 2.1), though admittedly the argument from silence is inconclusive; cf. *The Nighantu and the Nirukta*, Lakshman Sarup (ed. and tr.), Oxford University Press (London, 1920-1927) Three vols.

243RV 1.31.18, Geldner tr.

244RV 10.134.6, Geldner tr. It should be noted that here, too, Geldner challenges the traditional history of the language by allowing an alternative reading in his notes: "deinen Speer [*śakti*] wie einen Haken." That there is a third *śakti*, viz., "spear," is obvious in classical Sanskrit, and the DM itself uses this word (88.16, etc.). The attestation of the PW, however, does not include a single Vedic citation of this *śakti*. Geldner allows a similar alternative reading at 2.39.7.

245RV 10.88.10ab, Geldner tr. Cf. also 10.25.5, where Soma is endowed with multiple *śaktis*.

246The only exception to this statement that is worthy of note is an intriguing passage we have encountered in the Kashmirian (Paippalāda) recension of the AV. (It apparently does not occur in the Śaunaka recension.)

particularly surprising, of course: we have already noted [247] Gonda's remarks on the facility with which, in non-modern societies, "ideas" can be given substance and form, and it is fair to say that the Vedic notion of *śakti* gives it a status that is quasi-independent of its possessor.

It is in late Vedic times that *śakti* begins to become a philosophically pregnant word, and once again it is that watershed of theistic thought, the ŚU, that presents the germane material. To be sure, it does not present a systematic case, and there are vestiges of the familiar usage as well: strength (*śakti*) belongs to the devotee of controlled mind (2.2), and the supreme power (*parā śakti*) of Maheśvara is simply said to be various (*vividhā*: 6.8). We might be tempted to take this latter instance as similar to the traditional appreciation of divine or human versatility, were it not for the fact that, in the same verse, Maheśvara is said to be without action (*kārya*) or organ (*kāraṇa*), for such Sāṃkhya terminology is pervasive of the language of the ŚU. It is beyond the scope of this study to examine the role of the ŚU in effecting a rapprochement between theism and the atheistic, dualistic Sāṃkhya,[248] but we may point out that at the very outset of the ŚU, where the text is setting forth its initial formulation of the Lord's relationship to the material world, the word *śakti* is employed in a very interesting way:

---

It seems to be an invocation of Agni, and, if so, represents an interesting convergence of language and symbols on the Goddess, for in addition to its use of the word *śakti*, the passage also establishes a relationship between the god and the earth, *pṛthivī*. However, in the absence of sufficient critical work on the Kashmirian AV, it is impossible to assay its significance, and we can do no more than present the evidence (19.44.16-19):

*divo reto 'si pṛthivyā nabhyam/ nabhyam asi nabhyam mā kṛṇu//*
*divo reto 'si pṛthivyās śaktiḥ/ śaktir asi śaktaye te vidheyam//*
*divo reto 'si pṛthivyā vittiḥ/ vittir asi vittaye te vidheyam//*
*divo reto 'si pṛthivyā bhūtiḥ/ bhūtir asi bhūtaye te vidheyam//*

*The Kashmirian Atharva Veda*, Leroy Carl Barret (ed.; except Book 6, F. Edgerton, ed.) American Oriental Society (New Haven, 1906-1940).

[247] See the refs. given at Proleg., nn. 251, 252.

[248] For a substantial study of this, see Johnston, E. H., "Some Sāṃkhya and Yoga Conceptions in the Śvetāśvatara Upaniṣad," *Journal of the Royal Asiatic Society* (Oct., 1930), pp. 855-878.

Those who followed meditation and *yoga* saw the self-power of God (*devātmaśakti*), hidden by its own qualities (*svaguṇa*);
He is the one who rules over all these causes (*kāraṇa*), from "time" to "the soul."[249]

The text then proceeds (1.4-5) to articulate its understanding of God as comprising the material world, in which the individual soul "flutters about" (1.6), an exegesis which is obviously based on the Sāṃkhya understanding of *prakṛti*.[250] The precise nature of this *śakti* of God is not clear, nor is it specified whether the *guṇas* which mask the *śakti* are the same as the three *guṇas* of *prakṛti* alluded to in 1.4.[251] But the suggestiveness of this passage is enormous. That *śakti* is identical with *prakṛti* is at least implicit here, and their subsequent identification, in which the DM is a primary agent, is clearly facilitated by the ŚU's conceptualization.

To this emerging vision, the epic contribution is fragmentary, but intriguing. There is a male seer by the name of Śakti in both the Mbh and Rām, but neither seems to have a bearing on our epithet.[252] There is, however, the rather haunting figure of Śakti in the Mbh account of Skanda's birth, where she is a goddess, but seen only dimly. It is as if familiarity with her identity is assumed, so that she never has to emerge fully on-stage. The first glimmer we have of her occurs in the prologue to the birth story: in the first Mbh account, Agni is the father of Skanda,[253] and by way of introduction, the text gives the genealogy of various fires, one of which is "the fire called

[249]ŚU 1.3 :
*te dhyānayogānugatā apaśyan devātmaśaktiṃ svaguṇair nigūḍhām|*
*yaḥ kāraṇāni nikhilāni tāni kālātmayuktāny adhitiṣṭhaty ekaḥ||*

[250]See Hume's notes which indicate the precise correspondences between the ŚU's enumerations and the categories articulated in the *Sāṃkhya Kārikā*.

[251]We shall return to the ŚU's vision of the material world, *infra*, s. v., "*prakṛti*."

[252]The Mbh story of Śakti, son of Vasiṣṭha, father of Parāśara by Adṛśyantī, and consequently grandfather of Kṛṣṇa Dvaipāyana, appears at 1.166, though his name receives occasional mention in the sequel. The Rām reference at 7.96.3 merely cites one Śakti as belonging to a group of *ṛṣis* counseling Rāma.

[253]For more extended remarks on the Mbh accounts of Skanda's birth, see Appendix A.

Śiva [which] is bent upon the worship of Śakti, and it is always *śiva* because it gives succor to all that are afflicted with suffering."[254] After the birth of Skanda, we have another glimmer: the *ṛṣi* Viśvāmitra has secretly witnessed the encounter of Agni and Svāhā in the guise of six of the wives of the seven seers, from which encounter Skanda is born. Aware of the child's true stature, Viśvāmitra attends upon him:

> All the thirteen sacraments pertaining to childhood the great hermit performed for him, from the sacrament of birth onward. He sang of the glory of the Six-faced God, and the efficacy of the cock, [the efficacy of] the Goddess Śakti [*śaktyā devyāḥ sadhanam*], and the Companions [*pāriṣadam*], and he performed rituals for the good of the world.[255]

The final glimmer occurs at the very end of a discussion of Skanda's companions,[256] where the concluding comment is offered: "know that the sixth face of Skanda from among the six heads is a goat's face, king, and it is worshipped by the band of the Mothers. The foremost among his six heads is the one called Bhadraśākhā, through which he created the divine [*divyām*] Śakti."[257]

Since these three passages constitute the entire epic testimony on Śakti, any conclusions based thereon must be correspondingly modest. Yet the association of Śiva and Śakti is surely noteworthy,[258] not so much for its relevance to the DM where its only viability is in Māheśvarī's emergence from Maheśvara, as for its forecast of that pervasive association in the ensuing Śaiva mythology.[259] One might go even further and say that it is through their mutual involvement here with Śakti that Śiva and Skanda subsequently become related as father to son: the

[254]Mbh 3.211.2, van Buitenen tr.

[255]Mbh 3.215.9-11ab, van Buitenen tr. The "Six-faced God" is, of course, Skanda himself (see our next quotation), and we have seen the cock to be associated with Skanda-Kumāra *supra*, s. v. "*kaumārī*."

[256]See our much fuller quotation of this passage, and discussion of it, in connection with the Seven Little Mothers, in Appendix A.

[257]Mbh 3.217.12-13, van Buitenen tr.

[258]In his textual note on 3.211.2, van Buitenen says it is "at least remarkable."

[259]O'Flaherty, *Asceticism and Eroticism*, *passim*, esp. chap. VII.

initial Mbh account portrays Agni as the father of Skanda, almost without exception,[260] yet later Mbh and Purāṇic accounts know Skanda predominately as the son of Śiva.[261] Such reflections, however, run beyond our immediate concern, and the significance of the epic's account of Śakti for understanding the DM can be put more briefly. Śakti is intimately bound up with the identity of Skanda, for she appears only in the Mbh episode of his birth. As Appendix A makes clear, the identity of the Seven Little Mothers is also related to that of Skanda, though in a very different way. What the DM seems to have done is to systematize the diverse strands.[262] It has done this, on the one hand, by ascribing a particular *śakti* to each individual deity, suggesting in passing that they are seven in number; on the other hand, it has subsumed all of these *śaktis* into Śakti, the metaphysical ultimate, the Goddess herself, conceived along the lines suggested by the ŚU.

*gaurī*

In its four applications of the epithet Gaurī,[263] the DM clearly understands it as a true epithet, even a proper name, and employs it in rather subtle fashion. It is, on the one hand, inclined to apply it to the supreme form of the Goddess, as suggested by the fact that three of its appearances are in hymns. Yet, on the other, our text senses in it certain Śaiva associations, for its first instance proclaims, "You are Gaurī, whose abode is made with the one who is crowned with the moon (*śaśimaulikṛtapratiṣṭhā*)," i.e., Śiva, and a subsequent one speaks of Gaurī, Śivā, and Tryambakā all in the same breath.[264] Even more revealing, however, are the associations deriving from its non-hymnic usage. At the end of the second *carita*, the text

[260]See Appendix A, n. 35 for the two weak claims that the first Mbh account makes for Śiva's fatherhood.

[261]For the later Mbh accounts, see Appendix A, n. 17; in general, see O'Flaherty, *Asceticism and Eroticism, passim.*

[262]Or, if it is not responsible for this work, it reflects a systematization effected elsewhere.

[263]84.10, 35; 85.8; 91.9.

[264]91.9: this is the curious verse that also appears in the Śrī Sūkta and the Jodhpur inscription; see Proleg., n. 204.

creates a bridge to the third by having the *ṛṣi* say that he has described how the Goddess was "born from the bodies of the gods" for the good of the world (84. 34), and now he will describe how "she was born from the body of Gaurī" in order to slay wicked Daityas, including Śumbha and Niśumbha (84.35). This sets the stage for the third *carita's* opening hymn to Pārvatī and for the ensuing (85.38-41) emanation from Pārvatī, an emanation called *śivā*, *kauṣikī*, and *ambikā*, that informs Pārvatī, "This hymn is addressed to me" (85.39), i.e., to us who are, in fact, the same. We have commented above upon this particular event,[265] but here we may draw out some further implications. It is clear that our text understands Gaurī as synonymous with that common name for Śiva's spouse, Pārvatī.[266] What is significant, however, is that, in the dynamics of the ensuing events, our text makes virtually nothing of Gaurī-Pārvatī's relationship to Śiva: the prime actress throughout the third *carita* is this "auspicious emanation," and Gaurī-Pārvatī does not again appear.[267] If our text is impressed by anything here, it is by the *coincidentia oppositorum* in the Goddess: as an adjective, *gaurī* means "bright, fair-complexioned, beautiful" and this is precisely how the *emanation* of Pārvatī is described,[268] while Pārvatī herself, having produced this emanation, is described as having become black (*kṛṣṇā*) and consequently known as Kālikā, "The Black One."[269] What our text appreciates here is the symbiotic relationship between these forms of the Goddess, her enormous metamorphic potential, and this appreciation far transcends the mythological or sectarian resonance of any particular epithet, such as Gaurī.

Vedic usage of the word *gaurī* has been limited, but highly suggestive. In the RV, the word appears, sometimes in the plural, either in a literal sense as "buffalo cow," or possibly in

[265]S. v. "*ambikā*," text given at n. 31; see also n. 70.

[266]See *infra*, s. v. "*pārvatī*," however, for the rather meagre use of *pārvatī* in this regard in Vedic and epic literature.

[267]Except for the mention of Gaurī in the concluding hymn, cited above, n. 264.

[268]Cf. the description offered by Caṇḍa and Muṇḍa at 85.42-45.

[269]As observed at n. 70, this is the only occurrence of Kālikā in the DM, and it therefore carries quite a different weight than the epithet Kālī does.

a symbolic reference to the milk with which the Soma is ritually mixed.[270] The major occurrence, however, is in a hymn to the *viśve devāḥ*:

> Die Büffelkuh [*gaurī*] hat gebrüllt, Wasserfluten hervorbringend, einfüssig, zweifüssig, achtfüssig, neunfüssig geworden, tausendsilbig im höchsten Raum. Von ihr strömen Meere aus, davon leben die vier Weltgegenden. Davon strömt das Unvergängliche aus, von dem zehrt alles.[271]

One might, of course, see this as a "mere" glorification of the Büffelkuh, but to do so would be to overlook the fact that RV 1. 164 is the famous, and puzzling, riddling hymn. While we cannot trace the full range of commentary on this hymn, we can note that as early a text as the *Nirukta* remarks that "Gaurī is derived from (the verb) *ruc*, meaning to shine" and then ascribes these two verses to her,[272] an ascription with which the BṛDe concurs (4. 36). Moreover, this latter text also identifies Gaurī as belonging to Indra's sphere (1. 129) and, most significantly in the long run, as one of the middle forms of Vāc, which "(are) in the hymns to the All-gods (praised) incidentally only."[273] While these two RV verses have engendered some further commentary in the Taittirīya school,[274] it is in YVMai that the next major elaboration of Gaurī's identity occurs. In that text's version of the Śatarudrīya hymn, there is an introduction which does not seem to occur in the other recensions. In it there occurs a series of variations on the Gāyatrī *mantra* to such diverse deities as Skanda, Dantī (Gaṇeśa?), Brahmā, Viṣṇu, Bhānu, Candra, Vahni, Dhyāna, and Sṛṣṭi, the first of which, after Rudra himself, is one Gaurī, daughter of the mountain, from whom the Ganges streams forth:

> *tadgāngaucyāya vidmahe girisutāya dhīmahi/tan no gaurī pracodayāt//*[275]

[270]See RV 9.12.3 and 1.84.10, and Geldner's notes thereon; also 4.12.6 which, however, is obscure.

[271]RV 1.164.41-42, Geldner tr.

[272]*Nirukta* 11.39-41, Sarup tr.

[273]BṛDe 2.81, Macdonell tr.

[274]TB 2.4.6.11; TA 1.9.4.

[275]YVMai 2.9.1. Cp. the text of the Gāyatrī *mantra* given at n. 110. Ingalls has pointed out to us (personal note, undated) that if this introduction does refer to Gaṇeśa, then it must be a very late addition to the hymn.

While this description surely seems to fit the Gaurī of Purāṇic times, the text says no more, and the only additional Vedic mention of Gaurī is at ŚDS 116.22 where she is paired with Varuṇa, as whose consort she occasionally appears in later times.[276]

That Gaurī lacks a distinct identity in the epic is clear from the diversity of ways in which the name is applied: it is the name of an Apsaras,[277] of a river,[278] of a daughter of Matināra and mother of Māndhātṛ,[279] and there are some efforts to apply it to the earth.[280] The most frequent usage of the name is as the wife of Varuṇa,[281] but these are mere passing references, and there is also some evidence for a Śaiva association to the name: there is a *tirtha* known as the peak of Gaurī Mahādevī,[282] and on the first occasion that the Mbh applies the name Pārvatī to Śiva's spouse Umā, one Gaurī is said to be in her retinue.[283] Moreover, in later portions of the text, Śiva is referred to as "husband of Gaurī" and "dear to the heart of Gaurī."[284]

It is against this background, with its early suggestion of a cosmic role of Gaurī and its growing intuition of a relationship between Gaurī and Śiva, that the DM's use of the epithet occurs.

[276]Cf. Banerjea, *Development*, p. 526 and Sahai, *op. cit.*, p. 47 for instances of Gauri's iconographic relation to Varuṇa. The occurrence of *gaurī* at *Vaikhānasa Gṛhya Sūtra* (VaiGS) 6.12 barely bears mention, for it is used there purely as a technical term for a girl of marriageable age, "one between ten and twelve years, whose menses have not yet set in": *Vaikhānasasmārta* [*gṛhya* and *dharma*] *sūtra*, W. Caland (tr.), Asiatic Society of Bengal (Calcutta, 1929), Bibliotheca Indica 251.

[277]Mbh 3.44.30.

[278]Mbh 6.10.24, HV 9.82.

[279]HV 360*.

[280]Mbh *v. l.* on 13.134.8; HV App. I 40, lines 1484, 1519, 1529.

[281]Mbh 5.115.9; 13.134.4; 13.151.6.

[282]Mbh 3.82.131.

[283]Mbh 3.221.20. This is the first epic account of Skanda's birth. See also van Buitenen's n., p. 834.

[284]Mbh 14.8.28 and 10.7.8, *gaurīśa* and *gaurīhṛdayavallabha*, respectively.

*lakṣmī*

Of the epithets we have met so far, *lakṣmī* is the second, after *śakti*, that has currency as a common noun as well as, or instead of, adjectival or proper nominal usage. In fact, the DM's four instances of this epithet can be understood almost entirely in terms of its meaning "good luck, fortune," without clear personification. Thus the "good fortune of kings" is praised (85.9), the Goddess is said to abide in the form of good fortune (*lakṣmīrūpeṇa*) in all beings (85.26), and *lakṣmī* is hymned in a sequence of feminine nouns (91.20). The clearest sense of the DM's usage is obtained from its one non-hymnic occurrence—

> In times of well-being, she is the *lakṣmī* of men,
> granting (them) prosperity (*vṛddhi*) in (their) home(s);
> In times of privation, then she exists as *alakṣmī*,
> for the sake of destruction.[285]

—where we again have the intuition that the Goddess constitutes both poles of a polarity.

In treating the antecedents of *lakṣmī*, we find that the word has a single occurrence in the RV, and that in a late hymn to *jñāna*:

> Wo die Weisen mit Nachdenken die Rede gebildet haben, sie wie Schrotmehl durch ein Sieb reinigend, da erkennen die Genossen ihre Genossenschaft. Deren gutes Zeichen ist ihrer Rede aufgeprägt.[286]

In light of the fact that, from a Purāṇic perspective, it almost seems redundant to call *lakṣmī bhadrā*, and in order to cut through the later Vedic discussion[287] of the relationship, here implied, between *lakṣmī* and *lakṣman*, we may here cite the distinction of Gonda:

> ... a *lakṣmī*—is an object or a being the very existence or presence of which means something auspicious... or evil...; a *lakṣman*—is, more vaguely, a token or mark, a fact connected

[285]MarkP 92.36cd-37ab. The only other instance of *alakṣmī* in our text is at 84.4, where it is similarly juxtaposed with *śrī*.

[286]RV 10.71.2, Geldner tr. The text of the last clause reads: *bhadraiṣāṃ lakṣmīr nihitādhi vāci.*

[287]E.g., *Nirukta* 4.10; ŚB 8.4.4.8; 8.4.4.11; 8.5.4.3.

with the external form of beings or objects as perceived by the senses, which may induce man to infer that there is something auspicious, favorable, etc.[288]

What this means, first, is that a *lakṣmī* is closer than a *lakṣman* to the source of effective power—Gonda's way of putting it is that some "polysyllabic-ī-stems in Vedic... refer to power-substances believed to lead an independent existence"[289]—and thus begins to approximate the notion of *śakti* examined above. Second, however, the Vedic *lakṣmī* need not be auspicious, but may be profoundly ambivalent. Consequently, we frequently find *lakṣmī* characterized as either *puṇyā* (sometimes *bhadrā*) or *pāpā*, the classic example of which occurs in a hymn of the AV:

Fly forth from here, O evil sign [*pāpilakṣmī*] ...;
disappear from here; fly forth from yonder....
The unenjoyable flying sign [*lakṣmīḥ patayālūr ajuṣṭā*]
that hath mounted me, as a creeper a tree—that, O Savitar, mayest thou put hence elsewhere than on us....
A hundred and one[ are ]the signs [ *lakṣmyaḥ*] of a mortal...;
the worst of these we send forth
out from here; to us, O Jatavedas [Agni], confirm propitious ones.
These same have I separated...; let the good...
signs stay ; those that are evil have I made disappear.[290]

For all this original ambivalence, however, there is a discernible development within the Vedic texts,[291] so that by the time of Varāhamihira (sixth century C.E.)[292] *lakṣmī* had come to be understood as denoting the purely positive phenomenon of "luck" or "fortune."[293] What the DM thus seems to do is to emphasize the positive features of *lakṣmī*, but to retain some of the original ambivalence by juxtaposing it with the less ancient word *alakṣmī*.[294]

[288]Gonda, *Aspects*, p. 215.

[289]*Loc. cit.*

[290]AV 7.115.1-4, Whitney-Lanman tr.

[291]See Gonda, *Aspects*, pp. 216-217 for the relevant passages.

[292]Banerjea, *Development*, p. 25.

[293]Gonda, *Aspects*, p. 217.

[294]*Alakṣmī* seems to occur for the first time in the Śrī Sūkta (q. v. in Part III) and in the *Nirukta* (6.30), though it does not become common until the *sūtra* literature. (VPK's indication that it occurs in the Paippalāda AV

With regard to Lakṣmī understood as a goddess and not merely as a common noun, it seems clear that, for all their subsequent identification, originally Lakṣmī and Śrī were different divinities, though Gonda's claim[295] that they tended to merge in the Upaniṣads must be refined: Lakṣmī does not appear at all in the early Upaniṣads that we are considering. Surely the Śrī Sūkta, to be considered in Part III, plays a major role in this mergence. Lakṣmī's relationship to male deities, prior to her definitive relationship with Viṣṇu, is somewhat various. In the Śrī Sūkta her primary relationship is with Agni, but at YVMai 31.22 she appears as the co-consort (with Śrī) of Puruṣa (Prajāpati, Brahmā), a relationship she maintains at TA 3.13.2 where, however, her co-consort is Hrī. In the Mbh she appears in a number of roles, including that of daughter of Dakṣa and wife of Dharma (1.60.13), daughter of Brahmā and sister of Dhātṛ and Vidhātṛ (1.60.50), consort of Nārāyaṇa (1.191.6), co-consort (with Śacī and Śrī) of Indra (2.7.5),[296] attendant of Skanda (3.218.48), and even Skanda's wife Devasenā herself (3. 218.47). It would appear, then, that in spite of its eventual significance,[297] the relationship between Śrī-Lakṣmī and Viṣṇu is not, in fact, very ancient, a judgment with which Gonda concurs.[298] We may conclude our treatment of this epithet, however, by noting that at least one passage in the *sūtra* literature anticipates subsequent developments. VDS 99 consists entirely of an exchange between the goddess of the earth, one of the chief interlocutors of that text, and Lakṣmī, a name that is here used interchangeably with Śrī. Śrī-Lakṣmī is here described as "stroking the feet of Viṣṇu... shining with the splendour of her austerities,... [with a] face... radiant like melted gold,"[299] and is hymned briefly (99.2-6). She goes on to identify at some length (99.7-22) her various

is not supported by that text itself.) The more recent provenience and development of *alakṣmī* can, of course, be seen as a counter-balance to the growing auspicious denotation of *lakṣmī*.

[295]Gonda, *Aspects*, p. 214.

[296]Gonda is particularly fascinated by her relations with Indra, *ibid.*, pp. 223-225 : see *infra*, s. v. "*śrī*".

[297]*Ibid.*, pp. 229, 229n.

[298]*Ibid.*, p. 230.

[299]VDS 99.1, Jolly tr.

abodes in the cosmos, most of which are in auspicious mundane phenomena, and then concludes by declaring : "I do not remain separated from Puruṣottama for a single moment."[300]

*varadā*

The occasions on which the Goddess is known as *varadā* are when she is hymned as "the gracious giver of boons to men, for the sake of (their) release (*mukti*)" (81.43), as "she who grants boons to the three worlds" (84.21), when the gods request her to be a "boon-grantress" (91.33), and when she consents (91.34). Although this unpersonified characterization is variously applied in masculine form throughout the Mbh,[301] the feminine is of only isolated antecedent usage. The target of its predication in a one-verse hymn at AV 19.71 is not clear, but is suggested by the commentary to be either the Veda that one has studied, or the Gāyatrī *mantra*.[302] The latter hypothesis is supported by its occurrence at TA 10.26, while at the conclusion of VDS, *varadā* is applied to Lakṣmī in the earth goddess's description of her (99.6).

*buddhi*

The four occurrences of *buddhi*, "intelligence," in our text are all in hymns, so its signification is not discursively developed. Nonetheless, the fact of hymnic location implies its application to the supreme form of the Goddess, and it does receive some specific characterization: as "bearing the marks of understanding (*bodhalakṣaṇā*)" (81.60), and as "abiding in the hearts of the wise (*kṛtadhiyāṃ*)" (84.4). Even this latter limitation is removed, however, when it is declared that the Goddess abides in the form of intelligence (*buddhirūpeṇa*) in all beings (85.14; 91.7).

The word *buddhi* is not attested at all in the earliest stratum of Sanskrit, first appearing in the early Vedāṅgas. There it occurs in Yāska's etymological analysis of *ācārya*, where one

[300]*Ibid.*, 99.23.
[301]Cf. also ŚU 4.11.
[302]Cited in Whitney-Lanman notes.

suggestion is that the *ācārya* is so called "because he systematically develops the intellectual faculty."[303] It is also used at the very end of the BṛDe where it is said that the deities who have been discussed are "to be adored with concentration [*yoga*], assiduity [*dākṣya*], self-control [*dama*], intelligence[ *buddhi*],deep learning [*bāhuśrutya*], austerity [*tapas*], and by injunctions (to others) [*niyogāḥ*]."[304] That *buddhi* is seen as a particular endowment of the sage is evident from its sole occurrence in the Brāhmaṇas : a prayer at *Mantra Brāhmaṇa* (MB) 2.4.14 asks for the suppliant to be endowed with certain qualities, like certain exemplars, and Bṛhaspati is the standard for *buddhi*.[305]

It is in the Upaniṣads that *buddhi* receives its major Vedic elaboration. The most famous occurrence here is probably the KU's parable, in which the *ātman* is compared to the lord of the chariot, the body (*śarīra*) to the chariot itself, the *buddhi* to the charioteer, and the mind (*manas*) to the reins.[306] The text here is clearly employing the terminology of the *Sāṃkhya Kārikā* (SK)[307]—a not uncommon practice in philosophical discourse[308] —wherein *buddhi* is the first product of the evolution of *prakṛti*. But the KU transforms that dualistic terminology and, with it, the notion of *buddhi*, for in the inductive "upward" flow from the sense world, *buddhi* is understood as the penultimate reality, transcended only by the *ātman* (1.3.10). Even more dramatic is the ensuing suggestion that *buddhi* is the instrument for "seeing" the *ātman*:

[303]*Nirukta* 1.4, Sarup tr. The Sanskrit reads *ācinoti buddhim iti vā*.

[304]BṛDe 8.130, Macdonell tr.

[305]*Das Mantrabrāhmaṇa*, I Prapāṭhaka, Inaugural Dissertation zur Erlangung der Doktorwürde (Halle-Wittenberg) vorgelegt von Heinrich Stönner, s. n. (Halle, 1901); II Prapāṭhaka (Kiel), vorgelegt von Hans Jörgensen, C. P. Wintersche Buchdruckerei (Darmstadt, 1911).

[306]KU 1.3.3.

[307]Cf. *The Sāṃkhya Kārikā* in *A Source Book in Indian Philosophy*, Sarvepalli Radhakrishnan and Charles A. Moore (edd.), Princeton University Press (Princeton, 1970), pp. 426-445.

[308]In light of the pervasiveness of Sāṃkhya language throughout the Gītā, to say nothing of later Vedāntic thought, even to make such a statement may seem unnecessary, to document it, fatuous. We do the former simply because other Vedic instances of *buddhi* (PU 4.8; MaiU 6.30) have a Sāṃkhya resonance to them.

The *ātman*, hidden in all creatures, does not shine forth.
But it is seen by subtle seers with (their) pre-eminent,
subtle *buddhi* (1.3.12).

It is this notion of *buddhi* as having the potential to be a "divine eye"[309] that also underlies the ŚU's use of the word. On three occasions the prayer is offered to Rudra, "May he endow us with luminous intellect."[310] It is also clear, however, that for the ŚU *buddhi* itself is intrinsic to the individual, not a divine gift. More precisely, one might say that when one speaks of the lower (*apara*) *ātman*, it will necessarily be endowed with *buddhi*,[311] which is therefore universal. In this regard, the ŚU approximates the DM's conceptualization: *buddhi* is woven into the ontology of every individual, but is more developed in some than in others.

Mention of a specific goddess by the name of Buddhi is rare, for we have encountered only two such instances in the literature surveyed: at VaiGS 5.3 there is a *svāhā* for her and for a host of other deities including other personifications of Sāṃkhya categories (Ahaṃkāra, the *indriyas*), in conjunction with the sacrifice offered at the funeral pyre ; and she is cited at Mbh 1.60.14 as one of the ten daughters of Dakṣa who are wives of Dharma.[312]

### *lajjā*

On four occasions, the quasi-personification Lajjā, "modesty, bashfulness" is applied to the Goddess, once in each of the DM's four hymns.[313] Though one of these hymns (85.7ff) seems to universalize the presence of the Goddess in the form of Lajjā (*lajjārūpeṇa*) through its refrain *yā devī sarvabhūteṣu*, a

[309]Cp. Gītā 11.8.

[310]ŚU 3.4; 4.1; 4.12. The phrasing is uniform in all three instances: *sa no buddhyā śubhayā saṃyunaktu.*

[311]See ŚU 5.8cd: *buddher guṇenātmaguṇena caiva ārāgramātro hy aparo 'pi dṛṣṭaḥ.*

[312]Sørensen gives other instances of a goddess Buddhi, but they are inconsequential: at 12.45.18, Kṛṣṇa is said to have relied on *tāṃ devīṃ buddhiṃ*, of whom no further mention is made; at 12.291.17 and 12.301.13, the usage is simply a formalization for the Sāṃkhya category.

[313]81.60; 84.4; 85.22; 91.20.

more helpful characterization of Lajjā, the only one offered by our text, occurs at 84.4: the Goddess is there called "the modesty of (or, in the heart of) one of good birth (*kulajana-prabhava*)." She is, then, somewhat interpretatively, "graceful reticence."

*Lajjā* is a relatively young word in Sanskrit, for it has no occurrences in the Vedic literature we are examining. The Mbh knows her only as another of Dakṣa's ten daughters who are wives of Dharma (1.60.14). With this, a late passage in the HV concurs, while another late passage includes her in a list of personified feminine nouns associated with Śrī.[314]

*parameśvarī*

While each of the elements in this compound has been analyzed above and should therefore be consulted regarding its resonance, for the sake of completeness we may mention the four occasions, on which they are combined to call the Goddess *parameśvarī*. None of the usages is particularly pregnant, and *parameśvarī*, "the supreme queen," seems to be a straightforward characterization of the supreme form of the Goddess: in a hymn (81.62), slaying Mahiṣa's hordes (83.18), in combat with Śumbha (90.9), and in whom Suratha and Samādhi are advised to take refuge (93.3).

Though the masculine form of this compound is previously attested in conjunction with various male deities, neither the Vedic material examined nor the epic literature knows the feminine.

*svadhā-svāhā*

As we turn now to epithets of three occurrences in the DM, we would do well to recall that, among epithets with the same number of occurrences, priority in our order of treatment goes to those with the greatest resonance in the pre-DM Sanskritic tradition. While other epithets of three occurrences may be more important philosophically (e.g., *prakṛti*) or mythologically

[314]Appendix I 42, line 350 and Appendix I 42B, line 2457, respectively.

(e.g., *yoganidrā*), *svadhā* takes historical precedence. This is particularly the case when it is considered in conjunction with the similar epithet *svāhā*, which occurs twice in the DM, paired both times with *svadhā*,[315] for between them the two words appear well over five hundred times in the Vedic literature. Though both words are primarily simple ritual exclamations, their importance as bearers of the Sanskritic tradition is surely not lost upon our text, for the first line of the first hymn in the DM begins, "You are *svāhā*, you are *svadhā* . . ." (81.54). Aside from this, the only internal evidence bearing on our text's understanding of these epithets occurs at 84.7:

> Whose complete divinity, by means of utterance, attains satisfaction at all sacrifices, O Goddess,
> You are *svāhā*, and, (as) the cause of satisfaction among the *manes*, you are proclaimed by men to be *svadhā*.

The PW distinguishes two separate words, both *svadhā*. One is not attested beyond the Vedic literature and means "one's own particular nature or inclination." The flavor of this sense is conveyed well in a hymn to Uṣas: "Uṣas, sei nach eigenem Ermessen [*svadhā*] gnädig!"[316] A secondary meaning of this first *svadhā*, "a customary pleasure or enjoyment,"[317] spills over quite naturally into the more specific second *svadhā*, where it means "the refreshment that nourishes the manes" Originally this seems to have meant a physical offering, as at AV 18.4.39: "These waters, rich in honey, satisfying (*abhi tṛp*) son [and] grandson, yielding to the Fathers *svadhā* and *amṛta* – let the heavenly waters gratify both sides."[318] Increasingly, however, *svadhā* comes to be a mere ritual exclamation, uttered in lieu of (perhaps sometimes along with) the material offering. Among the almost innumerable instances, we may cite YVT 6.3.2.5: " '*svadhā* to the Pitṛs,' he says, for the *svadhā* call is the

[315]*Svadhā* and *svāhā* both occur at 81.54 and 84.7, *svadhā* alone (in a hymn) at 91.20.

[316]RV 4.52.6, Geldner tr.

[317]E.g., "Nach seinem Belieben [*svadhā*] strömten die Gewässer": RV 1.33.11, Geldner tr. Cf. also AV 18.2.52; 19.49.2, etc.

[318]Whitney-Lanman tr. and punctuation. The antiquity of the manes-*svadhā* relationship is indicated by its presence in the BṛDe (8.112).

due of the Pitṛs."[319] It is in this sense that *svadhā* is used throughout the epic. Though the phrase is occasionally identified with various deities—only Śrī,[320] and Kṛṣṇa[321] in the constituted text—and is once cited as the mother of certain *pitṛs*,[322] *svadhā* by and large seems to have resisted personification.[323]

The phrase *svāhā* has had a less specific liturgical association than *svadhā*, for it appears from RV times onward as a simple benediction—"hail ! praise be ! welcome !"—offered to the full range of divine figures. However, from early times *svāhā* has been associated with Agni, for the BṛDe (8.111) proclaims that "the call 'Svāhā' has Agni as its deity." Elsewhere (3.29-30) that text acknowledges the diversity of opinion as to the identity of the *svāhākṛtis*, but then proposes that what is meant by the term is simply a form of Agni: "while there are many *svāhās*, there is only one maker of them, that is Agni, the source of all beings."[324] While *svāha* shares with *svadhā* the capacity to be identified with different deities—Śrī,[325] Kṛṣṇa,[326] Sarasvatī[327]—in the epic, the Mbh testimony is primarily important for its account of Svāhā, personified as the consort of Agni. We have elsewhere encountered the Mbh episode in which Svāhā looms large, viz., in our accounts of *śakti* and of the Seven Little Mothers, and this convergence of themes is surely not insignificant. That episode is the account of Skanda's birth. Supplementing our remarks made elsewhere,[328] we may

[319]Keith tr.

[320]Mbh 12.221.22.

[321]Mbh 6.31.16 (this is the Gītā); 12.43.15.

[322]HV 13.61.

[323]The closest thing to an exception to this statement occurs in a late addition to the HV (Appendix I 42B line 2243), where Agni is called *svadhādhipaḥ*, which may well be a generalization from his relationship to Svāhā, q. v. below. By way of contrast with *svāhā*, cf. the two hymns to the latter cited *supra*, n. 224.

[324]This is Macdonell's gloss on 3.30. While the relation of the one and the many is a (the?) pervasive issue in Indian religiousness, the parallel between Agni's integration of many *svāhās* and the Goddess's integration of many goddesses is striking.

[325]Mbh 12.221.22.

[326]Mbh 12.43.15.

[327]Mbh 9.41.31.

[328]In Appendix A.

note that if anyone in that account can be said to be Skanda's "natural" mother, it is Svāhā, and then summarize her role as follows.[329] When Svāhā, the daughter of Dakṣa,[330] heard that Agni was setting out for the forest and was heartsick for the wives of the seven sages, she saw the opportunity to consummate her long unrequited love for him. Assuming the guise of one of the seers' wives, she had intercourse with Agni, and subsequently deposited his seed in a golden basin on Mount Śveta, a process which she repeated five times in the guise of other wives. That seed became Skanda. After[331] the appearance of various other candidates for the motherhood of Skanda, and their satisfaction in various ways by him, Svāhā made her own request, that she be able to dwell forever with Agni. Skanda then ordained that whatever offerings were subsequently made into the fire should always be accompanied by the exclamation "*svāhā*!" Gratified, Svāhā then withdraws from the epic account, except for an occasional subsequent passing remark.[332]

While the DM clearly does not emphasize the Agni-Svāhā relationship, that it is in the background can scarcely be doubted since we have seen the Goddess's identity intertwine with Agni under several other rubrics (Kālī, Durgā, the Seven Little Mothers), and since standard iconographic canons prescribe that the portrayal of Agni show him in Svāhā's company.[333]

### *Śrī*

Two of the three instances of *śrī* in the DM, all of which are in hymns, employ the word as virtually synonymous with *lakṣmī*.

[329]The following three sentences are a précis of Mbh 3.213.42-3.214.18.

[330]Svāhā is so identified at 3.213.50. She does not appear in the earlier (1.60.14) list of Dakṣa's daughters who were wives of Dharma, where we have met Buddhi, Lakṣmī, and Lajjā, though it is apparent (1.60.10) that Dakṣa had other daughters as well.

[331]This and the following sentence are a précis of Mbh 3.220.1-6.

[332]In addition to the scattered references in the Mbh, we may note that, in the HV, Svāhā appears as Agni's spouse only in the Appendices: I 29A, line 34; I 42B, line 2244.

[333]See Banerjea, *Development*, p. 524, Sahai, *op. cit.*, p. 28, both quoting the *ViṣṇudharmottaraP*.

On one occasion, it appears in a sequence of feminine nouns (81.60), and on another (84.4) it is juxtaposed with *alakṣmī*: "She who is *śrī* in the abodes of those who do good, (who is) *alakṣmī* (in the abodes) of those of wicked soul... (is the one we bow down to)." Here, as with *lakṣmī*, no more than common nominal force seems intended. Yet the third instance is a clear personification, for of the Goddess it is said : "(You are) Śrī, whose sole abode is in the heart of Kaiṭabha's enemy,"[334] i.e., of Viṣṇu.

Unlike *lakṣmī*, *śrī* is widely attested in the earliest strata of Sanskrit literature, for it occurs on literally hundreds of occasions throughout the Vedas and Brāhmaṇas. To survey these in a brief account is clearly impossible. We are fortunate, however, in that Gonda has examined the word, with his usual thorough documentation, in almost precisely the same way that we have been examining the DM's epithets, beginning with a survey of its common usage, then examining its history as a personification.[335] We may therefore depart from our usual practice of relying directly on the textual material and, instead, make use of Gonda's comprehensive discussion.

The central meaning of the word is not, as some translators would have it, "radiance, splendour, beauty," but "riches, prosperity, welfare, abundance, fortune," as is evident from its frequent citation as the benefit of sacrificers.[336] At one level, this means that *śrī* is often identified with the natural powers of growth and increase, such as food, earth, rain, a fertile woman, or even a complete lifetime.[337] But at another level, the identification is with the social pre-eminence that is a function of being prosperous, of being possessed of *śrī*, so that it is often correlated with *kṣatra*, "ruling power, dominion," with the royal throne, with *yaśas*, "honour, glory, dignity," and, through the related adjectives *śreyas* and *śreṣṭha* with superiority in general.[338] In both cases, *śrī* is understood as "a power substance" which may, to be sure, have external manifestations that are

[334]84.10c: *śrīḥ kaiṭabhārihṛdayaikakṛtādhivāsā*.

[335]Gonda, *Aspects*, pp. 176-212 and 212-225, respectively. A brief section on "Viṣṇu's Female Partners" follows, pp. 226-231.

[336]*Ibid.*, pp. 176-177.

[337]*Ibid.*, pp. 184, 185, 208-209, 183.

[338]*Ibid.*, pp. 188-189, 185-186, 196-204.

prone to magical manipulation: the word itself, however, includes both concrete and abstract dimensions, which are not formally distinguished.[339] In this regard, there is a certain affinity with *lakṣmī-lakṣman*, as discussed above, but it is interesting to note that *śrī* lacks the early ambivalence of *lakṣmī*. Its character is intrinsic, obviating adjectival specification: thus *śrī* is very frequently opposed to *pāpman*, "evil, misfortune, unhappiness, misery, wickedness, the state of being affected by sin," and the privative adjective *aśrira* is known from Vedic times in the sense of "shrunken, lean, weak, emaciated."[340]

In his discussion of Śrī as a goddess, Gonda generally affirms the judgment of Hartmann that "Śrī, who as a distinct female divinity does not appear before the Vājasaneyi Saṃhitā, is a pre-Aryan goddess of fertility and other phenomena relative to it (Fruchtbarkeit, Fülle, Glück), whose symbol is the lotus, the plant growing in mud and slime, and whose cult, mythology and iconography show a variety of traits characteristic of deities concerned with fertility and prosperity in general."[341] Much of Gonda's analysis is an exegesis of the Śrī Sūkta, which we shall present in Part III, and Śrī's particular relationships are virtually identical with those of Lakṣmī, presented above. We may supplement this material with three further comments. (1) Prior to her relationship with Viṣṇu, which "is not reached before the younger parts of the Mahābhārata," Śrī is commonly associated with Kubera, "the god of wealth and material happiness, the lord over all treasures, who was held to be immanent in a king..., and doubtless represents a fecundating divinity, a promoter of productivity."[342] (2) She also seems related to Indra, for it is in her company that he pours bounty upon the world, and there is the curious story of her being lost by Indra and giving herself to Viṣṇu, on which Gonda ruminates : "Would it be too rash to consider this narrative a reminiscence

[339] *Ibid.*, pp. 178-180. Cf. Gonda's more general remarks on Indian semantics, discussed in our Prolegomenon, section 5.

[340] *Ibid.*, pp. 186-187, 202, 182-183.

[341] *Ibid.*, p. 213. These are Gonda's words, presenting the position of Hartmann, Gerda, *Beiträge zur Geschichte der Göttin Lakṣmī*, Thesis Kiel, 1933, pp. 6ff.

[342] *Ibid.*, pp. 223, 195.

of a former association between Śrī-Lakṣmī and Indra, which was broken off in favour of Viṣṇu when he came to be, in many respects, Indra's successor ?"[343] (3) Finally, attention may be drawn to a passage in the ŚB which begins :

> Prajāpati was becoming heated (by fervid devotion), whilst creating living beings. From him, worn out and heated, Śrī ...came forth. She stood there resplendent, shining and trembling. The gods, beholding her thus resplendent, shining and trembling, set their minds upon her. They said to Prajāpati, "Let us kill her and take (all) this from her." He said, "Surely, that Śrī is a woman, and people do not kill woman, but rather take (anything) from her (leaving her) alive."[344]

The gods then proceed to take from her food, royal power, universal sovereignty, noble rank, power, holy lustre, dominion, wealth, prosperity, and beautiful forms, which are returned to her only after she sacrifices to the various gods. On this, Gonda remarks : "This passage must no doubt be understood to mean that power, kingship, prosperity, etc., are Śrī's spheres, the phenomena in which, and through which, her presence and activity manifest themselves, and to make it clear that she is only able to perform her functions through the mighty influence and the cooperation of Prajāpati and the ten gods...."[345] Such an image may well be operative in the DM's account of the Goddess's earthly form crystallizing out of the *tejas* of the different gods (82.8-18). But the DM goes much further: from this initial portrayal of her as implicitly dependent on the gods, it proceeds to establish not only her own autonomy and independence, but also the *de facto* dependence of the gods on her.

### *Śraddhā*

Although the DM applies the word *śraddhā*, "faith," to the Goddess on three occasions,[346] it does not make much of an

[343] *Ibid.*, p. 224. That the Śrī-Viṣṇu relationship was well-known by the time of our text is suggested by the VDS passage cited *supra*, s. v. "*lakṣmī*"; cf. also ViṣṇuP 1.8.15ff.
[344] ŚB 11.4.3.1-2, Eggeling tr.
[345] Gonda, *Aspects*, p. 223.
[346] 84.4; 85.24; 91.20.

effort to distinguish it from other nouns that are grammatically feminine, in a hymnic sequence of which it always appears. The only distinguishing characteristics of *śraddhā*, according to our text, are that it is in the form of *śraddhā* (*śraddhārūpeṇa*) that the Goddess abides in all creatures (85.24),[347] and that she is the "*śraddhā* of (or, in the hearts of those who are) the good (or true: *satām* ; 84.4)."

Of the various epithets used in the DM, it would appear that there are few that are as conceptually important to an understanding of Indian religiousness as a whole as *śraddhā*. At one end of the historical spectrum is its frequent attestation in the Vedic literature and, at the other, is its emergence as a critical term in recent scholarly efforts to understand the dynamics of Hindu and Buddhist religiousness. Here, more than anywhere else in the relatively brief epithetical discussions that comprise Part I of our study, it is simply impossible to convey the full resonance of the word *śraddhā,* or the significance of calling the Goddess Śraddhā. In an effort to strike a balance between the considerable significance of the word in the larger context, and the rather modest role that it plays in the DM itself, we shall take the following course: we provide hereunder in our notes an introductory bibliography for the study of *śraddhā* in the Indian tradition,[348] and now proceed to make a few selected

[347]While this is a powerful statement, on which we shall comment below, its impact is somewhat muted by the fact that the refrain of the hymn in which it occurs universalizes the Goddess's presence in twenty other forms (*-rūpeṇa*) as well.

[348]In chronological order, we may cite the following, all of which provide still further references: (1) Oldenberg, H., *Die Religion des Veda,* J.G. Cotta (Stuttgart, 1917), pp. 566ff. and notes; (2) Oldenberg, H., "Vedische Untersuchungen 4," ZDMG 50, pp. 448-450; (3) Das Gupta, Mrinal, "Śraddhā and Bhakti in Vedic Literature," IHQ 6 (1930), pp. 315-333 and 487-513; (4) Hacker, Paul, "Über den Glauben in der Religions-philosophie des Hinduismus," *Zeitschrift für Missionswissenschaft und Religionswissenschaft* 38 (1954), pp. 51-66; (5) Hacker, Paul, "*śraddhā*," *Wiener Zeitschrift für die Kunde Süd- und Ostasiens und Archiv für Indische Philosophie* 7 (1963), pp. 151-189; (6) Hara, Minoru, "Note on Two Sanskrit Terms : Bhakti and Śraddhā," *Indo-Iranian Journal* Vol. 7 2/3 (1964), pp. 124-145; (7) Rao, K. L., Seshagiri, *The Concept of Śraddhā* (*in the Brāhmaṇas, the Upaniṣads and the Gītā*), Ph.D. dissertation, Harvard University, 1966; (8) Smith, Wilfred Cantwell, *Faith and Belief,* Princeton University Press (Princeton, 1979), chap. 4, esp. pp. 59-68.

remarks about *śraddhā* in relation to our text without claiming comprehensiveness for them.

First, we may note that while *śraddhā* appears in a half dozen hymns of the RV, it is the explicit subject of one entire hymn. Since it is the watershed from which later developments flow, it is worth quoting in its entirety.

> 1. Mit Glauben [*śraddhā*] wird das Feuer angezündet, mit Glauben wird die Spende geopfert. Auf dem Gipfel des Glücks lege ich mit meiner Rede Zeugnis ab von dem Glauben.
> 2. O Glaube! Mache diese meine Rede dem Schenkenden lieb, O Glaube, dem zu schenken Gewillten lieb, den gastfreien Opfernden lieb!
> 3. Wie die Götter bei den mächtigen Asura's sich Glauben verschafft haben, so mache diese unsere Rede bei den freigebigen Opferern (vertrauenswürdig)!
> 4. Den Glauben ehren die opfernden Götter unter Vāyu's Hut, den Glauben mit herzlichem Vorsatz; durch den Glauben gewinnt man Gut.
> 5. Den Glauben rufen wir morgens an, den Glauben um Mittag, den Glauben, wann die Sonne untergeht. O Glaube, mach, dass man uns hier Glauben (Vertrauen) schenke.[349]

The seeds of personification sown in this imprecation are subsequently nourished in a variety of ways. The BṛDe knows Śraddhā as a terrestrial deity connected with Agni, as a terrestrial form of Vāc, and as a female seer.[350] The Brāhmaṇas know her variously as daughter of Sūrya[351] or Prajāpati,[352] eldest daughter of Ṛta,[353] and the early rising queen (*rājñī*) of the gods.[354] The diversity of such characterization makes vivid

[349]RV 10.151, Geldner tr. As Geldner remarks, the Asuras of v. 3 are certainly opponents of the *devas* but not simply demons. On 5d, the text of which is *śraddhe śraddhāpayeha naḥ*, he notes "nämlich bei den Opferherren."

[350]BṛDe 1.112; 2.74; 2.84.

[351]ŚB 12.7.3.11.

[352]TB 2.3.10.1.

[353]TB 3.12.3.2.

[354]*Jaiminīya Brāhmaṇa* (JB) 168: *Jaiminīya Brāhmaṇa*, W. Caland (ed. and tr.), Johannes Müller (Amsterdam, 1919) Verhandlingen der Koninklijke Akademie van Wetenschappen te Amsterdam, Afd. Letterkunde Deel I—Nieuwe Reeks, Deel XIX No. 4.

what may already be obvious: that, unlike some other epithets, *śraddhā's* significance does not lie in its being the name of a goddess. Even the Mbh knows *śraddhā* as a name on only two occasions, neither of major significance: as another daughter of Dakṣa and wife of Dharma, and as daughter of Vivasvat.[355]

It is, rather, as a concept, "faith," or as a process, "the putting of one's heart," that *śraddhā* is of such enormous significance. While there are various ways of conceptualizing human religiousness, "faith" surely looms as a critical feature of that phenomenon. But let us be more specific. Paul Hacker has surveyed many of the occurrences of *śraddhā* and we may excerpt his summary as follows :

> In philosophical and religious contexts, two sorts of *śraddhā* can be distinguished: intellectual *śraddhā* and ritual *śraddhā*. Intellectual *śraddhā*—faith, belief, reliance on the teacher's teaching—is a prerequisite to *jñāna*, but it occurs in the practices of *karman*, *bhakti*, and *yoga* also. In the hymns of the Ṛgveda, (ritual) *śraddhā* means trust in a god who, it is hoped, will fulfil one's desires. . . . This *śraddhā* is, as it were, the vehicle that carries the desire to the deity to whom sacrifices are offered and on whom one relies for the fulfilment of one's desire. In the epoch of the Brāhmaṇas, personal religion disappears and, as a consequence of this change, the object of *śraddhā* is no longer a god but either the officiating *ṛtvik* or the rite performed. *Śraddhā* becomes the firm belief that the rite will bring about the fulfilment of one's desire. Performance of rites without *śraddhā* is invalid; *śraddhā* is the particularly religious element in all religious actions.[356]

While Hacker's study also examines other nuances in the dynamics of *śraddhā*, we may focus on this instrumental, ritual role of *śraddhā*, for it converges rather strikingly with the conclusion arrived at by Minoru Hara. Hara's effort to illuminate the relationship between *śraddhā* and *bhakti* through a philological examination of their respective contexts suggests that

[355] Mbh 1.60.13 and 12.256.7, respectively. The latter instance, however, does introduce a rather lovely rapsody on the nature of faith.

[356] Hacker, "*śraddhā*," p. 188.

> though both *śraddhā* and *bhakti* are "Glauben," the one concerns an objective element of religion, the efficacy of sacrifice; the other concerns the personal and human element of theistic religion. Furthermore, from an Indological point of view, the one is particularly a vedic and brahmanical concept, whereas the other is rather Hinduistic, though we do not go so far as to say non-vedic or non-brahmanic.[357]

Since we have seen that one of the DM's major tasks, perhaps the primary one, is to portray the Goddess's role in the "orthodox" Sanskritic tradition, to call her *śraddhā* is to place her in the very center of that tradition: it is she who makes effective the whole ritual structure, without whom that structure would be hollow.

But we may go even further. Having established the contrast between *śraddhā* and *bhakti*, Hara goes on to inquire into how the two might be related. He finds the semantic evidence to be highly suggestive: "from such evidence I think one may conclude that there does exist a connecting link between the two concepts *śraddhā* and *bhakti*, the former being the fundamental principle ["the innate nature of a human being"[358]], and the latter being a developed mode of it, although the connotations of the two are in sharp contrast."[359] Precisely this kind of conclusion is suggested by the DM as well, for while it does seem to affirm Hacker's correlation of *śraddhā* and *satya*,[360] it also affirms that *śraddhā* is a universal phenomenon:

> Praise to the Goddess who abides in all creatures in the form of faith (*śraddhārūpeṇa*).
> Praise to her! Praise to her! Praise to her! Hail! Hail! (85.24)

Although the Goddess is praised in other forms (*rūpa*) in this hymn, there is a logic in calling her *śraddhā* with regard to human faith that is similar to the logic in calling her *śakti* with

[357]Hara, "Bhakti and Śraddhā," p. 139. For his separate conclusions on the semantics of *bhakti* and *śraddhā*, see pp. 132 and 142, respectively.

[358]*Ibid.*, p. 143.

[359]*Ibid.*, p. 145.

[360]Hacker, "*śraddhā*," pp. 170-171, 189; cp. MarkP 84.4.

regard to divine forms. Just as she is Śakti, which is the bedrock for all of the myriad divine manifestations of power, so is she Śraddhā, the bedrock for all human commitments of faith, which may be brought to fruition in diverse ways, in *bhakti*. It is of a piece with Hara's findings that the DM does *not* say that the Goddess is, or has the form of, *bhakti*. Rather, *bhakti* is what suffuses the actions of those who are actively engaged in the expression of their faith, particularly in a cultic context.[361] What our text seems to affirm, then, is that the Goddess as *śraddhā* is an ontological (more precisely, anthropological) fact : she is the movement of the heart, as a universal phenomenon. To the extent that the direction of movement is toward the Goddess herself, she may be said to elicit *bhakti* in the hearts of her devotees. Since movement may occur in other directions, there may, of course, be *bhaktas* of other deities. Nonetheless, inasmuch as the Goddess herself is *śraddhā*, she is *ipso facto* the starting-point of all faith, the prerequisite for all such movements.

### *kalyāṇī*

When our text thrice applies the word *kalyāṇī* to the supreme form of the Goddess,[362] it seems to understand it as "auspicious" when it appears in the gods' solicitation of her (85.9). On other occasions, it might be translated as "beautiful, lovely," for it is used in Caṇḍa and Muṇḍa's description of her to Śumbha (85.53), and when the Goddess gives Kālī her name of Cāmuṇḍā, the former is described as *kalyāṇī*, as if to emphasize the contrast between their respective appearances.

The earlier use of *kalyāṇī* shows a semantic association with symbols or times of fertility, such as herbs,[363] the cow,[364] or a

[361]The DM uses the word *bhakti* on nine occasions, on all of which it is applied to those engaged in the active demonstration of their faith. Thus it characterizes the gods' and *ṛṣis'* praising of the Goddess (82.34; 84.2; 85.36), their perfuming of her (84.28; Vid has an unintelligible misprint here; read *bhaktyā* with Jag and Veṅk), and the desired mode of listening to the recitation of the DM (92.3, 6); it also is what fills the devotee (91.31; 93.16) at the autumnal festival (92.11).

[362]85.9,53; 87.24.

[363]AV 6.139.3; JB 140.

[364]YVT 7.1.6.6; AV 5.17.18; AiB 5.25.

productive year.[365] On a number of occasions, *kalyāṇī* modifies a word for a verbal or mental process, such as the report (*kīrti*) given on a successful sacrifice,[366] the words (*vāc*) of consolation at a funeral,[367] or the favorable opinion (*mati*) that one seeks in the eyes of the gods.[368] The most common usage, however, is when it is applied to a woman. Thus Indra's spouse is said to be *kalyāṇī*,[369] the dalliance of a youth with maidens who are *kalyāṇī* is twice used in simile,[370] and throughout the literature one of the valued standards of a woman is that she be *kalyāṇī*.[371] On at least two occasions, rather interesting stories become associated with the word. In the BṛDe's account of Saramā and the Paṇis, she is accosted by those demons, who call her *kalyāṇī* (8.26). Also, a parable in the ŚB employs a vivid image of "two women, one beautiful [*kalyāṇī*], one over-beautiful [*atikalyāṇī*]: between them stood a man, black, with yellow eyes, and a staff in his hand,"[372] who are explained in the sequel (11.6.1.12-13) to be faith (*śraddhā*), absence-of-faith (*aśraddhā*) and wrath (*krodha*), all of which are subdued through knowledgeable performance of the Agnihotra. The literature also knows one instance where *kalyāṇī* is a quasi-personification of "auspicious beauty" (AV 6. 107.3-4), and on one occasion, in the proto-Upaniṣadic speculation of the AV, it is cryptically declared of the ultimate:

> This beautiful one (f.)[is]unaging, an immortal in the house of a mortal; for whom she [was] made, he lies; he who made [her] grew old.
>
> Thou art woman, thou [art] man, thou boy, or also girl;

[365]AiB 4.25.

[366]YVT 7.4.8.3.

[367]*Jaiminīya Gṛhya Sūtra* (JGS) 2.5.10; *Jaiminigṛhyasūtra*, W. Caland (ed. and tr.), Motilal Banarsidass (Lahore, 1922), The Punjab Sanskrit Series No. II.

[368]*Nirukta* 2.11; 7.22; 11.11, 19; 12.39.

[369]RV 3.53.6.

[370]RV 4.58.8; 10.30.5: for the ghee streams' flirtation with Agni, and Soma's with the waters, respectively.

[371]E.g., AV 5.17.12; JB 186, 205.

[372]ŚB 11.6.1.7, Eggeling tr. On *atikalyāṇī*, Eggeling notes that Sāyaṇa takes it as *aśobhanā* and suggests its real meaning may be " 'one of past beauty,' [i.e.] one whose beauty has faded."

thou, when aged, totterest (*vañc*) with a staff ; thou, when born, becomest facing all ways.[373]

The only specificity that the Mbh adds is at 9.45.7 where Kalyāṇī is one of several hundred *mātṛs* in the wake of Skanda.

*iśā*

It is not surprising to find the Goddess called *iśā*, "the queen, the powerful one, she who rules," or more impersonally, "supremacy," and the three occasions[374] on which the Goddess is hymned as such seem straightforward enough: the gods reverence her as *iśā* (85.36), she is the restrained (*niyatā*) ruler (91.21), and she is queen of all (*sarveśā*). There may, however, be a Śaiva undertone to the word, for on the occasions when our text uses the masculine *iśā* or *iśāna*, the reference is clearly to Śiva.[375]

*Īśā* appears only sporadically in the earlier literature and when it does, it is usually as an abstract feminine noun, "capacity, dominion, lordship."[376] If there is a particular association to the word, it is with hostile or threatening forces over whom one seeks, or is grateful for, this mastery or dominion. Thus the serpent-sage Arbuda is reminded of all those who have *iśā* over him (AV 11. 9. 25), Triṣandhi is "tamed" through knowledge of his dominion (AV 11.10.2), and Nirṛti is denied dominion through performance of a certain ritual (ŚB 5.3.1. 13). A perhaps related usage occurs when the Vrātya is said to have "compassed the lordship (*iśā*) of the gods; he became the Lord (*iśāna*)."[377] That the word could connote a female rule and have an auspicious connotation is, however, apparent both from AV 11.8.17, where *iśā*, wife of *vaśa*, brought color (*varṇa*) to the constitution of the human frame, and from its

[373]AB 10.8.26-27, Whitney-Lanman tr. and punctuation; "beautiful one," *kalyāṇī*.

[374]85.36; 91.21, 22 (here read vocative *īśe* with Veṅk and Jag for Vid *īśa*).

[375]See 82.3; 88.12 for *iśā*; 81.65; 88.21, 23 for *īśāna*.

[376]Thus TB 2.6.14.6 and parallels.

[377]AV 15.1.5, Whitney-Lanman tr.

repeated application to Śrī in the *Jaiminīya Upaniṣad Brāhmaṇa*.[378]
The Mbh uses the masculine *īśa* and *īśāna* for various gods, but does not know the feminine as a proper name.

*pārvatī*

To one familiar with the later history of the worship of the Goddess, wherein her identity as Pārvatī, spouse of Śiva, is so pervasive, it will seem strange to find this epithet placed so low in our ordering of the DM's epithets. Yet surely one of the striking features of the DM is the relative dearth of motifs that have subsequently become elaborated as Śaiva, and the presence of motifs that have not received much subsequent elaboration at all.[379] We have alluded to the DM's use of Pārvatī in association with a number of other epithets, and may summarize the evidence as follows. At the outset of the third *carita*, the afflicted deities, recalling (from the second *carita*) the Goddess's promise of succor, proceed to the lord of mountains, Himavān (85.5-6). There they hymn the Goddess, called Viṣṇumāyā in the prologue (85.6) and Pārvatī in the epilogue (85.37, 40, 41). Pārvatī does not know to whom the hymn is addressed, and an auspicious emanation comes forth from her body to remind her, "This hymn is addressed to me" (85.39). The auspicious form, which is called Ambikā, is said to be known as Kauṣikī, by virtue of having arisen from the sheath (*koṣa*) of Pārvatī's body (85. 40), and it is round her that the subsequent action rages.[380] Pārvatī does not make a formal exit, and the text simply ignores her after offering the parting comment :

> When she (Kauṣikī) had come forth, Pārvatī became black (*kṛṣṇā*) ;
> Known as Kālikā ("The Black one"), she makes her abode in the Himālayas (*himācalakṛtāśrayā*).[381]

[378]JUB 2.3.1.5, 7, 9: *The Jaiminīya or Talavakāra Upanishad Brāhmaṇa*, Pandit Rama Deva (ed.), D. A. V. College (Lahore, 1921), Dayanand Anglo-Vedic Sanskrit Series No. 3.

[379]As examples of the latter, we may cite two aspects which the Goddess prophecies for herself: Śākambharī, "bearer of vegetables" (91.44), and Bhrāmarī, "female bee" (91.48).

[380]See *supra* s. v. "*ambikā*," "*gaurī*," and n. 70, also *infra*, s. v. "*kṛṣṇā-tāmasī*," and Part II, n. 125, for further remarks on this passage.

[381]85.41. Since we have already remarked on the DM's distance from later Śaiva developments, we may go on to note in passing the absence

There is, so far as we have been able to ascertain, only one use of *pārvati*, "pertaining to rock or mountains," in the Vedic literature, whose recurrence through the liturgical commentaries accounts for all of its occurrences. It appears in three of the recensions of the YV,[382] and even here its integrity is not secure, for other recensions offer variant readings.[383] All readings agree that the word, or its variant, occurs in a *mantra* at the new or full moon sacrifice, and that it modifies *dhiṣaṇā*. While Pischel takes *dhiṣaṇā* as a goddess of earth,[384] we may follow Keith and Eggeling in taking it as a bowl, so that the *mantra* runs, "Thou art a bowl of rock," which accompanies the placing of one millstone upon another.[385]

That this should be the extent of the Vedic testimony on *pārvati* seems extraordinary, in light of its later history. There is, to be sure, Vedic material, tangential to our epithet proper, that suggests a broader process. For example, Macdonell observes that

> Mountains (*parvata*) are often in the RV conceived as divinely animate. ... They are invoked as manly, firmly fixed, rejoicing in plenty. ... Parvata is even three times lauded with Indra in the dual compound *Indraparvatā*. ... Here Parvata seems to be a mountain god conceived anthropomorphically as a companion of Indra.[386]

Such an association surely figures in the background of the sudden emergence of Umā Haimavatī as the instructor of Indra

---

of any reference to Pārvatī as Himavān's daughter (cf. also 82.28). Apart from this episode, there is a possible play on the word *parvata* at 82.11: when the *tejas* of the different gods becomes integrated into the mass (*kūṭaṃ*) that becomes the Goddess (82.12), it is compared to a flaming mountain (*jvalantaṃ parvatam*).

[382]YVKā 1.6; YVMai 1.1.7; YVKap 1.6 (*Kapiṣṭhalakaṭhasaṃhitā*, Raghu Vira [ed.], Mehar Chand Lachhman Das [Lahore, 1932], Mehar Chand Lachhman Das Sanskrit and Prakrit Series vol. I).

[383]YVT 1.1.6.1 reads *parvatyā*, YVMā 1.19 and YVKāṇ 1.7.2 read *parvatī*. These different readings persist through the respective *brāhmaṇa* portions and Brāhmaṇas.

[384]Cited by Keith in his note on YVT 1.1.6.1.

[385]ŚB 1.2.1.15,17. That there is, nonetheless, a Vedic goddess of abundance called Dhiṣaṇā is clear: see Macdonell, *Vedic Mythology*, p. 124.

[386]Macdonell, *Vedic Mythology*, p. 154.

at KeU 3.12-4.1.[387] As a second example, we may note that a Prajāpati named Dakṣa is said to have performed a sacrifice that was afterwards performed by one Dakṣa Pārvatī, [388] which seems to be a harbinger of the well-known mythological interpenetration of Dakṣa, his sacrifice, Śiva, and Satī (Pārvatī).[389] None of these examples, however, nor all of the material together, is sufficient to dissuade us from the conclusion that the major drama in the development of the name Pārvatī occurs outside of Sanskritic circles.

Even the epic material seems to confirm this judgment, for while it is common knowledge there that Śiva has a consort, the name Pārvatī is employed on only a handful of occasions.[390] All of the instances pair her with Śiva, and the only embellishment is when six females or goddesses are identified as being in Pārvatī's train.[391] Indeed, it is almost as if the Mbh is engaged in sorting out opinions on the identity of Śiva's spouse, for on one occasion it declares: "She who is Mahādevī, consort of Maheśvara, is known as Pārvatī."[392] The Rām is even less explicit,[393] and the HV constituted text does not know Pārvatī at all.[394]

We may conclude by noting that, for all of this dearth of material prior to, and in, our text, there *was* a drama being played out, for not only is the name known to Kālidāsa in his Kumārasaṃbhava, but in Bāṇa's *Caṇḍīśataka*, for which we earlier accepted a seventh-century date,[395] Pārvatī is the

[387]Since Umā does not occur in the DM, we have not investigated it systematically. However, we have not encountered any evidence to controvert the common opinion that this is the first Sanskritic appearance of Umā, or at least of Umā in a guise that is recognizably continuous with later developments.

[388]ŚB 2.4.4.1-2, 6.

[389]See O'Flaherty, *Asceticism and Eroticism, passim,* and pp. 30-32 for a convenient overview.

[390]In addition to the instances cited immediately hereafter, "Pārvatī" occurs at 3.221.1; 7.57.36; 7.172.64; 10.7.45; 13.14.115.

[391]Viz., Gaurī, Vidyā, Gāndhārī, Keśinī, Sumitrā, and Sāvitrī.

[392]14.43.14.

[393]We have located only a passing reference, at 7.4.27.

[394]*Pace* Böhtlingk and Roth: all references given by them are relegated to Appendices. In the constituted text, *pārvatī* is known only in the generic sense: cf. 36.24, 33; 45.48.

[395]*Supra*, n. 16.

favorite epithet for the Goddess, more common even than *devī*.[396]

*prakṛti*

In our above discussions of *mahāmāyā* and *śakti*, we have seen that the DM's use of those epithets is interwoven with its use of *prakṛti*, "primordial matter, nature," so that a full understanding of the latter requires that the former two be borne in mind. With that proviso, we may proceed to examine the three specific instances[397] of *prakṛti* in our text. The first occurs in the first hymn, Brahmā's praise of Mahāmāyā, where it is declared: "You are the *prakṛti* of all, manifesting the triad of constituent strands."[398] The second occurrence is in the second hymn, where *prakṛti* has one of the *vasantatilaka* verses all to itself:

> (You are) the cause of all the worlds; although possessed of the three qualities (*triguṇā*), by faults (or defects, *doṣaiḥ*) you are not known;[399] (you are) unfathomable even by Hari, Hara, and the other gods.
>
> (You are) the resort of all, (you are) this entire world which is composed of parts, for you are the supreme, original, untransformed *prakṛti*.[400]

The final usage (85.7) is a simple, unelaborated hymnic invocation.

As is the case with certain other epithets, a thorough investigation of the history of the word *prakṛti* would constitute a major

[396]Quackenbos, *op. cit.*, p. 258. For a further appraisal of the role of Pārvatī in our text, drawing on mythological material yet to be presented, see Part II, n. 125.

[397]81.59; 84.6; 85.7.

[398]81.59ab: *prakṛtis tvaṃ ca sarvasya guṇatrayavibhāvinī.*

[399]The point seems to be one of theodicy: though as *prakṛti* she may be said to have three qualities, viz., the three constituent strands (*guṇas*) of *prakṛti* (of which, more below), one cannot take *guṇa* in its more generic sense of "quality" and impute negativity (*doṣa*) to her. Alternatively, it may be saying, together with the following clause: "even the gods cannot comprehend you—how much less can (those who are marred) with flaws."

[400]84.6:
*hetuḥ samastajagatāṃ triguṇāpi doṣair na jñāyase hariharādibhir apy apārā/*
*sarvāśrayākhilam idaṃ jagad aṃśabhūtam avyākṛtā hi paramā prakṛtis tvam ādyā//*

study in its own right. Failing that, we may limit our attention to some of the highlights of that history. Initially most striking is the fact that the word is unknown in any of the Vedas. Even in the Brāhmaṇas, it seems to occur in but one passage, and that is in a late Brāhmaṇa.[401] The word does, to be sure, occur in the early Vedāṅgas and in the Sūtra literature, but the second striking fact is that its predominant usage throughout this literature is not philosophical at all, but grammatical. *Prakṛti* is the primary, radical form of a word, and is contrasted with the secondary, derivative *vikṛti* form.[402] Occasionally it simply means "the norm, the usual way."[403] Thus the internal evidence of the Vedic literature itself is enough to suggest that *prakṛti* as a dynamic and provocative philosophical term is not of Vedic provenience.

The external corroboration of this hypothesis stems, of course, from Sāṃkhya sources.[404] While the SK falls outside the purview of our investigation, we may here[405] quote Brown's crisp summary of the critical issues.

> In the classical Sāṃkhya of the SK, *puruṣa* and *prakṛti* are the spiritual (conscious) and material principles of the universe. It is the apparent involvement of *puruṣa* with *prakṛti* that initiates material evolution. There is actually a plurality of *puruṣas*, existing as the individual souls or

[401]GoB 1.1.24, 29; on the "late" dating of this text, see Macdonell, *History*, pp. 203, 217-218.

[402]*Nirukta* 2.2, 28.

[403]E.g., AiA 5.3.1; *Śāṅkhāyana Śrautasūtra* 6.1.2; 14.1.1 (W. Caland [tr.], International Academy of Indian Culture [Nagpur, 1953], Sarasvati-Vihara Series vol. 32).

[404]A helpful way of organizing the historical data here has been suggested to us by Prof. J. B. Carman (personal communication, Feb. 2, 1976; see Proleg., n. 13): rather than understanding the dynamism of Indian culture as involving only two "strands," the Aryan and Dravidian, one may conceptualize it as also involving a third, viz., Sāṃkhya-Yoga. Whether or not such a model has any larger validity, it does make intelligible the history of the word *prakṛti*.

[405]I.e., before turning to texts which do fall within our scope, viz., the Mbh and ŚU. The difficulty of establishing a relative chronology of texts and concepts here may legitimate our starting with the classical formulation, to serve as a foil for the others.

spirits in every body. Liberation is the discrimination of the spirit from *prakṛti*. *Puruṣa*, then, is ultimately distinct from *prakṛti*.[406]

To this we need add only (1) that in the SK *prakṛti*, composed of the three constituent elements (*guṇas*),[407] is seen as evolving into the totality of the material universe, including various mental processes;[408] and (2) that Sāṃkhya wants to maintain the philosophically difficult position of imputing a teleological function to the evolutionary process, viz., the liberation of *puruṣas*, while at the same time denying both that *prakṛti* is sentient and that *prakṛti* and *puruṣa* actually become involved with one another.[409]

With this background, we may return to our usual focus. In the later Upaniṣads that we are considering, *prakṛti* appears twice: once in the MaiU (6.10), where the usage does not differ substantially from the Sāṃkhya, and once in the ŚU. We have already commented[410] on the extent to which the ŚU effects a theistic transformation of Sāṃkhya concepts, and we have already quoted its use of *prakṛti* (under the epithet *mahā-māyā*), which we here reiterate:

> Know *māyā* to be *prakṛti*, the possessor of *māyā* to be the great Lord.
> This whole world is pervaded by beings that are parts of him.[411]

In light of their philosophical weight, we may note other points at which the ŚU addresses these issues, even though it there uses the neuter *pradhāna* instead of the feminine *prakṛti*. The

[406]Brown, C. M., *op. cit.*, p. 68.

[407]SK 11-14.

[408]SK *passim*, esp. 22-24.

[409]This position becomes particularly problematical in trying to account for why *prakṛti* should ever *start* to evolve, i.e., change from the condition at *pralaya* when all three *guṇas* are in equilibrium. For a general appraisal of the above features of the Sāṃkhya position, see Hiriyanna, *op. cit.*, pp. 270-283. For a particularly apt appraisal of its philosophical difficulties, see Dasgupta, Surendranath, *A History of Indian Philosophy*, University Press (Cambridge, 1932), vol. I, pp. 245-248.

[410]*Supra*, s. v. "*śakti*."

[411]ŚU 4.10. Cf. *supra*, n. 145.

basic intuition (1.7-9) is that the Lord exists in three forms, the supreme soul, the individual soul, and the world (*pradhāna*). Although all are unborn (*aja*), of these

> What is perishable is *pradhāna*; what is immortal and imperishable is Hara;[412] the one God rules (both) the perishable and the *ātman*.
>
> By meditating on him, by union with him, by becoming (his very) essence more and more, there is finally the cessation of all illusion (*māyā*).[413]

Elsewhere it is said that the one God covers himself like a spider with threads that he has spun forth from *pradhāna*, according to his own very nature (6.10). In sum, the ŚU seems to understand the material world (*prakṛti-pradhāna*) not as the antithesis of spirit, as Sāṃkhya does, but as its evolution. While it does allow that life under the conditions of *prakṛti* has an illusory quality to it, it does not say that *ipso facto* such life is "less spiritual." It does suggest that the illusion can cease ("what is perishable is *pradhāna*"), at least for individuals.[414]

While the primary use we have made of the Mbh has been to focus on its use of the DM's epithets as proper names, in the case of *prakṛti* we must broaden our scope slightly. *Prakṛti*, as we shall see, is associated with proper names, but its usage there grows out of its broader role as a common noun and a brief examination of that role is therefore apposite. A preliminary point of interest is that, in contrast to the ŚU, where the glorification of Rudra gives *prakṛti* a Śaiva, or proto-Śaiva,

[412]Ordinarily an epithet of Rudra-Śiva; here (cf. the next clause) it seems to mean the individual soul.

[413]1.10:

> *kṣaram pradhānam amṛtākṣaraṃ haraḥ kṣarātmānav īśate deva ekaḥ/*
> *tasyābhidhyānād yojanāt tattvabhāvād bhūyaś cānte viśvamāyānivṛttiḥ//*

For a similar verse, which further justifies understanding *hara* as the individual soul, cf. ŚU 6.16.

[414]We have emphasized the ŚU's reconciliation of Sāṃkhya's fundamental dualism since that bears most directly on the status of *prakṛti*. We may also note in passing that it has further eroded Sāṃkhya's atheism by affirming (under Yoga influence? See Hiriyanna, *op. cit.*, pp. 282-283; S.N. Dasgupta, *op. cit.*, vol. I, pp. 258-259) the subordination of all individual souls to "the one God."

resonance, in the Mbh the association is almost always with Viṣṇu (Nārāyaṇa, Kṛṣṇa).[415] The primary agent in this association is, of course, the Gītā, whose use of *prakṛti* we may summarize as follows.[416] First, upon occasion the word is understood in almost a pure Sāṃkhya sense, as at 3.27 where actions are said to be performed (merely) by the *guṇas* of *prakṛti*, and at 13.19 where both *puruṣa* and *prakṛti* are said to be beginningless.[417] In the latter case, however, the ensuing reference (13.22) to the *paramātmā's* existence in the body does modify the Sāṃkhya position, and once (7.4-5) the Gītā seems deliberately to confound the Sāṃkhya notion of *prakṛti*: having enumerated eight traditional Sāṃkhya *prakṛti* categories, the Bhagavān says, in effect, "that is all my lower nature; now let me tell you about my higher nature," using *prakṛti* in both cases. Elsewhere, the Gītā's view approximates that of the ŚU, which it even quotes verbatim.[418] Thus, when the Bhagavān discloses the dynamics of his incarnations, he proclaims :

> Tho unborn, tho My self is eternal, tho Lord of Beings,
> Resorting to My own material nature I come into being
> by My own mysterious power.[419]

Similarly, there is a description of life under the conditions of *prakṛti* as "My divine strand-composed trick-of-illusion, hard to get past" (7.14). Yet we may detect a subtle difference from the ŚU on this matter, for whereas the ŚU grounds *prakṛti* in the Lord, with the latter evolving into the former, the Gītā seems to maintain a distinction between the two. This is implicit in the passage (4.6) quoted above and is even clearer

[415]The only apparent exception to this is the declaration at 13.16.54 that Śiva is the eight *prakṛtis*, and beyond the eight *prakṛtis*. (On plural *prakṛtis*, see our ensuing discussion.) More paradigmatic is the excision of Śaiva material at 5.109,452* and 13.14, 73*.

[416]All references here are not to the Mbh critical edition, but to Edgerton's edition and translation of the Gītā, except as noted. We do not raise the interesting, but still more tangential question of what the Gītā means by "*sāṃkhya*."

[417]Similar usages occur at 13.29 and 18.59.

[418]Gītā 13.13-14ab equals ŚU 3.16-17ab.

[419]Gītā 4.6, Edgerton tr.; the text is:

*ajo 'pi sann avyayātmā bhūtānām īśvaro 'pi san/*
*prakṛtiṃ svām adhiṣṭhāya saṃbhavāmy ātmamāyayā//*

at 9.7-8 where it is affirmed that, at *pralaya* and at creation, all creatures pass into and out of the *prakṛti* of the Bhagavān.[420] Finally, we may note that on one occasion the Gītā resumes its list of the five elements, plus *manas*, *buddhi*, and *ahaṃkāra*, with the phrase "eight-fold *prakṛti*" (7.4). This conceptualization ramifies in both directions chronologically: retrospectively, because there is evidence for a pre-SK notion of there being eight *prakṛtis*;[421] prospectively, because at the outset of the Nārāyaṇīya section of the Mbh, the seven seers are identified with the seven *prakṛti* elements which, together with Svāyambhuva Manu as eighth, constitute the original prakṛti;[422] subsequently, they are again identified by name and it is maintained that from them the whole universe sprang.[423] While we cannot here undertake exploration of the relationship, if any, between the DM and the Pāñcarātra system,[424] we may note that there are certain external resemblances—the seven seers at Skanda's birth and in the Nārāyaṇīya section, the Seven Little Mothers

[420]I.e., and not into and out of the Bhagavān himself. This not being a study of the Gītā, we limit ourselves to an examination of the word *prakṛti* therein. That our conclusion differs from that suggested by other passages (e.g., 7.7-11; 10.19-39) which identify certain aspects of the world with the Bhagavān is obvious. But it is also clear that this is not mere inconsistency, but deliberate paradox on the part of the Gītā: cf. 9.4-5. Since the ŚU's position is hardly unambiguous on such matters, we may perhaps limit our contrast: the ŚU shows a greater willingness to use the evolutionary language of Sāṃkhya in describing the Lord's relationship to the material world than does the Gītā.

[421]See Johnston, E.H., *Early Sāṃkhya*, Royal Asiati c Society (London, 1937), pp. 25-29.

[422]Mbh 12.322.28ff.

[423]Mbh 12.327.29ff.

[424]To undertake such an inquiry here would far exceed the scope of our study. For more on the Pāñcarātra, see Matsubara, Mitsunori, *The Early Pāñcarātra with Special Reference to the Ahirbudhnya Saṃhitā*, Ph.D. dissertation (Harvard, 1973). The similarities noted in our next clause may, of course, be purely coincidental. For instance, Sørensen (s. v. "saptarṣi") notes a confusion between the seven seers and the seven mind-born sons of Brahmā. Nonetheless, there is at least some overlap in names between the two groups in the Nārāyaṇīya section and in Skanda's birth episode. Moreover, there are other accounts of plural *prakṛtis* and/or seven seers in late epic, but non-Pāñcarātra, material (Mbh 12.203.26; 12.298.10; HV 7.22-23) which stand in curious contrast to the one *prakṛti* of both the ŚK and the DM.

as *śaktis* and the Goddess as Śakti, the seven (or eight) *prakṛtis* and the Goddess as Prakṛti—which might bear investigation.

The upshot of all this is that when the DM uses the word *prakṛti*, it is using a word that has been used to designate the material world in varying relationships to the divine—and it is going one step further, calling the material world itself supremely divine, the Goddess herself.

*kātyāyanī*

On two of the three occasions[425] on which this epithet is employed, the only noteworthy feature is that it is predicated of the Goddess in her supreme form (88.28; 91.1). In the final instance, we have somewhat more detail—

> May this lovely face of yours, graced with three eyes,
> Protect us from all ghosts;[426] O Kātyāyanī, praise be to you !

—where there is a hint of Śaiva iconography in her triocularity.

An understanding of Kātyāyanī that one encounters from time to time is that she is the family or clan deity of Aryan sages known as the Kātyas.[427] Though her precise status is the very matter that we are here investigating, the acceptance of this epithet as a proper name, a patronymic,[428] is a helpful starting-point, for it immediately establishes a link with the mainstream of the Vedic tradition. The name of Kātyāyana is associated with one of the Śrauta Sūtras, an index (*anukramaṇī*) to the RV, an index and several appendices to the YV, some "Notes" (*vārttikas*) on the rules of Pāṇini, and, since the author of the last of these has been identified as the author of the *Vājasaneyi Prātiśākhya*, with that text as well.[429] Though the

[425]88.28; 91.1,23.

[426]Veṅk's reading of *sarvabhītibhyaḥ*, "from all dangers," is perhaps preferable to the *sarvabhūtebhyaḥ* read here.

[427]Banerjea, "Aspects," p. 229; Bhandarkar, R. G., *op. cit.*, p. 144.

[428]As the PW does; cf. also HV 23.87.

[429]On the "associations", see Macdonell, *History*, pp. 245, 273-275, 431. On the "identification", see Thieme, Paul, "On the Identity of the Vārttikakāra", *Indian Culture* 4 (1937-38), pp. 189-209, reprinted in Staal, J. (ed.), *A Reader on the Sanskrit Grammarians*, The MIT Press (Cambridge and London, 1972), pp. 332-356.

Mbh does not know the name, "Kātyāyana" recurs throughout the Rām in lists of venerable sages.[430] It is to this orthodox family that Kātyāyanī belongs.

We have already met what is probably the earliest Sanskritic occurrence of Kātyāyanī in our discussion of the epithet Durgā at TA 10.1, for on one occasion the names Kātyāyanī, Kanyākumārī, and Durgī are all employed in one of the variations on the Gāyatrī *mantra*.[431] While the text subsequently expatiates on Durgā, it does not on Kātyāyanī. Elsewhere in the Vedic literature, she is known as the mother of famous teachers: at ŚāṇA 8.10 Jātūkarṇya is called *kātyāyanīputra*, and in the BU's concluding genealogy of its teaching, two unnamed sages are called "the son of Kātyāyanī."[432] The most famous appearance of this name is earlier in the BU:

> Now then, Yājñavalkya had two wives, Maitreyī and Kātyāyanī. Of the two, Maitreyī was a discourser on Brahman, (while) Kātyāyanī had just a woman's knowledge on such matters.[433]

This is, to be sure, no flattering remark and, in the sequel, only Maitreyī is engaged in conversation by Yājñavalkya. And yet any association with a teacher of Yājñavalkya's stature is not to be taken lightly, and this fact perhaps partially redeems the disparagement of Kātyāyanī's intellectual prowess.[434]

In the absence of any epic testimony on Kātyāyāṇī,[435] we may, in conclusion, note that there is evidence from material

[430]Rām 1.7.5; 1.69.4; 2.67.3; 6.128.60; 7.74.4. No specific characterization is offered in any of these instances.

[431]For the precise text, see *supra*, s. v. "*durgā*."

[432]BU 6.5.1. On this passage, Radhakrishnan cites Śaṃkara's observation that "teachers are named after their mothers because the mother holds the important place in the training of children."

[433]BU 4.5.1. The text of the second sentence runs *tayor ha maitreyī brahmavādinī babhūva strīprajñaiva tarhi kātyāyanī*.

[434]The earlier BU account of Yājñavalkya and Maitreyī (2.4) does mention Kātyāyanī, but lacks the deprecatory remark.

[435]The PW and Sørensen references are all in excised hymns.

contemporary with the DM for the Śaiva resonance of this epithet and for its association with the slaying of Mahiṣa.[436]

*mahāvidyā-vidyā*

The Goddess is called *mahāvidyā*, according to Vid, on three occasions, though our two other editions use the word only twice. However, since all editions agree in also calling her *vidyā* twice, both times modified by *paramā*, it is appropriate that the two epithets be treated here, and together. The sense is the same for both epithets: she is the great, supreme knowledge.[437]

There are two points to be made regarding the DM's designation of the Goddess as *mahāvidyā*. The first is that here again the formulation is deliberately paradoxical, the paradox being one we have noted under *mahāmāyā*: she is both the Great Illusion and the Great Knowledge together. The Goddess is even hymned with these words consecutively at 81.58.[438] The second point is that this knowledge is salvific, "the supreme, eternal knowledge that becomes the cause of release (*mukter hetubhūtā*)" (81.44). An entire verse is devoted to this characterization :

> You who are the cause of release and of inconceivable austerities, your name is repeated by sages, who hold the

[436]Bāṇa's *Kādambarī* refers (text, p. 11) to Kātyāyanī's feet being reddened with the blood of Mahiṣa and (p. 29) to Kātyāyanī's marking of her servant with her trident. The Nagarjuni Hill Cave Inscription of Anantavarman (Fleet, J.F., *Gupta Inscriptions*, Superintendent of Govt. Printing (Bombay, 1888), Corpus Inscriptionum Indicarum, vol. III, pp. 226-228), which records the installation in a cave of an image of Kātyāyanī, also called Bhavānī, opens with a romantic account of her victory over Mahiṣa that is strikingly similar to the verses of Bāṇa's *Caṇḍīśataka*. See also our discussion of the VāmanaP mythology in Part II.

[437]The discrepancy in readings arises because Vid, after reading *mahāvidyā* at 81.58, reads it twice at 91.20, a hymnic verse comprised of feminine vocatives. For the second of these, Jag and Veṅk read *mahāmāyā*, which is preferable, since (1) it avoids repetition, (2) it re-emphasizes the paradox of the Goddess being both *mahāvidyā* and *mahāmāyā* (cf. our following paragraph). *Vidyā* is the Goddess at 81.44 and 84.8; at 93.2 it is made (*kriyate*) by her.

[438]And their further juxtaposition at 91.20 seems intended; see our preceding note.

> essence of truth because they have restrained their senses,
> Intent upon *mokṣa*, with all faults shed: you are this blessed, supreme knowledge, O Goddess.[439]

In other words, she is the knowledge upon which all seekers after *mokṣa* converge.

*Mahāvidyā* is unknown in either the Vedic or epic literature. While considerations of scale prohibit a full investigation of the word *vidyā*, we may note that the word does not occur in the RV. Thereafter, its history follows a course predictable by anyone familiar with the development of Vedic thought.[440] It occurs a total of some two dozen times in the AV and YV recensions, usually in the Brāhmaṇa portions of the latter, with a meaning of "knowledge, teaching, science," often characterized as "threefold" in reference to the three Vedas. The ruminative character of the Brāhmaṇas themselves is reflected in the occurrence of *vidyā* some hundred times therein, a density of occurrence that is maintained under the speculative impetus of the Upaniṣads. Of personification, the Mbh knows but two instances: of the singular, Vidyā, as a figure in the train of Pārvatī (3.221.20), and of the plural, Vidyās, who attend upon Brahmā (2.11.15).

*vārāhi*

The name of Vārāhī, the sixth of the Seven Little Mothers, is used by our text on three occasions.[441] The first of these is when she emerges as a *śakti* (88.18):

[439]84.8:

*yā muktihetur avicintyamahāvratā ca abhyasyase suniyatendriyatattvasāraiḥ/*
*mokṣārthibhir munibhir astasamastadoṣair vidyāsi sā bhagavatī paramā hi devi//*

[440]The cursory history that follows is based upon a tabulation of the instances indicated by the VPK, together with a selected consultation of the passages. While a detailed study of the nuances of *vidyā*, particularly in the Upaniṣads, might be desirable here, an awareness of the general trend in its usage, and of the fact that, however interpreted, it is a critical term in late (and post-) Vedic times, will suffice as background to the DM's usage.

[441]88.18, 48; 89.37.

> The *śakti* of Hari bearing the matchless form of a sacrificial boar (*yajñavarāha*)
> Then came forth, bearing the body of a sow (*vārāhī tanu*).

In the sequel, our text is impressed by the destructiveness of her sword (88.48) and snout (89.37), but it is under related words, clearly applied to the same figure, that the Vaiṣṇava motifs show most readily. Thus at 88.35, she who is *varāhamūrti* slays with snout, tusk, and discus, and when the Mothers are hymned, Vārāhī's verse (91.15) gives a still fuller description—

> O (you) who have grasped a great terrible discus, by whom the earth was upraised with your tusks,
> O auspicious one with the form of a boar (*varāharūpiṇī*), O Nārāyaṇī, praise be to you !

—in which the text's familiarity with Varāha's iconography and mythology is evident.[442]

In the Vedic literature, only a single usage of *vārāhī* is known, though it occurs in a number of texts:[443] that is as a modifier of *upānah*, meaning the "sandals of boar-skin" that the king puts on during the Rājasūya sacrifice. To this, the Mbh adds only one usage, in an excised passage (9.45,271*) where the long roster of *mātṛs* is embellished with a note that some "belonged to Varāha."

*bhadrakālī*

In the case of Bhadrakālī, which is employed in the DM and elsewhere simply as a proper name,[444] we seem to have an epithet with an intriguing history behind it, though we can see only a fragment of it. In the DM's use of Bhadrakālī, it is a simple synonym for Caṇḍikā or Ambikā, the supreme form of the Goddess (83.8; 84.33). The third of its usages (91.24)

[442]Cf. Banerjea, *Development*, pp. 412-415.

[443]YVMai 4.4.6; TB 1.7.9.4; ŚB 5.4.3.19; KāGS 3.8 etc.

[444]If one had to translate the name, it would be something like "the auspicious black one," but nowhere in the literature, even in the *BhāgavataP*'s account of Bhadrakālī's cult [5.9.16ff.; Venkaṭeśvara Press (Bombay, 1949)], have we seen the name analyzed. And in a tradition that delights in etymologies, that is curious.

occurs in a hymn where it is difficult to know whether the epithet has been deliberately associated with certain characteristics, as occurs, say, with the Mothers, or whether Bhadrakālī has been chosen simply as one of a number of names that might have sufficed. The verse reads—

> That fearsome (trident), terrible (*karāla*) with flames, laying waste the Asuras without remainder,
> May (that) trident protect us from danger; O Bhadrakālī, praise be to you!

—where a similarity to Durgā, Kālī and Māheśvarī is evident.

What little light is shed on this epithet by the earlier tradition comes from an interesting source, viz., the Gṛhya Sūtras. Bhadrakālī, theretofore unknown, emerges with an identity on which a number of texts are agreed:[445] in the householder's performance of the *vaiśvadeva* sacrifice, invoking different deities at different points in the house, it is Bhadrakālī who is to be invoked at the foot of the bed, while it is Śrī who is to be invoked at the head. Unfortunately, the literature we are surveying sheds no further light on the implied symbiosis between the two goddesses, for the only additional appearance of Bhadrakālī is as one of the hundreds of *mātṛs* in the train of Skanda, at Mbh 9.45.11.[446]

*yoganidrā-nidrā*

Although *yoganidrā* occurs in the DM on only three occasions,[447] there are few epithets that are of greater importance to

[445] VaiGS 3.7; *Śāṅkhāyana Gṛhya Sūtra* (H. Oldenberg [tr.], in *The Gṛhya Sūtras*, Part I, Clarendon Press [Oxford, 1886], SBE 29) 2.14.14; *Mānava Dharma Śāstra* (G. Bühler [tr.], Dover Publications [New York, 1969], SBE 25) 3.89; cf. also KāGS 19.7.

[446] The other reference that Sørensen and the PW give, in addition to the one in the Durgā Stotra, is not in the constituted text: Bhadrakālī appears in a battle scene in Mbh 12, App. I 28, lines 109-110, the whole of which Appendix has parallels in the *Vāyu* and *Brahmā Purāṇas*. In fact, if one were to investigate the whole fascinating process by which Bhadrakālī came from being the "goddess of the foot of the bed" to a designation for the Goddess, other early Purāṇas provide teasing suggestions: the VāmanaP, whose account of the Goddess's exploits may antedate the DM (see Part II), knows her only as the spouse of Śiva at a particular *tīrtha* (57.63), while the ViṣṇuP (5.1.83) includes her in the names that Viṣṇu applies to Yoganidrā after soliciting her aid in carrying out the plan for their respective births.

[447] 81.41, 49, 52.

our text in establishing the identity of the Goddess and in structuring its account of her. This is not to say that this importance is Sanskritic, for the Vedic tradition does not know the word at all. Even if we include the related word *nidrā*, which the DM applies to the Goddess on two occasions,[448] the Sanskritic antecedents are unimpressive. The word is not known in the Vedas at all, but first appears in the Brāhmaṇas where it means simply "sleep" or "drowsiness." It maintains this meaning in subsequent Vedic usage virtually without alteration or embellishment, except for one occasion when *nidrā* is identified with the Goddess Śrī.[449] Since the structure of the first part of our study is determined by the criteria of the frequency of an epithet's occurrence in the DM, and the depth of its Sanskritic heritage, *yoganidrā-nidrā* would seem to merit its relatively low position in the rank order of epithets.

There are, however, other criteria of importance. And if we notice that one of the instances of *nidrā* is in the third *carita's* hymn, where the Goddess is said to abide in all creatures in various forms, including *nidrārūpeṇa*, then a significant pattern to the remaining instances of *yoganidrā-nidrā* becomes apparent: they are all clustered at the "seam" between the frame story and the Madhu-Kaiṭabha myth. In fact, it is through the epithet *yoganidrā-nidrā* that the DM moves from the former to the latter. In a larger sense, because the text can move readily from one myth to another, having the narrator say, in effect, "Now I have told you one story of the Goddess's redemptive activity; let me tell you another," [450] it is through the epithet *yoganidrā-nidrā* that our text is able to recount any myths at all.

In our treatment of the epithet Mahāmāyā, we have seen that that epithet "introduces" the Goddess in a double sense. It is used in the second verse of the DM as part of the *rapprochement* with the preceding chapter of the MarkP, and it is used by the

[448] 81.53; 85.15. Cf. also 81.64.

[449] VDS 99.4. For examples of its ordinary usage, see ŚB 3.9.3.11; GoB 1.2.2; ŚDS 90; MaiU 3.5; 6.25. The last of these references does compare the practice of *yoga* to the indrawing of the senses in sleep, characterizing a *yogin* as *nidrevāntarhitendriya*, but this is as close as the Vedic tradition comes, at least in the texts we have examined, to the idea of *yoganidrā*.

[450] Cf. MarkP 81.77; 84.34-36.

*ṛṣi* Medhas to introduce the two woebegones to the Goddess. With the auditors' attention thus captured, the critical link is forged: "the *yoganidrā* of the lord of the worlds, Hari, is (this same) Mahāmāyā, and through her is this world being deluded" (81.41). As the tale of Madhu and Kaiṭabha then unfolds, the other occurrences of *yoganidrā-nidrā* follow in quick succession:

> ...When the universe dissolved into the primordial waters at the end of the age, the blessed lord, Viṣṇu,
> Having stretched out the (serpent couch) Śeṣa betook himself (*abhajat*)[451] to *yoganidrā*.

When the two Asuras arose and began to assail Brahmā, the latter

> With single-pointed concentration, for the sake of awakening Hari,
> Praised *yoganidrā* who had made her abode in the eyes of Hari.
> The lord of splendor (praised) the blessed sleep of Viṣṇu,
> The incomparable queen of all, supportress of the world who causes (its) maintenance and destruction.[452]

In order to appreciate the impact of this proclamation, we would do well to recall the enormity of Viṣṇu's stature in the Sanskritic tradition, relative to the Goddess, at the time of our text. Still further appreciation will ensue upon our consideration of the pre-DM accounts of the Madhu-Kaiṭabha myth in Part II. Suffice it to say at this juncture that by the time of our text, Viṣṇu's identity as executioner of Madhu and Kaiṭabha is secure. The pervasiveness of his epithet *madhusūdana* suggests

[451]The richness of the word *bhaj*, which is, we recall, the root of *bhakti*, precludes easy translation. One might equally as well say that Viṣṇu "partook of, resorted to, enjoyed, possessed, attended upon, worshipped, was devoted to, was engaged in" *yoganidrā*.

[452]The text of these verses is:

*yoganidrāṃ yadā viṣṇur jagaty ekārṇavīkṛte/*
*āstīrya śeṣam abhajat kalpānte bhagavān prabhuḥ//*81.49
*tuṣṭāva yoganidrāṃ tām ekāgrahṛdayasthitaḥ/*
*vibodhanārthāya harer harinetrakṛtālayām//*52
*viśveśvarīṃ jagaddhātrīṃ sthitisaṃhārakāriṇīm/*
*nidrāṃ bhagavatīṃ viṣṇor atulāṃ tejasaḥ prabhuḥ//*53

just how secure.[453] More narrowly, the only approximations of the term *yoganidrā* that we have found in the Mbh, which also seem not to be personifications there, have a Vaiṣṇava tone to them. On one occasion, it is said that "the boundlessly powerful Viṣṇu at the beginning of the Eon . . . sleeps the sleep of Yoga within the self [*adhyātmayoganidrā*],"[454] and, on another, Kṛṣṇa is praised as one "whose self (reposes) in the sleep of yoga (*yoganidrātma*)."[455] What our text has done is to personify that *yoganidrā*,[456] to suggest that one's entry into a particular state gives one a certain dependence upon it, a relationship that is most vividly portrayed through the reification, or personification, of that state.[457] That our text intends such a portrayal, such an interpretation of the verb *bhaj* at 81.49, is apparent in the sequel. After she is hymned by Brahmā, the Goddess, here called Tāmasī, "the Dark One," comes forth from the eyes, mouth, nose, arms, heart and breast of Viṣṇu[458]

[453]Considering just the Mbh, Sørensen lists 217 instances of *madhusūdana*, occurring in fifteen of the eighteen books of the Mbh. While some of these are excised from the constituted text of the critical edition, their pervasiveness is still impressive. The DM itself applies this epithet to Viṣṇu at 82.8.

[454]Mbh 1.19.13, van Buitenen tr.

[455]Mbh 12.47.39; cp. *nidrāyogam upāgatam* at 12. 335. 17, 57.

[456]We do not mean to imply that the DM was the sole agent, in this process, for clearly the notion of *yoganidrā* was very much in flux at the time. We have noted the Mbh's application of the term to Viṣṇu's (unpersonified) condition at *pralaya*, which the HV characterizes more diffusely: *viṣṇuṃ nidrāmayaṃ yogaṃ praviṣṭaṃ tamasāvṛtam* (40.15; on *tamasāvṛtam*, cp. the Goddess as *tāmasī*, noted below). In its account of Viṣṇu's solicitation of the assistance of the goddess of sleep in effecting their respective births, the HV calls her simply *nidrā*, which is employed throughout virtually as a proper name (47.26; 48.3ff; cp. Rām 7.13.1). However, in *its* account of the same material, the ViṣṇuP [Orientalia Press (Bombay, 1889) ] uses the designation *yoganidrā* throughout (5.1.70ff). In light of this shifting phraseology, what we may credit the DM with is the initial use of *yoganidrā* as a personification of Viṣṇu's condition at *pralaya*.

[457]The logic is very much the same as with *śakti* and *māyā*: the attribute or quality is so important to the very identity of its possessor that it comes to be conceptualized as distinct from, and eventually as more important than, that possessor.

[458]Our paraphrase does not mention the fact that, having emerged from Viṣṇu's different parts, the Goddess presents herself to Brahmā (81.69),

so that he may awaken and slay the two Asuras (81.68-69), which he then proceeds to do. The conclusion is inescapable: it is solely through the grace, the graceful withdrawal, of the Goddess Yoganidrā that Viṣṇu can fulfil his familiar role of slaying Madhu and Kaiṭabha. In fact, it is only through this grace that he can act at all. By extrapolation, it is only with her consent that the cosmos exists,[459] or that human beings can experience a waking state of consciousness.[460]

It is thus that, for all its Sanskritic innocence, *yoganidrā-nidrā* in our text carries an enormous weight structurally, mythologically, ontologically, psychologically.

### *viṣṇumāya*

Having seen the tendency that our text has to associate the epithets *mahāmāyā*, the Great Illusion, and *yoganidrā-nidrā*, the Sleep of Yoga or the Sleep of Viṣṇu, and to cluster their usage in the first *carita*, it is curious that it shows no such inclination with the potentially related *viṣṇumāyā*, the Illusion or Magic Power of Viṣṇu. The three instances of this epithet all occur in the third *carita*,[461] as a fairly straightforward designation for the supreme form of the Goddess. This does not mean, however, that its usage is casual. For instance, it is first used when the gods, having reflected on their affliction by Śumbha and Niśumbha and on the Goddess's promise to assist them, "went to Himavān, lord of mountains, (and) there praised the goddess

---

a sequence which is clearly similar to the Goddess's coalescence out of diverse manifestations of *tejas* at the outset of the second *carita* (82.9ff.).

[459]That there is a creation motif implicit in the Madhu-Kaiṭabha myth is evident in the frequent etymological association of the fat or marrow (*medas*) of the dead Asuras and the earth as *medinī*: see our discussion in Part II.

[460]Is this not the implication of Viṣṇu's relationship to *yoganidrā*, in conjunction with that of all creatures to *nidrā*, described at 85.15 (in the *yā devī sarvabhūteṣu* hymn)? It is tempting to associate the Goddess as *yoganidrā* with the deeper levels of consciousness enumerated in the MU's famous meditation on the syllable OM. That we do not press the case is because the MU does not use *nidrā*, but *svapna* and *suṣupta* (MU 4, 5), to label the different levels of sleep.

[461]85.6, 12; 93.2.

Viṣṇumāyā" (85.6). After the ensuing hymn, this goddess is designated by the name Pārvatī (85.37ff.), which, as we have seen, is inclined to be a name of Śiva's spouse. To call the spouse of Śiva "The Magic Power of Viṣṇu" is, at least, paradoxical. The same may be said for the formulation at 93.2-3, where it is said that knowledge (*vidyā*) is created by Viṣṇumāyā, who leads even men of discrimination into delusion. While the language here is very similar to the language used in the description of Mahāmāyā and Yoganidrā,[462] our text establishes continuity, not explicitly, but by letting the nature of the Goddess emerge as continuous, even unchanging, in different contexts, under different epithets, in the first and last chapters of its account.

This epithet is unknown in either the Vedic or epic literature.[463]

*sanātanī*

On the three occasions when the supreme form of the Goddess is called *sanātanī*, it may be taken simply as a descriptive adjective, "eternal." What it seeks to emphasize is that through all the variations of form and diversity of function, of which our text is gloriously aware, the Goddess remains unchanging, eternal. Thus, while she is the deluder and confounder, the "cause" of samsāric life, she is also the "supreme, eternal knowledge (*vidyā sanātanī*) that becomes the cause of release" (81.44). Similarly, she is the eternal one (*sanātanī*) who is the power (*śakti*) of creation, maintenance, and destruction (91.10), a judgment which 93.36 confirms when it sees "the eternal one" operative in different guises at different times.

As a descriptive adjective, *sanātana* is a middle-aged word in Sanskrit. It appears in the masculine as early as the AV and ŚB, but it does not seem ever to have modified a grammatically feminine word in the Vedic literature. Nor is it known as a feminine epithet in the epics.

[462]81.41-42, quoted *supra*, s. v. "*mahāmāyā*".

[463]For an archetype that may, however, be operative here, cf. the ŚU passage on *māyā* and *māyin* quoted *supra*, s. v. "*mahāmāyā*".

*mahādevī*

The logic behind calling the subject of the DM *mahādevī*, the Great Goddess, is clear enough, and its three occurrences are evenly distributed across the three episodes. At 81.58 the word serves to portray the Goddess as reconciling and transcending the Deva-Asura conflict, for she is hymned in consecutive words as *mahādevī mahāsurī*.[464] In the second *carita* the word simply identifies Mahiṣa's opponent (93.23), while in the third the Goddess is hymned as "the auspicious (*śivā*) Mahādevī (85.7).

It is surprising, at first blush, to find the word Mahādevī here used in such a mythological vacuum, i.e., devoid of any reference to Śiva, except to the extent that her characterization as "auspicious (*śivā*)" constitutes such a reference. It is surprising because, although the word Mahādevī does not appear in the Vedic corpus, the word Mahādeva is used on several occasions,[465] apparently in reference to the then embryonic figure of Rudra-Śiva, and in the Mbh Mahādeva is used pervasively as a designation of the god Śiva.[466] In fact, in the handful of Mbh instances of *mahādevī*, the predominant understanding is that she is the consort of Śiva Mahādeva.[467] Thus a *tīrtha* is identified as the peak of Mahādevī Gaurī (3.82.131), the gods lament that they have been cursed by Mahādevī Umā (13.84.51), and, most decisively, the text declares "the Great Goddess of the Great Lord is known as Pārvatī."[468]

On further reflection, this avoidance of mythological reference may be seen to be deliberate and of a piece with our text's diction regarding the Seven Little Mothers. In our discussion of Aindrī and Māheśvarī, we have seen that while our text acknowledges the relation of these *śaktis* to Indra and Maheśvara,

[464]For the significance of calling her *mahāsurī*, see "*mahāmāyā*," esp. n. 141.

[465]Usually in short lists of deities, e.g., YVT 1.4.36.1; AV 5.21.11; 9.7.7; 12.5.19; 13.4.4; ŚB 11.5.3.5. Although the ŚU uses some close approximations, such as *maheśvara* (4.10; 6.7), it never uses the word *mahādeva*.

[466]Sørensen lists 184 such applications, found in twelve of the eighteen books of the Mbh.

[467]Other applications of the epithet are to Earth (*pṛthivī*: 13.61.6) and Aditi (13.83.26).

[468]14.43.14cd: *māheśvarī mahādevī procyate pārvatīti yā.*

it wants to portray that relationship as far more profound than the merely "external" one between consorts. Consequently, it deliberately avoids the then current names for the consorts of the two gods. Similarly, our text does not draw out the Śaiva associations of *mahādevī* for the same reason it never calls her Umā. She is the Great Goddess intrinsically, on her own terms, not in a derivative sense nor by virtue of her relationship to some other deity.[469]

*viśveśvarī*

We have met most of the nuances of this epithet under other epithets with a common element : *īśvarī*, *māheśvarī*, *parameśvarī*. To the remarks made there we may add only that, in thrice calling the Goddess *viśveśvarī*,[470] "queen or ruler of all," the DM emphasizes her protective role. Thus (91.2) she protects all because she is mother of all (*mātṛ jagato 'khilasya*) and (91.31) she protects all because she has all for her very soul (*viśvātmikā*), thereby supporting (*dhṛ*) it. The epithet thus links two rather different notions of protectiveness, the maternal and the mighty.

Though the masculine *viśveśvara* is applied to various gods in both Vedic and epic literature, the feminine is unknown in either.

*muktihetu*

On two of the three occasions when this epithet is applied to the Goddess, it is in the context of calling her *vidyā*,[471] reflecting the tradition that knowledge is the "cause of release." In the third case (91.4), the Goddess herself is hymned as "the cause of release on earth," but in none of these instances is the epithet elaborated upon. It is not known in the Vedic literature, nor does Sørensen cite it for the epic.

[469]At the risk of belaboring the obvious, we might note the reflection of this in the very title of our text: it is the *Devī-*, not *Daivī-*, *Māhātmya*.

[470]81.53; 91.2, 31.

[471]Q. v.: both passages (81.44; 84.8) are quoted in full thereunder. The former of these is not the compound but the simplex *mukter hetu*.

*ambā*

Of the epithets of two occurrences in the DM that seem to merit formal recognition,[472] *ambā*, "mother," claims primacy, for although its usage is fairly simple—once the world is said to be filled (*puritaṃ*) by *ambā* (91.5), and it is the vision of *ambā* that the devout *vaiśya* seeks (93.6)—it is obviously akin to the very popular epithet Ambikā.

We may, in fact, begin our examination of the Vedic antecedents of *ambā* with a cross-reference to our discussion of Ambikā, for the two YV passages wherein the latter first occurs, and which engender subsequent commentary in Vedic literature, also contain the word *ambā*. Those passages, which deal with Ambikā's relation to Rudra and with fertility, have to be supplemented in the case of *ambā*, however, for it is attested in the RV as well. There it is used as a vocative in a verse to Sarasvatī that also calls her "best of mothers"

[472]Since we are now dealing with epithets of only a few instances in the DM, it sometimes happens that neither the internal evidence of our text, nor the external Vedic and epic evidence, proves very illuminating, as in the last two epithets above. The four epithets of two occurrences which fall into this category are listed here for the sake of convenience, with a brief comment on each. (1) *bhadrā* (MarkP 85.7, 66), "auspicious, favorable, gracious": a very common word from RV times on, it may be understood as close to *śivā* but without the euphemistic undertone; a personified Bhadrā appears in the epic in various roles—consort of Vaiśravaṇa (Mbh 1.191.6), abductee of Śiśupāla (2.42.11), wife (or daughter, as Subhadrā, *passim*) of Vasudeva (16.9.18), etc.,—but none of these is definitive. (2) *aparājitā*, "invincible, unconquered," is applied to the Goddess as she is remembered by the afflicted gods (85.4), and as she dispatches Śiva as messenger (88.23): the masculine receives occasional use in the RV, with the feminine subsequently modifying a brick (*iṣṭakā*) in the sacrificial altar(YVT 4.4.5.2), an army (*senā*) which is taken as an approximate definition of Brahman (BU 2.1.6; ŚāṇA 6.7; cp. CU 8.5.3) and, most commonly, the north-east direction (*diś*; AiB 1.14; 8.9; ŚāṇGS 2.12.1; 4.6.2, etc.); the Mbh understands Aparājitā as a distinct goddess when it identifies her with Skanda's spouse Devasenā (3.218.47), and there is evidence for Aparājitā as a militantly sectarian Buddhist goddess (Sahai, *op. cit.*, pp. 235-237, 259-261). (3) *alakṣmī*, "misfortune, ill-luck," is employed in the DM only in contrast with *śrī* (84.4) or *lakṣmī* (92.37), q. v. for remarks on the point of the contrast and on *alakṣmī*'s antecedents. (4) *mahārātri*, "the great night," is applied to the Goddess once in a hymnic sequence, along with *kālarātri*, "the death night," and *moharātri*, "the night of delusion" (81.59), and once in a sequence of grammati-

(*ambitamā*),[473] and in Vṛṣākapi's address to Indrāṇī (10.86.7). The association with fertility emerges most clearly when it is used collectively of sacred plants : "Hundert, o Mütterchen, zählen eure Arten und tausend eure Gewächse. So machet ihr, hundertfachen Rat wissend, mir diesen Mann gesund !"[474]

There are, in addition, other passages in the YV which are highly suggestive. In a passage that has given the commentators considerable difficulty, the god Soma is once invoked with the feminine *ambā*.[475] A *mantra* portion that is particularly intriguing in light of our earlier remarks[476] on the Goddess as the great Asurī occurs at YVT 4.1.9.1-2. While Agni is the primary focus of invocation here, there are others:

> O mother [*ambā*], daringly show thy heroism...;
> With Agni wilt thou do this deed.
> Be firm, O goddess earth [*devī pṛthivi*], for prosperity;
> Thou art the wile of the Asura, made with power [*āsurī māyā svadhayā kṛtā 'si*] ;
> Let this oblation be pleasing to the gods....[477]

Finally, another *mantra* portion makes the seemingly innocent remark that one of the sacrificial altar bricks (*iṣṭakā*) is called Ambā (YVT 4.4.5.1), but the commentaries on this passage (or its parallels in other recensions) establish a link with a motif we have encountered elsewhere:[478] Ambā and the other

---

cally feminine words (91.20). Although of these *-rātris* only *kālarātri* has a prior usage in the literature here surveyed (q. v. under "*kālī*"), we shall encounter hymnic elaborations on this theme in the Rātrī Sūkta and its *khila* in Part III.

[473]RV 2.41.16. In light of the integrative vision of the DM, it is striking that it only employs the name Sarasvatī, one of the few Ṛg Vedic goddesses of note, on one occasion (91.22), and that is an unelaborated hymnic reference.

[474]RV 10.97.2, Geldner tr. Two verses later, the herbs are again invoked as mothers, but this time with the plural *mātaraḥ*.

[475]YVT 1.4.1.2. For attempts at resolving the difficulties, see Keith's notes on this passage and ŚB 3.9.4.21 with Eggeling's notes.

[476]S. v. "*mahāmāyā*".

[477]Keith tr. This passage occurs in other recensions at YVKā 16.7, YVMai 2.7.7, YVMā 11.68-69, YVKāṇ 12.7.3-4.

[478]Viz., in the Mbh account of the Seven Little Mothers; see Appendix A.

bricks named there are said to be the constellation of the Kṛttikās.[479]

From elsewhere in the Vedic corpus we may cite the BṛDe's contention (5.58) that the daughter of a seer ought only to marry a seer, for thus she becomes a mother (*ambā*) of the Vedas, and the ŚāṅA's use of Ambā as a proper name (3.3) : in a description of the world of Brahman, the Apsarases are named Ambā and Ambāyavī, while the streams are called Ambayāḥ.

With regard to the epic testimony, we have already met[480] Ambā as the sister of Ambikā and Ambālikā, who was excused from marrying Vicitravīrya because of her previous engagement to Śālva. When the Mbh resumes her story in the fifth book, it gives her name to one of the hundred minor books of the Mbh, the Ambopākhyānaparvan.[481] The entry into the story does not, in fact, involve Ambā herself, but, rather, Duryodhana's inquiry of Bhīṣma (5. 170. 1-2) as to why the latter did not slay Śikhaṇḍin, by whom he (Bhīṣma) would eventually be slain. In response, Bhīṣma recounts the sad story of Ambā. After leaving her sisters, she turned to Śālva, but he refused to marry her as she was now to be wedded to another (5. 172.4-7). Disconsolate, she sought revenge against Bhīṣma by invoking the aid of Rāma Jāmadagnya, who engaged Bhīṣma in a long battle (5.177-186) that ended, however, in a stalemate. Thereupon, Ambā engaged in fierce austerities (5. 187) in order to slay Bhīsma. Enraged at this attempt on her son's life, Gaṅgā cursed her to become a crooked river, but by virtue of her ascetic merit, she did so with only half her body, remaining a maiden with the other half (5.187.39). Vowing to obtain manhood in order to avenge herself on Bhīṣma, and receiving a promise to that effect from Śiva, she then immolated herself on the bank of the river (5.188). Subsequently, concludes Bhīṣma, she was born as Śikhaṇḍin, but since he (Bhīṣma) had vowed

[479]Cf. YVT's *brāhmaṇa* portion on this at 5.3.9; also TB 3.1.4.1; *Āpastamba Śrauta Sūtra* (Richard Garbe [ed.], Asiatic Society [Calcutta, 1882-1902], Three vols.) 17.5.4; also note VDS 67.7 and KāGS 54.3.

[480]S. v. "*ambikā*".

[481]The balance of this paragraph is a précis of Sørensen's account of Ambopākhayanaparvan insofar as it bears on Ambā, with references to the critical edition on the salient points.

not to fight anyone resembling, or previously, a woman (5.193. 60ff.), he could not slay Śikhaṇḍin.

Though one could hardly argue for a precise correspondence between the Mbh Ambā and the DM *ambā*, such features as commitment to another, intense passion, and ascetic prowess suggest an underlying continuity, to supplement the subliminal association that we have argued for in the realm of diction.

*medhā-puṣṭi-śānti-kṣānti-tuṣṭi*

In light of the integration that the DM effects in the realm of particular goddesses and, as we shall see in Part II, of previously distinct myths, it is not surprising that it also integrates certain abstract feminine nouns. That our text does not originate such a practice is evident from the Gītā's identification of a cluster of feminine nouns with the deity(10.34), but the logic of such an identification is, if anything, even more inexorable in our text where the deity, too, is feminine. We have already encountered other words which might fall into this category (*lakṣmī*, *śrī*, *lajjā*, *śraddhā*). They, however, are not only of more frequent occurrence but most also have some degree of qualification, or an important Sanskritic history. By contrast, the five words that we consider here as a group receive virtually no elaboration in our text and have relatively unextraordinary histories. They occur only in hymns, usually in a sequence of feminine nouns.[482] What they have in common beyond their gender is their beneficent, desirable, auspicious quality.

*Medhā* is the only one of the five to receive any characterization at all and that is at 84.10, which exclaims, "O Goddess, you are *medhā*, knowing the essence of all scripture (*viditākhilaśāstrasārā*)." This phrase nicely conveys the dual thrust of *medhā*: the word, which is as old as the RV, is analyzed in the *Nirukta* (3.19) as "wisdom [which]... is stored...in the mind," yet Renou points out[483] that it means primarily the poetic faculty, which, as noted in our Prolegomenon, is at least partially a

[482]The words occur as follows: *medhā* (84.10; 91.21; *mahāmedhā* at 81.58); *puṣṭi* (81.60, 91.20); *śānti* (81.60; 85.23); *kṣānti* (81.60; 85.20); *tuṣṭi* (81.60; 85.30).

[483]Renou, *Études*, I, p. 3.

function of mastery over the multi-valent scriptural language. *Medhā*, then, is the insight, with an undertone of power, that comes from mastery over the Vedic material. The Mbh knows a personified Medhā on two occasions : as one of the daughters of Dakṣa who became the wives of Dharma, and as one figure in the multitude in Indra's palace.[484]

*Puṣṭi* is also known from Ṛg Vedic times and, like *medhā*, occurs upwards of a hundred times in the Vedas. In the pastoral context, it frequently means the "breeding" or "upbringing" of livestock, but in a larger sense it is "growth, prosperity, well-being." The Mbh knows her (1.60.13) as another of Dharma's daughters and Dakṣa's wives.

*Śānti* is not known to the RV but is widely used in the Black YV and Brāhmaṇas. Though the PW gives it a range of meanings, its sense here is quite specific: it appears usually in the dative case, meaning "expiation, atonement, appeasement," specifying the consequences of a particular course of action. From this, it easily spills over into the meaning of "peace" or "tranquillity." It is unknown as the proper name of a female in the epic.

*Kṣānti* is a word of far more recent provenience, first occurring in the Dharma Sūtras, where it is identified as "patience, forebearance, forgiveness" in accounts of the various virtues.[485] *Tuṣṭi* is of comparable youth in the Sanskritic tradition and, like *kṣānti*, has only a handful of occurrences therein. Meaning "contentment, gratification," on one occasion Tuṣṭi is personified as a goddess.[486]

### *kṛṣṇā-tāmasī*

Each of these epithets meaning "black, blue-black, dark" is applied to the Goddess on two occasions. Each of them appears

[484] Mbh 1.60.13 (where we have also seen Lakṣmī, Śraddhā, Buddhi, and Lajjā enumerated) and 2.7.17, respectively. The HV references of the PW are not in the constituted text. We may note that a late HV addition (App. I 42, lines 349-350) does know a roster of Dharma's wives who are Dakṣa's daughters, but it varies the order from the Mbh account and substitutes Vasu for Śraddhā.

[485] VDS 22.90; *Gautama Dharma Sūtra* (Georg Bühler [tr.], in *The Sacred Laws of the Aryas*, Part I, Clarendon Press [Oxford, 1879], SBE 2) 8.21.

[486] BDŚ 2.5.9.10.

in a hymn, without elaboration,[487] but each also appears in non-hymnic material where the force of the epithet is more clearly discernible. Thus at 85.41, when the emanation named Kauṣikī has come forth from her, Pārvatī is said to have become black (*kṛṣṇā*), and known as Kālikā, as if in counterpoint to the auspicious (*śivā*), beautiful emanation.[488] Similarly, in the first *carita*, when Brahmā completes his hymn, the Goddess who responds by coming forth from the parts of Viṣṇu's body is called *tāmasī*. Since the prologue to this hymn had called the goddess Mahāmāyā and Yoganidrā, now to call her "the one who shares in the obfuscating, disíntegrating quality of *tamas*"[489] is to maintain a continuity of characterization.

Although *tāmasī* has no history in the earlier literature, there are clearly discernible semantic associations of *kṛṣṇā*. At times to be sure, it has a merely descriptive function, particularly when it modifies a word for "cow";[490] to the extent that cows represent wealth and prosperity, the word may even have a positive resonance[491] Far more common, however, is a sense of the inauspicious or threatening quality of that which is *kṛṣṇā*. In the RV it appears on several occasions as the modifier of (or implying) night or darkness,[492] and in its commentary on RV 1.113.2ab, where Dawn (Uṣas) is described—"Resplendent, having a resplendent calf, the white one [*śvetyā*] has come; the black one [*kṛṣṇā*] has left places for her"[493]—the *Nirukta*'s interpretation is unequivocal :

> Having a resplendent calf, i.e., the sun.... Resplendent, the white one has come.... The black one has left places for her: the one of black colour, i.e., the night.

[487]*kṛṣṇā* at 85.10, *tāmasī* at 81.68.

[488]See *supra*, s. v. "*ambikā*," "*gaurī*," "*pārvatī*," and n. 70, and Part II, n. 125 for further remarks on this passage.

[489]For an interpretation of *tamas*, originally one of the *guṇas* of Sāṃkhya philosophy (cf. SK 23), see Danielou, *op. cit.*, pp. 22-24, 26-28.

[490]E.g., RV 1.62.9; 4.3.9; 10.61.4; YVT 2.1.9.1-2; ŚB 2.2.4.15.

[491]This same resonance is evident in its use in the AV's hymn to the earth (12.1.11).

[492]RV 1.113.2; 3.15.3; 9.66.24; 10.3.2.

[493]Sarup tr., when the passage occurs at *Nirukta* 2.20, whence also the following quotation.

> *Kṛṣṇam* (black) is derived from (the root) *kṛṣ* (to drag away): it is the despised colour.

While here, as with the Goddess herself, the force of that which is "despised" or threatening is mitigated by its being in symbiosis with its opposite, the fundamentally alien character of that which is *kṛṣṇā* is not in doubt. This is borne out by other Vedic texts where it is associated with an unfit altar brick,[494] sacrificial fees at death,[495] a cow killed at a funeral rite,[496] a cow offered to Nirṛti, the goddess of death,[497] and a cow that is black and decrepit, to be offered for a barren wife, for Nirṛti possesses them both.[498]

In the epic Kṛṣṇā appears primarily as an epithet of Draupadī, to whom it is applied on hundreds of occasions, and of whom it is simply descriptive: "she who is dark of complexion."[499] A hint of its more sinister aspect is evident when it appears as the name of one of the horde of *mātṛs* accompanying Skanda (9 45.21). In the HV it appears in the constituted text in Viṣṇu's invocation of Nidrā (47.39), where it may be merely descriptive—"(you are) *kṛṣṇā*, resembling my color (*macchavisadṛśi*)"—but where a "tamasic" undertone may be detected.

### *dhātrī-jagaddhātrī*

On two occasions the Goddess is called "supportress of the universe," *jagaddhātrī* (81.53; 93.9), a conceptualization that is also once found in uncompounded form, *jagatāṃ dhātrī* (84.27), and on one occasion she is simply called *dhātrī* (85.8). This epithet is used in the prologue and epilogue to hymns, and once appears in apposition with Caṇḍikā when the latter is worshipped. The instance of Dhātrī inclines toward being understood as a proper name, for it occurs in a hymnic sequence of proper names. Otherwise, the instances of this epithet are unextraordinary.

494 ŚB 8.7.2.16.
495 YVT 5.7.5.1.
496 YVT 6.1.6.7.
497 YVT 1.8.9.1.
498 ŚB 5.3.1.13. The DM praises the Goddess as *nairṛtī* at 85.9.
499 This explanation of Draupadī's designation as Kṣṛṇā is given at 1.155.50.

*Jagaddhātrī* is unknown in the earlier literature, while *dhātrī* is attested in various ways, none widely. Its oldest usage is at YVMai 4.4.2: the waters (*āpaḥ*) grant (*dhā*) splendor or power (*varcas*) to the *kṣatriya*, and hence are the supportresses (*dhātrīḥ*) of the *kṣatriya*. There are also instances of its use, as with other epithets we have seen, to modify a feminine word for verse, which verse is offered to a masculine deity. In the case of *dhātrī*[500] the corresponding male is Dhātṛ, the creator, variously identified in the RV as Indra or Viśvakarman, later as Brahmā or Prajāpati.[501] Finally, Dhātrī is the goddess who is to be worshipped after the successful delivery of an infant by Caesarean section from a dead mother.[502] In this case, the force of the word is close to the later generic understanding of it as "nurse" or "wet-nurse," which is the primary way that the Mbh knows the word, from a different root *dhā*, "to suckle."[503]

*nārasiṃhī*

Nārasiṃhī is the seventh of the Seven Little Mothers in our enumeration, appearing twice in the DM (88.19, 36), with an additional reference to the Goddess as *nṛsiṃharūpeṇa* (91.16). The description of her is not particularly detailed :

> Nārasiṃhī, having a form like the man-lion (*nṛsiṃha*),
> Then went forth, with multitudes of constellations cast down by the shaking of her mane (88.19).

In the sequel, our text focuses, as with other *mātṛs*, on her destructive potential, specifically her clawing and devouring of Asuras (88.36). It is worth noting in this regard that, while this description of Nārasiṃhī is general enough to say that it corresponds to that of Viṣṇu as Narasiṃha, Vaiṣṇava representations of the latter often incline toward a more explicitly gracious portrayal.[504]

[500] BṛDe 7.12; *Hiraṇyakeśin Gṛhya Sūtra* (J. Kirste [ed.], Alfred Hölder [Vienna, 1889]; H. Oldenberg [tr.] in *The Gṛhya Sūtras*, Part II, Clarendon Press [Oxford, 1892], SBE 30) 2.1.2.

[501] Keith, *op. cit.*, p. 206.

[502] VaiGS 7.4.

[503] E.g., 1.75.15ff.; 3.57.3. The Mbh does not know the word as a proper name.

[504] Banerjea, *Development*, pp. 415-417.

This epithet is unknown in Vedic or epic literature.

*mahāmārī*

Finally, we may note that one verse twice calls the Goddess *mahāmārī*, "the great pestilence."

> O king, this whole egg of Brahmā is pervaded by her,
> (Who is) Mahākālī at the end of time,[505] having the very form of the great pestilence.
> She herself is the great pestilence at one time, she herself, unborn, becomes the unborn creation (at another).[506]

Although some have subsequently seen the names here employed as distinguishing secondary and primary goddesses,[507] it seems preferable to take the passage at its face value, as a portion of the *ṛṣi*'s summary of the Goddess's diverse activity.[508] Furthermore, earlier in the same chapter (92.7), the Goddess has proclaimed that her glorification (*māhātmya*) cures all sicknesses that arise from the great pestilence (*mahāmārīsamudbhava*). We have repeatedly seen the delight that our text takes in paradoxical formulations, such as the ensuing application of *mahāmārī* to the Goddess herself dramatically presents.

This epithet is unknown in the earlier literature.

Our study so far has proceeded analytically, taking the epithets of the Goddess in the DM as "atomic units" and drawing on pre-DM Sanskritic literature in order to fathom their significance when employed at the time of the DM itself. To the

[505]See *supra*, n. 69.

[506]92.34cd-35. The text of 35 is:

> *mahākālyā mahākāle mahāmārīsvarūpayā* |
> *saiva kāle mahāmārī saiva sṛṣṭi bhavaty ajā* ||

Editions of the DM vary in their numbering and division of verses here. Our translation, which contrasts the forms of the Goddess at different times, is justified by 36ab :

> *sthitiṃ karoti bhūtānāṃ saiva kāle sanātanī* |

[507]Banerjea, *Development*, p. 496, discussing the *Prādhānikarahasya* of the DM.

[508]Which begins at 92.29 and ends two verses after the mention of *mahāmārī*.

extent that Hindus themselves have taken the names of "God" seriously, as indicative of the salient features and nuances of the divine character, such an inquiry needs no further elaboration.

However, as indicated in our Prolegomenon, the power of the DM derives not just from its use of particular epithets, but from the way they are integrated in its *stotras*. Our epithetical investigation therefore must also be seen in the larger context of providing historical leverage on the intrinsically ahistorical hymnic material.[509] To be complete, our study must examine the over-all structure that is comprised of the atomic units. It must proceed, as the DM itself does, from analysis to synthesis.

Before turning to the hymns themselves, however, we may examine a secondary integrative mechanism that is employed by our text, viz., its mythology. This is necessary, first, simply because the hymns refer to the myths, and to appreciate the former, some familiarity with the latter is essential. Second, and more important, is the fact that the DM's deployment of its myths itself reflects a crystallization of previously discrete motifs. It is as a preliminary step in the appreciation of the integrative quality of the DM that we turn to an examination of those myths in Part II.

[509] This is true even though we have not endeavored to provide a "complete history" of the individual epithets. As noted in our introductory remarks to Part I (*supra*, pp. 91-93), our task here has been to examine the Sanskritic resonance of the words at the time of the DM. The historical leverage that such a study exerts is that of setting the text (i.e., its diction) in its literary context.

Part II

# The Myths

# The Myths

The basic point of this second portion of our study can be put quite simply: in the DM we have the first discursive account in Sanskrit of the Goddess's role in the demise of the Asuras (1) Madhu and Kaiṭabha, (2) Mahiṣa, and (3) Śumbha and Niśumbha.[1] Mythological accounts of the encounter between these Asuras and various deities are known, with varying degrees of richness and detail, prior to the time of our text, and there is some evidence to suggest an earlier association of the Goddess with one or two of the myths. But, to our knowledge, there is no antecedent occasion on which (1) the three myths have been recounted together as a group, or (2) the Goddess has been portrayed as instrumental in effecting the divine triumph in all three encounters.

Documentation of this point, in comparison with our investigation of epithets, is more limited, for the liturgical nature of the Vedic corpus is such as to disincline it from the recounting of myths.[2] Our study, therefore, examines how the epics—Mbh, HV, and Rām—have dealt with these myths, proceeding in the order in which the DM recounts them, and supplementing the epic accounts with other material as necessary. In conclusion, we examine one other early Purāṇic account of the Goddess's salvific activity, that provided by the *Vāmana Purāṇa*.

## 1. *Madhu and Kaiṭabha*

In our discussion of the epithet "*yoganidrā-nidrā*," we have suggested that, by the time of our text, the Madhu-Kaiṭabha

[1]The three myths here enumerated correspond to the three *caritas* of the DM.

[2]Even the Vedic texts which do not show this reluctance do not know the myths of the DM: cf. Macdonell's appendix "Index of words in the *Bṛhaddevatā*," and Sarup's "An alphabetical list of stories related in the *Nirukta*."

myth is firmly linked to the figure of Viṣṇu, and have given preliminary support to that claim by noting how pervasive is the use of the epithet Madhusūdana, "slayer of Madhu," for Viṣṇu in the Mbh.[3] That this is how we should understand this epithet is made clear by the epic itself :

> The great Asura named Madhu, born from the secretions of (Viṣṇu's) ear,
> Fearful (*ugra*), of fearful deeds, entertaining a fearful design,
> Did Puruṣottama slay, showing respect for Brahmā.
> Because of his (Madhu's) destruction, gods, Dānavas, men,
> And seers call Janārdana "Madhusūdana."[4]

Further evidence for the integrity of this relationship is found in the fact that all but one of the references to Madhu and Kaiṭabha appear in the constituted text of the Mbh, not in the critical apparatus:[5] the story is no late-comer to the bardic tradition. Most conclusively, on the occasions when the agent of the Asuras' destruction is specified, the epics invariably cite Viṣṇu.[6]

The sequence of events which the epithet and passing references call to mind are recounted on several occasions in the epics. In order to provide ourselves with a standard against which to assess later versions of the myth, we here present the archetype, the first Mbh account, in full. In response to Yudhiṣṭhira's inquiry into the genealogy of the demon Dundhu,

[3]See Part I, n. 454.

[4]Mbh 6.63.12-13. These verses are repeated, with variants, at 12.200. 14-16. Note also the ubiquitous epithet Mādhava, which, however, is open to more equivocal interpretation.

[5]The one exception is 50*, inserted after 3.13.34. The context is Arjuna's praise of Kṛṣṇa's past accomplishments, to which this interpolation adds: at the beginning of the age, Brahmā sprang from your navel and, when M. and K. arose, Śiva from your forehead—"thus have the two commanders of the gods arisen from your body." Śiva's association with this myth is, at least, anomalous.

[6]The Goddess, however, is called *kaiṭabhanāśinī* in the Durgā Stotra, q.v. in Part III. Otherwise, see in addition to the passages already cited, and to the more extended accounts to be considered in the sequel, the following passing references to this agency of Viṣṇu: Mbh 5.128.49; 9.48.21; HV 31.17-18; 38.5-6; Rām 7.63.19-22; 7.69.26-27. The two Asuras very occasionally appear without any reference to the myth, e.g., Mbh 9.54.25; 12.220.52-53.

who had been called "the son of Madhu and Kaiṭabha,"[7] Mārkaṇḍeya replies:[8]

When there was but a single, dreadful ocean, and the moving and standing creation had perished, and all the creatures had come to an end, bull of the Bharatas, the blessed Viṣṇu, the everlasting source of all creatures, the eternal Person, slept [*suṣvāpa*] solitarily on his ocean bed in the vast coil of the boundlessly puissant snake Śeṣa. The maker of the world, the blessed lord Acyuta Hari slept, my lord, while encompassing the girth of this earth with the vast coil of the snake. While the God was sleeping, a lotus of the luster of the sun sprouted from his navel; and there, in that sun-like and moon-like lotus, Grandfather himself was born, Brahmā, the guru of the world, the One of the four Vedas, the four forms, the four faces, unassailable because of his own puissance, and of mighty strength and prowess.

Madhu[9] and Kaiṭabha saw the lord Hari of great splendor as he lay in his divine lair, the coil of the snake, which was many leagues wide and many leagues long. He wore his diadem, the Kaustubha jewel, and a yellow robe of silk; and he blazed with fortune, splendor, and beauty, O king, with the light of a thousand suns, of the most wondrous aspect. Madhu and Kaiṭabha were greatly astonished, when they saw the lotus-eyed Grandfather in the lotus. Thereupon those two began to intimidate boundlessly mighty Brahmā; and, repeatedly terrified by the pair, glorious Brahmā shook the lotus stalk and Keśava woke up. Govinda then saw the powerful Dānavas; and upon seeing them the God said, "Be welcome, mighty ones. I shall give you a superb boon, for I am pleased with you."

[7]Mbh 3.193.16; cf. also 3.195.1, 8, 35.

[8]The following quotation is Mbh 3.194.8cd-30, van Buitenen tr. Throughout, we emend his reading of dental "t" in Kaiṭabha to retroflex "ṭ", for the text so reads. Van Buitenen does maintain this phonetic distinction in other words but he always reads Kaitabha for Kaiṭabha.

[9]Van Buitenen here omits 13a: *kasyacit tv atha kālasya,* "after some time." In light of the fact that the account is silent on the origin of the Asuras, the phrase is perhaps important in indicating that the text is deliberately indefinite on such matters.

The powerful Asuras began to laugh at Hṛṣīkeśa, great king, and both replied to Madhusūdana, "Ask *us* for a boon, God, we are your benefactors, best of celestials; we shall surely give you a boon, ask without hesitation."

*The blessed lord said:*

I accept your boon, heroes, there is a boon I desire; for you are both of great prowess, and there is no man who is your equal. Now, for the good of the world, I wish to fulfill this desire: that the two of you, who are strong in the truth, may be killed by my hand !

*Madhu and Kaiṭabha said:*

Not even in jest have we ever spoken a lie before, let alone in fact. Know, best of persons, that we are devoted to truth and Law [*dharma*]. No one is our equal in strength, beauty, bravery, serenity, Law, austerity, generosity, and in character, mettle, and self-control. A great calamity looms before us, Keśava. But carry out your word, for Time is unavoidable. Yet we wish you to do one thing, God our lord, that you, greatest of celestials, do the killing where space [*ākāśa*] is uncovered [*anāvṛta*] and we shall become your sons, fair-eyed one. Know that this, O God who are the first of the Gods, is our boon.

*The blessed lord said :*

I shall certainly do so; thus shall it all be.

*Mārkaṇḍeya said :*

Thereupon Govinda reflected; but Madhusūdana saw no place on earth or in heaven that was uncovered. Then the great God looked at his own uncovered thighs; and glorious Madhusūdana cut off the heads of Madhu and Kaiṭabha with the sharp edge of his discus, O king.

For all of this account's conciseness, its "meaning," to use Biardeau's phrasing,[10] is not exactly vivid. As is so often true in mythological accounts, the progression of events seems determined by a logic that is more implicit than explicit, and the events themselves raise as many questions as they answer : if this is the universal dissolution of *pralaya*, whence come the two Asuras ? Why should Viṣṇu, when awakened, be pleased

[10]See Proleg., pp. 31-32.

with the Asuras? Given the certainty of the outcome, in light of the initial boon received by Viṣṇu, what is the critical issue in the ensuing dialogue and course of events? While a truly adequate answer to such questions must await, *inter alia*, a full structural analysis of this myth that has so captured Hindu fancy,[11] we may suggest some of the issues that are teased out by other epic versions.

The predominant interpretation is that this is a cosmogonic myth: the setting is, after all, *pralaya*, and what is of interest is the movement from that condition of disintegration to the manifestation of the universe. Consequently, one finds that the "point" of the myth is often made explicit at the end of the account. One HV account of Madhu, for instance, does not conclude with the death of the Asura, but goes two verses further :

> Like an alluring young woman in autumn, clad in a red garment,
> Did the earth (*pṛthivī*) appear, filled with the fat (*medas*) and marrow (*vaśā*) of Madhu.
> Thus was the name Medinī received by the earth, O king,
> (And) the name of Dharaṇī put forward by thousands of Asuras.[12]

[11]On the extent of this capturing of the Hindu fancy, we may note that, in addition to the epic versions about to be discussed, we have encountered fifteen full accounts in Purāṇas other than the MarkP, along with a host of brief allusions. Also, we may note that Ingalls has pointed out to us (personal note, undated) that the Mbh version misses the point of the myth's ending, a point that is clear in the MatsyaP version [*Matsyamahāpurāṇam* 170: Venkaṭeśvara Press (Bombay, 1923)]: M. and K., seeing the universal flood, cleverly asked to be slain "where the earth is not covered with water" (*na yatrorvī salilena pariplutā*); Viṣṇu, however, understood *ūrvī* as the feminine dual of *ūru*, "thigh," rather than as the singular of *urvī*, "earth," and so killed them on his thighs. In fact, none of the epic instances hereafter cited appreciates this play on words.

[12]Appendix I 41, lines 1431-1434. There is a second implicit etymological association here of *vasā* and the earth as *vasudhā* and *dharaṇī*. The myth which these verses conclude is somewhat different from the archetype and there seem, in fact, to be two stories about Madhu: one where he is paired with Kaiṭabha in their pranks at *pralaya*, and another where he appears alone as a Vaiṣṇava foe. The latter is also attested at HV 44.22-23 where Madhu is cited as a great Dānava who was the father of Lavaṇa. The Rām also knows this

Still more explicit is the occasion on which the story is put in the first person, narrated by the goddess Earth herself (*dharaṇī*) in her solicitation of divine relief from oppression.[13] One of the past favors she recalls is Viṣṇu's destruction of Madhu and Kaiṭabha, her account of which also has an etymological conclusion:

> The Daityas, immersed in the water, with their two bodies became one.
> Being churned by the waves of the water, they released fat (*medas*).
> The water was pervaded by them, with (their) fat; then they disappeared,
> And the blessed Nārāyaṇa again created creatures.
> Thus covered by the fat of the two Daityas, (I am) known as Medinī,
> Made eternal for mankind by the power of the lotus-naveled (Viṣṇu).[14]

So pervasive has this understanding of the myth become that, at times, the etymological reference is given alone, without a full version of the story. Thus the HV's introductory myth-history affirms:

> This earth is the supportress, creatrix, purifier,
> Support, and womb of all that does and does not move,
> The milker (who) milks every desire, putting forth every kind of produce.
> This is she, bordered by the ocean, known as Medinī,

---

relationship (7.61.17), along with the further details that Madhu is the brother-in-law of Rāvaṇa (7.25.22ff.), and had received from Śiva a mighty spear (7.61.5-14) with which Lavaṇa now belabors the world (7.61.20ff.). Although our concern is with the *pralaya* myth, since that is the DM's story, it is clear that the two stories are often intertwined: in the Rām, the instrument of Lavaṇa's demise at the hands of Śatrughna (7.68-69) is an arrow that the latter had received from Rāma (7.63.19-22), an arrow that was originally fashioned by Viṣṇu, reclining on the primordial waters, in order to slay Madhu and Kaiṭabha (*loc. cit.*) !

[13]Her speech is found at HV 42.13-53, with the Madhu-Kaiṭabha story being related in the first twenty-one verses.

[14]HV 42.31-33.

Utterly suffused with the fat (*medas*) of Madhu and Kaiṭabha.[15]

Even the Rām, which does not know a discursive account of the myth, is aware that it is only after slaying Madhu and Kaiṭabha that Viṣṇu began to create (7.63.23), though it misses the etymological association by affirming that it was from the heaps of bones (*asthicaya*) of Madhu and Kaiṭabha that the earth (*medinī*) was produced (7.104.5-6).

In some versions of the myth, its cosmogonic nature emerges in a rather different manner. Although the archetypal account ignores the issue of the Asuras' origin, we have seen that the Mbh passage that etymologizes Madhusūdana indicates they were born from the secretions of Viṣṇu's ear, with which the DM account concurs (81.50). Variant accounts, however, go much further in delineating the ontological status of the Asuras. For instance, in the Nārāyaṇīya section of the Mbh there is a version of the myth that seeks to account for the Asuras' presence by assimilating them to the raw material with which creation is accomplished, viz., *prakṛti*.[16] This account affirms that from the primordial darkness arose the Puruṣa Aniruddha, otherwise known as *pradhāna* or Hari. From him, while under the influence of *nidrāyoga* and lying on the waters, the thought of creation sprang forth as the four-faced Brahmā. Sitting on the lotus in Aniruddha's navel, Brahmā adopted the *guṇa* of *sattva* and began to create. Also in the lotus, however, were two drops of water that had been cast there by Nārāyaṇa.

One of those drops resembled honey (*madhvābhaḥ*), of brilliant radiance.
At the command of Nārāyaṇa, it engendered Madhu, of (the *guṇa* of) *tamas* (*tāmasaḥ*).
The other drop, a hard one (*kaṭhinaḥ*), (engendered) Kaiṭabha, of (the *guṇa* of) *rajas* (*rājasaḥ*)[17]

Later (12.335.64), the formulation is offered that the bodies of the two Asuras were pervaded by the two less-than-perfect

[15]HV 6.38-39.
[16]The following three sentences are a précis of Mbh 12.335.14-21.
[17]Mbh 12.335.22cd-23.

*guṇas* (*rajastamoviṣṭatanū*). With this, another version in the HV agrees nearly verbatim,[18] although it also admixes the *medas-medinī* motif by having the two Asuras declare, "By us is all (this) covered over with *tamas* and *rajas*."[19]

A second theme that runs through the different versions of the Madhu-Kaiṭabha myth is the gracious, facilitating activity of Viṣṇu. At a minimum, as in the Mbh archetype, this activity is no more than his termination of the Asuric harrassment of Brahmā, an activity on which all variants agree. But sometimes greater specificity is provided. In the Nārāyaṇīya account, for example, the offense of the Asuras is that they steal the Vedas from Brahmā, the implications of which are made clear in the latter's plaint to Nārāyaṇa:

> The Vedas are my great eye, my supreme strength.
> The Vedas are my primary dwelling-place, the Vedas my highest Brahman.
> All my Vedas have been taken from me by the two Dānavas,
> (And) deprived of the Vedas, the worlds created by me are (nought but) darkness.
> Without the Vedas, how can I, even with perseverance, create the worlds?[20]

That Viṣṇu becomes known via this myth as the great retriever of the Vedas, through whose redemptive activity creation occurs, is clear from a hymnic verse in the HV :

> The Vedas, formerly taken away from the onlooking Brahmā by the two Dānavas,
> Were rescued by you, O god; with that truth, release (me).[21]

It is worth noting that, as Viṣṇu becomes known as possessed of many forms and incarnations, one of them becomes commonly associated with this myth, viz., his *hayaśiras* or "horse-headed" form.[22]

[18]HV App. I 41, lines 381 and 437.

[19]HV App. I 41, line 406.

[20]Mbh 12.335.29-30.

[21]HV App. I 42B, lines 3008-3009. *Pāda* d (*tena satyena mokṣaya*) is a hymnic refrain.

[22]Cf. Mbh 12.335.44ff.; HV App. I 41, line 1422; App. I 42B, line 3010.

A third and final theme that runs through the pre-DM accounts of the Madhu-Kaiṭabha myth is that of deceit, trickery, illusion. At the simpliest level, it is not surprising to find such a motif associated with Asuras, for we have seen in our discussion of the epithet "*mahāmāyā*" that *māyā* has been associated with Asuras since Ṛg Vedic times. Some epic accounts of this myth merely particularize this association. Thus when the HV is setting the stage for its primary narrative, it remarks :

> It is said that of yore the earth was milked (*dugdhā*) by Asuras,
> Having taken an iron vessel; (their) magic tricks (*māyāḥ*) are destructive of (their) enemies,

and then goes on to identify a mighty, two-headed Madhu as the milker (*dogdhā*) for the Daityas.[23] More striking, however, in light of our earlier discussion of the Goddess, is one of the descriptions that Madhu and Kaiṭabha give of themselves to Brahmā:

> There is nothing superior to us in the world, O great sage.
> By us is all this world covered over with darkness (*tamas*) and passion (*rajas*).
> We who consist of *rajas* and *tamas* bear the marks of suffering (*duḥkha*) among ascetics,
> Are deceitful among those of virtuous conduct, are invincible (*dustara*) to all embodied ones.
> The world is deluded by us, who are born in age after age.
> We are wealth, desire, sacrifices, and all possessions,
> Where there is happiness, where there are joys, where fortune, humility, and prudence.
> Know, then, that what is desired by these (folk), that is the two of us.[24]

[23]HV 6.25-26.

[24]HV App. I 41, lines 405-412:

*nāvayoḥ paramaṃ loke kiṃcid asti mahāmune |*
*āvābhyāṃ chādyate viśvaṃ tamasā rajasā tathā ||*
*rajastamomayāv āvāṃ yatīnāṃ duḥkhalakṣaṇau |*
*chalakau dharmaśīlānāṃ dustarau sarvadehinām ||*
*āvābhyāṃ muhyate loka ucchritābhyām yuge yuge |*
*āvām arthaś ca kāmaś ca yajñāḥ sarvaparigrahāḥ ||*

While there are some critical correspondences between this description and that given of the Goddess by the seer Medhas in the first *carita* of the DM, it is important to note that, in the epic accounts of this myth, wiliness and guile are not only Asuric qualities. On the contrary, one version maintains that, prior to the actual physical encounter of Viṣṇu and Madhu, the latter's mind had been disturbed through the sensuous music of the Gandharvas and the Yogic eye of Viṣṇu.[25] Similarly, in the Nārāyaṇīya account, Viṣṇu's method of retrieving the Vedas is through trickery. His melodious, enchanting recitation of Vedic *mantras* fills the earth and induces the two Asuras to put down their booty and hurry off in search of the sounds' source; thereupon he scoops up the Vedas and returns them to Brahmā.[26] Sometimes, the distorted perception of reality comes about, not through the agency of another, but through self-delusion, as when the Asuras are described as "swollen and drunk with pride."[27] Such swashbuckling egoism is also apparent in their insistence on granting the initial boon in the Mbh archetype quoted above. It seems, in fact, that the encounter between Madhu-Kaiṭabha and Viṣṇu is as much a battle of wits as a physical combat. Though different accounts of the myth have preserved only isolated skirmishes, we may reconstruct that battle as follows. Infatuated with themselves, the Asuras make a commitment that promises their own undoing. Viṣṇu, ever gracious, and impressed by their martial prowess, then allows conditions to be set on meeting that commitment. Now the Asuras see a glimmer of hope for a total reprieve: perceiving that, it being *pralaya*, only the universal ocean exists, they attempt to outsmart Viṣṇu by requiring that their destruction be accomplished on a dry spot. Momentarily baffled, Viṣṇu then notices that his thighs are dry. He slays Madhu and Kaiṭabha thereon.[28]

---

*sukhaṃ yatra mudo yatra yatra śrīḥ saṃnatir nayaḥ /*
*eṣāṃ yat kāñkṣitaṃ caiva tad tad āvāṃ vicintaya //*

[25]HV App. I 41, lines 1335-1344.

[26]Mbh 12.335.50-53.

[27]HV App. I 41, line 384.

[28]See also *supra*, n. 11. Although this sequence of events, reconstructed on the basis of the epic accounts previously cited, does not appear *in toto* in any one text, such a reconstruction may be justified on the same grounds as

When the DM recounts this myth, then, there are several points of consequence. The first is that the story has previously been "owned" by Viṣṇu, for all previous accounts portray him as the agent of the Asuras' demise. Now, in our text, Viṣṇu's very capacity to act as agent is shown to be derivative, contingent upon the withdrawal from him of the Goddess as Yoganidrā. Second, the cosmogonic concern of the myth enables our text to begin its discursive account of the Goddess on a cosmic, even ontological, scale. Since the Asuras arose from strands of *prakṛti* and, in diffused form, became fashioned into the earth itself, it is utterly appropriate that Brahmā should hymn the Goddess as *mahāsurī* (81.58), for she herself "is *prakṛti*, manifesting the triad of constituent stands (81.59)."[29] She *is* the cosmos. Finally, we should recall that the epithet to which the DM links its version of the Madhu-Kaiṭabha myth is Mahāmāyā.[30] It is the Goddess, as the Great Illusion, who deludes the two Asuras into thinking they can outwit the divine (81.73). But it is also she who leads human beings to impute solidity to life in this world,[31] thereby making their own individual attempts to outwit the divine, for only the divine truly abides. And just as the former attempt ends in failure, though not without redemption — the promise of becoming "sons of God"—so, implies our text, must the latter.

## 2. *Mahiṣa*

Of the three myths that the DM associates with the Goddess, that of her encounter with Mahiṣa is of greatest moment in her on-going identity, for her designation as *mahiṣāsuramardinī* is

---

O'Flaherty's reconstruction of the much broader Śaiva mythology (*Asceticism and Eroticism*, pp. 30-32): it gives one an overview, wherein the individual episodes and particular textual fragments, may be better understood. One additional recurrent motif is the Asuras' request to become sons of Viṣṇu: we have not mentioned this in our reconstruction because Viṣṇu's consent does not seem to affect the course of events, whereas the request for a dry place of execution does. We offer an interpretation of this motif, the request for sonship, below.

[29]*guṇatrayavibhāvinī*: See Part I, s. v. "*prakṛti*".

[30]See Part I, s. v. "*mahāmāyā*" and "*yoganidrā*".

[31]MarkP 81.40. Cp. the Asuras' self-description given *supra*, n. 24.

pervasive of the later Indian religious tradition.[32] Yet, when we look at the antecedent versions of the myth, the material is far more modest than is the case with the Madhu-Kaiṭabha myth. In fact, anticipating our discussion of the Śumbha-Niśumbha episode, we may discern a pattern in the DM's account. The length at which it recounts the different myths is inversely proportional to the extent of a myth's attestation in the earlier literature: the familiar Madhu-Kaiṭabha myth provides a ready entry-point for establishing the Goddess's cosmic, transcendent status, which is accomplished in one chapter, of 77 verses;[33] the less familiar Mahiṣa episode establishes her origin on earth and provides one example of her salvific activity in three chapters (145 verses); the Śumbha-Niśumbha account, which is almost unknown heretofore, recounts in glorious detail her diverse mundane forms and accomplishments in nine chapters (351 verses).[34]

When the DM employs the Mahiṣa myth, there is only a single discursive account in the epics as precedent, and its influence upon our text's version seems more oblique than direct. Yet that something important is afoot here is clear, for that one epic precedent is in the Mbh's initial account of the figure of Skanda, and it is to Skanda that the destruction of Mahiṣa is originally ascribed (3.221). We have already met this account on several occasions in our discussion of epithets: Śivā is the seer's wife in whose guise Svāhā first cohabits with Agni; the goddess Śakti appears as a somewhat mysterious figure at a number of points; Lakṣmī is cited as both attendant and spouse of Skanda; and Gaurī appears in

[32]For a rough indication of this, see the wealth of material provided by Sahai in his chapter on "Mahiṣāsuramardinī" (pp. 181-195) and the comparatively meagre iconographic representation of Madhu and Kaiṭabha (Banerjea, *Development*, pp. 275, 408, 513, 538), which representation, in any case, involves Viṣṇu, not the Goddess. For an impressive analysis of Tamil versions of the Mahiṣa myth, see Shulman, David D., *Tamil Temple Myths: Sacrifice and Divine Marriage in the South Indian Śaiva Tradition*, Princeton University Press (Princeton, 1980), pp. 176-192.

[33]Actually, if one rules out the frame story, the DM's account of the Madhu-Kaiṭabha myth is accomplished in only 28 verses.

[34]Or, if one excludes the concluding frame (chapter 93) of the frame story, 344 verses. Even if one counts everything after Śumbha's demise (chapter 90) as part of the concluding frame, the third *carita* still runs to 248 verses.

Pārvatī's retinue on the first occasion that the Mbh applies the latter name to Śiva's spouse. We have also seen[35] that the identity of the Seven Little Mothers, and of "The Mothers" in general, is intertwined with the identity of Skanda, particularly when he is understood as the offspring of Agni. That the mythologies of Skanda and the Goddess should dovetail on the figure of Mahiṣa may be initially startling, then, but it is not, in the larger context, utterly anomalous.

Before turning to the Mbh account itself, it may be helpful to recall van Buitenen's appreciation of the dilemma that Skanda poses for the Mbh, viz., "there is the notion that *a God is born.* Incarnations of God are legion, but the birth of a completely *new* God is unique."[36] Consequently, this first Mbh account of his birth manifests diverse traditions regarding his genealogy, particularly on the maternal side, although "by the time of Kālidāsa Kumāra's parental parentage [sic] has been sorted out"[37] into the figures of Pārvatī and Śiva. We have noted elsewhere that, although this Āraṇyaka Parva account seems to prefer Agni as sire of Skanda, later Mbh accounts are inclined toward the fatherhood of Śiva,[38] and even this initial account presents two brief claims on behalf of Śiva.[39] These facts are important, apart from indicating the general fluidity of the mythology, because it is after the second of these claims in the Mbh 3 account that the Mahiṣa story occurs. After the complex discussion of Skanda's birth and companions, in which the fatherhood of Agni is preferred, Brahmā informs Skanda (3.220.8-10) that, in fact, Śiva and Pārvatī are his parents, having "permeated" (*samāviśya*) Agni and Svāhā, and *this* genealogy is accepted without cavil throughout the balance of this account.[40] Consequently, when Skanda slays Mahiṣa in the following chapter, it is in a Śaiva context.

Although that battle is not extraordinary by epic and Purāṇic standards, it is clear that the Mbh understands it as the

[35]In Appendix A.

[36]Mbh, van Buitenen tr. vol. II, p. 206, his italics; also cited in our Appendix A, section II.

[37]*Ibid.*, p. 207.

[38]Appendix A, n. 17.

[39]Appendix A, n. 35.

[40]Which ends after 3.221.

culmination of its account of Skanda, wherein the son visibly works out his relationship to his father. Also, some features of that account recur in the DM's version. We may see both of these aspects in the following salient events. (1) After Skanda acts upon Brahmā's advice by honoring Śiva as his father, a great Śaiva parade is described (3. 221. 1-25).

> Then the Great God [Śiva] spoke to Mahāsena [Skanda] this weighty word : "Always protect the seventh division [*skandha*] of the Maruts carefully."
>
> *Skanda said:*
>
> My lord, I shall guard the seventh division of the Maruts. Tell me quickly what else I should do, God.
>
> *Rudra said :*
>
> You must always look at me in your affairs, son. From looking at me and from devotion [*bhakti*] for me you shall attain the supreme good.[41]

(2) Immediately thereafter, the demonic assault upon the divine host begins, in the course of which, as in the DM, Indra looms as the chief spokesman for the gods.[42] (3) The battle appears to turn when

> From the dreadful army of the Daityas there emerged a powerful Dānava, Mahiṣa by name,[43] who had grabbed a great mountain; and the celestials seeing him hold high a mountain—like the sun that is completely decked with clouds—ran, king, ran. Mahiṣa fell on the Gods and hurled his mountain; and the grim-looking stone mass in its fall felled

[41]Mbh 3.221.26-28, van Buitenen tr.

[42]3.221.39-42. Cp. the opening verses of the second *carita* in the DM (82. 1-2):

> Once upon a time there was a battle between the gods and Asuras lasting a full hundred years,
> When Mahiṣa was leader of the Asuras, (and) Indra of the gods.
> There the gods' army was conquered by the mighty Asuras,
> And having conquered all the gods, the Asura Mahiṣa became lord (lit., "Mahiṣa became Indra": *indro 'bhūn mahiṣāsuraḥ*).

[43]Like the Mothers (cf. Appendix A, n. 24), Mahiṣa suddenly erupts into the account, without comment. Although the Mbh later makes passing reference to his having received a boon from Brahmā (3.221.73), neither it

a myriad God soldiers and crushed them to the earth, O lord.[44]

(4) That the text is concerned to portray Śiva as giving Skanda an identity of his own is evident in the sequel, for when the angry "Mahiṣa...attacked Rudra's chariot,...ran to and grabbed hold of Rudra's chariot pole..., even in this pass the blessed lord [Śiva] declined to kill off Mahiṣa in battle, for he remembered [sic : *sasmāra*] that Skanda was to be the death of the miscreant."[45] (5) The demise of the villain is described more succinctly than in the DM :

> ...when this grisly danger beset the Gods, out came Mahāsena.... And, great king, puissant Mahāsena threw his blazing, shattering spear [*śakti*] at Mahiṣa; and Mahiṣa's head was split, and he fell down relinquishing life. Throw after throw the spear smote the foes in their thousands and then, as witnessed the Gods and Dānavas, it returned again to Skanda's hand. Mostly killed off by the cunning [*dhīmat*] Mahāsena with his missiles, the remnant of the gory Daitya troops, frightened and panicked by Skanda's unstoppable Companions [*pārṣadāḥ*], fell and were eaten by the hundreds. They feasted on the Dānavas and gulped their blood....[46]

(6) Finally, that the Mbh intends this victory as the glorious climax of its account of Skanda is clear from Indra's concluding declaration : "This deed shall be thy first claim to fame and

---

nor the DM is interested in his origin, apparently. However, other Purāṇas do explore this matter: see section 4 below.

[44]Mbh 3.221.52-54, van Buitenen tr. The DM also knows Mahiṣa as the great hurler of mountains: cf. 83.24, 26, 34. Elsewhere (e.g., ViṣṇuP 2.4.27) "Mahiṣa" is the name of a mountain.

[45]3.221.57, 60, van Buitenen tr.

[46]3.221.62abc, 65-69ab, van Buitenen tr. Far simpler than the DM's account, this passage nonetheless does have certain subtle correspondences with our text. Though the Mbh knows nothing of Mahiṣa's changes of form (MarkP 83.28-32, 38),it does sense the presence of mysterious, extraordinary power in the reiterative flight of Skanda's spear. Also, the DM similarly assigns certain companions to the Goddess, although they are here called *gaṇas* (82.52, 53), rather than *pārṣadas*, and their blood-thirsty nature does not emerge until the third *carita*, in conjunction with the Seven Little Mothers.

thy glory shall be imperishable in the three worlds—the Gods shall be in thy power, son of a God, Mahāsena."[47]

Although one may justifiably conclude from this account that the Mahiṣa myth in the epics is predominantly a "Skandic" or quasi-Śaiva motif, one should temper this conclusion with an awareness that those texts are, as with the genealogy of Skanda, engaged in a winnowing process, sorting out the mythology of this god. The constituted text of the Mbh is, to be sure, consistent, for its two additional passing references to Mahiṣa cite Skanda as his conqueror, as does one later interpolation.[48] Elsewhere in the critical apparatus, however, some equivocation is apparent. In the Durgā Stava, the "slayer of Mahiṣa" (*mahiṣāsuranāśinī*) is none other than the goddess there praised,[49] while on another occasion it is Śiva who is hymned with such a title (*mahiṣaghna*).[50] The Rām does not know Mahiṣa at all, though it occasionally describes the demon Dundubhi as having assumed the form of a buffalo (*māhiṣaṃ rūpam*).[51] The constituted text of the HV is similarly void of reference to the Asura Mahiṣa. The critical apparatus, however, in two separate hymns praises the goddess (Goddess?) as his vanquisher.[52] And, as we shall see in the next section, Bhāsa's *Bālacarita* gives one passing suggestion of a convergence of the Mahiṣa and Śumbha-Niśumbha myths. Furthermore, if we exclude the MarkP's knowledge (which is limited to the account provided by the DM),[53] among the Purāṇas that

[47]Mbh 3.221.76, van Buitenen tr.

[48]Mbh 7.141.15; 9.45.65; and App. I 22, line 6 in the Āraṇyaka Parva (the Kārttikeya Stava, inserted after 3.221).

[49]Line 29; see Part III.

[50]Mbh 13, App. I 6, line 45; cf. also Mbh 13, App. I 5, lines 44ff.

[51]E.g., Rām 4.11.25.

[52]Pradyumna's Hymn, line 371, q. v. in Part III; also, 13* in HV App. I 35, i.e., an insertion in Aniruddha's hymn, the basic text of which we cite in Part III.

[53]This parenthetical comment holds true insofar as the MarkP is understood to be one of the three editions consulted in the course of this study. However, it appears that there is another edition, or another text under the same title: W. T. Elmore, (*Dravidian Gods in Modern Hinduism*, published by the author [Hamilton, N.Y., 1915], reprinted from University Studies of the University of Nebraska Vol. XV, No. 1 [1915], p. 126) cites the following account from "*Durga Sapta Shati*, in the *Markandaya Purana*, Bangalore,

O'Flaherty calls "early" (i.e., 300 B.C.E. — 500 C.E., viz., *Brahmāṇḍa*, *Mārkaṇḍeya*, *Matsya*, *Vāyu*, *Viṣṇu*),[54] only the MatsyaP knows Mahiṣa as a demon. Though he appears as a fairly nondescript Asura at several junctures,[55] there is one intriguing occasion on which Viṣṇu refrains from slaying him with the remark that Brahmā has foretold that Mahiṣa will die at the hands of a woman (152.17-24). But this Purāṇa never recounts such an event.[56] Yet by the time of Bāṇa, as we have seen in considering the epithet "*caṇḍikā*," the Mahiṣa myth is so firmly associated with the Goddess that it can form the very backbone of his *Caṇḍīśataka*.

If we turn to iconographic material for assistance in tracing the Goddess's involvement with Mahiṣa, we may note that the prevailing opinion for years has been that "extant Mahiṣāsuramardinī images... can hardly be dated before the Gupta period, and some miniature stone figurines unearthed at Bhitā are a few of the earliest summary representation[s] of this aspect of the goddess."[57] Of late, however, this dating has been called into question on two fronts. The first is occasioned by the discovery of a terracotta plaque of Mahiṣāsuramardinī at Nagar, Rajasthan which "appears to belong to the beginning

1893" (p. 126n): "Diti, the mother of the Asuras, lost all of her sons in a fight with the gods. Another son was born to her, and he took the form of a buffalo in order to annihilate the gods. He was called Mahisasura. The story goes on to tell of the terrible fight between Durga and this buffalo. Durga at last conquered him, and cutting off his head, drank his blood." W. Crooke (*The Popular Religion and Folklore of Northern India*, Munshiram Manoharlal [Delhi, 1968; reprint of the second edition, 1896], vol. 2, p. 237) cites what seems to be the same account, at somewhat more length, the source being identified as "Mārkandeya Purāṇa," without bibliographic details. We have been unable to locate the text that these authors cite, let alone compare its account with that of our editions, which seem, on balance, to be the "normative" MarkP text.

[54]*Asceticism and Eroticism*, p. 14.

[55]MatsyaP 147.28; 148.42; 150.109-140.

[56]It does, however, subsequently treat the iconography of Mahiṣāsuramardinī (260.55ff.). The VāmanaP, which O'Flaherty calls a "middle" Purāṇa; i.e., 500-1000 C.E. (*Asceticism and Eroticism*, p. 14), does present interesting testimony regarding Mahiṣa. We shall consider it, along with the rest of the VāmanaP account, in section 4 below.

[57]Majumdar, *HCIP* vol. 3, p. 447; J. N. Banerjea is the author of this passage.

of the first century A.D. or the middle of the first century B.C." and which

> depicts the four-handed deity, her lower right hand being placed on the back of the buffalo (*mahisha*). The upper right hand holds a *triśūla* (trident). The tail of the animal appears erect while its front legs are raised. Its mouth is just below the lower left hand of the goddess. Her left leg is placed on the head of a recumbent lion,... [which, in such an] early plaque,... is a feature of high interest.[58]

The second questioning of tradition stems from

> six statues of the Kuṣāṇa age, preserved in the Mathurā Museum, [which] appear to contain some other early representations of the Mahiṣamardinī form. The Devī is shown in these as holding a buffalo raised to her waist, the demon being represented in his animal form. The weapons in the Devī's hand are the spear and trident; but the animal is killed more with her hands than with the weapons. The lion is absent in the sculptures.[59]

While we cannot trace the full discussion[60] of this image here, we may note that iconographers are sharply divided on the course of the image's development. Implicit in the above dating of the Nagar goddess-with-lion is the claim that this is the earliest mode of representing the Goddess-Mahiṣa encounter. Viennot, however, prefers to date this image in late Kuṣāṇa-early Gupta times and argues for a process of development: from the simple Kuṣāṇa statuary, through the Nagar addition of the lion motif, to the mature portrayals of Gupta and later

[58]Agrawala, R. C., "A Terracotta-Plaque of Mahishamardinī from Nagar, Rajasthan," *Lalit Kalā* 1-2 (April 1955- March 1956), pp. 73, 74. This dating is often presented elsewhere: Agrawala, R. C., "Some sculptures of Durgā Mahiṣāsuramardinī from Rājasthāna," *Adyar Library Bulletin* NS Vol. XIX (1955), pp. 37-46; Chatterjee, A.K., "Characteristics of Skanda-Kārttikeya," *Indian Museum Bulletin* (Calcutta) IV 1 (1961), pp. 60-66; Sircar, D. C., *Studies in the Religious Life of Ancient and Medieval India*, Motilal Banarsidass (Delhi, 1971), p. 231; Sahai, *op. cit.*, p. 184.

[59]Sircar, *Religious Life*, p. 231.

[60]Which often revolves around the number of arms that the images have: see Sahai, *op. cit.*, pp. 181-195; Banerjea, *Development*, pp. 497-500.

times.[61] We are inclined toward the more balanced appraisal of Bhattacharyya—some of "the earlier Mahishamardinī figures seem to have had their inspiration from some other source than the *Mārkaṇḍeya Purāṇa* as the Devī's leonine mount is absent from some of the earliest images"[62]—for this seems most congruent with the textual material: just as there are various traditions about the identity of the slayer of Mahiṣa, so is it likely that there were varying accounts of the Goddess's encounter with him, which manifest themselves in the variations of representational art.[63] In iconography, as in mythology, it seems unlikely that the tradition has known a univocal development.

Finally, we may say word about a feature of the DM's account of the Mahiṣa myth that does not appear in the epics, viz., the initial crystallization of the Goddess out of the *tejas* of the different deities (82.8-18). We have argued that, in the over-all dynamic of our text, the function of the second *carita* is to move from the cosmic-transcendent orientation of the first *carita* to the exuberant exemplification of her mundane activity in the third. Its task is to demonstrate not only that the Goddess has an earthly career, but that of earthly creatures, she is the supreme ruler. Put more pointedly, when we ignore the eternal and focus on the temporal, ignore power as a religious phenomenon and focus on it as a secular one, the Goddess has to be shown to be the ultimate agent. What our text has done in its portrayal of the Goddess in this role is to draw on the model which, in Indian culture, most nearly fits these requirements, viz., the model of the king. Manu begins his account of this figure and his function as follows:

> I will declare the duties of kings, (and) show how a king should conduct himself, how he was created, and how (he can obtain) highest success.
>
> . . . . . . . . . . . . . . . . . . . . . .
>
> ...When these creatures, being without a king, through fear dispersed in all directions, the Lord created a king for

[61]Viennot, Odette, "The Goddess Mahishāsuramardinī in Kushāna Art," *Artibus Asiae* 19 (1956), pp. 372-373.

[62]In Majumdar, *HCIP*, vol. 4, p. 339.

[63]The force of this comparison will be felt still more strongly after our subsequent consideration of the VāmanaP's mythology.

> the protection of this whole (creation),
> Taking (for that purpose) eternal particles of Indra, of the Wind, of Yama, of the Sun, of Fire, of Varuṇa, of the Moon, and of the Lord of Wealth (Kubera).
> Because a king has been formed of particles of those lords of the gods, he therefore surpasses all created beings in lustre [*tejas*[64]];
> And, like the sun, he burns eyes and hearts; nor can anyone on earth even gaze on him.
> Through his (supernatural) power he is Fire and Wind, he Sun and Moon, he the Lord of justice (Yama), he Kubera, he Varuṇa, he great Indra.
> Even an infant king must not be despised, (from an idea) that he is a (mere) mortal; for he is a great deity in human form.
>
> . . . . . . . . . . . . . . . . . . . . .
>
> Having fully considered the purpose, (his) power, and the place and time, he assumes by turns many (different) shapes for the complete attainment of justice.
> He, in whose favour resides Padmā, the goddess of fortune, in whose valour dwells victory, in whose anger abides death, is formed of the lustre of all (gods).[65]

That this model of secular power underlies[66] the DM's vision of the Goddess's earthly origin is obvious enough. That its appropriateness is utter is equally obvious, for only one who is of peerless power on the world's own terms can cope with that great disturber of the mundane equilibrium, Mahiṣa.

### 3. *Śumbha and Niśumbha*

In the elaborate third *carita* of the DM, there are a number of subsidiary episodes, such as the Goddess's encounter with Dhūmralocana (chapter 86), Caṇḍa and Muṇḍa (87), and Raktabīja (88), yet it is clear that the account is primarily

[64]That "lustre" is a translation of *tejas* is clear from Bühler's notes.

[65]*Mānava Dharma Śāstra*, 7.1, 3-8, 10-11, Bühler tr.

[66]That this text is prior to the DM is affirmed by Macdonell (*History*, p. 428) who says "it probably assumed its present shape not much later than 200 A.D."

concerned with the Asuras Śumbha and Niśumbha. The first verse of the *carita* (85.1) cites them as villains, thereby providing a point of departure for its ensuing account, and in the order of demise, these two come last (89-90). Yet, as noted preliminarily at the beginning of the last section, the antecedent usage of the names Śumbha and Niśumbha is exceedingly modest. To be sure, there is such usage, and the consistency of the context in which it occurs makes it of unusual significance. Before turning to such matters, however, we may allow for the possibility that, upon occasion, the familiar reversion of the palatal sibilant *ś* to the guttural mute *k* has occurred, and that we should therefore be inquiring into the names Kumbha and Nikumbha. Such an inquiry will also enable us to consider some of the other Asuric names in the third *carita*.

To put our conclusion first: many of the demons' names in the final episode of our text are known in the epic literature, where they seem to belong to a "pool" of minor figures, usually but not always demonic in nature, and rarely given more than cursory characterization. Thus, the Mbh makes the following passing references to Kumbha and Nikumbha, always as Asuras: (1) they, along with Virocana, are the sons of Prahrāda (1.59.20); (2) Nikumbha is the son of Dānu (1.59.26); (3) Nikumbha was born on earth as king Devādhipa (1.61.27); (4) Nikumbha is the descendant of Hiraṇyakaśipu and father of Sunda and Upasunda (1.201.1-4). The Rām provides a more extensive account of two demons named Kumbha and Nikumbha: they are ministers or generals of Rāvaṇa[67] and sons of Kumbhakarṇa,[68] whose houses were fired by Hanumān;[69] they participate in the great battle,[70] and the demise of each of them is described at some length, Kumbha's at the hands of Sugrīva,[71] Nikumbha's at the hands of Hanumān,[72] but in none of these cases is there a distinctive description or mythology. As suggested by the penultimate reference here, the DM's characterization

[67]Rām 5.49.11; 6.9.1, 3.
[68]6.8.19; 6.75.46-47.
[69]5.54.14-15.
[70]6.59.20-21. Nikumbha's preliminary skirmish with Nila occurs at 6.43.9, 29-31.
[71]6.76.36-93.
[72]6.77.1-24.

of figures with these names occasionally differs from that of the epics. Sugrīva appears throughout the Rām as a monkey ally of Rāma and company, a verdict with which the Mbh's account of the Rāma story concurs,[73] whereas in our text he is an Asura, messenger of Śumbha to the Goddess (85.54-76). Dhūmralocana, "Smoky Eyes," does not appear in the epics, though a demon with the same characterization, Dhūmrākṣa, is known in the Rām as one of the miscellaneous malefactors,[74] in which capacity he also appears in the Mbh account.[75] Not all of the figures in the third *carita*, however, are drawn from this epic pool, for Raktabīja, who comes close to having a unique character, is unknown in epic accounts, and Caṇḍa and Muṇḍa appear as demons only in one late account.[76] If there is continuity, then, between the DM and the epics with regard to the figures of Kumbha, Nikumbha, and their associates, it seems to be rather casual, without undue ramification.

If, however, we consider the names of the chief demons without phonetic change, i.e., as they appear in our text, as Śumbha and Niśumbha, then the situation is quite different. The Mbh does not know these names at all, and the Rām knows a Śumbha and Niśumbhaka only in a roster of villains slain by Viṣṇu (7.6.35). The evidence from three other sources, however, is as follows.

(1) In the HV, when Viṣṇu descends to the nether regions (*pātāla*) in order to solicit the aid of the goddess Nidrā, he proposes a plan for their respective births to Devakī and Yaśodā (47.23-37) and then recounts the future course of events, in which she will be dashed against a rock by Kaṃsa (47.38). Viṣṇu then provides a description of the goddess which we will present in Part III, here quoting only the critical verse (49):

> Then the two Dānavas Sumbha and Nisumbha [sic], who frequent mountainous regions,

[73]Mbh 3.263-275, *passim*.

[74]The closest the Rām comes to providing a personal portrait is to identify him as one of the offspring of the demon Sumali and the Gandharvī Ketumati (7.5.39) and to describe his last battle with Hanumān (6.51-52). Other passing references occur at 5.6.23; 6.9.3; 7.14.2; 7.15.10-12; 7.31.35.

[75]Mbh 3.270.5-14.

[76]HV App. I 42B, lines 70, 76. In another reversal, however, Caṇḍa is cited as one of the monkey warriors at Rām 6.26.27-28.

You will slay, along with their followers, having fixed your mind on me.[77]

When the text proceeds to describe Kaṃsa's slaying of the female infant, there is no mention of Śumbha and Niśumbha in her ensuing transfiguration (48.27-36). However, when Kaṃsa is ruminating upon the identity of who it is that could be responsible for Kṛṣṇa's marvelous deeds, he recalls an encounter in the woods with Nārada, where the sage addressed him thus:

O Kaṃsa, that great effort which you exerted for the sake of (destroying Devakī's) infants
Has been made a fruitless action by Vasudeva, (acting) at night.
That daughter whom you struck upon a rock at night, O Kaṃsa,
Know her to be the daughter of Yaśodā and Kṛṣṇa to be the son of Vasudeva.
The two infants were exchanged at night, for the sake of your destruction,
By Vasudeva in alliance (with others), an enemy in the guise of a friend.
That daughter of Yaśodā, on the best of mountains, Vindhya,
Having slain the two Dānavas Śumbha and Niśumbha who wander on the mountains,
(Now) consecrated, a boon-giver, honored by a host of spirits,
(And) fond of great animal sacrifices, is worshipped by terrible outcastes (*dasyu*).
With two urns filled with liquor and flesh, resplendent,
Bedecked with various peacock (-like) ornaments and peacock feathers,
(She inhabits) a wood that resounds with the cries of wild cocks and crows,
Filled with throngs of goats and wild birds,
Resounding with the cry of lions, tigers, and boars,

[77]Lit, "having put me in your mind": *kṛtva manasi mām*. All ensuing refs. in the HV employ the palatal sibilant in the names of Ś. and N., but all manuscripts at the passage cited here attest the dental.

Thick and impenetrable with trees, surrounded on all sides
with deep woods.
Her palace on Vindhya mountain, fashioned by her own
splendor,
Is adorned with heavenly golden vases, chowrie fans, and
mirrors,
Reverberating with the sounds of the gods' musical
instruments.
The mother who strikes terror (*trāsajananī*) into (her)
enemies there constantly in ecstacy (*manorame*)
Dwells, supremely beloved (and) worshipped, even by the
gods.[78]

(2) In its version of the same story, the *Viṣṇu Purāṇa* does not know such a lengthy identification of this goddess, but it does associate her with Śumbha and Niśumbha in precisely the same context as the HV. After Viṣṇu has proposed his plan to the goddess, here called Yoganidrā (5.1.70), he describes her, rather more briefly than in the HV account, but including the line: "having slain Śumbha and Niśumbha, and numerous other demons, you shall sanctify the earth in many places."[79]

(3) Finally, although the date of the plays ascribed to Bhāsa is uncertain, it is generally accepted that they are prior to Kālidāsa, and one of them contains a version of these events that merits our attention.[80] While in some ways the *Bālacarita*

[78]HV 65.48-57. The text of the central description of the Goddess (52-53) runs:

*kṛtābhiṣekā varadā bhūtasaṅghaniṣevitā* |
*arcyate dasyubhir ghorair mahāpaśubalipriyā* ||
*surāpiśitapūrṇābhyāṃ kumbhābhyām upaśobhitā* |
*mayūrāṅgadacitraiś ca barhabhāraiś ca bhūṣitā* ||

There are other references to Śumbha and Niśumbha in the HV, in App. I 30. We shall mention them in introducing Pradyumna's Hymn in Part III.

[79]ViṣṇuP 5.1.81, Wilson tr., which we emend by reading *ś* for *s*, as the text does.

[80]Basham, *op. cit.*, p. 435. We here accept Basham's date for the dramatist and do not enter into the still undecided question of whether all the plays ascribed to him in fact come from his hand. For an important discussion of the date of the *Bālacarita*, and of its place in the Kṛṣṇa literature, see Hawley, John Stratton, *The Butter Thief*, Ph.D. dissertation, Harvard University, 1978, pp. 12-17, a revision of which is forthcoming from Princeton University Press under the title *Krishna, The Butter Thief.*

seems to present a simpler (and therefore earlier?) account of the Kṛṣṇa story, its portrayal of the goddess's transfiguration is more complex than the HV and ViṣṇuP accounts. At the end of the second act, Kaṃsa dashes the infant girl upon a rock, the stage directions read "Enter Kārtyāyanī and her retinue," and they speak as follows.

> *Kārtyāyanī.* [81] The demons Sumbha and Nisumbha and the Buffalo [*mahiṣa*] I slew, smiting the ranks of the celestials' foes. Now am I Kārtyāyanī born in Vasudeva's house [sic] to destroy the Kaṃsa brood.
>
> *Pot-belly* [*kuṇḍodara*]. Pot-belly am I, invincible, of fierce deeds in battle. Dreadful in my mighty hissing issued at the Goddess's wish. Swiftly I glide from the sky to the wide earth, eager to slaughter the haughty demons vainglorious of their powers.
>
> *Spear* [*śūla*]. I am the Spear, a spirit brought down to this earth and given a beautiful gleaming form by the favour of the Goddess. Kaṃsa will I strike down and drag him hither and thither on the battle-field as the God of War [*kārttikeya*] dragged Tāraka rooted in the ocean.
>
> *Nīla*. And I am Nīla ["blue-black"], stirer up of strife, a hero of the battle, who never turns his back. I shall slay the wicked Kaṃsa as the great Spear-wielder [Kārttikeya[82]] split the Kraunca rock.
>
> *Speed of Thought* [*manojava*]. I am Speed of Thought, swift as the wind. Hither I come to fulfil the Goddess's purpose. I do away with demons in the forefront of the fight just as fire goes through a house of reeds.
>
> *Kārtyāyanī.* Pot-belly, Pointed-ears, Big Blue, and Speed of Thought, come here. We'll disguise ourselves as cowherds and go down to the herdsmen's station to observe the Blessed Viṣṇu's exploits as a child.

[81] The spelling of this and the following names is that of the text itself: see Bhāsa, *Bālacaritam*, with introduction in English and Hindi and Hindi translation by S.R. Sehgal, foreword by Dr. V. Raghavan, Munshiram Manoharlal (Delhi, 1959).

[82] So identified in a note of the translators (who are themselves identified in our following note). Cf. also the VāmanaP's account of the events alluded to in this simile, which is discussed in our next section.

*All.* As the Goddess bids. (*Exit Kārtyāyanī with her train.*)[83]

Bhāsa's version is unique, among accounts here surveyed, for several reasons, e.g., its reference to the destruction of Śumbha and Niśumbha as a *fait accompli*, its suggestion that among the *gopīs* whom Kṛṣṇa enchants are this goddess and her retinue, etc. In a broader context, the appearance of some familiar motifs is arresting: the notion of the Goddess as having manifold strange companions, the ready reference to Skanda-Kārttikeya, and particularly the Goddess's claim to having slain Mahiṣa. But rather than pursuing these particular matters, we must turn to the more pressing question of the significance of this recurrent appearance of the Śumbha-Niśumbha myth in a Kṛṣṇa Gopāla context.[84]

What we want to know is not how Kṛṣṇa Gopāla became part of the larger Vaiṣṇava complex, nor how his worship ramified in later times, both of which have received a

[83] *Bālacarita* 2.20-25: *The Adventures of the Boy Krishna* (*Bāla-caritam*), in *Thirteen Trivandrum Plays Attributed to Bhāsa*, A. C. Woolner and Lakshman Sarup (tr.), Oxford University Press: Humphrey Milford (London, 1930, 1931), vol. II, pp. 109-141.

[84] We may offer one parting remark on *Bālacarita*. After working with the early Sanskritic "Goddess material" for a while, one becomes accustomed to having apparently hard evidence turn soft, to finding that hymns are excised from critical editions, texts are interpolated, interpreters biased. Our most extraordinary such experience involves Bhāsa's *Bālacarita*. We turned to it specifically for the light it sheds on Śumbha and Niśumbha. It is, then, at least remarkable to find that in the introduction to the Sanskrit text, the editor's entire argument against Bhāsa's authorship of this drama turns on these two words (pp. 39-42). Having argued that the Goddess is not a Vedic figure, he goes on to maintain that these two Asuras' names are a corruption of the verbal forms *śundhasva* and *niśumbhasva* that are first found in YVKā, a corruption effected by the DM as well as by the *Bālacarita*, which is, bluntly, an "indication of gross ignorance" ! Though he agrees with our general dating of Bhāsa (p. 39), his conclusion—"to carry the worship of the Durgā as far back as the time of Bhāsa does not stand to reason and the attempts to connect the practice with Vedic tradition is [sic] entirely baseless and puerile" (pp. 41-42)—seems questionable in light of evidence presented throughout our study, as well as devoid of appreciation of the whole Vedicization-Sanskritization process. His consequent decision regarding authorship—"The *Bālacarita*, therefore, cannot be accepted as an original work of Bhāsa" (p. 42)— thus stands in need of a more cogent rationale.

fair amount of scholarly attention.[85] What we want to know is: who is this goddess who is credited with slaying Śumbha and Niśumbha in texts that are primarily concerned with recounting the wondrous events of Kṛṣṇa's youth? What is her relationship to Kṛṣṇa, and that of her worship to his ?

A preliminary answer to these queries may be based on an iconographic reinterpretation first offered some years ago by J. C. Ghosh.[86] Ghosh's primary concern is with the correct identification of (1) a relief of three figures in the Lucknow museum, previously identified as Lakṣmana, Sītā, and Rāma (p. 43), and (2) the triad worshipped in the Jagannātha temple at Puri, previously identified as the Buddhist *triratna*, Buddha, Dharma, and Saṅgha (p. 46). In his reinterpretation, which suggests that both triads should be understood as Balarāma, Subhadrā (Ekānaṃśā), and Kṛṣṇa,[87] Ghosh quotes extensively from the HV, often from what now turns out to be interpolated material, though that does not seem to affect the integrity of his interpretation. His argument, which is concerned to account for how Subhadrā came to be deified, runs as follows:

> It appears to us that Ekānaṃśā was being worshipped by the Yādavas [who knew the Kṛṣṇa Gopāla cycle at an early date] as their tribal guardian deity.... The worship of *Śakti* prevailed there before the rise of the Kṛṣṇa cult. When they [the Yādavas] found that the daughter of Yaśodā was the means of saving directly the life of Kṛṣṇa, and indirectly that of Valadeva [sic], their favourites, they thought that she is no other than their household goddess Ekānaṃśā.

[85]On the former, see the references given at I, n. 62. As an example of the latter, cf. Singer (ed.), *Krishna: Myths, Rites, and Attitudes*. For an attempt at both (which is rather shallow regarding early textual material and which is silent on our primary concern—see our next sentence) see White, Charles, S. J., "Kṛṣṇa as Divine Child," *History of Religions* 10 2 (Nov. 1970), pp. 156-177. For a wide-ranging series of articles on these and related topics, see Hawley, John S. and Wulff, Donna B. (edd.), *The Divine Consort: Rādhā and the Goddesses of India*, Berkeley Religious Studies Series (Berkeley, forthcoming).

[86]Ghosh, Jogendra Chandra, "Ekanaṃśā and Subhadrā," *Journal of the Royal Asiatic Society, Letters*, vol. II (1936), pp. 41-46 and plate 7.

[87]For a helpful visualization of the way Balarāma, Subhadrā, and Kṛṣṇa are related in the epic account, see the genealogical chart in Mbh, van Buitenen tr., vol. I, facing p. 12.

> Valarāma and Kṛṣṇa, most probably, came to be associated with the goddess as her wards, or as two notable representatives of her votaries. When the Kṛṣṇa cult rose into prominence, the popular worship was not rejected altogether, but appropriated and given a subordinate position. Thus she came to be worshipped along with her two deified wards.[88]

When this worship came under Pāñcarātra influence, certain features of Śākta worship were found repugnant,[89] so that devotees

> had recourse to the expediency of changing Ekānaṃśā to inoffensive Subhadrā. This required only the change in name. This was helped by the fact that Ekānaṃśā having been born as the daughter of Yaśodā, the foster-mother of Kṛṣṇa, she was a sister to him. Subhadrā also held the same relationship.[90]

This intuition that the Kṛṣṇa Gopāla cycle originated in a Śākta context that was eventually outgrown has recently been explored in a brilliant study by Charlotte Vaudeville.[91] From it, we may excerpt a number of points that have a bearing on our inquiry, a procedure that is most readily followed by working backwards from her conclusion, viz.,

> Il semble que l'entrée de Kṛṣṇa-Gopāla dans le cycle de Viṣṇu-Nārāyaṇa se soit accomplie lentement, vers la fin de l'ère Gupta, en dehors de l'aire géographique ou son culte avait pris naissance et en dehors des castes pastorales, qui ne furent jamais vishnouites. Célèbre et partout répandue par le chant et la danse, sa légende resta longtemps en

[88]Ghosh, *op. cit.*, p. 44.

[89]Ghosh here quotes what is, in the critical edition, HV 47.50cd-51, q.v. in Part III, s. v. "Viṣṇu's Praise of Nidrā."

[90]*Ibid.*, p. 45.

[91]Vaudeville, Charlotte, "Aspects du Mythe de *Kṛṣṇa-Gopāla* dans l'Inde Ancienne" in *Mélanges d'Indianisme,* à la Mémoire de Louis Renou, Éditions E. de Boccard (Paris, 1968), Publications de l'Institut de Civilisation Indienne, fasc. 28, pp. 737-761. One point at which we might question the author's usually exquisite judgment is when without justification (or, it seems, necessity) she claims that the ViṣṇuP account of Kṛṣṇa's exploits is older than that of the HV and BhāgavataP (p. 753), for, as Ingalls has shown ("The *Harivaṃśa* as a *Mahākāvya,*" pp. 383-384), the sequence runs HV, ViṣṇuP, BhāgavataP.

dehors de la synthèse vishnouite. Si le dieu bouvier vient des rives de la Yamunā, s'il est "enfant de la Mathurā du Nord", c'est pourtant dans l'Inde méridionale qu'il fit fortune et que sa légende, tout imprégnée de ses origines primitives, fut progressivement décantée et assimilée par la bhakti vishnouite. Ce processus s'achève, dans le sud, vers le Xe siecle, avec la compilation du Bhāgavata-Purāṇa, véritable Bible krishnaïte....[92]

Within this context, the first point of note is that, having established the northern, pastoral origin of Kṛṣṇa Gopāla in Gupta times on iconographic, textual (Mbh and ViṣṇuP), and ethnographic grounds,[93] Vaudeville reflects on the curious fact that devotion to Kṛṣṇa does not really flourish in north India until after Caitanya in the fifteenth century.

L'infériorité de Kṛṣṇa-Gopāla, au moins en tant qu'object de culte, durant cette longue période, ne peut s'expliquer simplement par le statut inférieur des castes pastorales, Abhīras et Gurjāras, où ce culte avait pris naissance. Bien que considérés comme Śūdras et Mlecchas par la tradition brahmanique, ces tribus, dont la plus célèbre est celle des Abhīras, étaient nombreuses et formaient des clans puissants qui avaient atteint une certaine importance politique dès les premiers siècles de notre ère.... ce sont probablement les Abhīras et les castes apparentées qui ont propagé dans toute l'Inde la légende de leur héros, Kṛṣṇa-Gopāla. Mais rien n'indique que ces tribus étaient vishnouites, ou même que leurs croyances et traditions particulières présentaient des affinités avec le culte brahmanique de Viṣṇu-Nārāyaṇa—et encore moins avec l'enseignement de la Bhagavad-Gītā. Comme toutes le castes anaryennes du Nord au Sud de l'Inde, les tribus pastorales reconnaissaient comme divinité supérieure la grande déesse, la Devī, sous sa forme guerrière de Durgā ou sa forme féconde et maternelle d'Umā, épouse de Rudra-Śiva. Aujourd'hui encore, même après l'invasion de la bhakti vishnouite, le culte de la Devī reste la religion dominate dans les couches inférieures

[92]Vaudeville, *op. cit.*, p. 761.
[93]*Ibid.*, pp. 739-749.

> des populations rurales, tout particulièrement dans l'ouest et au Bengal.[94]

This more systematic formulation of Ghosh's basic intuition can be supported by evidence on a number of fronts. Early references to Kṛṣṇa Gopāla seem more concerned with the literary, poetic potential of the story than with its religious significance,[95] and one may, in fact, see the *Bālacarita's* more explicit account of Kārtyāyanī as an indication of its early date: it unabashedly acknowledges the stature of the Goddess, whereas the later versions of the same material portray her with decreasing explicitness.[96] Even the BhāgavataP, however, gives vestigial attestation of this interplay of Kṛṣṇa Gopāla and the Goddess, for when Kṛṣṇa steals the clothes of the *gopīs*, it is after they have been worshipping Kātyāyanī.[97] One might go so far as to see Patañjali, in the third century B.C.E. suggesting that Vāsudeva-Kṛṣṇa and his followers are champions of Durgā-Kātyāyanī since the former are to be dramatically represented with the color red, the color of that goddess.[98] Finally, we may note that Vaudeville detects an extraordinary thematic parallelism, particularly in the myths of origin, between the two dancing gods, Kṛṣṇa and Skanda, and suggests that the former may have borrowed much from the latter.[99] Since we have repeatedly encountered Skanda's interplay with the Goddess, it may well be that such a process was facilitated by the fact that both Kṛṣṇa and Skanda bear a relationship to the divine female.

[94]*Ibid.*, pp. 749-750.

[95]*Ibid.*, pp. 750, 756-757.

[96]*Ibid.*, pp. 757-758. The BhāgavataP's account of Viṣṇu's prenatal solicitation of aid, there said to be of the goddess Yoganidrā, makes no reference to the Śumbha-Niśumbha myth and, in general, is less effusive than earlier accounts (10.2.6-13). Though it knows of Kaṃsa's slaying of the female infant, her subsequent transfiguration (10.4.9-13) emphasizes her beauty and solicitiousness of innocent children, rather than her status as the Goddess. However, see our next sentence.

[97]BhāgavataP 10.22, cited *ibid.*, pp. 758-759. Vaudeville here says "Kārtyāyanī", as in the *Bālacarita*, though the text reads "Kātyāyanī".

[98]*Ibid.*, pp. 741, 758, citing Patañjali's *Mahābhāṣya* on Pāṇini 3.1.26.

[99]*Ibid.*, pp. 759-760, 760n.

The conclusion seems clear. What we have in the Śumbha-Niśumbha myth is a fragment of the mythology of the great Goddess as it was current among the north Indian peoples who came to know of the heroic exploits of Kṛṣṇa Gopāla. The latter underwent religious elaboration as it became current in south India [100] Meanwhile, the former became integrated with other mythological motifs and received *its* religious elaboration in such texts as the one at the center of our study, the DM.[101]

## 4. *A Preliminary Integration: the Vāmana Purāṇa Account*

On several occasions we have mentioned that the VāmanaP recounts some of the same myths as the DM, and also associates them with the Goddess. A cursory glance would suggest that its version is later than the DM's: O'Flaherty calls the *Vāmana* a 'middle Purāṇa,' i.e., 500–1000 C. E., while the MarkP is an "early Purāṇa," i.e., 300 B.C.E.-500 C.E.,[102] and, on at

[100]Full documentation of this is the central point of the Vaudeville article, though we have not recapitulated her argument as it is tangential to our primary concern with the Goddess. Suffice it to say that the Alvars play a critical role (*op. cit.*, pp. 753-754; cf. also Vaudeville, Charlotte, "Evolution of Love-Symbolism in Bhagavatism," JAOS Vol. 82 [1962], pp. 31-40).

[101]In the absence of conclusive evidence, we have refrained from completing the implicit parallelism in this sentence and saying that the DM is a composition of north (or north-west) Indian provenience. Nonetheless, circumstantial evidence does suggest that this is the case. We have already cited Pargiter's claim (MarkP, Pargiter tr., Intro. pp. xi-xiii) that the DM came from the Narmadā river valley, probably at Mandhāta, while Renou and others prefer a location somewhat further north (cited by Viennot, *op. cit.*, p. 368n.). The early Mahiṣāsuramardinī icons (see *supra*, n. 58) come from Rajasthan, while the early plastic representations of the Kṛṣṇa Gopāla cycle, when Kṛṣṇa seems still to be only a human hero, are found in Rajasthan and in the Mathurā region (Vaudeville, "Aspects," p. 742). The inscriptions regarding the Seven Little Mothers (cited, Appendix A, nn. 40, 48, 49) come from Deogarh, Bihar, and Gaṅgdhar ("fifty-two miles south-west of Jhāhāpāṭan"), respectively; another undated one regarding the Goddess as slayer of Mahiṣa (Fleet, *op. cit.*, pp. 226-228) from "the Gayā district of the Bengal Presidency"; and the inscription which quotes a verse from the DM (cited, Proleg., n. 204) from Jodhpur. While it is thus likely that our text is a composition of north-west India, the presence of some scattered evidence to the contrary, as well as the danger of the argument from silence, keep this from being a certainty.

[102]*Asceticism and Eroticism*, p. 14; see her *Sexuality and Asceticism*, Appendix IV for the material on which she bases her dating.

least one occasion, Gupta has relied on the MarkP, in fact on a passage in the DM, for his constitution of the critical edition of the VāmanaP.[103] B. H. Kapadia, however, maintains that, in the VāmanaP, "the Devī Māhātmya, Mahisāsuravadha [sic], Caṇḍamuṇḍavadha, Śumbhaniśumbhavadha [,] etc., appear to be prior to those of Mārkaṇḍeya's Devī Māhātmaya [sic]."[104] The relative chronology of different Purāṇic accounts remains highly problematical here,[105] as elsewhere, but brief consideration of the VāmanaP version of the myths of the Goddess will help us discern further the uniqueness of the DM's account.

If we examine the myths in the same order as the DM presents them, we may note that the VāmanaP's understanding of the Madhu-Kaiṭabha myth seems to be the same as that of the epics. Viṣṇu is once cited as "slayer of Madhu and Kaiṭabha" (64.115) and is known throughout as "the slayer of Madhu."[106] A full version of the myth is unknown in this text.

The myths of Mahiṣa and Śumbha-Niśumbha, however, are recounted at some length in the VāmanaP. Since they differ both from the epic tradition and from the DM's versions, we may best appreciate their distinctive features by summarizing the salient events. Since the two myths are somewhat conflated, we simply follow the sequence of the text itself.

The occasion for the excursus upon the Goddess is Pulastya's presentation of a series of *mantras* (18.26-36), known as "that which contains Viṣṇu (*vaiṣṇavaṃ pañjaram*)," which were first uttered, it is said, to protect Kātyāyanī when she slew Mahiṣa and other demons (18. 37-38). An account of Mahiṣa's birth

[103]Gupta, "Constitution of the Vāmana Purāṇa Text", pp. 180-181. Given the difficulty and subtlety, of his task, however, such reliance does not imply absolutely that he thinks the MarkP is earlier.

[104]Kapadia, B. H., "Some Aspects of Vāmana Purāṇa", *Purāṇa* VII 1 (Jan. 1965), p. 181.

[105]P. V. Kane, for instance, maintains that it is the VārāhaP's account of the *mahiṣāsuravadha* that "appears to be the earliest Paurāṇika version of the slaughter of Mahiṣāsura" (*op. cit.*, vol. V, part 1 (1958), p. 155n). The imminent publication of the critical edition of the VārāhaP by the All-India Kashiraj Trust should enable us to get some clarity on the relative chronology of the mythology of the Goddess in the VāmanaP, VārāhaP, and DM.

[106]35.73, 75; 47.43, 45; 65.61; 68.58.

follows, wherein he is born, as a result of a boon from Agni to the demon Rambha, from Rambha's copulation with a she-buffalo (*mahiṣī*). Assailed by Mahiṣa, the gods betake themselves to Viṣṇu and Śiva and recount their woes (19. 1-4); from their anger, the collective *tejas* congeals into the Goddess in the *āśrama* of Kātyāyana, whence her name Kātyāyanī; the specifics of her constitution and weaponry are recounted (19. 5-17), as in the DM.[107] Subsequently, she is seen by the demons Caṇḍa and Muṇḍa and described to their leader Mahiṣa in overtly sensual language (20. 1-16). Mahiṣa dispatches Dundubhi as messenger, but he is rebuffed by the Goddess saying it is a family tradition that only one who bests a daughter in battle can be her husband (20. 17-34). When the Asuras attack, the Goddess, who is without armor (*kavacaṃ*),[108] protected only by the *viṣṇupañjara*, dispatches Mahiṣa with a kick (20. 35-44). Chapter 21 responds to the interlocutor Nārada's thirst to hear the specific details of the encounter, of which we may note the following: the Goddess beats on one Asura who turns into a drum, and, throughout, she seems musically inclined;[109] from her laughter are born various strange spirits (*bhūtā nānāvidhā 'dbhutāḥ*), possessed of assorted animal faces (21.18ff.); as in the DM, Mahiṣa attempts his metamorphic escape, but to no avail (21. 41-49). Though there is no hymn of victory, the concluding verse of the chapter is interesting :

> Being praised by throngs of gods and Siddhas, sitting at the feet of Śiva,
> Having said, "I will come into being again in this way for the sake of the gods," Durgā entered (back into) the gods.[110]

[107]Despite the similar accounts, there appear to be no direct borrowings between the texts. In fact, the whole of VāmanaP 19, and much of the rest of its first Mahiṣa story (through chapter 21) is in *triṣṭubh* or *jagatī* metres, whereas the DM reserves the elegant metres for hymnic usage, the balance (and some of the hymns) being entirely in *śloka*.

[108]One of the famous later hymns to the Goddess, said to be from the MarkP but not in our editions, is known as the *devīkavacam*, q. v. in Jagadīśvarānanda's translation of the DM, pp. xiv-xx.

[109]Cf. 21.17, 18, 34, 35, 37.

[110]VāmanaP 21.52:

> *saṃstūyamānā surasiddhasaṅghair niṣaṇṇabhūtā harapādamūle |*
> *bhūyo bhaviṣyamy amarārtham evam uktvā surāṃs tān praviveśa durgā ||*

When chapter 22 picks up the thread of continuity, it initially looks as if it will proceed along the lines of the DM, for in response to Nārada's request to hear about the reincarnation of the Goddess, Pulastya says he will tell of her destruction of Śumbha (22.1-2). Immediately thereafter, however, motifs are introduced that look more like epic or later Purāṇic accounts :

> She who is the ascetic daughter of Himavān was married by Śiva,
> And her name is Umā; from her sheath (*kośa*) was born Kauśikī.
> Having come into being again, and having gone to the Vindhya (mountains), surrounded by throngs of spirits,
> She will slay (sic : *vadhiṣyati*) both Śumbha and Niśumbha with the best of weapons.
> Nārada said :
> O Brāhmaṇa, it was recounted by you[111] that Satī, the daughter of Dakṣa died
> Now may you tell me (how) she was born (as) daughter of Himavān,
> And how Kauśikī was born from the sheath of Pārvatī,
> (And) how she slew Śumbha and the great Asura Niśumbha.
>
> . . . . . . . . . . . . . . . . . . . . . . .
>
> Pulastya said :
> I shall relate to you the birth of Pārvatī, O sage.
> Having become attentive, listen to the everlasting (account of the) birth of Skanda.[112]

The text then directly begins a second version of the Mahiṣa story, the structure of which resembles the basic Śiva cycle,[113] only with Mahiṣa replacing Tāraka : the Asura oppresses the gods, only a son of Śiva can slay him, Śiva is a reluctant householder, etc. This familiar story is the basic concern of the text.

[111] At VāmanaP 5.14-16.

[112] VāmanaP 22.3-6, 8.

[113] Cf. O'Flaherty, *Asceticism and Eroticism*, pp. 30-32.

through chapter 28.[114] Though we need not trace the story in its entirety, we may note certain features : (1) at the betrothal, it is declared that Śiva's son by Umā will slay both Mahiṣa and Tāraka (26.58), and earlier Umā has undertaken austerities to win Śiva, "so that the slayer of Mahiṣa will become associated with my name";[115] (2) the name Kālī is applied to Umā throughout, but it is a name about which Śiva teases her (28.6), and through austerity Umā gets rid of its concomitant dark complexion: from the externalized dark sheath (*kośa*) is produced Kātyāyanī-Kauśikī, whom Indra installs as Vindhyavāsinī;[116] (3) consequently, after recounting the love making of Śiva and Pārvatī, and its attendant problems, this chapter can conclude : "thus did that goddess Kātyāyanī come into being again, she who slew the great Daityas Śumbha and Niśumbha" (28.76).

Chapters 29 and 30 proceed to recount the story of Śumbha and Niśumbha, here slain by this subsidiary form, Kātyāyanī-Kauśikī-Vindhyavāsinī, in much the same fashion as in the DM.[117] There are, to be sure, differences, as when Śumbha and Niśumbha initially form an alliance with Raktabīja, Caṇḍa and Muṇḍa, whose lord, Mahiṣa, here seems to be already dead.[118] But most of the account is familiar, with the emergence of Kālī from Durgā's brow (29.55-57), her subsequent destruction of Caṇḍa and Muṇḍa and designation as Cāmuṇḍā (29.68-85), the appearance of various *śaktis* or *mātṛs* (30.2ff.), though here they emerge from different limbs of the *devi*, rather than from the male deities and there is no final resumption of them into her, and so on. The account concludes with a hymn (30.56-66) to the

[114]Between chapters 23 and 24, however, occurs one of those universally attested, but apparently interpolated, excursuses, on which we have already seen Gupta comment (Proleg., pp. 34-36), viz., the Saromāhātmya. It does not continue, or even seem to mention, the basic story line.

[115]25.18cd: *yathā mannāmasaṃyukto mahiṣaghno bhaviṣyati.*

[116]28.9-28.

[117]Here the verbal correspondence of the two texts is sometimes rather close (e.g., cf. VāmanaP 29.44 and MarkP 86.7), but the differences are major enough to suggest that, rather than one text being dependent on another, the two simply share certain stock phrases. This would, of course, be consistent with the method of bardic composition discussed in our Prolegomenon.

[118]See 29.16-19.

victorious goddess, using terms that are primarily circumstantial, i.e., that do not endeavor to understand her as the one Goddess, and with her promise to be born again in various guises (30.67-71).

Finally, chapters 31 and 32 resume the account of Skanda's birth and his destruction of Mahiṣa.[119] The former holds no particular interest for us here, though we may note that the account of his parentage is somewhat more cogent than that in Mbh 3.207ff. This is accomplished largely through the device of giving Skanda different forms for different claimants of parentage (31.39-40), in the use of which device, as in general tenor, there is a resemblance to the account in Mbh 9.43ff. More to the point is that there is a clamor for the consecration of the child, so that he may slay Mahiṣa and Tāraka (31.51-52), and when that is accomplished, he turns to the task at hand, accompanied by *gaṇas* and *mātṛs*. The account that the text gives of Mahiṣa's demise is truly curious. After an initial skirmish with Skanda, Mahiṣa withdraws from battle (32.71ff.) and, after seeing his brother Tāraka slain, retreats to the Himālayas (32.84). Pursued by Skanda, he flees to a cave (*guhā*) on Mount Krauñca, where Skanda, here called Guha, watches over him,[120] wondering how he can slay his own relative,[121] i.e., how he can strike Krauñca, a mountain, when he himself is the son of Pārvatī, daughter of Mount Himavān.[122] When Indra taunts

[119]Actually, this account has not totally dropped from sight during the Śumbha-Niśumbha episode, for towards the end of that battle a simile appears —one of the demons fell "just as (Mount) Krauñca did, together with Mahiṣa, (when) struck by Skanda" (30.54)—which anticipates the events in chapter 32. The Śumbha-Niśumbha episode thus presents the mythological perplexity of the VāmanaP in a nutshell: at the outset (see our preceding note), it knows Mahiṣa to have been already slain by Kātyāyanī, but here at the conclusion, it anticipates Mahiṣa's subsequent demise at the hands of Skanda.

[120]Or "hides," or "protects": *jugopa*.

[121]32.88cd: *svabandhuhantā bhavitā katham tv ahaṃ saṃcintayann eva tataḥ sthito 'bhūt.*

[122]That this is the crux of Skanda's dilemma is clear from the sequel, for he ruminates, "How can I slay the grandson of my maternal grandfather, my brother, the son of my mother's brother ?" (32.90cd) and then goes on to declare, "When the demon comes forth from the cave, then will I smite the enemy with (my) spear" (32.93cd). Skanda is known as the cleaver of Krauñca (but obviously without the hidden Mahiṣa motif) from the first

him, arguing that one must die for the sake of the many (32.97), Skanda challenges him to a race around Mount Krauñca. When that mountain lies as to who is the victor, Skanda strikes Krauñca with his spear, thereby piercing it and slaying Mahiṣa.[123] The account concludes with Skanda doing penance for having slain his maternal cousin Krauñca (32.113ff.).

What, then, shall we make of this involuted, intriguing account? Though we cannot deal with all its particulars, such as the epithets which it does not share with the DM,[124] certain conclusions are possible. Above all, it seems clear that the view of the Goddess here is less synthetic, less comprehensive, than in the DM. It is, more properly, a view of the goddess, with a small "g". Thus, the Vaiṣṇava story of Madhu and Kaiṭabha is not included in the mythology of the *devī*. Even when she does dispatch Mahiṣa, no effort is made to establish her as a permanent salvific presence in the world. She is finally diffused back into the bodies of the male deities (21.52), whereas the DM allows for her on-going and unique reality by saying simply, but suggestively, "she vanished" (84.33). Moreover, the VāmanaP is more aware that the vanquisher of Śumbha and Niśumbha is a particular goddess, Kātyāyanī-Kauśikī-Vindhyavāsinī, who is derivative from Umā-Pārvatī. Although the DM knows the Pārvatī-*kośa*-Kauṣikī association (85.37-41), our interpretation of that has suggested that our text seems there to be glorying in the metamorphic potential of the Goddess, rather than establishing her primary and secondary forms. In any case, Pārvatī's role in the DM is decidedly minor, and, as we have noted, the name Umā is never used in that text, whereas Umā-Pārvatī is a real presence in the VāmanaP account, sometimes in the background, but always there, as a distinct figure.[125] We may say that, in general, as the relative

Mbh account of him onward; see 3.214.30ff. Part of the logic of the eventual identification of Skanda as son of Pārvatī, "she of the mountain," is the homage that mountains here pay him as a consequence of his splitting them. Also, note again the coincidence of opposites, for Mahiṣa, too, is associated with mountains: see *supra*, n. 44.

123 32.100-109.

124 E.g., *caṇḍamārī* (29.67), *śuṣkarevatī* (29.82), *carcikā* (30.67).

125 Although we offer a remark below on the matter of the relative chronology of the VāmanaP and DM accounts, we may here comment on that matter

absence of hymnic material suggests, the Vāmana's account is inspired by motives other than the pure desire to glorify the Goddess for her own sake.

With regard to the myths themselves, the Śumbha-Niśumbha account clearly approximates that of the DM quite closely. If it is true, as our earlier analysis suggests, that this story derives from ancient, non-Aryan accounts of the great Goddess, then this similarity is not surprising. The Mahiṣa mythology is more puzzling. Gupta maintains that there are, in fact, two different

---

insofar as it has a bearing on the Pārvatī-*koṣa*-Kauṣikī episode in the DM, which has come up on a number of occasions (see Part I, s. v. "*ambikā, gaurī, pārvatī, kṛṣṇā-tāmasī*" and n.70). It seems to us that the evidence is such that the relationship between the two accounts, in general, may be variously interpreted, as follows. (1) The confused mythology of the VāmanaP, and its clear awareness that Kātyāyanī is a local goddess, primarily associated with the Vindhya mountains, and sharply distinguished from the more major figure of Pārvatī-Umā, show that it is the earlier text: it lacks the DM's later view of the Goddess as the fulfilment of the Vedic tradition, as well as of various local ones. (2) The DM's account, because it displays so little familiarity with such subsequently major themes as the Goddess being the consort of Śiva and daughter of Himavān, and because it seems simply to have heard of Pārvatī, but without much knowledge of her, must be earlier: the VāmanaP at least knows these themes, albeit in gestative form, and is therefore later. (3) The two accounts do not even admit of formal comparison, for they are generically distinct: the Vāmana account is simply a local *māhātmya*, of which India has known so many, while the DM takes as *its* tradition the pan-Indian Sanskritic heritage. (4) The DM, although it makes so little of Pārvatī and the Śaiva mythological cycle, is nonetheless the earlier text: it may well have known of those traditions, but it deliberately ignores them, and it does so in the name of devotion—the glorification of the divine reality is what commands its attention, not the presentation of a "cogent" account. Whatever the merits of these (or additional) arguments with regard to matters of chronology, the fourth is clearly most sensitive to the spirit of the DM: that text is simply not interested in being more specific about the relationship between Pārvatī and the auspicious emanation Kauṣikī. (And, it might be argued, to the extent that we are interested in *accounts* of the divine, rather than its reality, we have simply manifested the reality of the Great Illusion, Mahāmāyā !) Consequently, we have throughout this study interpreted this episode as "glorying in the metamorphic potential of the Goddess" (which our text consistently does), rather than as distinguishing secondary from primary forms. One final consideration may be adduced in favor of this interpretation. So comprehensive is the DM's account of the Goddess that there is simply no room left for some other divine reality. (Cf. BU 4.5.15: when all has become one, what else might one see ?) Though other accounts (whether earlier or later is really

demons, both named Mahiṣa, who have here been confused.[126] Moreover, the account of Rambha, brother of Karambha, as father of Mahiṣa, seems more a harbinger of later accounts than an outgrowth of the earlier tradition.[127] Yet, on balance, it seems to us that the VāmanaP's Mahiṣa mythology may be best understood as a mythology in transition. We have seen that the constituted text of the Mbh consistently affirms that Mahiṣa is vanquished by Skanda, but that the Mbh and HV critical apparatus is more equivocal in its designation of his conqueror. The Vāmana account seems to occupy a point mid-way between the epic preference for associating Mahiṣa and Skanda and the later tradition's association, definitively articulated in the DM, of Mahiṣa and the Goddess. It has inherited both versions of the myth, and therefore presents them both, with no attempt at reconciliation.

To call the Vāmana account "a preliminary integration" of the Goddess mythology thus seems fair enough. This may mean that it is chronologically prior to the DM, though not necessarily. The tradition of later résumés of earlier material, in keeping with local tradition, is a venerable one in India[128] and, as our Prolegomenon suggests, it is the very soul of the Purāṇic process. But that the Vāmana account is "preliminary" in the sense of "incomplete" or "prefactory" is patent when compared with the succinct, cogent, and yet also dazzling account of the DM.

---

beside the point) may explore dimensions of the divine reality that the DM only hints at, or ignores, it can scarcely be doubted that for the DM there is but one divine reality—*the* Goddess—on which all depends.

[126]Gupta, "Constitution of the Vāmana-Purāṇa Text," p. 159.

[127]Cf. SkandaP [Veṅkateśvara Press (Bombay, 1908-1910)] 92.138ff. and DevībhāgavataP [Paṇḍita-Pustakālya (Kāśī, 1969)] 5.2.18ff. Rambha and Karambha are unknown in the Mbh.

[128]See *supra*, note 125; also for a fine discussion of the issues involved in such situations, addressing the thorny matter of the relationship between the Rām and the Mbh's version of the Rāma story, see Mbh, van Buitenen tr., vol. II, pp. 207-214.

Part III

# The Hymns

# The Hymns

Having laid the historical groundwork through an examination of the DM's epithets and myths in the previous two Parts, we turn now to a translation of what we have maintained is the devotional core of our text, viz., its hymns. To an extent, the virtue of such an endeavor is self-evident. It enables us to appreciate how the power of the hymns derives from their multi-faceted allusions, compounding the impact of each reference by piling one upon another, and constructing, as a consequence, a truly comprehensive and synthetic vision of the Goddess. This power is, of course, in addition to that which derives from their metrical construction.[1]

There are two further considerations, however, which dictate that the hymns of the DM be accompanied by translations of other early Sanskritic hymns involving a feminine conceptualization of the divine. First, earlier portions of our study have been heavily analytical, breaking down our text's diction into small units and tracing the resonance of each. While this has proven illuminating of particular epithets and myths, what is masked in such an approach is the fact that certain such units have been associated with one another prior to the time of our text. Translation of other hymns may thus identify preliminary stages in this convergence of motifs. In addition, in certain cases, most notably that of Śrī, an examination of isolated

[1]Naturally, this latter is primarily evident in the Sanskrit metres themselves, and we have made no effort to imitate them in our translations. Since metrical considerations will be of interest primarily to Sanskritists, and since the texts of all the hymns to be dealt with in Part III (with the possible exception of the RVK) are readily available, we do not here present the full Sanskrit texts of the hymns.

words may fail to capture their larger ramifications, such as in the Śrī Sūkta. Consequently we here translate nine other hymns, as well as those of the DM, with a preliminary remark on each.

Second, we have suggested in our Prolegomenon that the significance of hymns is, in part, a function of their transcendent, ahistorical quality and it is precisely this that renders them so impervious to historical analysis. For all of the historical background provided in Parts I and II, we are still without the historical leverage that would enable us to determine such matters as the relative chronology of different hymns. What we can do, however, is to indicate correspondences between the hymns in the DM and other, apparently early, hymns in the Sanskrit tradition. In some cases, it seems reasonable to assume that those hymns are prior to the DM, while in others—primarily those from the epic—we have to leave the matter of relative chronology open. We can in all cases, however, indicate some of the relationships between the other hymns and those in the DM.

Our mechanism for doing this is as follows. Since the DM is the focus of our study, we translate its hymns last. In the preliminary hymns, we underscore those motifs which are also found in the DM, indicating significant verbal correspondences when appropriate. Usually these will have been dealt with in Parts I and II, but when this is not the case, the relevant passages in the DM are noted. Occasionally we have underscored a motif or characterization which, while not identical to one in the DM's language, seems sufficiently close to warrant inclusion. We have moved back and forth between translating a characterization, and using it as an untranslated proper name, as seems fit. Also, because of our focus on the DM, we refrain from comment upon the epithets in other hymns which, interesting though they may be, seem not to bear upon our text. Finally, when we come to the DM's hymns, we shall introduce a modification in our method of annotation that is appropriate to the understanding of hymnic material from an historical perspective.

1. *From the Ṛg Veda*

A. The Vāg Āmbhṛṇī Sūkta (10.125)

Although the RV hymn to Vāc or Speech has not emerged in the course of our study as having major verbal connections with the language of the DM, there are other grounds, some of which we have met in passing, for including it in our comparison of hymns to the Goddess. Renou, for example, sees the Vedic understanding of *vāc* to be a precursor of the later view of *ātman-brahman* as the ontological fundament.[2] More specifically, A.C. Das maintains that "the goddess Vāc... was the origin of the later Vedic Umā or the Purāṇic Durgā,"[3] and in general studies of the rise of Śāktism, *vāc* as a concept, and RV 10.125 in particular, are cited almost without exception.[4] Finally, that this hymn, often known as the Devī Sūkta, has been intertwined with our text both conceptually and liturgically is clear from the remarks of K.C. Chatterji that "... the Saptaśatī is regarded as an extensive commentary on this hymn," and that the hymn "has its ritual application in the Durgāpūjā as well as in the recitation of the Caṇḍī or Saptaśatī."[5] The hymn, then, may be translated as follows:

[2]Renou, *Études*, vol. I (1955), pp. 1-27. Our Prolegomenon touches on this view in its discussion of Renou's remarks on Vedic composition.

[3]Quoted by Sahai, *op. cit.*, p. 181n.

[4]See Banerjea, "Some Aspects of Śakti Worship in Ancient India," p. 228; Bhattacharyya, N., *op. cit.*, pp. 28-29; Dasgupta, S. B., *op. cit.*, pp. 61-62; Kumar, *op. cit.*, p. 2 and 2n; Sastri, *op. cit.*, p. 13; Sinha, B. P., *op. cit.*, pp. 48-49.

[5]Chatterji, Kshitish Chandra, *Devī-Sūkta*, Calcutta University (Calcutta, 1945), pp. iii, 2. The hymn is known as the Vāg Āmbhṛṇī Sūkta because it "is attributed to Vāc, daughter of Ambhṛṇa" (*ibid.*, p. iii). Chatterji notes (p. 2) that RV 10.125 is unusual in being an *ādhyātmika* hymn, i.e., it uses the first person, in which case "the seer is the same as the deity"; such hymns are, he remarks, rare, with the other well-known instances (10.48, 49, 119) all having Indra as speaker. He also observes (p. 32) that the DM's hymn at 85.7ff. (q. v., *infra*) is widely known as *devīsūkta*. Banerjea ("Some Aspects," p. 229) agrees in understanding the DM as an exposition of both the Vāc and Rātrī hymns in the RV. See also Bhattacharyya, N., *op. cit.*, p. 159 where he describes the position of Satya Deva as affirming that "what the *Devīsūkta* of the *Ṛgveda* says with reservation is explained in the *Devīmāhātmya* in the forms of legends."

1. I go about with the Rudras, with the Vasus, I with the Ādityas, and with the All-gods.
   I support both Mitra and Varuṇa, I both Indra and Agni, I the two Aśvins.
2. I support the impetuous Soma, and I Tvaṣṭṛ, Pūṣan, (and) Bhaga.
   I grant wealth to the skillful sacrificer who offers oblation, who presses the Soma.
3. I am *the queen,* who brings treasures together, *wise,* foremost of those worthy of worship.
   The gods have put me *in many places, variously abiding, of manifold presence.*
4. *Through me a man eats food: he who sees, who breathes, who hears what is spoken (does so through me).*
   *Unknowing, they depend upon me.* Hear, O famous one—I am telling you (something) worthy of faith.
5. I myself proclaim this (state of affairs) which is approved by gods and men.
   Whomsoever I wish I make mighty, a Brahman, a seer, a sage.
6. I draw the bow for Rudra, so his arrow may slay the foe of sacred speech.
   I stir up quarrels among people;[6] *I pervade heaven and earth*
7. On the summit of this world, I give birth to the father; *my origin is in the waters, in the ocean.*[7]
   Thence I spread through all worlds, and I touch yonder sky with my summit.
8. I blow forth like the wind, grasping all worlds.
   Beyond heaven, beyond this earth, in (my) greatness such have I become.

### B. The Rātrī Sūkta (10.127)

There is little direct correspondence between the language of a second Vedic hymn, the Rātrī Sūkta, and that of the DM,

[6]We adopt this reading as striking a balance between the two possible senses that Ingalls has suggested to us (personal note, Nov. 28, 1976): (1) "I bring about the common will to fight for mankind" (as in a peptalk), or (2) "I stir up rivals in oratorical contests."

[7]Cf. MarkP 91.3, translated *infra*.

but again, as with the Vāc hymn, there is much secondary evidence for the association of the two texts. Thus, this hymn to Night is frequently cited in general histories of Śāktism, though with somewhat less consistency than the Vāc hymn,[8] and the DM itself appreciates the nocturnal nuances of the Goddess's character by calling her *kālarātri*, *mahārātri*, and *moharātri*.[9] Sinha notes that "the Rātri [sic] hymn...occupies a very prominent position in the Śākta ritual of subsequent times,"[10] though he provides no details on this matter. Finally, much depends on this hymn, for it is after the Rātrī Sūkta at RV 10.127 that the Rātrī Khila stands, as an hymnic elaboration.[11] As we shall see, that Khila has some very intimate connections with the motifs of the DM. The Rātrī Sūkta itself reads :

1. The goddess *Night* approaches, *illuminating manifold places* with her eyes:
   She has put on *all her glories* (*śriyaḥ*).
2. The *immortal* goddess has filled up the broad expanse, the heights and depths;
   With (her own) light, *she drives out the darkness* (*tamaḥ*).
3. The goddess approaches, replacing her sister Dawn.
   May (this) *darkness* also disappear.
4. (May you stand) by us now, at whose coming we go to rest,
   Like birds to their nest in a tree.
5. To rest have gone the villagers, as have all legged and winged creatures,
   Even the greedy hawks.
6. Ward off the she-wolf and the wolf, ward off the thief, O *Night*,
   And *be easy for us to get through.*
7. Distinctly has the plastering *black darkness* come unto me.
   O Dawn, may you collect (it) like a debt !

[8]Banerjea, "Some Aspects," p. 228; Dasgupta, S. B., *op. cit.*, pp. 62-63; Kumar, *op. cit.*, pp. 9, 16; Sinha, B. P., *op. cit.*, p. 49.

[9]81.59; cf. also 91.20. The editors of our text are clearly undecided as to whether the word is the classical *rātri* or the Vedic *rātrī*: all three eds. read *-rātriḥ* as the nominative singular of all three words at 81.59, while at 91.20 Vid and Jag read *mahārātri* as the vocative, while Veṅk reads *mahārātre.*

[10]Sinha, B. P., *op. cit.*, p. 49.

[11]RVK, Scheftelowitz ed., p. 110.

8. Accept, O daughter of heaven, what I have presented
you as if (it were a herd) of cattle,
(Viz.,) this hymn, (presented) as if to a *conqueror*, O *Night*.

2. *From the Ṛg Veda Khila*

C. The Śrī Sūkta (2.6)

There is little need to defend the inclusion of the Śrī Sūkta in our collection of hymns, for we have seen in our discussion of Śrī and Lakṣmī that this hymn figures prominently in the identification of these two goddesses. Also, as will be seen in the sequel, several familiar feminine names and characterizations are employed in this hymn, and Agni is once again involved with a feminine deity. We must, however, say a preliminary word about the different historical strata of the Śrī Sūkta.

While our general predilection in Part III is to appreciate the ahistorical, eternal quality of the hymnic material by treating the hymns as discrete wholes, in the case of the Śrī Sūkta our translation cannot avoid recognizing the presence of historical factors. As Scheftelowitz has remarked, "Die Verszahl des Śrīsūkta ist in den Handschriften und Ausgaben sehr schwankend,"[12] and his edition of the text represents an effort to set the different versions in some kind of order. Our procedure in what follows is simply to take the text, given by Scheftelowitz in three portions,[13] and to present it in three corresponding stages. This is not to deny that, within each stage, further strata may exist[14] or that there may be a certain arbitrariness in the way that Scheftelowitz has assigned identically numbered verses to different strata.[15] Such an approach

[12]Scheftelowitz, I., "Śrīsūkta," ZDMG 75 (1921), p. 37.

[13]RVK, Scheftelowitz ed., pp. 72-73, 77-79 top, and the remainder of p. 79, respectively.

[14]E.g., Scheftelowitz ("Śrīsūkta, pp. 38, 42-44) maintains that, in the first stratum, vv. 3-12 are directed to Śrī , vv. 1-2, 13-17 to Lakṣmī. While this would seem to support the hypothesis of a prior distinction between the two goddesses, it does not vitiate the significance of their occurrence here together.

[15]It will be noted that the first stratum contains verses numbered one through nineteen, while the second has verses numbered sixteen through twenty-nine. All this means (see RVK, Scheftelowitz ed., p. 77) is that the versions of the text that comprise the second stratum omit vv. 16-19 of the first stratum,

does, however, obviate the renumbering of verses and, in an area where critical studies are so few, our continuity with extant ones may be deemed desirable. It also allows us to avert further fragmentation of the hymn, while nonetheless appreciating how the early verses, which are of interest primarily for the light they shed on Śrī and Lakṣmī, are nurtured into a vision that dovetails with that of the DM.[16] The reader may consult Scheftelowitz's critical notes for further information on the different versions of the hymn.

i. The first stratum. This is the most widely attested version of the Śrī Sūkta, which all texts agree comes at the end of the fifth *maṇḍala* of the RV, and the bulk of which seems to come from the period of the Brāhmaṇas, with a few verses from Upaniṣadic times.[17]

1. That *Lakṣmī* who has the color of gold, yellowish, with a gold and silver garland,
   Glittering, (and) consisting of gold, may you lead unto me, O *Jātavedas* (*Agni*).[18]
2. May you lead unto me, O *Jātavedas*, that unceasing *Lakṣmī*
   *In whom I may find gold, cattle, horses,*[19] (and) men.
3. She who is accompanied by horses, in the center of a chariot, delighting in the elephant's roar,

reading in their stead other verses (also numbered 16-19), to which additional verses are appended (20-29). There is a similar overlap in enumeration between the second and third strata.

[16]For an exegesis of the hymn in conjunction with other Indian and Southeast Asian material, see Scheftelowitz, "Śrīsūkta," pp. 38-43, and Gonda, *Aspects*, pp. 212-225.

[17]"The bulk" is vv. 1-12, "a few verses" are 13-17: cf. Scheftelowitz, "Śrīsūkta," pp. 41, 43, 44. Verses 18-19 are Vedic quotations, identified in the notes to our translation.

[18]We annotate the references to Agni because of his previously noted association with certain motifs in the DM: Durgā, Kālī, the Seven Little Mothers, etc. Note also the Vedic verses to Agni below (18, 19).

[19]Cp. MarkP 92.12: a devotee of the Goddess becomes "endowed with wealth, grain, and children;" cf. also 92.36. To the extent that the Goddess is understood in the DM as the great benefactress, virtually all of the lines in the Śrī Sūkta that speak of Śrī-Lakṣmī as such might be underscored. We have refrained from so marking them because of our concern with more precise verbal and conceptual correspondences.

The goddess *Śrī* do I invoke; may the goddess *Śrī* be pleased with me.

4. A supplicator am I; her whose cloak is of gold, the moist one, flaming, satisfied, causing satisfaction (in others),
Abiding in a lotus, of lotus color, this *Śrī* do I here invoke.

5. In the glittering, shining *Śrī*, flaming with beauty, beloved of the gods in the world, *generous*,
Enclosed in a lotus, do I take refuge. May my *ill-luck* (*alakṣmī*) perish, (for) you do I choose.

6. O[20] one of solar hue, out of austerities is your tree produced, the Bilva tree:
May its fruits through (my) austerities *drive away illusion* (*māyā*) *and ill-luck*, both internal and external.

7. Along with this amulet, may friendship with the gods come unto me, and fame.
I have arisen in this realm; may it grant me fame (and) increase.

8. I destroy *hunger, thirst*,[21] impurity, utmost *ill-luck*,
Poverty, and failure: drive away all these from my house !

9. She who is perceptible through her odor, *hard to overcome*, the eternal fertilizer, abounding in dung,
The *queen of all creatures*, this *Śrī* do I invoke.

10. May we obtain what we mentally desire and intend, *what is true in* (*our*) *speech.*
May *Śrī* bestow upon me fame (and all) manner of cattle and food.

11. Those things that are alive are nourished into being by mud (earth: *kardama*); O mud, do your nourishing on my behalf:
Cause your mother *Śrī*, garlanded with a lotus, to dwell in my abode.

12. May the waters release their beloved streams; let *ciklītā*[22] abide in my abode,

[20]This and the following two verses are admittedly obscure. Scheftelowitz ("Śrīsūkta," p. 38) thinks they refer to an auspicious amulet derived from the fruit of the Bilva tree.

[21]Cf. MarkP 85.16, 19, translated *infra.*

[22]We leave untranslated this word which is unattested elsewhere and of unknown meaning.

And cause your mother, the goddess *Śrī*, to dwell in my house.

13. The ripe one with a lotus, in full bloom, tawny, garlanded with a lotus,
The daughter of the sun, consisting of gold, (that) *Lakṣmī* may you lead unto me, O *Jātavedas*.

14. The moist one with a lotus, slender, of beautiful color, garlanded with gold,
Glittering, consisting of gold, (that) *Lakṣmī* may you lead unto me, O *Jātavedas*.

15. May you lead unto me, O *Jātavedas*, that unceasing *Lakṣmī*
In whom I may find much gold, cattle, slave girls, (and) men.

16. He who is intent upon bliss (*ānanda*), making offering to the sun,
He should revere *all the goddesses of fortune* (*śriyaḥ*); O *ciklītā*, may you dwell in my abode.

17. Creatures[23] have come into existence through mud; you cause them to go to success;
He granted, he approached, to whom have we poured forth our desires.

18. O[24] *Jātavedas*, purify me and undergird (my) increase of wealth.
May *Agni* release me from every fault (and) sin.

19. O[25] *Agni*, great friendly deity, call forth (from) the gods benevolence toward heaven and earth for us.
Bring well-being (and) security to men from heaven; may we overcome enemies, sins, and difficulties; may we cross over with your protection.

ii. The second stratum. The following, less widely attested verses are clearly posterior to the ones just presented, for verses 16 and 22 presuppose the existence of another hymn, once even called the Śrī Sūkta. Nonetheless, Scheftelowitz argues

[23]Another obscure verse. Failing a logical alternative, or access to a commentary, we here follow Scheftelowitz's German translation ("Śrisūkta") quite literally.

[24]18a=RV 9.67.27; 18cd=YVT 3.1.4.3, et al.

[25]19=RV 6.2.11; 6.14.6.

on grammatical grounds that these, too, come from the Brāhmaṇa period.[26]

16. He who, having become pure and restrained in senses, offers ghee day after day,
Desirous of *Śrī*, he should constantly recite (this) hymn of fifteen verses.

17. O one of lotus-face, lotus-thighs, lotus-eyes, who are born in a lotus,
May you, the lotus-eyed one, grant me that through which I may attain felicity.

18. O grantor of horses, grantor of cattle, grantor of wealth, O one of great wealth,
May wealth be fond of me; O goddess, grant me all (my) desires,

19. Sons and grandsons, wealth, grain, elephants, horses and kine, a chariot.
*You are the mother of (all) creatures*: make me live my full span of life.

20. *Agni* pour forth wealth, Vāyu wealth, Sūrya wealth, Vasu wealth,
Indra (pour forth) wealth, Bṛhaspati (and) Varuṇa[27] wealth.

21. O Vainateya, drink the Soma, let the slayer of Vṛtra drink the Soma,
May those who have Soma grant me the Soma of wealth from the one who has Soma.

22. No anger and no spite, no greed, no impure thoughts
Are there for virtuous devotees; one should recite the Śrī Sūkta.

23. O one whose abode is in the lotus, one with lotus in hand, purest one, one with most purely sweet-smelling garland,
*O blessed one*, beloved of Hari, *beautiful one, one who makes the triple-world prosper*, be gracious to me.

24. One rejoices in the lustre of *Śrī*, full life, health resplendent until-?-[28]

[26]RVK, Scheftelowitz ed., p. 78.
[27]Read *varuṇo* for Scheftelowitz's *varuṇam*.
[28]The meaning of *āvidhāt* is not clear.

(Also) grain, wealth, cattle, acquisition of many sons, (and) long life of a hundred years.

25. The spouse of Viṣṇu, *tranquil goddess*, the sweet one (*mādhavī*), beloved of Mādhava,
Lakṣmī, the dear friend, the goddess who is dear to Viṣṇu, do I revere.

26. We both worship (?) the great *Lakṣmī* and would receive the spouse of Viṣṇu:[29]
Therefore may *Lakṣmī* inspire us.

27. O one of lotus-face, possessing a lotus, of lotus leaves, beloved of the lotus, with wide eyes (like) lotus petals,
Beloved of all, agreeable to the mind of all, put down your lotus foot on (my) heart.

28. Bliss (*ānanda*), Mud (*kardama*), Śrīta, like *ciklīta* and Viśrita
Are seers and the sons of *Śrī: the goddess Śrī is the deity of deities.*

29. *May my debts, illnesses, etc., poverty, sin, hunger, sudden death,*
*Danger, grieving mind, (and) torment perish forever.*[30]

iii. The third stratum. Although Scheftelowitz quotes the following verses from but a single text, they are striking for their addition of new "Goddess motifs" to the identity of Śrī-Lakṣmī. Especially noteworthy are the introduction of nocturnal and martial language, the references to triocularity, and especially, the entire last verse.

23. *Lakṣmī*, who has the lustre of the moon, *the queen*, who has the lustre of the sun, *the governess Śrī*,
In color like the sun, moon, and fire, *the great Lakṣmī* do we worship.

24. O *Night* (*vibhāvari*) may lightning flashes from your heavenly cloud shower down.

[29]We here understand the corresponding accusatives for nominative *mahālakṣmī* and *viṣṇupatnī*, though the vocative or dative (both of which are attested in the variants) would do equally as well. The significance of the verse clearly lies in its being a variation on the Gāyatrī *mantra*, rather than in its grammatical precision. Ingalls has commented to us that *vid* seems to be used for *vidh*.

[30]Cf. MarkP 92.1-28.

May all seeds grow; smite down the haters of Brahmā.

25. O one beloved of the lotus, possessing a lotus, of lotus-hands and lotus-face, with wide eyes (like) lotus petals,
Beloved of all, agreeable to the mind of Viṣṇu, put down your lotus-foot on me.

26. She who rests on a lotus throne, of wide hips, with wide eyes like lotus petals,
Bent down with the weight of her round (?) navel and breasts, with an upper garment of white cloth,

27. *Lakṣmī*, bathed by lordly elephants decked with jewels and with golden foreheads (or: [bathed] with golden water jars),
Constantly may she, with lotuṣ in hand, *endowed with all felicities* (*sarvamāngalyayuktā*), dwell in my house.

28. (May) the *Lakṣmī* of what is accomplished, the *Lakṣmī* of release, the *Lakṣmī* of victory, *Sarasvatī*,[31]
*Śrī*, *Lakṣmī*, the best *Lakṣmī*, be always gracious unto me.

29. The one *who carries* the finest *noose* of *kuśa* grass, making the gesture of protection with her hands, standing on a lotus-throne,
*With three eyes* like myriad risen suns, her, *the primal queen of the world* do I worship.

30. *O*[32] (*you*) *who are blessed with every felicity, auspicious, accomplishing every intent,*
O autumnal one, *three-eyed Gaurī, O Nārāyaṇī, praise be to you* !

## D. The Rātrī Khila (4.2)

Our introductory remarks to the RV's Rātrī Sūkta may also suffice as an introduction to the following *khila* on that hymn. While Scheftelowitz, on the basis of the textual evidence available to him, calls verses 5-14 "secondary," there is no conflicting enumeration of verses. Therefore we present the hymn as a whole, without subdivision of strata.

[31]Cf. MarkP 91.21, translated *infra*.

[32]This verse is identical with DM 91.9, and with a verse in the Jodhpur inscription (see Proleg., n. 204), the sole variant being its reading of *śaradhaye* for *śaraṇye*.

1. O[33] *night*, the earthly space hath been filled with the father's orderings; *great*, thou spreadest thyself to the seats of the sky; bright *darkness* comes on.
2. The men-watching skillful ones that are thine, O *night*, ninety (and) nine—eighty are they (and) eight, also seven (and) seventy of thine—
3. I take refuge in *the night, the mother, the resting-place of all creatures,*
   *(Who is) auspicious* (*bhadrā*) *blessed, black, the night of all the world,*
4. Occasioning rest, drawing (things) in, garlanded with planets and constellations.
   I take refuge in *auspicious* (*śivā*) *night* ; *O auspicious one,* may we obtain what is best.
   O *Agni*, may your splendor abide in my invocations.
5. Reverently I will praise the goddess, (our) *refuge*, beloved of well-versed poets,
   *Durgā*, (who is) equal to a thousand (others): "*To Jātavedas* (*Agni*) *we will press the Soma.*"[34]
6. *For the sake of* the tranquillity of those who are twice-born, (they are your) followers, along with the seers,
   *You have your origin in the Ṛg Veda : "may he burn up the possessions of the envious."*
7. The Brahmans who take refuge in you, the bearer of oblations, O goddess,
   Whether ignorant or knowing a great deal : "*he leads us over all difficulties.*"
8. Those twice-born who praise *the one who has the color of Agni, auspicious, beautiful,*

[33]Verses 1 and 2 correspond to AV 19.47.1 and 19.47.3, respectively, the sole variant being the latter's reading of *draṣṭāro* for *yuktāso*. With the exception of this variant, we here give the Whitney-Lanman tr., deleting their parenthetical Sanskrit phrases. They entitle the AV hymn "To Night: for protection."

[34]The phrase in quotation marks is a quotation of RV 1.99.1a with the other three *padas* being quoted seriatim in the following three verses. The significance of this quotation is major, for RV 1.99 is a one-verse hymn to Agni, a hymn that we have met before, in our discussion of the epithet Durgā, and that becomes known as the *durgā-sāvitrī*.

*She causes them to cross over difficulties : "Agni (does this) as one (crosses over) the stormy sea with a boat."*

9. *In difficulties, in battle that is painful or terrifying, in peril from enemies,*[35]

*In attacks of fire and theft, in the warding off of seizers, O one who wards off wicked seizers, (you abide) : Om,* hail !

10. *In difficulties, in calamities, in battles, and in forests are you. Having deluded (human beings ?), they take refuge (in you); make me unafraid of those (circumstances) ; make me unafraid of those: Om,* hail !

11. *May* the one with (beautiful) hair among all creatures, Pañcamī by name,

*The goddess, protect me from everything in every direction; may she protect from everything: Om,* hail !

12. *In*[36] *her who has the color of Agni, flaming with ascetic power, the offspring of Virocana, who delights in the fruits of one's actions,*

*In the goddess Durgā do I take refuge ; O one of great speed, (well) do you cross:* hail ! *O one of great speed, (well) do you cross:* hail !

13. *Durgā, in difficult places,* "the goddess(es) is for our welfare."[37]

He who always recites, night after night, this meritorious hymn to *Durgā,*

[35]A similar enumeration of perils in overcoming which the Goddess's aid is found efficacious is found at DM 92.23ff. We shall see other similar enumerations in subsequent hymns.

[36]Once again the convergence of Durgā and Rātrī is striking: except for the concluding refrain, this passage corresponds, without variant, to the (second) passage from TA 10.1 that we have discussed in Part I, s. v. "*durgā*".

[37]Prof. Alaka Hejib first called our attention to the significance of *pada* b—*śam nó devīr abhíṣṭaye*—and Prof. Ingalls has aided us in formulating that significance as follows. This phrase is found at AV, Śaunaka recension, 6.1.1, but it forms the first line of the whole AV in the Paippalāda recension (see AV, Whitney-Lanman tr., pp. cxvi-cxvii). In the AV, the "goddesses" are the waters, but the nominative plural *devīr* is here in the *khila* understood as nominative singular, which is an impossibility in the Vedic language. This is a striking instance of how the Veda is enabled to live on, as a religious presence in post-Vedic times.

14. Kuśika[38] Subharaḥ every night and Bhāradvājin every night, (should recite) the Rātrī-praising Gāyatrī.
One should recite the hymn of *Rātrī* constantly. It is appropriate for that time.

### 3. *From the Mahābhārata*

## E. The Durgā Stava

In setting the context for our translation of this hymn, which appears as an insertion near or at the end of Mbh 4.5, little need be said about its relationship to the constituted text at that juncture. The opening line establishes a thread of continuity with that text, and there seems to be no organic connection between the hymn and the main story-line.

The textual evidence for this hymn does bear remark, however. The Durgā Stava appears at Appendix I No. 4 in the Virāṭa Parvan of the critical edition, where seven different versions of the hymn are given, ranging in length from eight to eighty-seven lines, with some verses common to multiple versions. Five of these versions are attested by a single manuscript, one by three manuscripts, and one by five. What is noteworthy is that, except for one Telugu (T) version, all of this testimony occurs in Devanāgarī (D) manuscripts. That is, there are no Śāradā (Kaśmirī), Bengalī (B), Grantha, or Malayālam versions of the Durgā Stava, and the second T manuscript collated for this book also lacks it. While it is risky to rely too heavily on the Devanāgarī tradition, which has been open to influence from all directions, we may note (1) that the text-editor finds it "curious" that "the Durgāstava did not find its way into Bengal," for elsewhere in the texts "B and D are constantly running into one another";[39] and (2) that the textual evidence does not, at least, controvert our earlier remarks[40] on the likely geographic provenience of the DM in particular,

[38]Neither the syntax, nor the thrust of the specific references, is clear. Following Ingalls' suggestion, our translation requires reading *ratrīḥ* and *ratrīr* for *rātriḥ* and *rātrir*, as "accusatives of uninterrupted extent of space or time."
[39]Mbh 4, Introduction, p. xxi.
[40]Part II, note 101.

and, perhaps, of the Sanskritized worship of the Goddess in general.

We here present the most widely attested version of the Durgā Stava, the testimony for which includes the Vulgate. We follow the critical edition's convention in Appendices of indicating lines, rather than verses.[41]

Going, to the delightful city of Virāṭa, Yudhiṣṭhira
With his mind praised *the goddess Durgā, queen of the three worlds,*
(*Who was*) *born in the womb of Yaśodā,*[42] best beloved of Nārāyaṇa,
*Born in the family of the cowherd Nanda, auspicious* (*mangalyā*), causing the growth of the family,
Causing the destruction of Kaṃsa, *causing the destruction of Asuras,*
Dashed on a precipice of stone, going into the skies,
Sister of Vāsudeva,[43] adorned with a heavenly garment,
Wearing heavenly clothes, *the goddess who carries sword and shield.*

[41]Here we give the whole of what has been traditionally known as the Durgā Stava, even though it is not all technically hymnic material; we follow this practice with subsequent hymns as well. We do this, first, for the sake of continuity with that tradition: the appearance of the deity who has been hymned, and her granting of boons, are as much a part of the emergence of a Sanskritized worship of the Goddess as are the invocations proper. Moreover, it will be seen that illuminating characterizations of the divine emerge in the dialogues between devotee and deity. We have omitted from our translation phrases which simply identify the interlocutors.

[42]On the DM's association with the Kṛṣṇa Gopāla cycle, see, in addition to our analysis of the Śumbha-Niśumbha myth in Part II, the Goddess's remarks at the end of that myth (MarkP 91.36-37) where she enumerates her various future activities:

When the twenty-eighth *yuga* in the Vaivasvata Manu interval has arrived,
Two other great Asuras, Śumbha and Niśumbha, will arise.
Born in the house of the cowherd Nanda, born in the womb of Yaśodā,
I, dwelling on Vindhya mountain, will then slay those two Asuras.

[43]We do not underscore this phrase, even though being Vāsudeva's sister might be seen as being an implication of being "born in the house of the cowherd Nanda" (see our preceding note). The DM does not use the phrase "sister of Vāsudeva," although we shall encounter it in other hymns in this Part of our study.

Having[44] invoked the goddess, the king, together with his brothers, desirous of seeing (her),
Began to praise (her) again with various hymnic (verses).
"Hail, O *boon-giver, black one* (*kṛṣṇā*), chaste young virgin,
Whose form is like the newly-risen sun,[45] whose face is like the full moon,
O one of four arms (and) four faces, with full, high breasts,
*With bracelets of peacock's feathers*, wearing armlets on your arms.
You shine, O goddess, like *the wife of Nārāyaṇa*, the lotus.
Your form and chastity are pure, O sky-wanderer.
*Black* like dark clouds, your face rivals Saṃkarṣaṇa's.
You have two broad arms, upraised (like) Indra's standard.
(A woman) who is without stain among women in the world, born from the lotus, *carrying a vessel and bell*,
(*Carrying*) *a noose, a bow, a great discus, and assorted weapons*,
Endowed with well-shaped ears and earrings,
O goddess, you shine with a face rivaling the moon.
Shining with a many-colored diadem, with a hair-band,
Shining with a garment of snakes' hoods, with row(s) of thread,
With your serpentine bond you shine here like Mount Mandara (itself).
With your upraised standard of peacock-tails do you shine.
Having undertaken a vow of chastity, by you is the triple-world purified.
Therefore, *you are praised, O goddess*, and *even by the thirty* (*gods*) are you worshipped,
*For the sake of protecting the triple world, O destroyer of the Asura Mahiṣa.*

[44]Here, as elsewhere, for syntactical clarity our translation reads two lines of the text in reverse order.

[45]Although the DM is clearly appreciative of the physical beauty of the Goddess, particularly in its account of her mundane origin at the beginning of the second *carita*, we have not annotated all the details of her beauty that the Durgā Stava enumerates, for they are both more extensive, and more specific, than those remarked upon in the DM.

Be *gracious* to me, O *best of deities*, show *compassion*, be *auspicious*.
You are Jayā and Vijayā, and you grant victory (*jaya*) in battle :
May you, a *boon-giver*, now grant me victory (*vijaya*) in battle.
*Your eternal abode is upon that best of mountains, Vindhya.*[46]
*O Kālī, Kālī, O great Kālī,* fond of liquor, flesh, and beasts,
Wandering where you wish, of spirits is your retinue composed, you *a giver of boons*.
*Those men who call upon you for the removal of burdens,*
And those men on earth who honor you at daybreak,
*For them nothing is hard to obtain, even regarding sons or wealth.*
*O Durgā, you cause (people) to cross from difficulty (durgāt) (to safety); therefore are you known to the world as Durgā.*
*Of those who are lost in dreary forests, and of those sunk in the great ocean,*
*Or of men held up by thieves, you are the supreme refuge.*
*And in the crossing of waters, in dreary forests and woods,*
*Those men who remember you, O great goddess, they do not perish.*
You are fame, *fortune* (*śrī*), steadiness, *success*, *modesty*,[47] *knowledge* (*vidyā*), continuity, mind,
Twilight, *night*, light, *sleep*, moonlight, *loveliness*,[48] patience, *compassion*.[49]
(When) honored, you cause to perish the bondage of men, (their) delusion, death of sons, loss of wealth,
Sickness, death, and fear.
Fallen from my kingdom, I submissively take refuge in you,
Just as I have bowed my head to you, O goddess, *queen of the gods*.

[46]Cf. MarkP 91.37, where the Goddess says that in a future episode she will be *vindhyācalanivāsinī*.
[47]*siddhi*: cf. MarkP 85.9; *hrī*: cf. MarkP 81.60.
[48]*kānti*: cf. MarkP 85.25.
[49]*dayā*: cf. MarkP 85.29.

Protect me, one of lotus-leaf eyes; O truth, be true to us.
Be a refuge for me, O *Durgā*, O refuge, O one who is fond of her devotees."
Thus praised, the goddess showed herself to the son of Pāṇḍu.
Having approached the king, she spoke these words :
"O great-armed king, listen to my words, O lord.
Victory in battle will soon be yours.
Having by my grace conquered (and) slain the Kaurava army,
Having made (your) kingdom free from troubles, you will again enjoy the earth.
Together with your brothers, O king, you will obtain abundant favor,
And by my grace happiness and health will be yours.
And those who gloriously rejoice (in me), having (here) in the world cast off their sins,
I, delighted, will grant them dominion, long life, bodily beauty, (and) offspring.
And *those who in going abroad, or in the city, in battle, in danger from foes,*
*In a forest, in an impassable dreary wood, on the ocean, in an abyss, upon a mountain,*
*Will remember me*, as I have been remembered by you,
*For them nothing in this world will be hard to obtain.*
One should both listen to and recite this best of hymns with devotion.
(Then) will all one's endeavors be successful, O son of Pāṇḍu.
And by my grace neither the Kurus, nor men dwelling in the city of Virāṭa,
Will recognize all of you dwelling there."
The *boon-granting goddess*, having spoken thus to Yudhiṣṭhira, crusher of enemies,
And having given protection to the sons of Pāṇḍu, thence disappeared.

## F. The Durgā Stotra

The Mbh's second hymn to Durgā receives somewhat broader attestation in the manuscripts, for it is known in both the Bengalī and Devanāgarī traditions and, by conflation, in the Kaśmirī.[50] Elsewhere, however, it is not known. In general, it seems to have had a more clearly defined identity than the Durgā Stava, as is reflected in there being but a single version of the text, found in the critical edition as Appendix I, No. 1 in the Bhīṣma Parvan. There are, of course, a number of variant readings, but there is not the extreme difference of opinion as to the length of the hymn that was present regarding the Mbh's first hymn to Durgā.

Although the hymn has been excised from the constituted text, the juncture at which it appears as an insertion is noteworthy. The attesting manuscripts place it after 6. 22. 16, i.e., six verses before the end of that chapter, and it is with chapter 23 that the *Bhagavad Gītā* begins. This would appear to be a tacit recognition by those manuscripts of the enormous stature of the impending chapters of the Gītā—some of them even insert an identification of Kṛṣṇa as Śrī Bhagavān after line 2 of the Durgā Stotra[51]—and an effort to effect at least a *rapprochement* between Durgā and the Gītā, perhaps even a subordination of the latter to the former. As in the constituted text, Saṃjaya is recounting the course of events to the blind Dhṛtarāṣṭra, a fact which accounts for the admittedly abrupt, even awkward, references in the last few lines.

> Having seen the army of the sons of Dhṛtarāṣṭra drawn up for battle,
> Kṛṣṇa spoke (these) words for the sake of Arjuna's well-being :
> "Having become pure, O great-armed one, being about to engage in battle,
> Recite the Durgā Stotra for the sake of conquering (your) enemies."
> Thus addressed in battle by the illustrious Vāsudeva, Arjuna,

[50]Mbh 6, Introduction, pp. xviii-xix.

[51]As noted above, we omit such phrases from our translation.

The son of Pṛthā, having descended from (his) chariot, with his hands in reverent gesture, uttered (this) hymn :
"*Om*, hail to you, leader of the army of Siddhas, virtuous one, who dwells on (Mount) Mandara.
O young virgin, O *Kālī, adorned with skulls*, reddish, *black* and tawny one,
O *Bhadrakālī*, hail to you ! O *great Kālī*, hail to you !
O *impetuous Caṇḍī*, hail to you ! O *agent of crossing* (*tāriṇī*), fair woman,
O *illustrious Kātyāyanī*, *fierce one*, O Vijayā (and) Jayā,
*O one who bears a banner of peacock plumes, adorned with various ornaments.*
*O bearer of a lofty spear, bearer of sword and shield,*
O youngest sister of the lord of cowherds (Kṛṣṇa), O eldest one, *born in the family of the cowherd Nanda*,
*O one who is eternally fond of Mahiṣa's blood*, O *Kauśikī*, clothed in yellow,
O one of harsh laughter with the face of a wolf, hail to you, O one fond of battle.
O Umā, O *Śākambharī*,[52] white one, *black one, destroyer of Kaiṭabha*,
O one of gold eyes, of deformed eyes, of smoky eyes, hail to you !
O *Veda and Śruti*, O one of great virtue, well-versed in the Veda, *who has knowledge of beings*,[53]
O one whose abode is ever made in the *caitya* halls of Jambūkaṭaka,
*Of knowledges you are the knowledge of Brahman, of embodied creatures* (*you are*) *the great sleep* (*mahānidrā*).
O *blessed* mother of Skanda, *Durgā, who dwells in difficult places*,
(*You are*) *the syllable Svāhā and Svadhā*, the smallest part, the utmost extremity, *Sarasvatī*.

[52]Cf. MarkP 91.44.

[53]*jātavedasī*; as we have seen, the masculine *jātavedas* is frequently applied to Agni; such an application is as old as the RV, e.g., 1.77.5.

O *Sāvitrī*,[54] (you are the) mother of the Vedas; likewise are you called the end of the Vedas.
You are praised, O great *goddess*, by one whose inner soul is pure.
Through your grace may victory always be mine, in battle after battle.
*In dreary forests, fearful spots, and places of difficult access*, and in the abodes of (your) devotees,
(Even) in the nether regions do you constantly dwell; *in battle you conquer demons*.
You are the gaping one, the *one of delusion, delusion (itself)*, *modesty and fortune*, too,
The twilight and luminous *Sāvitrī*, likewise the *mother*,
*Contentment*, *growth*, *support*, light, causing the waxing of the moon and sun,
The prosperity of the prosperous; in battle you are regarded by Siddhas and celestial singers."
Then, having acknowledged the devotion of Pṛthā's son, she who is kindly disposed toward human beings,
Who goes through the sky, stood in front of Govinda (and) said :
"In a short time you will conquer (your) enemies, O son of Pāṇḍu.
O invincible one, you are a man possessing aid from Nārāyaṇa.
In battle you are unconquerable by enemies, even by Indra himself."
Having spoken thus, the *boon-grantress* immediately disappeared.
Having received the boon, the son of Kuntī knew that victory was his.
Then the son of Pṛtha mounted his well-made chariot.
Kṛṣṇa and Arjuna, on a single chariot, blew two heavenly conches.
The man who, having arisen at daybreak, recites this hymn,
Never knows any fear from Yakṣas, Rakṣas, or Piśācas,

[54]Cf. MarkP 81.55, translated *infra*.

And he has no enemies among those who are serpents, etc., who have tusks.
Even from the royal family, there is never any danger for him.
In controversy, he obtains victory; bound, he is released[55] from (his) bond.
*He inevitably crosses over difficulty,* and likewise is free from (the assaults of) thieves.
He is always victorious in battle, he obtains the whole of good fortune.
Likewise endowed with good health and strength, may he live for a hundred years.
This was seen by me through the grace of the splendid Vyāsa.
All your wicked sons in delusion do not know that these two are the seers Nara and Nārāyaṇa,
And that the proper time for these words has come (so) enveloped (are they) by the snare of death, under the influence of anger.
Dvaipāyana, and Nārada, Kaṇva, likewise the sinless Rāma
Restrained your son, but he did not accept it (their restraint).
Where *dharma* is, there are radiance and grace; where modesty, there fortune and intelligence;
Whence is *dharma*, thence is Kṛṣṇa; whence Kṛṣṇa, thence victory.

4. *From the Harivaṃśa*

## G. Viṣṇu's Praise of Nidrā

In our epithetical discussion, we have alluded on several occasions to the hymn that Viṣṇu offers to the goddess Nidrā in the course of arranging for their respective births to Devakī and Yaśodā, and we have commented elsewhere on the significance of this hymn.[56] The context in the HV for this hymn is, of

[55]Read *mucyate* for *mucyati.*
[56]Part I, n. 89.

course, the commencement of the familiar Kṛṣṇa Gopāla cycle: the wicked Kaṃsa, knowing that he is to be slain by one of the offspring of Devakī and Vasudeva, instructs his ministers to confine those two, so that Devakī's pregnancies might be watched over and the infants slain (47.1-8). Viṣṇu then descends to the nether regions (*pātāla*) where the Ṣaḍgarbhas ("six embryos"), of whom a brief history is given (47.11-22), are found sleeping in the waters like intra-uterine foetuses. Entering them in the form of a dream (*svapnarūpeṇa*), Viṣṇu draws forth their life breaths and sends them to Nidrā, to whom he then speaks (47.26). The first part of Viṣṇu's address pertains to the particulars of the plot, how Nidrā is to dispose the Ṣaḍgarbhas as Devakī's first six offspring, transferring the next foetus, a portion of Viṣṇu to be called Samkarṣaṇa, to Rohinī, and then being born herself to Yaśodā, thence to exchange places with Kṛṣṇa who will meanwhile have been born to Devakī. Our translation begins with Viṣṇu's comment on her mundane fate in this enterprise, which then grows into a eulogy of the goddess. We present the hymn in two strata, corresponding to the material found in the constituted text, and that appended in the critical apparatus.

i. The first stratum :

47.38 "Having seized you by the feet, (Kaṃsa) will dash you on a rock.
Being (thus) dashed, you will obtain an eternal place in the sky.

39. Being *black* like me in color, with a face like Samkarṣaṇa's,
Having broad arms like my arms on earth,

40. Raising up a three-pointed spear and gold-hilted sword,
And a vessel filled with honey and an utterly spotless lotus,

41. Wearing a dark-blue linen garment, with an upper garment in white,
With a necklace shining like the rays of the moon on your breast,

42. Ornamented, your two ears completed with heavenly earrings,

You will shine with a face that has become the rival of the moon.

43. With a crown of three discs, resplendent with braided hair,

With arms like iron bars, which russle like the coils of a snake,

44. With an upraised standard of peacock feathers nearby,

And shining with a bracelet made from peacocks' tails,

45. Surrounded by terrible throngs of spirits, following my command,

Having taken a vow of celibacy, you will go to the heavens.

46. There, in an action ordained by me, the thousand-eyed Indra,

Together with the (other) gods, will perform your heavenly consecration.

47. There Indra will take you as a sister;

Through the lineage of Kauśika, you will be (known as) *Kauśiki.*

48. He will give you *an eternal abode on Vindhya*, the best of mountains;

Then you will cause the earth to shine with a thousand (sacred) places,

49. *And the two demons Sumbha and Nisumbha*, who wander upon the mountain

*Together with their followers, you will slay*, having fixed your mind on me.

50. Wandering in the triple world, fulfilling requests on earth,

You will be a *boon-giver*, O illustrious one, taking form at will.

51. Followed by spirits, constantly delighted by offerings of flesh,

On the ninth lunar day you will receive worship, together with a sacrifice of wild beasts.

52. And those men who, knowing my majesty, will worship you,

For them *nothing will be hard to obtain*, including even sons and wealth.

53. *Of*[57] *those who are lost in dreary forests, and of those who are sunk in the great ocean,*
*Or of men held up by thieves, you are the supreme refuge.*

54. You[58] are *success, fortune*, support, fame, *modesty, knowledge*, obeisance, intellect,
Twilight, *night*, light, *sleep*, and also *the night of destruction*.

55. Human bondage, terrible death, the destruction of sons, the loss of wealth,
Sickness, death, and fear do you, (when) worshipped, put to an end.

56. Having *deluded* Kaṃsa, you alone will glory in the world;
For the sake of its enhancement, I will accomplish Kaṃsa's destruction."

57. Thus having instructed her, the lord disappeared.
And she, having bowed to him and saying "So be it," also vanished.

ii. The second stratum :

With the above denouement, *adhyāya* 47 of the constituted text ends, and in *adhyāya* 48 the account of the anticipated events begins. The only further elaboration upon this goddess that occurs therein is in Nārada's report to Kaṃsa (65.48-57), a passage that we have quoted in our discussion of the Śumbha-Niśumbha myth in Part II. However, the above hymn has been embellished with additional verses in more than half of the manuscript tradition. The verses are relegated to Appendix I, No. 8, for they are lacking in the southernmost manuscript tradition,[59] but we may here note the material that all other manuscripts read after, or near, 47. 52.[60]

[57]This verse equals Durgā Stava lines 40-41, without variant.
[58]Cf. 54-55 and Durgā Stava lines 44-47.
[59]Viz., M 1-3; cf. HV, Introduction, pp. xxx, xxxv-xxxvi.
[60]The manuscript tradition at this juncture is very complicated, with partially or wholly repeated verses and the like: cf. the critical apparatus. We may note that many of the manuscripts smooth over the "seam" by ending the *adhyāya* and beginning a new one, and read the following passage (591*) in effecting the transition from the material now found in the constituted text to that now found in Appendix I 8 :

Those men who devotedly praise you with this hymn, O fair one,
From him (sic: *tasya*) I do not disappear, and he does not disappear from me.

"(You are) the virtuous *Kātyāyanī, the goddess Kauśikī*,
practicing celibacy,
Mother of the one whose army is the Siddhas (Skanda),
the brave *Durgā*, of great austerities.
You are Jayā and Vijayā, *increase, patience, compassion,*
Eldest sister of Yama, wearing a blue silken lower
garment,
*Of many forms* and deformed, *of various sorts of forms,*
Of deformed eyes, of wide eyes, *protectress* of devotees.
On terrible mountain peaks, and in rivers, and in caves,
In forests and in groves is your dwelling, O *great
goddess.*
Well-honored by savages, barbarians, and mountain
folk,
With a standard of peacock feathers, you conquer the
worlds on every side.
Surrounded by cocks, goats, sheep, lions, and tigers,
Accompanied by the sounds of bells, famous, *dwelling
on Vindhya (mountain),*
*Carrying trident and sharp-edged spear,* having the sun
and moon as (your) emblem,
The ninth day of the dark (lunar) fortnight, the eleventh
day of the bright (fortnight), beloved (are you).
Sister of Vāsudeva, the *night, fond of a quarrel,*
*The abode, the basis, and the supreme goal of all creatures,*
*And the daughter of the cowherd Nanda,* bringing about
the victory of the gods,
Clothed in bark and (yet) well-clothed, *violent* and
(yet) the twilight are you.
With disheveled hair, likewise death (are you), fond
of flesh and boiled rice,
*Good fortune (lakṣmī) and (yet) with the form of ill-fortune
(alakṣmī)*, for the sake of slaying demons,
*Sāvitrī* among the gods, and mother of the throng of
spirits,

---

Colophon

Vaiśampāyana (who is also the narrator in the constituted text at this juncture) said:

I will recite the Āryā Stava, just as it was uttered by seers of yore.
I honor Nārāyaṇī, the goddess, queen of the three worlds.

The sacred ground among sacrifices, and sacrificial gift among priests,
The success of sea-farers, and seashore of those who go upon the ocean,
The foremost Yakṣī among Yakṣas, and Surasā among Nāgas,
A speaker of Brahman, initiation, likewise the supreme loveliness,
You are the light of lights, O goddess, and Rohiṇī among constellations.
And at the doors of kings, and holy places, and at the confluences of rivers,
And when the moon of the full moon day is full, (you are) known as Kṛttivāsā ("skin-clad"),
And the blessed words (*sarasvatī*) of Vālmīki, likewise the recollective power of Dvaipāyana (Vyāsa),
And the goddess of liquor among spirits, you are praised by your (very) deeds.
The fair appearance of Indra, you are known as "thousand-eyed."
The seers' *knowledge* of *dharma*, likewise Aditi among the gods,
And Sītā ("the furrow") among plowmen, and Dharaṇī ("the earth") among creatures,
And the goddess of ascetics, and the tinder-stick of Agnihotra sacrifices are you.
And *the hunger of all creatures*,[61] and the satisfaction of the gods,
*Svāhā*, *delight*, firmness, *wisdom*, of Vasus the wealthy one,
You are the hope of men, and the *delight* of those who have performed (proper) action,
The four directions and the intermediate directions, the tip of fire, light (itself),
Śakunī, Pūtanā, and the very terrible Revatī are you,
And *the sleep of all creatures, the deluding one, likewise she who rules.*
Among knowledges, you are the *knowledge* of Brahman, the syllable *om*, likewise *the* (*exclamation*) *Vaṣaṭ*.[62]

[61]Cf. MarkP 85.16, translated *infra*.
[62]Cf. MarkP 81.54, translated *infra*.

Among women (mentioned) in the Purāṇas, seers know you to be *Pārvatī.*
Among women with one husband (you are) Arundhatī, according to the words of Prajāpati,
Known by a heavenly succession of names to be Indrāṇī.
*By you, all this universe,* (*everything*) *that moves and is stationary, is pervaded.*
In all battles and flamings of fire,
On the banks of rivers, *in terrible dreary forests and dangers,*
*In journeying abroad,* in bondage to a king, and in the trampling down of enemies,
And *in all dangers to life, you are the great protectress,* without a doubt.
My heart is on you, O goddess, (my) intellect on you, (my) mind on you.
Protect me from all sins, and you will demonstrate graciousness.
The pure man who, having arisen in the morning, with disciplined mind shall recite
This heavenly hymn to the goddess, which is connected with historical tradition (*itihāsa*),
For three months, he receives the fruit that is desired;
(He who does this) for six months receives a single, most excellent boon;
(When the goddess is) praised for nine months, (the devotee) receives the divine eye;
(He who does this) for a year, he receives perfection, just as he desires,
And truth, and celibacy, according to the words of Dvaipāyana."

### H. Pradyumna's Hymn

The second hymn of note in the HV does not occur in the constituted text at all, but in an Appendix that constitutes an *upabṛṃhaṇam* upon an episode in the constituted text. The precipitating episode is inquired into by Janamejaya at 99.1 :

He whom you formerly called the slayer of Śambara,
That Pradyumna; just how did he slay Śambara ? Tell me that.

Pradyumna is then identified as the son of Rukmiṇī and Kṛṣṇa, and the balance of this *adhyāya* recounts the basic story. After verse 26, four additional *adhyāyas,* constituting Appendix I, No. 30, in the course of which our hymn occurs, are inserted by some texts. It is impossible to draw any geographical conclusions from this insertion, for it appears in all manuscripts except those at the geographic extremities, i.e., it is lacking only in the Śāradā, Newārī, and Malayālam versions, which are the very versions used to determine the constituted text.[63]

Before turning to the hymn itself, we may note that the dilemma confronting Pradyumna, which occasions his hymn, has been created, at least indirectly, by the goddess herself. There is thus an intriguing interplay and reversal of mythical motifs, not unlike that which we have seen in the Rām's integration of two stories about Madhu.[64] Prior to the battle between Śambara and Pradyumna, the former has reflected:[65]

My club, adorned with gold, is like the staff of Death,
Not[66] to be warded off in battle by gods, Dānavas, or men,
Created by me from my own body, having performed very difficult austerities.
It was formerly given to me by the supremely delighted Pārvatī (saying) :
"O Śambara, take this club adorned with gold,
Named Bringing-Illusion-to-an-End (*māyāntakaraṇa*), destroying all Asuras.
With it two terrible, mighty Dānavas, wanderers upon the mountain,
Śumbha and Niśumbha, together with their hordes, were slain by me.
When your life is in danger, it is to be loosed upon the enemy."
Having spoken thus, the goddess Pārvatī disappeared therefrom.

[63]See HV, Introduction, pp. xxiv, xxxi, xxxv-xxxvi.

[64]Cf. Part II, note 12.

[65]Here, as in the ensuing hymn, our marginal enumeration is of the lines in Appendix I 30.

[66]We read the accusatives, which are clearly intended to modify *mudgaraḥ* in line 305, as nominatives in this and the following line.

Now I shall release this best of clubs upon the enemy.

It is thus for protection against a former weapon of the goddess that Pradyumna now turns to the goddess herself.

After enumerating the inauspicious portents that appear when Śambara picks up his club, the account continues :

> Having seen these great omens, the brave Pradyumna quickly
> Having descended from his chariot stood, cupping his hands in obeisance.
> He called to mind the goddess *Pārvatī*, beloved of Śiva.
> Having bowed his head, he began to praise the goddess:
> "*Om*, hail to *Kātyāyanī* ! Hail to the mother of Guha !
> Hail to *the illusion of the triple world* ! To *Kātyāyanī* alleluia, alleluia!
> Hail to *the destructress of enemies* ! Hail to Gārgī, queen of the mountains !
> I reverence *the slayer to Śumbha, the piercer of Niśumbha's heart* !
> I bow to *Kālarātri*, and (I bow) to the ever-chaste maiden.
> With folded hands I bow to the goddess who dwells in dreary forests.
> To her *who dwells on Vindhya mountain, who destroys difficulties, who is hard to overcome in battle*, who is fond of battle,
> *The great goddess*, Jayā and Vijayā, do I bow down.
> I bow to the *unconquered*, the unconquered scorcher of enemies.
> I bow to *the one with a bell in her hand*, who is likewise adorned with a garland of bells.
> I bow to *the one with a trident, the slayer of the Asura Mahiṣa*.
> I bow to *the one mounted on a lion*, having as her emblem the best of lions.
> I bow to Ekānaṃśā, Gāyatrī, who possesses the virtue of the sacrifice.
> And with folded hands I bow to *Sāvitrī* of the sages.
> Protect me eternally, O goddess, give (me) victory in battle."
> Having heard these words of desire, *Durgā's* mind was well-pleased.

With greatly delighted soul, the goddess spoke (these) words :
"Behold, behold, O great-armed one, who increases the joy of Rukmiṇī.
Choose a boon, my dear, (for) beholding me is not in vain."
Having heard (these) words of the goddess, with thrilled mind,
Having bowed his head to the goddess, he began his entreaty:
"If you are pleased, O goddess, let what is desired by me be granted.
I ask for a boon, O *boon-giver*, (viz.,) victory over all my enemies.
That club which was given by you to Śambara, produced from his own (body),
May it, having touched my limbs, become a garland consisting of flowers."
Having said "So be it," she disappeared from there.
And the splendid Pradyumna, delighted, then mounted his chariot.

We may note that, immediately hereafter, Pradyumna's boon comes to fruition, thus completing the coincidence of opposites which has centered around the goddess and her weapon.

## I. Aniruddha's Hymn

The last hymn of note in the HV also appears as an obvious insertion into a familiar story. The story is, at the most general level, that of Aniruddha, who is known as the son of Pradyumna and Śubhāṅgī, and husband of Rukmavatī (89. 1-10). More specifically, the account is of Uṣā's infatuation with Aniruddha and of his confinement by her father, the Asura Bāṇa, son of Bali, for it is when he is thus imprisoned that some texts insert the following passage.[67] There is no obvious pattern in the geographical distribution of those texts.[68]

[67]This specific context is set in HV 106-108, with the following interpolation coming after *adhyāya* 108, except in one instance when it follows 109; in the critical edition it is found at Appendix I 35.

[68]This passage is found in the Śāradā manuscript, but is missing from the

When, in Bāṇapura, the brave Aniruddha together with Uṣā
Was confined by king Bāṇa, son of Bali,
Then for the sake of protection, he took refuge in the goddess *Kaumārī*.
Hear this hymn to the goddess as it was sung by Aniruddha.
"Having bowed down to the endless, indestructible, heavenly primal god,
The eternal Nārāyaṇa, the excellent, foremost lord,
I will sing praises to *Caṇḍī*, *Kātyāyanī*, the virtuous goddess, revered by the (whole) world,
The *boon-grantress*, with the names familiar to Hari.
(I will praise) the splendid one, who is extolled by seers and gods with flowery words,
*The goddess who abides in the body of all* (*sarvadehasthā*), reverenced by all the gods.
I bow down to the sister of Indra and Viṣṇu, for the sake of well-being.
With purity of mind, (eternally) pure, with folded hands do I hymn
Gautamī, who strikes fear into Kaṃsa, causing Yaśodā's delight to increase,
Sacrificially pure, born in (the town of) Gokula, *daughter of the cowherd Nanda*,
*Wise*, clever, *auspicious*, gentle, crushing the sons of Danu,
*The goddess who abides in the body of all*, reverenced by all creatures,
Wondrous, ancient, *illusion*, with a face like the moon, having the lustre of the moon,
*Tranquillity*, the firm one, the *mother*, *the deluding one*, also the emaciator,
To be honored by the gods together with throngs of seers, reverenced by all the gods,
*Kālī*, *Kātyāyanī*, the fear-striking goddess, (who) destroys (all) fears,

crucial Newārī and Malayālam versions, as it is also from various other editions: see HV, Introduction, pp. xxiv, xxxi.

*Kātyāyanī*, going about at will, *three-eyed*,[69] chaste,
Lightning, with the sound of a (thunder) cloud, goblin, of broad face,
Foremost of the host, illustrious, Śakunī, likewise Revatī,
Among lunar days the fifth, sixth, full-moon, (and) fourteenth (days),
The twenty-seven constellations, rivers, all the ten directions,
Dwelling in cities, woods, pleasure gardens, doorways, and upper stories,
*Modesty*, *fortune*, the Gangės, Gāndhārī, a *yoginī* and grantress of *yoga* to good men,
Fame, hope, space, touch, *Sarasvatī*, do I revere.
And (I revere) the mother of the Vedas, *Sāvitrī*, fond of (her) devotees,
Practitioner of austerities, peace-maker, the eternal Ekānaṃśā,
Kauberī, intoxicating, *fierce*, *sleepy*, dwelling in Malaya,
*Supportress of creatures*, instigator of fear, Kuṣmāṇḍī, fond of flowers,
*Destroying*, of fascinating abode, *dwelling on Vindhya* and Kailāsa,
A magnificent woman, *having a lion as conveyance*, of many forms, with a bull as emblem,
*Inaccessible*, *hard to conquer*, *Durgā*, *seeing whom terrified Niśumbha*,
Beloved of the gods, a deity, the goddess, younger sister of Indra, *auspicious*,
Barbarian, clothed in bark, revered by an army of thieves,
Drinker of ghee, drinker of *soma*, gentle, dwelling upon all mountains,
*Crushing Śumbha and Niśumbha*, with breasts like an elephant's frontal lobes,
Mother of Skanda, honored by Siddhas and Cāraṇas,
The excellent mother of Skanda, *Pārvatī*, *daughter of the mountain*,
Among the maidens of the fifty gods, the wives of the divine throngs,

[69]Cf. MarkP 83.18, 91.9.

The best wives of the sons and grandsons of the thousand sons of Kadru,
*Mother*, father, to be revered by the world, by throngs of gods and Apsarases in heaven,
Among the throngs of seers' wives, and among the wives of Yakṣas and Gandharvas,
Among the wives of Vidyādharas, and among virtuous human women,
Among these women, (you are) the refuge of all creatures.
You are reverenced in the triple world, O one who is honored by Kinnaras' songs;
She who is beyond conception, not to be measured : hail to you !
(You are) praised with these and other names, O Gautamī.
By your grace, may I freely (and) quickly be released from bondage.
Behold, O wide-eyed one, I take refuge at your feet.
You are able to effect release from all bonds.
Brahmā and Viṣṇu and Rudra, Candra, Sūrya, Agni, and the Maruts,
The Aśvins and the Vasus, the creator, the earth, the ten directions,
Cattle, collections of constellations, planets, rivers and lakes,
Streams and oceans, various Vidyādharas and serpents,
Likewise snakes and birds, hosts of Gandharvas and Apsarases:
All this whole world is said (to result) from the proclamation of the names of the goddess.
The well-composed man who recites this meritorious hymn to the goddess—
She *is* the goddess—he receives the foremost boon in the seventh month.
The goddess has eighteen arms, is adorned with heavenly jewels,
With all her limbs shining because of her necklace, ornamented with flames from her diadem.

O *Kātyāyanī*, you are praised (by me), O *boon-grantress*, coy-eyed one.
Hail to you, O *great-goddess*; well-pleased, may you attend upon me.
May you grant a boon, long life, increase, patience, and firmness."
Thus praised, the *great goddess Durgā*, whose valor is hard to surpass,
Came nigh unto Aniruddha in confinement.
The goddess, who is fond of her devotees, for the sake of Aniruddha's well-being,
Released the bound, brave Aniruddha (there) in Bāṇapura.
She pacified the brave, impetuous Aniruddha.
She manifested her grace, when Aniruddha was confined.
Having with the tip of her hand burst open the adamantine snare
Of the one who was bound with a serpent-noose, his mind carried away by Usā,
Then the goddess of gracious face spoke (these) words, by way of consolation,
To the brave Aniruddha, bound up in Bāṇapura.
"O Aniruddha, he whose weapon is the discus will release you from bondage soon; have patience;
Having cut off the thousand arms of Bāṇa, the pulverizer of Daityas will lead (you) to his own city."[70]
Then Aniruddha, delighted, his face as beautiful as the moon, again praised the goddess.
"Hail to you, O *auspicious, boon-granting* goddess!
Hail to you, O goddess, destroyer of the foes of the gods!
Hail to you, O *auspicious* one who goes where she wills![71]
Hail to you, O beloved one who desires the well-being of all!
Hail to you, who always put fear into enemies!
Hail to you, who effect release from bondage!

[70]The reference here is to Kṛṣṇa's impending rescue of Aniruddha.

[71]Somewhat more than half of the relevant manuscripts here, or after the next line, insert the following line (13** in App. I 35):
Hail to you, *crusher of the enemy of the gods, Mahiṣa* (*mahiṣasurārimardini*).

O *Brahmāṇi*, Indrāṇī, Rudrāṇī, past, future, and present, *auspicious*,

Protect me from all miseries; O *Nārāyaṇi*, praise be to you!

Praise be to you, O leader of the world, beloved, tranquil, great-vowed one!

Whose devotees are beloved, *mother of the universe*, *daughter of the mountain*, bearer of wealth (earth),

Protect me, wide-eyed one; O *Nārāyaṇi*, praise be to you!

Protect me from all miseries, O one who puts fear into Dānavas!"

The well-composed individual who recites this meritorious hymn to Aryā,

Free from all sin, goes to the world of Viṣṇu.

### 5. *From the Devi-Māhātmya*

As we turn now to the hymns of the DM itself, we face the following dilemma. On the one hand, our translation should be as unencumbered with critical apparatus as possible, allowing the hymns, as it were, to speak for themselves, approximating the rythmic flow of the text itself. On the other hand, as the hymns unfold, it would be convenient to be reminded of the historical resonances of particular phrases, which we have indicated in Parts I and II. In an effort to do partial justice to both of these considerations, we have here adopted the following method of annotation: whenever there occurs a phrase that has been discussed in Parts I or II, it is followed by an asterisk (*). Usually, the phrase will be a proper name, left untranslated, or an epithet in translation, the original of which may be recollected on the basis of our earlier discussion; where the underlying Sanskrit phrase is not obvious, we have provided the Sanskrit in parentheses. To encounter the hymns in this fashion, perhaps having reviewed the underscored phrases in the hymns translated above, is thus to approximate an encounter with the hymns in their original historical context. We shall offer some final remarks on such an encounter in our Conclusion.

## J. Brahmā-stuti[72]

In the first *carita*, when Brahmā hymns Yoganidrā, requesting her withdrawal from Viṣṇu so that he can slay Madhu and Kaiṭabha, he praises her as follows :

81.54 You are Svāhā*, you are Svadhā*, you are the exclamation Vaṣaṭ, having speech as your very soul.
You[73] are the nectar of the gods, O imperishable, eternal*(*nityā*) one; (you) abide* having the threefold syllabic moment (*mātrā*) as your very being.

55. (You are) the half-*mātrā*, steadfast*, eternal*, which cannot be uttered distinctly.
You are she; you are Sāvitrī (the Gāyatrī *mantra*); you are the Goddess, the supreme mother.

56. By you is everything supported, by you is the world created;
By you is it protected, O Goddess, and you always consume (it) at the end (of time).

57. At (its) emanation, you have the form of creation; at (its)protection, (you have) the form of steadiness;
Likewise at the end of this world, (you have) the form of destruction, O you who consist of the world !

58. You* (*bhavati*) are the great knowledge* (*mahāvidyā*), the great illusion* (*mahāmāyā*), the great insight* (*mahāmedhā*), the great memory,
And the great delusion, the great Goddess* (*mahādevī*), the great demoness.

59. And you are the primordial material* (*prakṛti*) of everything, manifesting the triad of constituent strands,
The night of destruction, the great night*, and the terrible night of delusion.

60. You are Śrī*, you the queen* (*īśvarī*), you modesty, you intelligence*(*buddhi*),characterized by knowing;

[72]The titles we here apply to the hymns in the DM are those given by Banerjea, J. N., "Some Aspects," p. 229, except for the third hymn, for which he gives no name, and which we here entitle with a portion of its distinctive refrain. Throughout we follow the reading of Vid, except as indicated; we correct obvious misprints without comment.

[73]For a discussion of the difficult readings in this and the following line, see Part I, s. v. "*nityā*".

Modesty*, well-being, contentment*, too, tranquillity* and forebearance* are you.

61. Terrible with your sword and spear, likewise with cudgel and discus,
With conch and bow, having arrows, sling, and iron mace as (your) weapons,

62. Gentle, more gentle than other gentle ones, exceedingly beautiful,
You are superior* to the high and low, the supreme queen*.

63. Whatever[74] and wherever anything exists, whether it be real or unreal, O (you) who have everything as your very soul,
Of all that, you are the power* (*śakti*); how then can you be (adequately) praised?

64. By you, the creator of the world, the protector of the world, who (also) consumes the world
Is brought under the influence of sleep* (*nidrā*); who here is capable of praising you?

65. Since Viṣṇu, Śiva, and I have been made to assume bodily form
By you, who could have the capacity of (adequately) praising you?

66. May you thus praised, O Goddess, with your superior powers
Confuse these two unassailable Asuras, Madhu* and Kaiṭabha*,

67. And may the imperishable lord of the world be quickly awakened,
And may his alertness be used to slay these two great Asuras.

## K. Śakrādi-stuti

At the end of the second *carita*, after the Goddess has vanquished Mahiṣa and his hordes, the gods, having Indra (Śakra) as first (*ādi*), praise her in this manner:

[74]For a discussion of this verse, see Part I, s. v. "*śakti*".

84.2 To the Goddess, by whom this world was stretched out through her own power*, whose body is comprised of the powers* of all the hosts of gods,
To Ambikā*, worthy of worship by all gods and great seers, are we bowed down with devotion; may she bring about auspicious things for us.

3. May she whose peerless splendor and might the blessed Viṣṇu, Brahmā, and Śiva cannot describe,
May she, Caṇḍikā*, fix her mind on the protection of the entire world, and on the destruction of the fear of evil.

4. May she who is Śrī* herself in the abodes of those who do good, Alakṣmī* (in the abodes) of those of wicked soul, intelligence* in the hearts of the wise,
Faith* (*śraddhā*; in the hearts) of the good, modesty* (*lajjā*; in the heart) of one of good birth, to you who are she are we bowed down: protect the universe, O Goddess!

5. How can we describe this unthinkable form of yours? Or your abundant, surpassing valor which destroys Asuras?
Or such deeds, which (you do) in battles, among all the throngs of Asuras and gods, O Goddess?

6. (You[75] are) the cause of all the worlds; although possessed of the three qualities, by faults you are not known; (you are) unfathomable even by Hari, Hara, and the other gods.
(You are) the resort of all, (you are) this entire world which is composed of parts, for you are the supreme*, original, untransformed Prakṛti*.

7. Whose complete divinity, by means of utterance, attains satisfaction at all sacrifices, O Goddess,
You are Svāhā*, and, (as) the cause of satisfaction of the multitude of manes, you are proclaimed by men to be Svadhā*.

8. You who are the cause of release* and of inconceivable austerities, your name is repeated by

[75]See our discussion of this verse, Part I, s. v. "*prakṛti*".

sages, who hold the essence of truth because they have restrained their senses,
Intent upon *mokṣa*, with all faults shed: you are this blessed*, supreme* knowledge*, O Goddess.

9. Having sound as your very soul, the resting-place of the utterly pure Ṛg and Yajur (hymns) and of the Sāmans, delightfully recited with the Udgītha,
The Goddess (are you), the blessed* triple (Veda), acting for the existence and production of all worlds, the supreme destroyer of pain.

10. O Goddess, you are insight*, knowing the essence of all scripture, you are Durgā*, a vessel upon the ocean of life (that is so) hard to cross, devoid of attachments.
(You are) Śrī*, whose sole abode is in the heart of Kaiṭabha's* foe (Viṣṇu); you are Gaurī*, whose abode is made with the one who is crowned with the moon (Śiva).

11. Slightly smiling, spotless, like the orb of the full moon, as pleasing as the lustre of the finest gold (is your face).
Wondrous it is that when the Asura Mahiṣa* saw (this) face, he suddenly struck it, his anger aroused.

12. But, O Goddess, the fact that Mahiṣa*, having seen (your face) angry, terrible with knitted brows, in hue like the rising moon, did not immediately
Give up his life is exceedingly wondrous—for who can live, having seen Death enraged?

13. O Goddess, may you*, the supreme* one, be gracious to life; enraged, you (can) destroy (whole) families in a trice.
This is now known, since the extensive power of the Asura Mahiṣa* has been brought to an end.

14. Honored are they among nations, riches are theirs, honors are theirs, and their portion of *dharma* does not fail,
Fortunate are they, with devoted children, servants, and wives, on whom you*, the gracious one, always bestow good fortune.

15. O Goddess, a virtuous man always attentively performs all righteous actions on a daily basis,
And then he goes to heaven by your* grace: are you not thus the bestower of rewards on the three worlds, O Goddess ?

16. O Durgā*, (when) called to mind, you take away fear from every creature; (when) called to mind by the healthy, you bestow an exceedingly pure mind.
O you who destroy poverty, misery, and fear, who other than you is always tender-minded, in order to work benefits for all ?

17. Since these (foes) are slain, the world attains happiness; although they have committed (enough) sin to remain in hell for a long time,
It is with the thought—"Having met death in battle, may they go to heaven"—that you assuredly slay (our) enemies, O Goddess.

18. Having, in fact, seen them, why do you* not (immediately) reduce all the Asuras to ashes, since you hurl your weapon at enemies ?
"Let even enemies, purified by (my) weapons attain (heavenly) worlds"—such is your most gracious intent even toward them.

19. Although the eyes of the Asuras were not destroyed by the terrible flashings of the light-mass of your sword, or by the abundant lustre of your spear-point,
While they looked at your face, which was like a portion of the radiant moon, that very thing happened.[76]

20. Your disposition, O Goddess, calms the activity of evil-doers, and this incomprehensible form (of yours) is unequalled by others,
And (your) valor is the slayer of those who have robbed the gods of their prowess: thus was compassion shown by you even towards enemies.

21. With what may this prowess of yours be compared? Where is there (such a) form, exceedingly charming (yet) striking fear into enemies?

[76] I.e., their eyes were destroyed.

Compassion in mind and severity in battle are seen in you, O Goddess, granter of boons* even upon the triple world.

22. This whole triple world was rescued by you, through the destruction of (its) enemies; having slain (them) at the peak of battle,
The hosts of enemies were led to heaven by you, and our fear, arising from the frenzied foes of the gods, was dispelled: hail to you!

23. With (your)spear protect us, O Goddess! And with (your) sword protect (us), O Ambikā*!
Protect us with the sound of (your) bell, and with the twang of your bow-string!

24. In the east protect (us) and in the west, O Caṇḍikā*; protect (us) in the south
By the wielding of your spear, likewise in the north, O queen*.

25. With your gentle forms which roam about in the triple world,
And with the exceedingly terrible ones, protect us, and also the earth.

26. And with the weapons, O Ambikā*, sword, and spear, and club, and the rest,
Which lie in your sprout (-like) hands, protect (us) on every side.

## L. The "Yā Devī" Hymn

At the beginning of the third *carita*, when the beleaguered gods recall the Goddess's promise to assist them, they repair to Mount Himavān and there offer the following hymn.

85.7 Hail to the Goddess, hail eternally to the auspicious* (*śivā*) great Goddess*!
Hail to Prakṛti*, the auspicious*! We, restrained, bow down to her.

8. To the terrible one, hail! To the eternal* Gaurī*, the supportress*, hail!
And to the moonlight, to the blissful one having the form of the moon, hail eternally!

9. To the auspicious one* (are we) bowed down; to growth, to success do we offer praise, alleluia !
To Nairṛti, to the Lakṣmī* of kings, to you, Śarvāṇī, hail, hail !

10. To Durgā*, the inaccessible further shore, the essential one who accomplishes all,
To fame, likewise the black one* (*kṛṣṇā*), the smoky one, hail eternally !

11. To the one who is exceedingly gentle and exceedingly terrible (are we) bowed down: hail, hail !
Hail to the support of the world, to the Goddess (who is) action: hail, hail !

12. The Goddess who is known as Viṣṇumāyā* in all creatures,
Hail to her, hail to her, hail to her: hail, hail !

13. The Goddess who is designated "consciousness" in all creatures,
Hail to her, hail to her, hail to her: hail, hail !

14. The Goddess who abides in all creatures in the form of intelligence*,
Hail to her, hail to her, hail to her: hail, hail !

15. The Goddess who abides in all creatures in the form of sleep*,
Hail to her, hail to her, hail to her: hail, hail !

16. The Goddess who abides in all creatures in the form of hunger,
Hail to her, hail to her, hail to her: hail, hail !

17. The Goddess who abides in all creatures in the form of shadow,
Hail to her, hail to her, hail to her: hail, hail !

18. The Goddess who abides in all creatures in the form of power*,
Hail to her, hail to her, hail to her: hail, hail !

19. The Goddess who abides in all creatures in the form of thirst,
Hail to her, hail to her, hail to her: hail, hail !

20. The Goddess who abides in all creatures in the form of patience*,
Hail to her, hail to her, hail to her: hail, hail !

21. The Goddess who abides in all creatures in the form of birth,
Hail to her, hail to her, hail to her: hail, hail !
22. The Goddess who abides in all creatures in the form of modesty*,
Hail to her, hail to her, hail to her: hail, hail !
23. The Goddess who abides in all creatures in the form of tranquillity*,
Hail to her, hail to her, hail to her: hail, hail !
24. The Goddess who abides in all creatures in the form of faith*,
Hail to her, hail to her, hail to her: hail, hail !
25. The Goddess who abides in all creatures in the form of loveliness,
Hail to her, hail to her, hail to her: hail, hail !
26. The Goddess who abides in all creatures in the form of Lakṣmī*,
Hail to her, hail to her, hail to her: hail, hail !
27. The Goddess who abides in all creatures in the form of activity,
Hail to her, hail to her, hail to her: hail, hail !
28. The Goddess who abides in all creatures in the form of memory,
Hail to her, hail to her, hail to her: hail, hail !
29. The Goddess who abides in all creatures in the form of compassion,
Hail to her, hail to her, hail to her: hail, hail !
30. The Goddess who abides in all creatures in the form of contentment*,
Hail to her, hail to her, hail to her: hail, hail !
31. The Goddess who abides in all creatures in the form of mother (*mātṛ*),
Hail to her, hail to her, hail to her: hail, hail !
32. The Goddess who abides in all creatures in the form of error,
Hail to her, hail to her, hail to her: hail, hail !
33. She who is the governess of the senses in all creatures,
And constantly in the elements, to the Goddess of pervasiveness, hail, hail !

34. She who abides*, having pervaded this whole world in the form of mind,
Hail to her, hail to her, hail to her: hail, hail !

35. Praised of yore by the gods because refuge was desired, similarly praised by the lord of gods day after day,
May she, the queen*, the cause of what is bright, accomplish for us bright things, auspicious things: may she destroy misfortunes.

36. She, the ruler* (*īśā*), is now reverenced by us, the gods, who are tormented by haughty demons.
And at this very moment, she who has been called to mind by us, whose bodies are prostrated in devotion (*bhakti*), destroys all (our) misfortunes.[77]

## M. Nārāyaṇī-stuti

At the conclusion of the third *carita*, after the Goddess has disposed of Śumbha and Niśumbha, but before the *phalaśruti* and concluding portion of the frame story, she is hymned by the gods as follows.

91.2. O Goddess, who takes away the sufferings of those who take refuge (in you), be gracious; be gracious, O mother of the entire world.
Be gracious, O queen of all*, protect all; you are the queen*, O Goddess, of all that does and does not move.

3. You have become the sole support of the world, for you abide* in the form of the earth.
By you who exist in the form of water, all this (universe) is filled up, O one of inviolable valor.

4. You are the power* of Viṣṇu*, of boundless valor; you are the seed of all, the supreme* illusion*.
Deluded, O Goddess, is this entire (universe); you, (when) resorted to, are the cause of release (right here) on earth.

[77]As Pargiter remarks in a note on this verse, it is tempting to read *hantu*, "may she destroy," for *hanti*. Yet all our editions read *hanti*, thus perhaps emphasizing the Goddess's ready availability: when invoked with utter sincerity and devotion (*bhakti*), her aid is utterly certain; there are no further conditions, and therefore the indicative is more appropriate than the imperative.

5. All the (various) knowledges, O Goddess, are portions of you, (as is) each and every woman in the (various) worlds.
By you alone as mother*(*ambā*) has this (world) been filled up; what praise (can suffice) for you (who are) beyond praise, the ultimate utterance?
6. When you, the Goddess who has become everything, granting heaven and ultimate freedom,
Are praised, what fine words could (suffice) for the eulogy?
7. O (you) who abide in the heart of every individual in the form of intelligence*,
Granting heaven and ultimate freedom, Goddess Nārāyaṇī*, praise be to you !
8. O (you) who bring about the process of change, in the form of minutes, moments, and so forth,
The (very) power* (manifest) at the destruction of the cosmos, O Nārāyaṇī*, praise be to you !
9. O (you) who are blessed with every felicity, auspicious*, accomplishing every intent,
O protectress, three-eyed Gaurī*, O Nārāyaṇī*, praise be to you !
10. O (you), the eternal*, who become the power* of creation, sustenance, and destruction,
Abiding in the qualities of primordial matter, (actually) consisting of (those) qualities, O Nārāyaṇī*, praise be to you !
11. O[78] (you) who are mounted upon a chariot yoked to swans, having the form of Brahmāṇī*,
Sprinkling water in which *kuśa* has steeped, Goddess Nārāyaṇī*, praise be to you!
12. O (you) who carry a trident, moon, and snake, having as your conveyance a massive bull,
Having the form of Māheśvarī*, O Nārāyaṇī*, praise be to you !
13. O (you) who are surrounded by peacocks and cocks, faultless, (and) carrying an enormous spear,

[78]In this and the following verses, the Seven Little Mothers are praised (followed by our text's distinctive additions to this group) in the same order as they appear at 88.14ff.

Having the form of Kaumārī*, O Nārāyaṇī*, praise be to you!

14. O (you) who have taken up the best of weapons, conch and discus, club and bow,
Be gracious, O one with Vaiṣṇavī's* form; O Nārāyaṇī, praise be to you!

15. O (you) who have seized a great terrible discus, by whom the earth was upraised with (your) tusks,
Auspicious* (and) having the form of a boar*, O Nārāyaṇī*, praise be to you!

16. O (you) who set out to slay the demons, having the terrible man-lion form*
In conjunction with the rescue of the triple world, O Nārāyaṇī*, praise be to you!

17. O (you) who are crowned and have a great thunder-bolt, flaming with a thousand eyes,
Aindrī*, the destroyer of Vṛtra's life-breath, O Nārāyaṇī*, praise be to you!

18. O (you) who slew the mighty army of demons, having the form of Śivadūtī*,
Of fearful form, of mighty roar, O Nārāyaṇī*, praise be to you!

19. O (you) whose mouth is terrifying with its teeth, who are ornamented with a garland of skulls,
O Cāmuṇḍā*, crusher of Muṇḍa*, O Nārāyaṇī*, praise be to you!

20. O Lakṣmī*, modesty*, great-knowledge*, faith*, prosperity*, Svadhā*, firm one,
O great-night*, O great-knowledge*,[79] O Nārāyaṇī*, praise be to you!

21. O wisdom*, Sarasvatī, choicest one, well-being, Bābhravī, the dark one*,
O restrained one, be gracious, O queen*; O Nārāyaṇī*, praise be to you!

22. O (you) who have the very form of all, queen* of all, endowed with the power* of all,

[79]Veṅk and Jag here read *mahāmāyā*, "the great illusion" : see Part I, n. 438.

Protect us from dangers, O Goddess; O Goddess Durgā*, praise be to you!

23. May this gentle face of yours, adorned with three eyes,
Protect us from all ghosts;[80] O Kātyāyanī*, praise be to you!

24. That fearsome (trident), terrible with flames, laying waste the Asuras without remainder,
May (that) trident protect us from danger; O Bhadrakālī*, praise be to you!

25. That (bell) which destroys the demonic splendors, having filled the world with its sound,
May that bell, O Goddess, protect us from evils as if we were children.

26. That (sword) of yours, smeared with mud and the blood and fat of Asuras, gleaming with rays,
May that sword be for (our) welfare; O Caṇḍikā*, we are bowed down to you!

27. (When) delighted, you destroy all afflictions, but (when) angered, (you destroy) all longed-for desires.
No accident befalls men who have resorted to you, for those who resort to you have truly entered a refuge.

28. This destruction of great *dharma*-hating Asuras, which you have now accomplished, O Goddess,
Having multiplied your own body into many forms—O Ambikā*, what other (goddess) can do that?

29. In the (various) knowledges, in the scriptures (requiring) the lamp of discrimination, and in the primordial sayings, who other than you
Causes all this (world) to whirl around so much, in (this) pit of egoism, (this) pitch-black darkness?

30. Where (there are) demons and serpents of terrible poison, where (there are) enemies, where armies of Dasyus,
Also where forest-fire (rages) in the middle of the ocean, abiding* there, you protect all.

31. O queen of all*, you protect all; having all for your very soul, you are said to support all.

80 Or "creatures", or possibly "dangers" : see Part I, n. 427.

You* are worthy of praise by the lord of all; those who bow down in devotion to you, they become the refuge of all.

32. O Goddess, be gracious, protect us always from the fear of enemies, just as you have now promptly (saved us) from bondage by the Asuras.

Quickly may you bring the sins of all the worlds to tranquillity, and the great calamities born of the ripening of portents.

33. Be gracious, O Goddess, to those who are bowed down, O (you) who take away the afflictions of all.

O (you) who are worthy of praise by (all) who dwell in the triple world, be a boon-giver* to the worlds.

# Conclusion

In terms of the question that we originally posed for ourselves—"how is the Sanskritic tradition made contemporary, and how is the worship of the Goddess made traditional [in the DM]?"[1]—the annotated hymns of the DM that we have presented in Part III constitute our fullest answer. Building upon our historical inquiry into the words that the DM applies to the Goddess and her forms, and into the myths that the DM associates with her, they present in graphic form how the Vedic-Sanskritic tradition is operative in the devotional core of our text. If we are to encounter the text in a way that approximates the way in which it was encountered in its original context, there is no substitute for the careful reading of those hymns, deliberately appreciating the rich and highly nuanced associations that the annotated words possess, in addition to the more obvious manifestations of devotion.

It may, however, be appropriate to conclude our study with some general remarks about the DM and its view of ultimate reality. These remarks will inevitably gloss over many of the subtleties of that vision, but they may be helpful in indicating the DM's relationship to both previous and subsequent expressions of Hindu religiousness.

If we first think about the DM retrospectively, in relation to its antecedents, eight brief remarks seem to be in order. First, ultimate reality is understood by our text as feminine, as the Goddess. Although this seems to be the first occasion on which such an understanding is articulated in Sanskrit, the DM does not argue that ultimate reality is feminine, nor does it propose

[1]Proleg., p. 9.

it as a deliberate alternative to understanding ultimate reality as masculine. Feminine motifs are, of course, pervasive of the DM. But insofar as the DM is concerned to "demonstrate" anything, it is that ultimate reality is really ultimate, not that it is feminine.

Second, the ultimate reality that is the Goddess is clearly understood as transcendent. We have seen that our text is explicit about establishing the transcendent status of the Goddess at the very outset of its account, and that it does so by incorporating the familiar Madhu-Kaiṭabha myth. By characterizing her as *mahāmāyā* and *yoganidrā*, under whose influence Viṣṇu lies at *pralaya*, it is indicated that it is solely through her grace—her graceful withdrawal—that he can act at all. The transcendent status that the myth traditionally ascribes to Viṣṇu is here seen to apply at least equally well to the Goddess.

Third, the ultimate reality that is the Goddess is understood as an inward, interior phenomenon. At one level, this is evident in the application of the Vedic ritual words *svadhā* and *svāhā* to her; though she is never explicitly called *vāc*, we have seen that that association is implicit on a number of occasions in our text and that the Vāc hymn in the RV is frequently linked with the DM. More conclusively, the same inwardness emerges from the characterization of the Goddess as *nityā*, "the inwardly eternal one," and *śraddhā*, the movement of the heart in faith. It is found most clearly in her designation as *śakti*, the universal manifestation of power or capability, regardless of who or what is the external form of its manifestation.

Fourth, our text also affirms that ultimate reality is immanent, operative both *as* the material world and *in* the material world. The former is the implication of calling the Goddess *prakṛti*, a designation that has been of philosophical consequence. But we have seen that our text is not inclined to pursue speculative matters, and it focusses instead on the myriad ways that the Goddess is operative within the world. Foremost of these ways is as the great protectress, the one who responds to the cry of the devout for assistance in adversity. Thus it is that the threat of hostile forces is what occasions her action in all three *caritas*. Moreover, the structure of our text suggests that it is particularly appreciative of the Goddess's immanence, for it moves from the compact, terse establishment of her transcendent status in the Madhu-Kaiṭabha myth, through the more deliberate account of her mundane origin and initial activity in the Mahiṣa story, to the florid account of her worldly forms and accomplishments in the Śumbha-Niśumbha myth. Finally, we may note that the non-DM hymns presented in Part III, which were selected primarily for their preliminary integration of words and motifs that converge in the DM, and which individually involve varying conceptions of the divine, have as a common thread a similar appreciation of the divine's efficacy in the face of mundane adversity: all of them except for the Vāc hymn involve a request for protection and deliverance from such adversity,[2] which may range from nocturnal terrors and foes in battle, to the state of being imprisoned and the fear of being lost in dreary forests. The DM thus is not alone in its glorying in the immanent protectress.

Fifth, we may simply note that the three features we have just mentioned—transcendence, internality, immanence—can be simultaneously predicated of ultimate reality because of our text's understanding of the Goddess as *śakti.* There need be no paradox or contradiction between transcendence and immanence, nor between either of these and internality, because all of these are manifestations of power. The forms of power are many, but the fact of power is one.

Nevertheless—and this is the sixth point—at another level, ultimate reality is understood by the DM to be inherently paradoxical. Indeed, it is understood to be gloriously paradoxical, and that in a variety of ways. Thus the Goddess is affirmed to be both *mahāmāyā* and *mahāvidyā,* both beautiful and grotesque, both maternal and martial. The tension of such paradoxes may emerge most clearly in the character of the Seven Little Mothers, of whom the DM offers its particular interpretation, and whose general importance we have seen to lie "in their proximity to the central issues of family life: the exhilaration and risk of pregnancy, the innocence and joy of childhood, the horror of infant

[2]Obviously such a request is not the central feature of all these hymns. Nonetheless, it does seem to be the most recurrent theme, and that fact is what we are calling attention to here.

mortality, and the mystery with which this joy and horror are intermingled."[3]

Seventh, the language that our text employs in characterizing ultimate reality seems, with remarkable frequency, to have been previously employed in association with the Vedic figure of Agni, and a number of these motifs, as well as some additional ones, also converge on the epic figure of Skanda. It is perhaps too strong to say that the "identity" of Agni lives on in the figure of the Goddess, but particular names that our text applies to the Goddess and her forms have clearly been nourished in proximity to the god of fire, e.g., Svāhā, Kālī, and especially Durgā. Agni has also been involved with the Seven Little Mothers as a group, and the Śrī Sūkta suggests a relationship with Śrī and Lakṣmī as well. With regard to Skanda, the occurrence of the Mahiṣa myth, along with the appearance of so many familiar names (Śivā, Svāhā, Śakti, Lakṣmī, Gaurī, the Mothers) in the one epic version of his birth that knows Agni as his father can scarcely be coincidence. At a minimum, we may say that the vision of the Goddess as ultimate reality arises out of a symbolic matrix in which Agni and Skanda prominently participate.

Eighth, it is apparent that in its theological integration of the many into the One, our text has also integrated myths from diverse backgrounds. One of the myths comes out of a Vaiṣṇava context, another has been associated with the figure of Skanda, while the third has been known by the tribes of north India who also came to know of the heroic exploits of Kṛṣṇa Gopāla. But in our text, just as apparently diverse goddesses are seen to be forms of the Goddess, so are apparently diverse myths seen to be myths about her.

[3]Appendix A, p. 330. Although our study has not particularly emphasized the role of paradox in the DM, we have noted its presence on a number of occasions and they appear to bear out Carman's suggestion that although "not all religious systems feed on paradox, yet it may frequently be the case that what is an intellectual problem or a point of rational inconsistency for the theologian is crucial for the worshipper's awe and adoration. This religiously significant 'inconsistency' is often a direct indication of, or at least a clue to, an effort on the part of the adherents of this tradition to hold together in both thought and worship two different sides of the Divine nature": Carman, John B., *The Theology of Rāmānuja*, Yale University Press (New Haven and London, 1974), Yale Publications in Religion 18, p. 254.

These, then, are the highlights of the view of ultimate reality that crystallizes in the DM. Insofar as the DM is a Purāṇic phenomenon, these are the salient features of our text's "confirming elaboration" or "harmonious revision" of the Vedic truth. This is how that truth was re-presented in a contemporarily relevant way in the fifth-sixth century C. E.

But, as we have seen, the DM is more than a Purāṇic phenomenon, and it has been involved not just in the religious life of one historical era, but in the on-going religious life of many Hindus to the present day. The DM is a watershed as well as a crystallization, and it may be viewed prospectively as well as retrospectively.

Two final comments are appropriate in conjunction with this fact. The first pertains to the DM itself. We have seen that, though appearing in a Purāṇa as *smṛti*, the DM has functioned in the continuing religious life of Hindus more in the fashion of *śruti*, more, we have suggested, as the RV has functioned. Originally occurring as one particular "moment" in the historical unfolding of the Hindu religious tradition, that moment has been frozen, captured as if in a photograph, and the text has been subsequently addressed as an eternal, immutable scripture. It is tempting, therefore, to conclude that our text's view of ultimate reality, the Sanskritic side of which we have examined in the course of this study, has continued through the centuries as a vital presence in the life of some Hindus. Such a conclusion may, however, be unwarranted. We have seen in our Prolegomenon that the interpretation of an orally transmitted scripture is a complex matter, and surely the relationship between the personal religious views of an individual and the views of a text which he or she recites as an act of devotion is no less complex. It is to the investigation of such matters, as part of an inquiry into how our text has been received and understood by later generations, that we shall turn in a sequel to the present study.

The second comment pertains, not to our text, but to the view of ultimate reality that it articulates, i.e., to the conception of ultimate reality as feminine. That India has known various conceptions of ultimate reality in which the feminine figures prominently is clear. Pārvatī and Rādhā provide two ready instances, and in both cases there appears to be some overlap between their respective conceptualizations and that of the Goddess in the DM.[4] It is, however, the Śāktas who have placed the feminine most clearly at center stage, and our Prolegomenon has cited a number of studies of Śāktism that appreciate the seminal role of the DM in the development of the Śākta tradition. What is striking, on the basis of our study of the DM, is the number of features in the DM's view of ultimate reality that are transformed in mature Śāktism. This point may be made briefly by reflecting on a broader scale:

> It would be worth investigating whether...the dominant polarity in a Hindu conception of the Deity is reflected in the distinction drawn between the God and the Goddess. Both in Śākta and in Śankara's Advaita, that polarity seems to be between transcendent undifferentiated consciousness and the active power immanent in a universe of constant activity and infinite differentiation. Quite opposite evaluations of the two poles are made in the two systems, but the same polarity exists, whether expressed as the distinction between Śiva and Śakti, or between Para-Brahman and Māyā.[5]

If we take this as a succinct account of the central theme of Śāktism, then a number of features of the DM's view of the Goddess are, by contrast, thrown into bold relief. For instance, although our text is particularly interested in the Goddess's immanent character, it is explicit in establishing her transcendence as well. Moreover, though the figure of Śiva is known in our text, the Goddess bears no special relationship to him. In fact, she bears no special relationship to anyone other than her devotees. While each god has a *śakti*, our text avoids characterizing such forms as consorts, for the Goddess is Śakti, Power itself, beyond

[4]Cf. O'Flaherty, *Asceticism and Eroticism*, *passim*, and Brown, C.M., *op. cit.*, *passim*, esp. Part C, for Pārvatī and Rādhā, respectively.

[5]Carman, *op. cit.*, p. 246. Carman is proposing this investigation in order to shed light on the fact that this polarity is not the critical one either for Rāmānuja or for later Śrī Vaiṣṇavism: for the former, the polarity that is central is the one between God's supremacy and his accessibility, while, for the latter, it is the one between God's justice and his mercy, which are ascribed to God himself and his consort Śrī, respectively (*idem*).

the realm of being a consort to anyone.[6] Finally, the DM does not know the conceptualization that *śakti* is feminine and its possessor or vehicle masculine, for, as we have seen, the Goddess herself can put forth a *śakti.*[7]

There are, of course, some major continuities between the DM's view of the Goddess as ultimate reality and later Śākta views, such as that of the *Saundaryalaharī.*[8] Much more work is necessary, however, before we can trace with clarity the developments within Śākta thought, as well as the relationship of those developments to other sectarian orientations. What we can say at present is that the Sanskritic strand of the Hindu tradition has both fed into and been nourished by the DM's vision of ultimate reality, as has the faith of many Hindus. Ultimate reality has, presumably, remained constant, though how we shall conceptualize that fact is not easily determined. Even as compelling a formulation as the following—"The traditions evolve. Men's faith varies. God endures."[9]—requires some modification with regard to our study. For some, the One who endures is not God, but Goddess.

[6]One is tempted to say that she is "one only, without a second" (CU 6.2.1).

[7]Viz., Śivadūtī, q. v. in Part I.

[8]*The Saundaryalaharī or Flood of Beauty*, W. Norman Brown (ed. and tr.), Harvard University Press (Cambridge, 1958), HOS 43.

[9]Smith, *Meaning and End*, p. 173.

# Appendices

# APPENDIX A

## The Seven Little Mothers

Taking our cue from Gonda's remarks on the significance of specific names applied to divine figures,[1] the primary focus of Part I of our study has been on the DM's use of epithets: we have structured our investigation around individual epithets, so that we could see the cluster of meanings associated with each one, given its earlier Sanskritic usage. One possibility that such a structure does not allow for is the significance of interrelationships between certain epithets. The more important of these relationships—e.g., between Kālī and Cāmuṇḍā, between Mahāmāyā, Yoganidrā, and Prakṛti—we have commented upon in the course of our discussion. There is one such relationship, however, that does not admit of ready discussion according to the structure of Part I and yet clearly requires treatment, for our text is at least as aware of the relationship as of the individual figures involved in it. The name that our text applies to the relationship is *mātṛgaṇa* (88. 38, 39, 61), "the group of mothers," or simply *mātṛs* (88.44, 49; 89.6), "the mothers." However, because our text enumerates the basic *mātṛs* as seven, we have chosen to entitle our discussion of that relationship with another label that the Indian tradition has frequently applied to it, viz., *sapta-mātṛkās*, "the seven little mothers."[2]

[1]See *supra*, Proleg. pp. 75-78.

[2]It should be noted here that our ensuing discussion is deliberately narrow in its focus, not because it lacks larger reverberation, but for pragmatic reasons. Many of the larger issues have been explored in a work that was not

Let us start with the view of the DM itself. All the figures whom our text calls *mātṛs* appear only in the third *carita*[3] and have a quite specific role: when Śumbha, angered at Kālī's destruction of Caṇḍa and Muṇḍa, sends forth his legions against the Goddess, she multiplies her own forces:

> At that very moment, O king, in order to destroy the enemies of the gods,
> (And) for the sake of the well-being of the gods, very valorous and powerful
> *Śaktis*, having sprung forth from the bodies of Brahmā, Śiva, Skanda,
> Viṣṇu, and Indra, (and) having the form of each (*tadrūpaiḥ*), approached Caṇḍikā.
> Whatever form, ornament, and vehicle a (particular) god possessed,
> With that very form did his *śakti* go forth to fight the Asuras.[4]

We have quoted the description that our text gives of each of these *śaktis* under the appropriate epithet in Part I, so that here we may simply list the names that our text applies to the seven *śaktis*, and the gods from whom they emerge, in the ensuing verses (88. 14-20):

---

available to us at the time of completing the core of this study. It is J. N. Tiwari's *Studies in the Goddess Cults in Northern India, with Special Reference to the First Seven Centuries A. D.*, Ph.D. dissertation, The Australian National University, 1971, a revised version of which is forthcoming from Agam Prakashan (Delhi) under the title *Goddess Cults in Ancient India.* Tiwari's treatment of the Mātṛs far surpasses our Appendix A in both scope and detail. We have nonetheless retained our discussion here as a synoptic effort to illuminate a particular facet of the DM, while referring readers to Tiwari's definitive discussion for further details.

[3]The one potential exception to this statement—the occurrence of *maheśvarī* at 84.31—proves upon closer examination actually to confirm it, for *maheśvarī*, "the great queen," is an appelation that could apply to the Goddess at virtually any point in our text. All the references in the third episode, however, are to *māheśvarī*, which has the quite different meaning and specific characterization of "one who (or the *śakti* which) is related to Maheśvara (Śiva)."

[4]88.11-13. This formulation presents an interesting development, indeed reversal, of the events in the second *carita*. There (82.8ff.) a multitude of gods had contributed their respective *tejas's* to the constitution of the Goddess.

Out of Brahmā: Brahmāṇī
Out of Śiva: Māheśvarī
Out of Skanda: Kaumārī
Out of Viṣṇu: Vaiṣṇavī
Out of Viṣṇu's boar-form incarnation: Vārāhī
Out of Viṣṇu's man-lion incarnation: Nārasiṃhī
Out of Indra: Aindrī

To this group of seven, our text makes an interesting addition: when Śiva, who was surrounded by these *śaktis*, asked Caṇḍikā to send them forth to kill Asuras for his gratification (88. 21), Caṇḍikā's own body put forth a *śakti*, which sent Śiva to summon the Asuras to battle (88. 22).[5] As we have seen in Part I, because Caṇḍikā's *śakti* engaged Śiva as messenger, she is known as Śivadūtī (88. 27) and Śivadūtī is clearly distinguished from that other, earlier (87.4ff.) emanation from Caṇḍikā, viz., Kālī (Cāmuṇḍā). Yet it is clear that all nine of these figures are fairly closely related, for, as we have seen in Part III, the Nārāyaṇī Stuti praises these *mātṛs* in consecutive *ślokas* (MarkP 91.11-18) in the same order as they appear at 88.14ff., at the end of which sequence there is a verse to Cāmuṇḍā (91.19). Similarly, while Kālī is clearly the primary agent in the demise of Raktabīja, the *mātṛs* seem to share in her basic character when they are described, after that demise, as "dancing about, intoxicated with (his) blood" (88.61). The view of our text, then, seems to be that there is a basic group of seven *mātṛs* who are *śaktis* of male deities, to which Śivadūti, *śakti* of the Goddess, is an addition that is a fairly easy extrapolation from the male model. Their primary role is to aid in the combat with Raktabīja, and with Niśumbha and his hordes, before being resumed into the Goddess (90.4).[6] Kālī (Cāmuṇḍā),

---

Here, the Goddess exists from the outset of the *carita* and summons forth secondary forms of herself from the gods when the need arises. This parallels the DM's mythical movement that we have noted in Part II: from concern with the cosmic status of the Goddess in the first *carita*, through the account of her mundane origin and activity in the second, to the extensive description of her redemptive activity in the world in the third.

[5]See our rumination on this curious fact, Proleg., pp. 41-43, and n. 265.

[6]It is worth noting that our text thus strikingly contrasts the entrance and exit of the *mātṛs* in its drama, for whereas the *mātṛs* had been summoned out

while not formally one of the *mātṛs* and possessing a more distinct identity than any one of them, seems to bear at least an informal relationship to them.

In order to shed light on this "group of mothers," we will consider three bodies of evidence. The basic question in each of them is: how and where have "mothers" been considered as a group, and particularly as a group of seven? Who are these Seven Little Mothers?

## I

The first body of evidence, the Vedic, is also the least conclusive. In the RV, heaven and earth are called "mothers" (9.68.4), as are rivers (1.23.16), waters in general (10.18.10), and plants (10.97.4), all of which are, to the phenomenologist, feminine symbols,[7] but which here lack sharp characterization. With regard to specific enumerations, we have already seen[8] that one way of understanding Rudra Tryambaka is as "Rudra who has three mothers," while the other Vedic occurrence of "three mothers" seems simply to refer to the three-fold earth.[9] "Having seven mothers" is predicated of Soma at RV 9.102.4, where the significance is not entirely clear: it may refer to the seven prayers or pious thoughts (*dhītayaḥ*) offered to Soma at RV 9.8.4, which are also called his seven sisters (RV 9.10.7) or seven fingers (RV 9.66.8).[10] To the extent that Soma resembles Agni,[11] we might see here a reference to the seven tongues

---

of the bodies of the gods, their dismissal is accomplished, not by returning them whence they came, but by having them subsumed into the Goddess herself. The movement of the *mātṛs*, out of the many into the one, thus presents in miniature the central point of the DM, that the various goddesses previously known in the Sanskritic tradition are, in fact, different forms of the Goddess.

[7]Eliade, Mircea, *Patterns in Comparative Religion*, Rosemary Sheed (tr.), World Publishing Co. (Cleveland and New York, 1958, 1963), Chapters V, VII, VIII, *passim*. Note, however, C. M. Brown's shrewd remarks (*op. cit.*, p. 116n) on the complex psychological, cross-cultural, and historical problems involved in deciding what qualities are "naturally" masculine or feminine.

[8]In our discussion of the epithet "*ambikā*".

[9]We follow Geldner in his reading of RV 1.164.10.

[10]Again, we follow Geldner, his notes and references.

[11]Keith, *op. cit.*, p. 166.

of fire, the occurrence of which at MuU 1.2.4 we have already commented upon.[12] Finally, we should note Renou's remarks, alluded to earlier,[13] to the effect that the Vedic hymns themselves are often called "mothers", with their youthful fecundity being emphasized in such characterizations of them as "virgins," "desiring a male," "setting out on a tryst."[14]

## II

When we come to the second body of evidence, that afforded by the Mbh, the material is far richer, though its interpretation is correspondingly difficult. The crux of the interpretative problem stems from the fact that most of the relevant material occurs in Mbh 3.215-219, which comprises a portion of the larger story (3.207-221) of the origin of Skanda (Kumāra, Kārttikeya, Guha): that origin is a matter about which the Mbh itself is not entirely clear. To be sure, the Mbh account does seem to be the oldest existing account of Skanda's birth, one in which he "leaps suddenly into view," but the very subject matter poses problems, for "there is the strange notion that *a God is born.* Incarnations of God are legion, but the birth of a completely *new* God is unique."[15] While this Mbh account is reasonably consistent in affirming that Agni is the father of Skanda, the uniqueness of the situation creates a real uncertainty as to the identity of his mother: although "the first, 'real' mother is Svāhā, the personification of a sacrificial call..., there are [ also ]... quite a few [other] candidates for honorary motherhood." In sum, "the *Mahābhārata* version obviously has not sorted out who should be the right mother of this new God."[16] All of this has a bearing on our current point of inquiry because one of the candidates for the motherhood of Skanda is a group known simply as "the Mothers (*mātaraḥ*)," and another involves a group of seven women, the wives of the seven seers, subsequently known as the Kṛttikās.[17]

[12]In our discussion of the epithet "*kālī*"; cf. RV 10.5.5.

[13]Proleg., n. 235.

[14]Renou, *Études*, vol. I (1955), p 8.

[15]Mbh, van Buitenen tr., vol. 2, pp. 205, 206, his italics.

[16]*Ibid.*, pp. 205, 206, 207.

[17]As we shall see, there actually may be a third group (the daughters of Tapas) and one might wish to distinguish between the sages' wives and

In an effort to thread our way through this tangled mythology, let us deal with the latter group, the seers' wives, first, for their relation to the Seven Little Mothers is, at most, indirect and can be dealt with briefly. In fact, our sole reason for introducing them is because of the likelihood that they reflect an implicit association of "seven-ness" and the Mothers, an intuition, so frequent in mythological accounts, that apparent contrasts are actual identities. At one level, the seers' wives are at odds with the Mothers in the Mbh account, because of their apparently conflicting claims to honorary motherhood of Skanda: the former base their claim on the fact that six of them were unfairly divorced by their husbands who suspected them of having borne Skanda illegitimately;[18] the latter base their claim on their being "Mothers of the world (*lokasya mātaraḥ*)" and their having nursed Skanda as a child.[19] Yet, at another level, the two groups are not at odds but are one, for Skanda can say to both of them, in virtually identical words, "Indeed, you are my mothers and I am your son."[20] And for both groups there is a tangible reward given as a symbol of honorary motherhood: the wives' reward is their appointment as a constellation, the Kṛttikās or Pleiades,[21] while we shall examine the Mothers' reward below. It is through this explicit parallelism,

---

Kṛttikās, thereby creating a fourth group. In our ensuing discussion, we focus on the account of Skanda's birth in Mbh 3, because it is the account that provides the most information on the Seven Little Mothers. There are other accounts of his birth in the Mbh: at 9.43-45 and at 13.83-84, but in these the role of the Mothers is much reduced. (See n. 24 for the extent of their involvement at 9.43-45; at 13.83-84, the Seven Little Mothers motif seems limited to the appearance of the Kṛttikās as Skanda's nurses.) It may well be that the major role of the Mothers in the Mbh 3 account is a function of the text being all but convinced here that Agni is the father of Skanda (see n. 35 for the equivocations). The later Mbh accounts are more inclined to ascribe paternity to Śiva, though not denying Agni a role, and here, too some uncertainty regarding Skanda's parentage remains (see 9.45.85-86). We might thus infer a relationship between Agni and the Mothers, for to reduce the role of the former seems also to be to reduce (or eliminate) the role of the latter.

[18]Mbh 3.215.1-6; 219.1-5.

[19]Mbh 3.215.16-19; 217.7; 219.14.

[20]Cf. 3.219.6ab where Skanda replies to the seers' wives and 3.219.15ab where he replies to the Mothers.

[21]3.219.7-11.

reflecting an awareness that a cluster of seven females is somehow involved in the phenomenon of plural motherhood, that the Kṛttikās contribute to the identity of the Seven Little Mothers.[22]

In the course of the Mothers' appearance in this episode, three events bear particular mention, and even they may perhaps be summarized in the simple observation that " 'mother' is [here] used euphemistically, expressing the hope that the demoness will act as a loving mother to the child."[23] The first event exemplifies just such a transformation. When the gods heard of Skanda's birth and power, they urged Indra to slay him posthaste, but he shrank from the task and proposed an alternative:

> "... let all the Mothers of the world [*lokasya mātaraḥ*] attack Skanda this time, for they have the power and the will to slay him." The Mothers agreed and went. Seeing that he was without peer in puissance, their faces fell; and reflecting that he was invincible they sought refuge with him. They said: "You are our son. We hold the world [*asmābhir dhṛtaṃ jagat*]. Welcome us all, we are yielding milk, overcome with love."[24]

Skanda then obliged them, and they, in turn, protected him.

[22]Though the Kṛttikās thus bear only an oblique relationship to the Seven Little Mothers—which is reflected in the fact that the heart of their story, Agni's cohabitation with Svāhā who assumed the guise of six of the seers' wives (Mbh 3.213-214), has not proven relevant to our discussion here—they do come to occupy an important place in the Indian mythological edifice, on which see O'Flaherty, *Asceticism and Eroticism* , Appendix G: Index of Characters, s. v. "Kṛttikās".

[23]Mbh, van Buitenen tr., vol. 2, p. 207n. Cf. the euphemistic use of *śivā* in the DM and elsewhere.

[24]Mbh 3.215.16-18, van Buitenen tr. The suddenness with which the Mothers are introduced here is striking. They simply appear (this is their first appearance in the Mbh), play out their role in these few chapters, and disappear. There are a few isolated references to them elsewhere in the Mbh—there is a passing reference to seven multitudes of them (*saptamātṛgaṇāḥ*) dwelling on the Himavān at 9.43.29, a reference which occurs in close conjunction with a reference to Skanda nursing on the Kṛttikās (9.43.12), and there is a list of about two hundred *mātṛs* who accompany Skanda in battle at 9.45.3-35 —but the primary epic characterization of the *mātṛs* occurs in the chapters here under discussion.

While it would be tempting to conclude from this passage that the essentially malevolent Mothers only become benevolent when at a disadvantage, it is clear that even a benevolent Mother retains her horrific potential: "The one woman among all the Mothers who had been born from Fury [*krodhasamudbhavā*] guarded Skanda with a spike in her hand, as a nursing mother guards her son. The cruel daughter of the blood sea, who feasts on blood, embraced Mahāsena [Skanda] and guarded him like her son."[25]

The second event of note occurs when the text describes the companions of Skanda. Here it is clear that the Mbh is as uncertain of the Mothers' origin as it is of Skanda's. On the one hand, it is claimed that certain powerful maidens (*kanyāḥ*) were born from the impact of Indra's thunderbolt (*vajra*) upon Skanda's side(3.217.2). On the other, when (the same?) maidens immediately thereafter solicitously approach Skanda, they are described as "begotten by the fire named Tapas"[26] and their request is introduced with the phrase *mātara ūcuḥ*, suggesting that they are the same Mothers who had previously suckled him (3.215). In spite of this uncertainty, and in spite of the obscurity of the ensuing passage, its importance in establishing the identity of the Seven Little Mothers leads us to quote it in its entirety.

*The Mothers said:*

May we by your grace be the ultimate Mothers [*mātaraḥ uttamāḥ*] of all the world, and worshipful [*pūjyāḥ*] to it: do us this favor.

*Mārkaṇḍeya said:*

He replied: "Surely!" and repeated noble-mindedly: "Ye shall be of different kinds, propitious [*śivāḥ*] and unpropitious [*aśivāḥ*]." After making Skanda their son

[25]3.215.21-22ab, van Buitenen tr. The text of the heart of this description runs *lohitasyodadheḥ kanyā krūrā lohitabhojanā*.

[26]3.217.6ab: *yās tās tu ajanayat kanyās tapo nāma hutāśanaḥ*. A fire named Tapas had appeared (3.210-211) at the outset of the narrative of Skanda's birth where he is pictured as the offspring of five ascetics and is himself the creator of the Gods and sire of various other fires. The logic of his abrupt reappearance here—unless it be to link the procreative power of fire with the procreative power of the Mothers—is not obvious.

the band of Mothers went. Kākī, Halimā, Rudrā, and Bṛhalī, Āryā, Palālā, and Mitrā became the seven mothers of newborn sons [*śiśumātaraḥ*]; they had each a most terrifying, red-eyed, and frightening son by the grace of Skanda, named the Newborn [*śiśuḥ*]; the Eight Heroes[27] are called they who were born from the band of the Mothers of Skanda [*skandamātṛgaṇodbhavaḥ*]; and are called the Nine together with the Goat-face [*chāgavaktreṇa*]—know that the sixth face of Skanda from among the six heads[28] is a goat's face, king, and it is worshipped by the band of the Mothers. The foremost among his six heads is the one called Bhadraśākha, through which he created the divine [*divyāṃ*] Śakti.[29]

It is beyond the scope of this inquiry to examine the growth of the mythology and cult of Skanda,[30] but we may make the following observations on the basis of this passage. Once again those who bear children are conceived as a heptad, and though those who bear offspring here may not belong to the formal category of Mothers,[31] yet the juxtaposition of innocent

[27]The eighth figure may be the youth Viśakha who was born from the split in Skanda's side, caused by Indra's spear, at the end of the previous chapter (3.216.13); the name is applied to Skanda himself at 3.217.2, where he is the one round whom lesser Kumāras (*kumārakāḥ*) gather.

[28]In the earlier account (3.214) of the infant Skanda, he is described as having six heads, a fact that other versions of the myth correlate with his having the six Kṛttikās as mothers: cf. the O'Flaherty ref. at n. 22, and Hopkins, E. Washburn, *Epic Mythology*, Karl J. Trübner (Strassburg, 1915), p. 230. The imputation of a *chagavaktra* to Skanda is an affirmation that Agni is his father, for the latter had been so described at 3.215.23 when he played with the infant Skanda. At the beginning of this account of Skanda's companions, Skanda himself is called *chagamukha* (3.217.3).

[29]Mbh 3.217.7-13, van Buitenen tr. *Bhadraśākha* has been used as a name of Skanda just prior to this passage (v. 4). The "divine Śakti" may well be connected with the Goddess Śakti whom the seer Viśvamitra hymned in Skanda's presence (3.215.10) and the Śakti whom the fire called Śiva worships (3.211.2), but, as we observed under the epithet "*śakti*", in none of these cases is it made clear who, or what, this Śakti is.

[30]For an introduction to such matters, see Bhandarkar, R. G., *op. cit.*, pp. 150-151; Chattopadhyaya, *op. cit.*, pp. 192-197; Hopkins, E. W., *op. cit.*, pp. 227-231; Sahai, *op. cit.*, pp. 99-117. For a full study, see Sinha, Kanchan, *Kārttikeya in Indian Art and Literature*, Sundeep (Delhi, 1979).

[31]The text implies this by referring to the departure of the Mothers before listing the seven figures who bore sons; also, the names of these seven figures

and horrific motifs in infancy is patent. Furthermore, the Mothers and Skanda are involved in something of a symbiotic relationship whereby the Mothers produce offspring who are homologous with one of Skanda's forms, a form that the Mothers themselves worship. There is even a hint of an Oedipal relationship whereby Skanda, the child of the Mothers, sires lesser Kumāras (*kumārakāḥ*: 3.217.1) upon those same Mothers. And finally, another of Skanda's forms is affirmed to be the creator of power, conceived as the feminine Śakti, which may be an extension of the Mothers-Skanda symbiosis, but the precise meaning of which is not clear. In any case, the Mothers and the notion of maternity as a septuple phenomenon are here intimately bound up with the identity of Skanda.

The third event involving the Mothers is the one alluded to in conjunction with the Kṛttikās, viz., their reception of a tangible badge in recognition of their being granted honorary motherhood of Skanda. The account of their request and Skanda's response runs as follows:

*The Mothers said:*

Let ours be the estate of those who before had been fabricated [*prakalpitāḥ*] as the Mothers of this world [*mātara lokasyāsya*], and it shall be no more theirs. Let us be worshipful to the world, and let *them* be not so, bull among Gods. They have robbed our progeny on your account, restore it to us ![32]

*Skanda said* [ :]

You cannot cherish progeny that have been given away. I'll bestow on you what other offspring you may desire.

*The Mothers said:*

We want to devour [*bhoktum*] the offspring of those Mothers —give them to us, them and their Gods who are different from yourself.

---

bear very little resemblance to names applied elsewhere to the Mothers. On the other hand, if the "Eight Heroes" (who are said to be born of the Mothers) include the previously mentioned seven sons known as Newborn (*śisuḥ*), then clearly the mothers of those seven sons *were* Mothers ( !).

[32]*prajāsmākaṃ hṛtās* [sic ] *tābhis tvatkṛte tāḥ prayaccha naḥ*.

*Skandă said:*

I give you the offspring, but you have spoken a dire thing [*kaṣṭam*]. Hail to ye—spare the offspring when they honor Ye well.... Afflict the young children of men in your various forms until they are sixteen years old.[33]

What seems to be transpiring here is that the Mothers seek to replace ordinary human mothers in their maternal, earthly role.[34] Skanda replies that this role has already been irrevocably assigned to human mothers, whereupon negotiations begin: if the Mothers cannot have the maternal role, then they want the offspring produced in that role. Skanda allows the legitimacy of this request, for all its hardness, and concludes the negotiations with a compromise: the Mothers may have jurisdiction over human progeny until they reach the age of sixteen.

In the balance of this chapter, the Mbh is concerned to show that, in the final actualization of this reward, Skanda's is the effective power: he grants the Mothers a "Rudra-like immortal soul [*raudrātmānam avyayam*]" to devour the offspring of mortals (3.219.23-24). This spirit (*puruṣa*) is called a Grasper (*graha*), and there follows a long passage correlating particular Graspers with particular Mothers. For our purposes, we may simply note some of the descriptions of these figures: one "aborts the foetus of women" (v.27); another "afflicts small children" (28); another "feasts gluttonously on children's flesh" (29); still another "enters a pregnant woman,... eats the foetus inside her and the mother gives birth to a snake" (36), and all of them "like flesh and strong liquor" (35). In order to propi-

[33]Mbh 3.219.16-20, 22, van Buitenen tr.

[34]Who is meant by "the Mothers of this world" in v.16 is not entirely clear, and one wonders why van Buitenen has employed capitalization in his translation, particularly since his note (p. 834) suggests that they are human mothers. In the Roy-Ganguli translation (*The Mahābhārata*, P. C. Roy [ed.], K. M. Ganguli [tr.], Bharata Press [Calcutta, 1927-32], nine vols.), the suggestion is made (following Nīlakaṇṭha ?) that the reference is to Brāhmī, Māheśvarī, etc., i.e., to the *śaktis* of various male deities (who, it will be recalled, are in the DM identical with the *mātṛs*). While this is possible, particularly in light of the Mothers' subsequent request (v. 19) for the *mātaraḥ* 'and their Gods who are different from you (*tvayā saha pṛthagbhūtā ye ca tāsām atheśvarāḥ*)," the interpretation we offer here seems to convey more consistently the sense of the dialogue and the logic of the conclusion reached.

tiate these figures, "who are malign for sixteen years, then turn benevolent" (41), "one should use oblations, incense, collyrium, thrown-offerings, and gifts, and especially the rite of Skanda. When thus propitiated they all bestow well-being on people, and long life and virility..., if properly honored with a *pūjā*" (43-44).

To summarize, then, the Mbh contribution to the identity of the Seven Little Mothers: there is a throng of females, known as Mothers, of indeterminate number, who are renowned for their physical strength and horrific appearance, but in whom the maternal instinct runs deep. When their procreative powers are emphasized, they are frequently enumerated in groups of seven. Their origin is not clear, for they are either the progeny of the Tapas fire, or the products of Indra's clash with Skanda: in either case, they are clearly assimilated to Agni who is, in one case, homologous with Tapas, and, in the other, the sire of Skanda.[35] The identity of the Mothers is closely intertwined with that of Skanda, with Skanda appearing as the offspring of the Mothers, and with the Mothers appearing as the devotees of Skanda; it is difficult, however, to know how much of this conception of an intertwined identity is intrinsic to the Mothers, and how much is a function of the text's fascination with Skanda in this episode. Finally, the Mothers, while potentially either benevolent or malevolent, have a distinct notoriety for the atrocities they wreak upon pregnant women and small children, and there is a cult of the Mothers which recognizes their power in this domain.

## III

The third body of evidence is the most eclectic, consisting of

[35]In light of the later, almost universal ascription of the fatherhood of Skanda to Śiva (see O'Flaherty, *Asceticism and Eroticism*, *passim*), it is interesting to note that this Mbh account is so consistent in ascribing this role to Agni. The only exceptions to this, where a hint of Rudra-Śiva's claim to fatherhood is evident, are: (1) at 3.218.25-30, where the crucial identification is "the brahmins call the Fire [Agni] Rudra, hence he [Skanda] is Rudra's son"; and (2) at 3.220.9-10, where the earlier account of Agni's and Svāhā's parentage is not denied, but the effective power is ascribed to Rudra and Umā, who had "permeated" (*samāviśya*) Agni and Svāhā. For further remarks on Śiva's "indebtedness" to Agni, see O'Flaherty, *Asceticism and Eroticism*, pp. 90-110.

assorted literary references, inscriptions, and sculptural representations. While the form of the evidence is diverse, the specific items converge sufficiently to provide substantial further insight into the identity of the Seven Little Mothers.

We have already seen that the Mbh record suggests the existence of a cult of the Mothers, and should any doubt remain, there is the sixth-century[36] testimony of Varāhamihira's *Bṛhat Saṃhitā* that "those who know the circle of Mothers [*mātṛmaṇḍalavidaḥ*]" constitute one of the most powerful sects of the time.[37] While the author does not here identify the Mothers, elsewhere he remarks that images of the "mothers are to be made with the cognizances of the gods corresponding to their names,"[38] implying that the Mothers are the *śaktis* of male gods, which approximates the DM's conception. To this cultic evidence, we might add Bāṇa's account of how Vilāsavatī, anxious for news of her son, visited a temple (*āyatana*) of the Mothers, and of how, when he subsequently returned, it was attributed to the favor shown by the Mothers.[39] In fact, we have the remains of at least one such temple, dating from the sixth century C.E., in Deogargh, where there are separate niches for individual images of the *mātṛs*, as well as a panel portraying the group and an inscription which begins: "May the group of Mothers, the mothers of the universe having their dwelling in... [mutilated]...and having prowess fit for the preservation of the world be for your welfare."[40]

While it is impossible for us to trace in detail the interplay between cultic activity and representational art with regard to the Mothers, it is clear that the presentation of seven of these goddesses as a group, with iconography closely approximating that given in the DM, is very common. Generalizations about such matters without reference to specific works of art are treacherous, so we may make reference to Sahai's fine discussion

[36]Banerjea, *Development*, p. 25.

[37]Text (*Bṛhat Saṃhitā* 60.19) and assessment thereof given by Hazra, *Studies*, p. 40n.

[38]*Bṛhat Saṃhitā* 57.56, quoted by Banerjea, *Development*, p. 504.

[39]*Kādambarī* text p. 199, Ridding tr. p. 330.

[40]Sahni, Daya Ram, "Deogarh Rock Inscription of Svamibhata," *Epigraphia Indica* 18 (1925-26), p. 127.

of the various *sapta-mātṛkā* representations,[41] and then simply quote his summary of iconographic trends :

> Earlier forms of the Mātṛkās in the Kuṣāṇa period are without any distinctive symbols and vehicles; they are rather shown standing or seated as ordinary female figures. They usually exhibit *abhaya mudrā* by their right hands, while the left hands either hold vessels (*kamaṇḍalu*) or are placed on the waists. They are flanked by two Āyudha-puruṣas, carrying [a] long spear in their left hands and exhibiting *abhayamudrā* by their right hands. Then certain changes are introduced even in the Kuṣāṇa period, i.e., the Mothers are associated with babies, either seated in their laps or on their knees or standing nearby, emphasizing their mother aspect. The two Āyudha-puruṣas continue to remain on either side of the Mātṛkās. Later on in the Gupta and the early medieval periods the Āyudha-puruṣas are replaced by the figures of Gaṇeśa and Vīrabhadra..., one of the forms of Lord Śiva himself. It is again in the Gupta period that the distinct attributes and the vehicles of the different Mātṛkās begin to appear; and consequently developed forms of the Mātṛkās are found in sculptural representations. Finally in more highly elaborate and developed forms, Brahmāṇī is four-faced...,Vārāhī is sow-faced and Nārasiṃhī is lioness-faced, exhibiting various weapons in their hands.[42]

Through all of these representations, it is worth noting that the standard identification of the particular Mothers differs somewhat from that offered by the DM, for ordinarily Cāmuṇḍā is portrayed as one of the basic seven,[43] replacing Nārasiṃhī in the DM list. Nonetheless, it is clear that there is a certain amount of flexibility in this matter: in his commentary on the above-noted *Bṛhat Saṃhitā* 57. 56, Utpala says that the "mothers" meant in the passage are Brahmī, Vaiṣṇavī, Raudrī (Māheśvarī), Kaumārī, Aindrī, Yāmī, Vāruṇī, and Kauberī, but that there are certain other mothers such as

[41] *Op. cit.*, pp. 207-219.
[42] *Ibid.*, p. 218.
[43] *Ibid.*, p. 208.

Nārasiṃhī, Vārāhī, and Vaināyakī.[44] Since even his basic list differs from the standard iconographic portrayal, as well as from the DM's list, it would appear that there was a "pool" of Mothers, of indeterminate number, from whom seven might be chosen for representation, and worship, in any particular context. That this is the case is also suggested by the fact that, while the usual visual portrayal of the Mothers is as a group of seven, the various Purāṇic lists often enumerate eight, or even sixteen.[45] And, as we have already seen,[46] the Mbh provides a list of the names of roughly two hundred *mātṛs*.

Given the floridity and kaleidoscopic nature of Indian mythology, this elasticity in the enumeration and identification of the Seven Little Mothers is not particularly unusual. What is striking, however, is the capacity that the Seven Little Mothers have shown *as a group*, apart from variations in the identity of individual goddesses, to transcend sectarian boundaries. As suggested by Sahai, the mature iconography of the *sapta-mātṛkās* has a strong Śaiva flavor to it, through the presence of Gaṇeśa, the son of Śiva, and Vīrabhadra, the form of Śiva responsible for destroying Dakṣa's sacrifice,[47] and there is no doubt that this is the predominant resonance of this representation. However, it has many other associations as well. For instance, in a Gupta inscription from Bihar, Skanda has maintained (or reaffirmed) his Mbh association with the Mothers,[48] while in the Gangdhar stone inscription of Viśvavarman, dated at 424 C.E., there is an apparent *rapprochement* of Viṣṇu with the *mātṛs*. This latter inscription is remarkable, not simply for its recording of a shrine of Viṣṇu in conjunction with an "abode" for the Mothers, but for the explicit characterization it offers :

> Also, for the sake of religious merit, the counsellor of the king caused to be built this very terrible abode... [mutilat-

[44]Cited by Banerjea, *Development*, p. 504.

[45]The various Purāṇic references are given by Sahai, *op. cit.*, pp. 207-208nn. Monier Williams (*A Sanskrit-English Dictionary*, New Edition, E. Leumann and C. Cappeller [collaborators], Clarendon Press [Oxford, 1899], s. v. "mātṛ") provides a convenient list of the names usually encountered.

[46]*Supra*, Appendix A, n. 24.

[47]For Gaṇeśa's identity, see Danielou, *op. cit.*, pp. 291-297. For one of the many marvelous accounts of Vīrabhadra's vendetta, see *Bhāgavata Purāṇa* 4.5.

[48]Fleet, J. F., *op. cit.*, p. 51.

> ed] ... (*and*) filled full of female ghouls, of the divine Mothers, who utter loud and tremendous shouts in joy, (*and*) who stir up the (*very*) oceans with the mighty wind arising from the magical rites of their religion.[49]

The mobility of the Seven Little Mothers moreover is not limited simply to the realm of "Hindu" deities. In the Khaṇḍagiri caves at Bhuvaneśvara, there is a series of Jain carvings dating from the late Gupta or early medieval period: one of these has along its rear wall two rows of carvings, the upper one of which is, not surprisingly, a representation of the first seven Tīrtaṅkaras. The lower row, however, consists of seven female figures, whose iconography shows them to be none other than our *sapta-mātṛkās*, complete with Gaṇeśa as guardian.[50] With regard to the Buddhists, it is clear that, in the general matter of the developing religious appreciation of the feminine, they have much in common with Hindus, primarily in the complex matter of the Tantra, but such matters exceed the scope of this study.[51] We cannot resist commenting, however, on the similarity, in both iconography and underlying motif, between the *mātṛs* and the Buddhist goddess Hāritī, "originally an ogress, an incarnation of destruction of the children, which [sic], in due course, came to be regarded as the goddess of fertility and child-birth, [and] is usually represented standing or seated with a child in her lap."[52] Beyond this, however, and more to our present point of inquiry, is the fact that the presence of the *sapta-mātṛkās* in the *Sādhanamālā* seems to attest to their incorporation into Buddhist cult practice, a conclusion that is supported by their appearance in a composite figure at the great Buddhist university of Nālandā.[53]

[49] *Ibid.*, p. 78. On purely impressionistic grounds, the tone of this passage strikes us as hardly that of mainstream Vaiṣṇavism!

[50] Majumdar, *HCIP*, vol. 3, pp. 418-419, 419n; Bhattacharyya, N., *op. cit.*, p. 66. For further instances of Jain employment of the *sapta-mātṛkā* motif, see Majumdar, *HCIP*, vol. 4, p. 300.

[51] The investigation of this common ground is the burden of Sircar (ed.), *op. cit.* Perhaps the best exploration of Tantra as a Hindu and Buddhist phenomenon is Bharati, Agehananda, *The Tantric Tradition*, Anchor Books (Garden City, N. Y., 1970).

[52] Sahai, *op. cit.*, p. 258.

[53] *Ibid.*, p. 208.

What, then, shall we make of these Seven Little Mothers and of their appearance in the DM? It seems to us, first, that the DM's conception of the *mātṛs* and of their role is unusually sharp and clear: they are summoned forth, fulfil their role, and exeunt. Particularly in comparison with the account of the Śumbha-Niśumbha myth at VāmanaP 30, wherein the *mātṛs* also figure, and which we have seen in Part II to be roughly contemporary with the DM, the picture is striking. In the VāmanaP account, the *mātṛs* come forth from various parts of the Goddess herself (30. 3-9), but then simply participate in the battle, without any dramatic denouement. In the DM, however, the status of the *mātṛs*, with regard both to the male gods and to the Goddess herself, is clearly defined, as befits its more intense effort to glorify the Goddess. And in contrast with the Mbh's testimony, the clarity of the DM's account of the *mātṛs* is overwhelming. In other respects, the identification, iconography, and characterization of the Seven Little Mothers—except for the somewhat increased stature it gives Cāmuṇḍā—the DM's view seems to be normative for the Indian tradition.

With regard to the Seven Little Mothers as a conceptualization of the divine, they seem to have undergone a process of development, at least so far as that conceptualization is expressed in Sanskrit,[54] that is fairly similar to a process that can be observed throughout Hindu religiousness, viz., the intertwining of the Sanskritic and non-Sanskritic. That the Mothers have Sanskritic roots, fragile though they may be, is clear. If those roots have a common sap running through them, that sap would seem to be Agni: he is implicitly there in the hymns to Soma, explicitly there in the enumeration of his tongues as seven and in his siring of Skanda, and implicitly there again in the Śaiva flavor of the *sapta-mātṛkā* motif. Yet it is also clear that these roots, while necessary to the identity of the Seven Little Mothers, can hardly be sufficient for it. One feels here, perhaps more than elsewhere in the DM's integrative vision, that the

[54]As our study has suggested, the issue of religious change is an enormous, and subtle matter. To say that the Seven Little Mothers have changed would be to make a (perhaps unwarranted) theological statement. But to say that the Sanskritic conceptualization of those Mothers has changed is simply to make an historical observation about textual material.

dynamism of faith stems not from Sanskritic but from popular sources. In fact, it seems to us that the Jain carvings described above constitute a graphic, almost palpable, presentation of the position of the Seven Little Mothers in Indian religious life. They are a group of seven, of somewhat indeterminate identity, whose importance lies in their proximity to the central issues of family life: the exhilaration and risk of pregnancy, the innocence and joy of childhood, the horror of infant mortality, and the mystery with which this joy and horror are intermingled. Over and above these simple but universal issues, one can address more cosmic concerns But no matter how those concerns are addressed—and India has provided a variety of ways—the domestic issues always form the bedrock from which they are addressed : the Seven Little Mothers are the lower register of Indian religiousness. Consequently, all efforts to "domesticate" the Seven Little Mothers, to put a particular sectarian stamp upon them, have proven futile. It seems likely that the Mbh account represents just such an effort, perhaps the first one, certainly the first one in Sanskrit, an effort to effect a *rapprochement* between Skanda and the *mātṛs*: the effort is "successful", but not irrevocable. Similarly, the DM has, as we have noted, a clear sense of the relationship between the Goddess and the *mātṛs*, but, for all its clarity, this, too, has failed to be the definitive statement, and the maternal mobility has continued. That this has been the case is perhaps the very significance of the Seven Little Mothers: because of the simple universality of the issues they speak to, they are relevant to virtually every context and sect; but because of that same universality, they cannot be permanently particularized by any one.

## APPENDIX B

### Correlation of Epithets and Myths According to Episode

Part I of our study has examined the resonance of individual epithets in the DM, on the basis of their Vedic and epic antecedents, as well as of the internal evidence that the DM affords. Part II has examined the integrative vision of the DM in terms of its myths: we have seen the Madhu-Kaiṭabha myth of the first *carita* to have a Vaiṣṇava background, the Mahiṣa myth (second *carita*) to be of "Skandic" or quasi-Śaiva provenience, while the Śumbha-Niśumbha myth (third *carita*) claims a Kṛṣṇa Gopāla background. In order to see at a glance if, and how, our text associates the epithets mythologically, we present here in tabular form the distribution of epithets according to *carita*. For details of the usage, one may consult the appropriate epithetical or mythological discussion.

| | Carita | | | | Carita | | |
|---|---|---|---|---|---|---|---|
| *Epithet* | 1 | 2 | 3 | *Epithet* | 1 | 2 | 3 |
| Caṇḍikā | 0 | 6 | 23 | Īśā | 0 | 0 | 3 |
| Ambikā | 0 | 10 | 15 | Pārvatī | 0 | 0 | 3 |
| Nārāyaṇī | 0 | 0 | 15 | Prakṛti | 1 | 1 | 1 |
| Kālī | 0 | 0 | 14 | Kātyāyanī | 0 | 0 | 3 |
| Bhagavatī | 2 | 3 | 4 | Mahāvidyā | 1 | 0 | 2 |
| Durgā | 0 | 2 | 5 | Vidyā | 1 | 1 | 0 |
| Vaiṣṇavī* | 0 | 0 | 7 | Vārāhī* | 0 | 0 | 3 |
| Mahāmāyā | 7 | 0 | 0 | Bhadrakālī | 0 | 2 | 1 |
| Bhavatī | 1 | 4 | 2 | Yoganidrā | 3 | 0 | 0 |
| Nityā | 4 | 0 | 2 | Nidrā | 1 | 0 | 1 |
| Aindrī* | 0 | 0 | 6 | Viṣṇumāyā | 0 | 0 | 3 |
| Paramā | 2 | 3 | 1 | Sanātanī | 1 | 0 | 2 |
| Cāmuṇḍā | 0 | 0 | 6 | Mahādevī | 1 | 1 | 1 |
| Śivadūtī | 0 | 0 | 6 | Viśveśvarī | 1 | 0 | 2 |
| Īśvarī | 1 | 2 | 2 | Muktihetu | 1 | 1 | 1 |
| Śivā | 0 | 1 | 4 | Bhadrā | 0 | 0 | 2 |
| Sthitā | 2 | 0 | 3 | Aparājitā | 0 | 0 | 2 |
| Kaumārī* | 0 | 0 | 5 | Alakṣmī | 0 | 1 | 1 |
| Māheśvarī* | 0 | 0 | 5 | Mahārātri | 1 | 0 | 1 |
| Brahmāṇī* | 0 | 0 | 5 | Ambā | 0 | 0 | 2 |
| Śakti | 1 | 0 | 3 | Medhā | 0 | 1 | 1 |
| Gaurī | 0 | 2 | 2 | Puṣṭi | 1 | 0 | 1 |
| Lakṣmī | 0 | 0 | 4 | Śānti | 1 | 0 | 1 |
| Varadā | 1 | 1 | 2 | Kṣānti | 1 | 0 | 1 |
| Buddhi | 1 | 1 | 2 | Tuṣṭi | 1 | 0 | 1 |
| Lajjā | 1 | 1 | 2 | Kṛṣṇā | 0 | 0 | 2 |
| Parameśvarī | 1 | 1 | 2 | Tāmasī | 1 | 0 | 1 |
| Svadhā | 1 | 1 | 1 | Dhātrī | 0 | 1 | 1 |
| Svāhā | 1 | 1 | 0 | Jagaddhātrī | 1 | 0 | 1 |
| Śrī | 1 | 2 | 0 | Nārasiṃhī* | 0 | 0 | 2 |
| Śraddhā | 0 | 1 | 2 | Mahāmārī | 0 | 0 | 2 |
| Kalyāṇī | 0 | 0 | 3 | | | | |

*designates the Seven Little Mothers: see Appendix A.

# BIBLIOGRAPHY

Sanskrit texts are listed alphabetically by title except when a title is commonly associated with, or ascribed to, an individual author; in such instances, the texts are listed alphabetically by author. Where the original date of publication of a secondary source is significantly prior to the date of an edition we have used, we cite both dates.

## I. Sanskrit Texts and Translations


*Aitareya Āraṇyaka.* Ed. with intro., tr., notes by Arthur Berriedale Keith. Oxford: The Clarendon Press, 1909. Anecdota Oxoniensia Aryan Series No. 9.

*Aitareya Brāhmaṇa.*

1. *aitareyabrāhmaṇa.* [Bombay: Tukārām Tātya, 1890.]
2. *Aitareya Brāhmaṇa.* In *Rigveda Brāhmaṇas*, tr. by Arthur Berriedale Keith. Cambridge : Harvard University Press, 1920. HOS 25.

*Āpastamba Śrauta Sūtra.*

1. *The Śrauta Sūtra of Āpastamba.* Ed. by Richard Garbe. 3 vols. Calcutta: Asiatic Society, 1882-1902.
2. *Das Śrautasūtra des Āpastamba.* Übers. von W. Caland. 2 vols. 1-7 Buch, Göttingen: Vandenhoeck and Ruprecht, 1921; 8-15 Buch, Amsterdam: Koninklijke Akademie van Wetenschappen te Amsterdam, 1924.

*Atharva Veda.*

1. Śaunaka recension.
   a. *Atharva Veda Sanhita.* Herausgegeben von R. Roth und W. D. Whitney. Berlin: Ferd. Dümmler's Verlagsbuchhandlung, 1855.
   b. *Atharva-Veda Saṃhitā.* Tr. with a critical and exegetical commentary by William Dwight Whitney, revised and brought nearer to completion and edited by Charles Rockwell Lanman. 2 vols. Cambridge: Harvard University, 1905. HOS 7,8.
   c. [Selections.] *Hymns from the Atharva Veda.* Tr. by Maurice Bloomfield. Oxford: Clarendon Press, 1897. SBE 42.
2. [Paippalāda recension.] *The Kashmirian Atharva Veda.* Ed. by Leroy Carr Barret [Book 6 by F. Edgerton]. New Haven: American Oriental Society, 1906-40.

Bāṇa. *Harṣacarita.*
1. *Harṣa-Carita of Bāṇabhaṭṭa with the commentary of Raṅganātha.* Ed. and published by Śūranāḍ Kuñjan Pillai. Trivandrum: 1958.
2. *The Harshacarita of Bāṇabhaṭṭa.* Ed. by P. V. Kane. Delhi: Motilal Banarsidass, 1973.
3. *Harṣa-carita of Bāṇabhaṭṭa.* Tr. by E. B. Cowell and F. W. Thomas. Delhi: Motilal Banarsidass, 1961.

———. *Kādambarī.*
1. *Bāṇa's Kādambarī.* Ed. by Peter Peterson. Bombay: Central Book Depot, 1883. Bombay Sanskrit Series XXIV.
2. *The Kādambarī of Bāṇa.* Tr. with occasional omissions by C. M. Ridding. London: Royal Asiatic Society, 1896. Oriental Translation Fund New Series [V]II.

———. See Mayūra.

*Baudhāyana Dharma Śāstra.*
1. *The Baudhāyanadharmaśāstra.* Ed. by E. Hultzsch. Leipzig: F. A. Brockhaus, 1884. Abhandlungen für die Kunde des Morgenlandes [herausgegeben von der Deutschen Morgenländischen Gesellschaft VIII Band No. 4].
2. [*Baudhāyana Dharma Śāstra.*] Tr. by Georg Bühler in *The Sacred Laws of the Āryas* Part II. London: Clarendon Press, 1882. SBE 14.

[*Baudhāyana Gṛhya Sūtra.*] *The Bodhāyana Gṛihyasūtra.* Ed. by R. Sama Sastri. Mysore: University of Mysore, 1920. Oriental Library Publications, Sanskrit Series 32/55.

[*Bhagavadgītā.*] *The Bhagavad-Gītā.* Tr. and interp. by Franklin Edgerton. 2 vols. Cambridge: Harvard University Press, 1944. HOS 38, 39.

*Bhāgavata Purāṇa*
1. *Bhāgavatapurāṇa* [*with Curṇika commentary*]. 2 vols. Bombay: Veṅkaṭeśvara Press, 1949.
2. *Bagavadam ou Doctrine Divine, Ouvrage Indien, canonique; sur l'Être Supreme, les Dieux, les Géans, les hommes, les diverses parties de l'Univers,* & c. [traduit du Sanskrit d'après une version tamoule, par Méridas Poullé, un Malabare Chrétien]. Paris: [Foucher d'Obsonville,], 1788.

Bhāsa. *Bālacarita*
1. *Bālacaritam.* With intro. in English and Hindi and Hindi tr. by S. R. Sehgal. Delhi: Munshiram Manoharlal [1959].
2. *The Adventures of the Boy Krishna* (*Bāla-caritam*). In *Thirteen Trivandrum Plays Attributed to Bhāsa.* Tr. by A. C. Woolner and Lakshman Sarup. London: Oxford University Press: Humphrey Milford, 1930-31. Panjab University Oriental Publications 13. Vol. II, pp. 109-141.

Bhavabhūti. *Mālatīmādhava.*
1. *Mālatī-Mādhava, with the commentary of Jagaddhara.* Ed. by Ramakrishna Gopal Bhandarkar, second ed. Bombay: Government Central Book Depot, 1905.
2. *Mālatī and Mādhava; or The Stolen Marriage.* In *Select Specimens of the Theatre of the Hindus.* Tr. by Horace Hayman Wilson, third ed. London: Trübner and Co., 1871. Vol. II, pp. 1-123.

3. *Mālatīmādhava*. Ed. and tr. by M. R. Kale. Delhi: Motilal Banarsidass, 1967.

[*Bṛhad Devatā.*] *The Bṛhad-Devatā*. Critically ed. and tr. by Arthur Anthony Macdonell. 2 vols. Cambridge : Harvard University, 1904. HOS 5,6.

[*Devībhāgavata Purāṇa.*] *śrīmaddevībhāgavatam*. Kāśī: Paṇḍita Pustakālya, 1969.

*Devī-Māhātmya*. See *Mārkaṇḍeya Purāṇa*.

[*Gautama Dharma Sūtra.*] Tr. by Georg Bühler in *The Sacred Laws of the Aryas* Part I. Oxford : Clarendon Press, 1879. SBE 2.

[*Gopatha Brāhmaṇa.*] *Gopatha Brāhmaṇa of the Atharva Veda*. Ed. by Rājendralāla Mitra and Harachandra Vidyābhushana. Calcutta: Ganeśa Press, 1872. Bibliotheca Indica, New Series Nos. 215, 252.

*Harivaṃśa*.

1. *The Harivaṃśa, Being the Khila or Supplement to the Mahābhārata*. For the first time critically ed. by Parashuram Lakshman Vaidya. 2 vols. Poona: Bhandarkar Oriental Research Institute, 1969, 1971.
2. *Harivansa ou Histoire de la famille de Hari*. Tr. par A. Langlois. 2 vols. Paris: Oriental Translation Fund of Great Britain and Ireland, 1834-35. Oriental Translation Fund 36.

[*Hevajra Tantra.*] *The Hevajra Tantra: A Critical Study*. Ed. and tr. by David Snellgrove. 2 vols. London: Oxford University Press, 1959. London Oriental Series vol. 6.

*Hiraṇyakeśin Gṛhya Sūtra*.

1. *The Gṛihyasūtra of Hiraṇyakeśin, with extracts from the commentary of Mātṛidatta*. Ed. by J. Kirste. Vienna: Alfred Hölder, 1889.
2. *Hiraṇyakesin Gṛihya-Sūtra*. Tr. by Hermann Oldenberg in *The Gṛihya-Sūtras* Part II. Oxford: Clarendon Press, 1892. SBE 30.

[*Jaiminīya Brāhmaṇa.*] *Das Jaiminīya-Brāhmaṇa in Auswahl*. Text., Übers., Indices von W. Caland. Amsterdam: Johannes Müller, 1919. Verhandelingen der Koninklijke Akademie van Wetenschappen te Amsterdam, Afdeeling Letterkunde Deel I—Nieuwe Reeks, Deel XIX No. 4.

[*Jaiminīya Gṛhya Sūtra.*] *The Jaiminigṛhyasūtra, belonging to the Sāmaveda, with extracts from the commentary*. Ed. and tr. by W. Caland. Lahore: Motilal Banarsidass, 1922. The Punjab Sanskrit Series No. II.

[*Jaiminīya Upaniṣad Brāhmaṇa.*] *The Jaiminīya or Talavakāra Upanishad Brāhmaṇa*. Prepared from the edition in Roman script of Shri Hanns Oertel by Pandit Rama Deva. Lahore: D. A. V. College, 1921. [Dayanand Anglo-Vedic Sanskrit Series No. 3].

Kālidāsa. *Kumārasaṃbhava*. Ed. by Nārāyana Rāma Ācharya, 14th ed. Bombay: Nirṇaya Sāgara Press, 1955.

———. [*Raghuvaṃśa.*] *Raghuvaṃśa, with the commentary of Mallinātha*. With tr. and notes by Gopal Raghunath Nandargikar, 3rd ed. Bombay : Radhabai Atmaram Sagoon, 1897.

[*Kāṭhaka Gṛhya Sūtra.*] *The Kāṭhakagṛhyasūtra, with extracts from three commentaries*. Ed. by Willem Caland. Lahore: Research Department, D. A. V. College, 1925. Dayanand Anglo-Vedic Sanskrit Series vol. 9.

*Kūrma Purāṇa.*

1. *The Kūrma Purāṇa.* Text critically edited by A. S. Gupta and others. Varanasi: All-India Kashiraj Trust, 1972.
2. *The Kūrma Purāṇa (with English translation).* Ed. by Anand Swarup Gupta. Tr. by A. Bhattacharya, S. Mukherji, V. K. Varma [Verma], G. S. Rai. Varanasi: All-India Kashiraj Trust, 1972.

*Mahābhārata.*

1. *The Mahābhārata.* For the first time critically edited by Vishnu S. Sukthankar (and others). 19 vols. Poona: Bhandarkar Oriental Research Institute, 1933-1959.
2. *The Mahābhārata of Krishna-Dwaipayana Vyasa.* Ed. by Protap Chandra Roy. Tr. by Kisari Mohan Ganguli. 9 vols. Calcutta: Bharata Press, 1927-32.
3. *The Mahābhārata.* Tr. by J. A. B. van Buitenen. Vol. 1: *The Book of the Beginning.* Vol. 2: *The Book of the Assembly Hall, and the Book of the Forest.* Chicago and London: University of Chicago Press, 1973, 1975.

[*Mahānārāyana Upaniṣad.*] *The Mahānārāyaṇa-Upanishad of the Atharva Veda, with the Dīpikā of Nārāyaṇa.* Ed. by Colonel G. A. Jacob. Bombay: Government Central Book Depot, 1888. Bombay Sanskrit Series No. XXXV.

[*Mānava Dharma Śāstra.*] *The Laws of Manu.* Tr. by Georg Bühler. New York: Dover Publications, 1969.

[*Mānava Gṛhya Sūtra.*] *Das Mānava-gṛhya-sūtra, nebst Kommentar in kurzer Fassung.* Herausgegeben von Friedrich Knauer. St. Petersburg: l'Academie Imperiale des Sciences, 1897.

[*Mantra Brāhmaṇa.*] *Das Mantrabrāhmaṇa.* 1. Prapāṭhaka: Inaugural Dissertation Halle-Wittenberg von Heinrich Stönner. Halle: s. n., 1901. 2. Prapāṭhaka: Inaugural Dissertation Kiel von Hans Jörgensen. Darmstadt: C. F. Wintersche Buchdruckerei, 1911.

*Mārkaṇḍeya Purāṇa.*

1. [*Mārkaṇḍeya Purāṇa.* Edited by Śrīdharātmajatryambaka Gondhalekara. Poona (?) : Jagaddhihecchu Press, 1867.]
2. *mārkaṇḍeyapurāṇam.* [Edited by] Jīvānanda Vidyāsāgara. Calcutta: Sarasvatī [Press], 1879.
3. *śrīmanmārkaṇḍeyapurāṇam.* [Bombay: Veṅkateśvara Press, 1910.]
4. *The Mārkaṇḍeya Purāṇa.* Tr. with notes by F. Eden Pargiter. Calcutta: The Asiatic Society [1888-] 1904. Bibliotheca Indica New Series Nos. 700, 706, 810, 872, 890, 947, 1058, 1076, 1104.

*Mārkaṇḍeya Purāna. Devī-Māhātmya.*

1. *Saptaśatī or Chaṇḍī-Pāṭha (Devimāhātmya).* Translated from the Sanscrit into English by Cavali Vaṅkata Ramasswami, Calcutta: Columbian Press, 1823.
2. *Devimahatmyam.* Markandeyi purani sectio edidit latinam interpretationem annotationesque adiecit Ludovicus Poley. Berolini: Impensis F. Duemmleri, 1831.

3. Δουργα. μεταφρασθεισα εκ του βραχμανικου παρα Δημητρ Γαλανου. Αθηναισ: Γ. Χαρτοφυλακος, 1853.

4. "Translation of Books 81-93 of the Mārkandeya Purāṇa" by B. Hale Wortham. *Journal of the Royal Asiatic Society* New Series XVII part I (Jan. 1885), pp. 221-274.

5. *Devī-māhātmya: The Glorification of the Great Goddess.* [Text with English tr. and annotations] by Vasudeva S. Agrawala. Varanasi: All-India Kashiraj Trust, 1963.

6. *The Devī-Māhātmyam or Śrī Durgā-saptaśati.* [Ed. and translation by] Swāmī Jagadīśvarānanda. Madras: Śrī Rāmakrishna Math, 1969.

7. See Burnouf.

[*Matsya Purāṇa.*] *matsyamahāpurāṇam.* [Bombay: Veṅkateśvara Press, 1923.]

[Mayūra.] *The Sanskrit Poems of Mayūra.* Ed. with a translation and Notes and an Introduction together with the text and translation of Bāṇa's *Caṇḍīsataka* by George Payn Quackenbos. New York: AMS Press, 1965.

[*Nighantu.*] *The Nighantu and the Nirukta.* By Lakshman Sarup. 3 vols.: Introduction (1920); English Translation and Notes (1921); Sanskrit Text, with an Appendix showing the relation of the *Nirukta* with other Sanskrit works (1927). London: Oxford University Press.

*Original Sanskrit Texts: On the Origin and History of the People of India, Their Religion and Institutions.* Collected, translated, and illustrated by J. Muir, 2nd rev. ed., vol. IV. London: Trübner and Co., 1873.

*Pāṇini.* [*Aṣṭādhyāyi.*] *Grammatik.* Hrsg., übers., erläutert und mit verschiedenen Indices versehen von Otto Böhtlingk. Leipzig: H. Haessel, 1887.

*Ṛg Veda.*

1. *Ṛg Veda Samhitā: The Sacred Hymns of the Brahmans, together with the commentary of Sāyana.* Ed. by F. Max Müller, 6 vols. London: W. H. Allen and Co., 1849-1874.

2. *Der Rig-Veda.* Übers. von Karl Friedrich Geldner. Four vols. Cambridge: Harvard University Press, 1951-1957. HOS 33-36.

[*Ṛg Veda. Devī-Sūkta.*] *Devī-Sūkta.* [Text, tr., and notes by] Kshitish Chandra Chatterji. Calcutta: Calcutta University, 1945.

[*Ṛg Veda Khila.*] *Die Apokryphen des Ṛgveda* (*Khilāni*). Herausgegeben und bearbeitet von J. Scheftelowitz. Breslau: M. und H. Marcus, 1906. Indische Forschungen, herausgegeben von Alfred Hillebrandt, I. Heft.

[*Ṛg Veda Khila. Śrī Sūkta.*] "Śrīsūkta". [Intro., notes, and German tr. by] I. Scheftelowitz. ZDMG 75 (1921), pp. 37-50.

*Ṣaḍviṃśa Brāhmaṇa.* Introduction, tr., extracts from the Commentary and Notes, Proefschrift door Willen Boudewijn Bollée. Utrecht: Drukkerij A. Storm, 1956.

[*Sāṃkhya Kārikā.*] Tr. in Sarvepalli Radhakrishnan and Charles A. Moore (edd.), *A Source Book in Indian Philosophy.* Princeton: Princeton University Press, 1970, pp. 426-445.

[*Śaṅkha-likhita Dharma Sūtra.*] *Dharma-sūtra of śaṅkha-likhita.* [Ed.] by P. V. Kane. *Annals of the Bhandarkar Oriental Research Institute* Vol. VII, Parts I and II (1926), pp. 101-128.

*Śāṅkhāyana Āraṇyaka.*

1. *ṛgvedāntargataṃ śāṅkhāyanāraṇyakam.* [Poona:] ānandāśrama mudranālya, 1922. ānandāśramasaṃskṛtagranthāvaliḥ 90.
2. *The Śāṅkhāyana Āraṇyaka.* [Tr.] by Arthur Berriedale Keith. London: The Royal Asiatic Society, 1908. Oriental Translation Fund New Series Vol. XVIII.

*Śāṅkhāyana Brāhmaṇa.*

1. *ṛgvedāntargataṃ śāṅkhāyanabrāhmaṇam.* [Edited by] Gulābrai Vajeśamkar Chāyā. [Poona:] ānandāśrama mudraṇālya, 1911. ānandāśramasaṃskṛtagranthāvaliḥ 65.
2. *Śāṅkhāyana Brāhmaṇa.* In *Rigveda Brāhmaṇas*, tr. by Arthur Berriedale Keith. Cambridge: Harvard University Press, 1920. HOS 25.

[*Śāṅkhāyana Gṛhya Sūtra.*] Tr. by H. Oldenberg in *The Gṛhya Sūtras* Part I. Oxford : Clarendon Press, 1929. SBE 29.

[*Śāṅkhāyana Śrauta Sūtra.*] *Śāṅkhāyana-śrautasūtra.* Tr. by W. Caland, ed. with an introduction by Lokesh Chandra. Nagpur: International Academy of Indian Culture, 1953. Sarasvatī-Vihāra Series Vol. 32.

*Śatapatha Brāhmaṇa.*

1. *The Śatapatha-Brāhmaṇa, in the Mādhyandina-śākhā with extracts from the commentaries of Sāyaṇa, Harisvāmin, and Dvivedaganga.* Ed. by Albrecht Weber. Berlin: Ferd. Dümmler's Verlagsbuchhandlung, London : Williams and Norgate, 1855. The White Yajurveda edited by Albrecht Weber in Three Parts: Part Two.
2. *The Śatapatha-Brāhmaṇa, according to the text of the Mādhyandina School.* Tr. by Julius Eggeling. 5 vols. Oxford: Clarendon Press, 1882-1900 SBE 12, 26,41,43, 44.

[*Saundaryalaharī.*] *The Saundaryalaharī or Flood of Beauty.* Ed. and tr. by W. Norman Brown. Cambridge: Harvard University Press, 1958. HOS 43.

[*Skanda Purāṇa.*] *skandapurāṇa.* 7 vols. [Bombay:] Veṅkateśvara [Press, 1908-1910].

*Śrī Vishnu Sahasranāma Bashya* (*Commentary by Śrī Parāsara Bhaṭṭarya*). Tr. by L. Venkatarathnam Naidu. Tirupati: Tirumala Tirupati Devasthanams, 1965.

[*Taittirīya Āraṇyaka.*] *The Taittirīya Āraṇyaka of the Black Yajur Veda, with the Commentary of Sāyaṇāchārya.* Ed. by Rājendralāla Mitra. Calcutta: Asiatic Society of Bengal, 1872. Bibliotheca Indica New Series Nos. 60, 74, 88, 97, 130, 144, 159, 169, 203, 226, 263.

[*Taittirīya Brāhmaṇa.*] *kṛṣṇayajurvedīyaṃ taittirīyabrāhmaṇam śrīmatsāyaṇācāryaviracitabhāṣyasametam.* [Edited by] Nārāyaṇa Śāstri. 3 vols. [Poona:] Āpte, 1898. Ānandāśrama Sanskrit granthāvali 37.

[*Tāṇḍya Brāhmaṇa.*] *Tāṇḍya Mahābrāhmaṇa with the commentary of Sāyaṇa ācharya.* Ed. by Ānandachandra Vedāntavāgīśa. 2 vols. Calcutta: Asiatic Society of Bengal, 1870, 1874. Bibliotheca Indica New Series Nos. 170, 175, 177, 179, 182, 188, 190, 191, 199, 206, 207, 212, 217, 219, 221, 225, 254, 256, 268.

Upaniṣads.

1. *The Principal Upaniṣads.* Ed. and tr. by S. Radhakrishnan. London: George Allen and Unwin Ltd., 1968.
2. *The Thirteen Principal Upanishads.* Tr. by Robert E. Hume. Oxford, London, New York: Oxford University Press, 1971.

[*Vaikhānasa Dharma and Gṛhya Sūtras.*] *Vaikhānasasmārtasūtra: The Domestic Rules and Sacred Laws of the Vaikhānasa School belonging to the Black Yajurveda.* Tr. by W. Caland. Calcutta : Asiatic Society of Bengal, 1929. Bibliotheca Indica No. 251.

[Vālmiki. *Rāmāyaṇa.*] *The Rāmāyaṇa of Vālmīki, with the commentary (Tilaka) of Rāma-* [*varman*]. Ed. by Kāśināth Pāṇḍuraṅg Parab. 2 vols. Bombay: Nirṇaya-Sāgara Press, 1888.

*Vāmana Purāṇa.*

1. *The Vāmana Purāṇa.* Text critically ed. by A. S. Gupta and others. Varanasi: All-India Kashiraj Trust, 1968.
2. *The Vāmana Purāṇa (with English translation).* Ed. by Anand Swarup Gupta. Tr. by A. Bhattacharya, N. C. Nath, V. K. Verma. Varanasi: All-India Kashiraj Trust, 1968.

[*Vāsiṣṭha Dharma Śāstra.*] Tr. by Georg Bühler in *The Sacred Laws of the Aryas* Part II. Oxford: Clarendon Press, 1882. SBE 14.

[Vidyākara. *Subhāṣitaratnakoṣa.*] *An Anthology of Sanskrit Court Poetry: Vidyākara's "Subhāṣitaratnakoṣa".* Tr. by Daniel H. H. Ingalls. Cambridge: Harvard University Press, 1965. HOS 44.

[*Viṣṇu Dharma Sūtra.*] *The Institutes of Vishnu.* Tr. by Julius Jolly. Oxford: Clarendon Press, 1880. SBE 7.

*Viṣṇu Purāṇa.*

1. [*Viṣṇu Purāṇa with Ratnagarbha Bhaṭṭa's Commentary.* Bombay: Oriental Press, 1889.]
2. *The Vishṇu Purāṇa: A System of Hindu Mythology and Tradition.* Tr. by H. H. Wilson. Calcutta: Punthi Pustak, 1972. Also published as vols. VI-X of Wilson's *Works,* ed. by Fitzedward Hall. London: Trübner and Co., 1864-1877.

*Yajur Veda.*

1. [*Kapiṣṭhala-kaṭha Saṃhitā.*] *Kapiṣṭhalakaṭhasaṃhitā.* Critically ed. by Raghu Vira. Lahore: Mehar Chand Lachhman Das, 1932. Mehar Chand Lachhman Das Sanskrit and Prakrit Series vol. I.
2. [*Kāṭhaka Saṃhitā.*] *Kāṭhakam. Die Saṃhitā der Kaṭhaśākhā.* Herausgegeben von Leopold von Schroeder. 3 vols. Leipzig: F. A. Brockhaus, 1900-1910. Gedruckt auf Kosten der Deutschen Morgenländischen Gesellschaft.
3. [*Mādhyandina and Kānva Saṃhitās.*] *The Vājasaneyi-Sanhitā in the Mādhyandina-and the Kānva-sākha with the commentary of Mahīdhara.* Ed.

by Albrecht Weber. Berlin: Ferd. Dümmler's Verlagsbuchhandlung, London: Williams and Norgate, 1852. The White Yajurveda edited by Albrecht Weber in Three Parts: Part One.

4. [*Maitrāyaṇīya Saṃhitā.*] *Maitrāyaṇī Saṃhitā.* Herausgegeben von Leopold Schroeder. Leipzig: F. A. Brockhaus, 1881-1886. Gedruckt auf Kosten der Deutschen Morgenländischen Gesellschaft.

5. *Taittirīya Saṃhitā.*
   a. *kṛṣṇayajurvedīyataittirīyasaṃhitā sāyaṇācāryaviracitabhāṣyasametā.* [Ed. by] Kāśināthaśāstri Āgāśe. 9 vols. [Poona:] Āpte, 1900-1908.
   b. *The Veda of the Black Yajus School entitled Taittiriya Sanhita.* Tr. by Arthur Berriedale Keith. 2 vols. Cambridge: Harvard University Press, 1914. HOS 18, 19.

## II. Secondary Sources

Agrawala, R. C. "Some Sculptures of Durgā Mahiṣāsura-mardinī from Rājasthāna," *Adyar Library Bulletin* NS XIX 1-2 (May 1955), pp. 37-46.

———. "A Terracotta-Plaque of Mahishāsuramardinī from Nagar, Rajasthan," *Lalit Kalā* 1-2 (April 1955-March 1956), pp. 72-74.

Agrawala, V. S. "Editorial," *Purāṇa* I 2 (Feb. 1960), pp. 115-119.

———. "The Glorification of the Great Goddess," *Purāṇa* V 1 (Jan. 1963), pp. 64-89. Reprinted as the Introduction to *Devī-māhātmya: The Glorification of the Great Goddess.* [Text with English tr. and annotations] by Vasudeva S. Agrawala. Varanasi: All-India Kashiraj Trust, 1963.

———. "Original Purāṇa Saṃhitā," *Purāṇa* VIII 2 (July 1966), pp. 232-245.

———. "Purāṇa Vidyā", *Purāṇa* I 1 (July 1959), pp. 89-100.

Banerjea, Jitendra Nath. *The Development of Hindu Iconography.* Calcutta: University of Calcutta, 1956.

———. "Some Aspects of Śakti Worship in Ancient India," *Prabuddha Bharata* 59 (Mar. 1954), pp. 227-232.

———. "Some Folk Goddesses of Ancient and Mediaeval India," IHQ XIV (1938), pp. 101-109.

Banerji-Sastri, A. "Ancient Indian Historical Tradition," JBORS XIII 1 (Mar. 1927), pp. 62-79.

———. "Asura Expansion by Sea," JBORS XII 3 (Sept. 1926), pp. 334-360.

———. "Asura Expansion in India," JBORS XII 2 (June 1926), pp. 243-285.

———. "Asura Institutions," JBORS XII 4 (Dec. 1926), pp. 503-539.

———. "The Asuras in Indo-Iranian Literature," JBORS XII 1 (Mar. 1926), pp. 110-139.

Basham, A. L. *The Wonder That Was India.* New York: Grove Press, 1959.

Beane, Wendell. *Myth, Cult and Symbols in Śākta Hinduism : A Study of the Indian Mother Goddess.* Leiden: E. J. Brill, 1977.

Bedekar, V. M. "Principles of Mahābhārata Textual Criticism: The Need for a Restatement," *Purāṇa* XI 2 (July 1969), pp. 210-228.

Bhandarkar, D. R. "Epigraphic Notes and Questions," *Journal of the Bombay Branch of the Royal Asiatic Society* XXIII (1909), pp. 61-74.

Bhandarkar, R. G. *Vaiṣṇavism, Śaivism, and Minor Religious Systems.* Varanasi: Indological Book House, 1965. [Reprint of 1913 ed.]

Bharati, Agehananda. *The Tantric Tradition.* Garden City, N. Y.: Anchor Books, 1970.

Bhattacharya, A. K. "A Non-Aryan Aspect of the Devī," in D. C. Sircar (ed.), *The Śakti Cult and Tārā*, pp. 56-60.

Bhattacharyya, Narendra Nath. *History of the Śākta Religion.* New Delhi: Munshiram Manoharlal, 1973 [1974].

Bhattacharyya, Sivaprasad. "Indian Hymnology," in Haridass Bhattacharyya (ed.), *The Cultural Heritage of India.* 4 vols. 2nd rev. ed. Calcutta: Ramakrishna Mission Institute of Culture, 1953-62. Vol. IV, pp. 464-478.

Biardeau, Madeleine. "Letter to the Editor," subtitled "Dr. Madeleine Biardeau's rejoinder to Shri V. M. Bedekar's article written in reply to her article on the critical editions of the Mahābhārata and the Purāṇas," *Purāṇa* XII 1 (Jan. 1970), pp. 180-181.

———. "Some More Considerations about Textual Criticism," *Purāṇa* X 2 (July 1968), pp. 115-123.

———. "The Story of Arjuna Kārtavīrya without Reconstruction," *Purāṇa* XII 2 (July 1970), pp. 286-303.

Böhtlingk, Otto von und Roth, Rudolph. *Sanskrit-wörterbuch.* 7 vols. St. Petersburg: Buchdr. der K. Akademie der Wissenschaften, 1855-1875.

Bogatyrev, P. and Jakobson, R. "Die Folklore als ein besondere Form des Schaffens," *Donum Natalicium Schrijnen.* Nijmegen-Utrecht: N. v. Dekker and van de Vegt, 1929, pp. 900-913.

Bolle, Kees. "Reflections on a Purāṇic Passage," *History of Religions* II 2 (Winter, 1963), pp. 286-291.

Bowra, C. Maurice. *Heroic Poetry.* London: MacMillan and Co., Ltd., 1961.

Brown, Cheever Mackenzie. *God as Mother: A Feminine Theology in India.* [Foreword by Daniel H. H. Ingalls.] Hartford, Vt.: Claude Stark and Co., 1974.

Brown, W. Norman. "Class and Cultural Traditions in India," in Milton Singer (ed.), *Traditional India: Structure and Change*, pp. 35-39.

———. "The Content of Cultural Continuity in India," *Journal of Asian Studies* XX 4 (Aug., 1961), pp. 427-434. Reprinted as chap. 1 of his *Man in the Universe.*

———. *Man in the Universe: Some Continuities in Indian Thought.* Berkeley: University of California Press, 1966.

———. "Mythology of India," in Samuel Noah Kramer (ed.), *Mythologies of the Ancient World.* Garden City, N. Y. : Doubleday and Co., Inc., 1961, pp. 277-330.

———. "Proselytizing the Asuras," JAOS XXXIX 2 (April 1919), pp. 100-103.

Buck, Harry M. and Yocum, Glenn E. (edd.), *Structural Approaches to South India Studies.* Chambersburg, Pa.: Wilson Books, 1974.

Burnouf, Eugène. "Analyse et extrait du *Dévi Mahatmyam*, fragmens du *Markandéya Pourana*," *Journal Asiatique* ler série IV (1824), pp. 24-32.

Carman, John Braisted. *The Theology of Rāmānuja*. New Haven and London: Yale University Press, 1974. Yale Publications in Religion 18.

Chakravarti, Chintaharan. "The Mārkaṇḍeya Purāṇa: Editions and Translations," *Purāṇa* III 1 (Jan. 1961), pp. 38-45.

Chatterjee, A. K. "Characteristics of Skanda-Kārttikeya," *Indian Museum Bulletin* (Calcutta) IV 1 (1961), pp. 60-66.

Chatterji, S. K. "The Indian Synthesis, and Racial and Cultural Intermixture in India. Presidential Address, All-India Oriental Conference. Poona: s. n., 1953.

———. "Purāṇa Legends and the Prakrit Tradition in New Indo-Aryan," *Bulletin of the School of Oriental Studies* (*University of London*) VIII parts 2 and 3 (1936), pp. 457-466.

Chattopadhyay, K. P. "Ancient Indian Cultural Contacts and Migrations," *Our Heritage* 9 (1961), pp. 75-109.

Chattopadhyaya, Sudhakar. *Evolution of Hindu Sects: Up to the Time of Śaṃkaracārya*. New Delhi: Munshiram Manoharlal, 1970.

Coburn, Thomas B. "Consort of None, *Śakti* of All: The Vision of the *Devī-Māhātmya*," in John S. Hawley and Donna B. Wulff (edd.), *The Divine Consort*: *Rādhā and the Goddesses of India*. Berkeley: Berkeley Religious Studies Series 3, 1982 pp. 153-165.

———. "The Study of the Purāṇas and the Study of Religion," *Religious Studies* 16 3 (Sept. 1980), pp. 341-352.

Coomaraswamy, Ananda. "A Pallava Relief: Durgā," *Bulletin of the Museum of Fine Arts, Boston* XXV 148 (April 1927), pp. 22-25.

Crooke, W. *The Popular Religion and Folklore of Northern India*. Delhi :Munshiram Manoharlal, 1968. [Reprint of the 2nd ed., 1896.]

Danielou, Alain. *Hindu Polytheism*. New York: Pantheon Books, 1964. Bollingen Series LXXIII.

Das Gupta, Mrinal. "Early Viṣṇuism and Nārāyaṇīya Worship," IHQ VII (1931), pp. 93-116, 343-358, [735-759, incorrectly paged as] 655-679; VIII (1932), pp. 64-84.

———. "Śraddhā and Bhakti in Vedic Literature," IHQ VI (1930), pp. 315-333, 487-513.

Dasgupta, Shashi Bhushan. *Aspects of Indian Religious Thought*. Calcutta: A. Mukherjee and Co., 1957.

Dasgupta, Surendranath. *A History of Indian Philosophy*. Vol. I. Cambridge: University Press, 1932.

"Delhi scholar rebuts new Ramayana theory," in unidentified Delhi newspaper, Jan. 1976.

Deshpande, V. V. "Nature and Significance of Itihāsa and Purāṇa in Vedic Puruṣārtha Vidyās," *Purāṇa* XVI 1 (Jan. 1974), pp. 47-66; XVI 2 (July 1974), pp. 245-260, XVIII 2 (July 1976), pp. 197-211.

Dimmitt, Cornelia and van Buitenen, J. A. B. (edd. and tr.). *Classical Hindu Mythology: A Reader in the Sanskrit Purāṇas*. Philadelphia: Temple University Press, 1978.

Dumont, Paul-Émile. *L'Aśvamedha: Description du sacrifice solennel du cheval dans le culte védique d'après les textes du Yajurveda Blanc*. Paris: P. Geuthner, 1927.

———. "The Horse Sacrifice in the Taittirīya Brāhmaṇa: The Eighth and Ninth Prapāṭhakas of the Third Khaṇḍa of the Taittirīya-Brāhmaṇa with Translation," *Proceedings of the American Philosophical Society*, Vol. 92 (1948), No. 6, pp. 447-503.

Eliade, Mircea. *Patterns in Comparative Religion*. Tr. by Rosemary Sheed. Cleveland and New York: World Publishing Co., 1958, 1963.

———. *The Quest: History and Meaning in Religion*. Chicago and London: University of Chicago Press, 1969.

———. *The Sacred and the Profane*. Tr. by Willard R. Trask. New York: Harcourt, Brace and World, Inc., 1957, 1959.

Elmore, Wilber T. *Dravidian Gods in Modern Hinduism*. Hamilton, N. Y.: published by the author, 1915. Reprinted from University Studies of the University of Nebraska vol. XV No. 1 (1915).

Farquhar, J. N. *An Outline of the Religious Literature of India*. London: Oxford University Press, 1920.

Fleet, J. F. (ed.). *Gupta Inscriptions*. Bombay: Superintendent of Government Printing, 1888. Corpus Inscriptionum Indicarum Vol. III.

Ghate, V. S. *The Vedānta: A Study of the Brahma-sūtras with the Bhāṣyas of Śaṃkara, Rāmānuja, Nimbārka, Madhva and Vallabha*. Poona: Bhandarkar Oriental Research Institute, 1960.

Ghosh, Jogendra Chandra. "Ekānaṁśā and Subhadrā," *Journal of the Royal Asiatic Society of Bengal. Letters*. Vol. II 1 (1936), pp. 41-46 and plate 7.

Ghoshal, Pratāpachandra. *Durga Puja : With Notes and Illustrations*. Calcutta: Hindoo Patriot Press, 1871. "Originally published in the 'Hindoo Patriot' for the 23rd October, 1871."

Ghoshal, U. N. *Studies in Indian History and Culture*. Bombay: Orient Longmans, 1957.

Ghurye, K. G. *The Preservation of Learned Tradition in India*. Bombay: The Popular Book Depot, 1950.

Gonda, Jan. *Aspects of Early Viṣṇuism*. Utrecht: N. V. A. Oosthoeck's Uitgever's Mij, 1954.

———. *Epithets in the Ṛgveda*. 's-Gravenhage: Mouton and Co., 1959. Disputationes Rheno-Trajectinae IV.

———. "The Etymologies in the Ancient Indian Brāhmaṇas," *Lingua* V 1 (1955-56), pp. 61-85.

———. *Notes on Names and the Name of God in Ancient India*. Amsterdam, London: North-Holland Publishing Co., 1970. Verhandelingen der Koninklijke Nederlandse Akademie van Wetenschappen, Afd. Letterkunde, Nieuwe Reeks, Deel 75, No. 4.

Gonda, Jan. *Some Observations on the Relations between "Gods" and "Powers" in the Veda, apropos of the Phrase Sūnaḥ Sahasaḥ*. 's-Gravenhage: Mouton and Co., 1957. Disputationes Rheno-Trajectinae I.

Gopinatha Rao, T. A. *Elements of Hindu Iconography*. 2 vols. in 4. Madras: Law Printing House, 1914-16.

Gupta, Anand Swarup. "Constitution of the Vāmana-Purāṇa," *Purāṇa* IX 1 (Jan. 1967), pp. 141-194.

———. "In Memoriam: Dr. Vasudeva S. Agrawala," *Purāṇa* IX 1 (Jan. 1967), pp. 197-201.

———. "The Problem of Interpretation of the Purāṇas," *Purāṇa* VI 1 (Jan. 1964), pp. 53-78.

———. "A Problem of Purāṇic Text-Reconstruction," *Purāṇa* XII 2 (July 1970), pp. 304-321.

———. "Purāṇa, Itihāsa, and Ākhyāna," *Purāṇa* VI 2 (July 1964), pp. 451-461.

———. "Purāṇas and their Referencing," *Purāṇa* VII 2 (July 1965), pp. 321-351.

Gyani, Siva Datt. "The Date of the Purāṇas," *Purāṇa* I 2 (Feb. 1960), pp. 213-219; II 1-2 (July 1960), pp. 68-75.

Hacker, Paul. "Eigentümlichkeiten der Lehre und Terminologie Śaṅkaras: Avidyā, Nāmarūpa, Māyā, Īśvara," ZDMG C, pp. 246-286.

———. "*śraddhā*," *Wiener Zeitschrift für die Kunde Süd-und Ostasiens und Archiv für Indische Philosophie* 7 (1963), pp. 151-189.

———. "Über den Glauben in der Religionsphilosophie des Hinduismus," *Zeitschrift für Missionswissenschaft und Religionswissenschaft* 38 (1954), pp. 51-66.

———. *Untersuchungen über Texte des fruhen Advaitavāda, I. Die Schüler Śaṅkaras*. Wiesbaden: Franz Steiner Verlag, 1951. Akademie der Wissenschaften und der Literatur in Mainz, Abhandlungen der Geistes- und Sozialwissenschaftlichen Klasse, Jahrgang 1950, Nr. 26.

Hale, Wash E. *Ásura—in Early Vedic Religion*. Ph.D. dissertation: Harvard, 1980.

Hara, Minoru. "A Note on the Sanskrit Word *Ní-tya-*," JAOS 79 (1959), pp. 90-96.

———. "Note on Two Sanskrit Terms: *Bhakti* and *Śraddhā*," *Indo-Iranian Journal* Vol. 7 2/3 (1964), pp. 124-145.

Haraprasad Shastri, M. "The Maha-Puranas," JBORS XIV 3 (Sept. 1928), pp. 323-340.

Hastings, James (ed.). *The Encyclopedia of Religion and Ethics*. 13 vols. New York: Charles Scribner's Sons and Edinburgh: T. and T. Clark, 1908-27.

Hawley, John Stratton. *The Butter Thief*. Ph.D. dissertation: Harvard, 1978.

———. *Krishna, The Butter Thief*. Princeton: Princeton University Press, 1984.

———, and Wulff, Donna M. (edd.). *The Divine Consort : Rādhā and the Goddesses of India*. Berkeley: Berkeley Religious Studies Series 3, 1982.

Hazra, Rajendra Chandra. "The Problems Relating to the Śiva Purāṇa," *Our Heritage* I 1 (1953), pp. 46-68.

Hazra, Rajendra Chandra. "The Purāṇas," in Haridass Bhattacharyya (ed.), *The Cultural Heritage of India*. 4 vols. 2nd rev. ed. Calcutta: Ramakrishna Mission Institute of Culture, 1953-62. Vol. II, pp. 240-270.

———. *Studies in the Purāṇic Records on Hindu Rites and Customs*. Dacca: University of Dacca (Bulletin No. XX), [1940].

Hiriyanna, M. *Outlines of Indian Philosophy*. London: George Allen and Unwin Ltd., 1932.

Hopkins, E. Washburn. *Epic Mythology*. Strassburg: Karl J. Trübner 1915. Grundriss der Indo-Arischen Philologie und Altertumskunde (Encyclopedia of Indo-Aryan Research) III Band 1 Heft B.

Hopkins, Thomas J. *The Hindu Religious Tradition*. Encino and Belmont, Calif.: Dickenson Publishing Co., Inc., 1971.

Huizinga, Johan. "A Definition of the Concept of History," in R. Klibansky and H. J. Patton (edd.), *Philosophy and History*. Oxford: Clarendon Press, 1936, pp. 1-10, tr. by D. R. Cousin.

*The Hymnal of the Protestant Episcopal Church in the United States of America*. Greenwich, Conn.: The Seabury Press, 1940.

Ingalls, Daniel H. H. "The Brahman Tradition," in Milton Singer (ed.), *Traditional India: Structure and Change*, pp. 3-9.

———. "The *Harivaṃśa* as a *Mahākāvya*," in *Mélanges d'Indianisme, à la Mémoire de Louis Renou*. Paris: Éditions E. de Boccard, 1958. Publications de l'Institut de Civilisation Indienne fasc. 28, pp. 381-394.

———. "Śaṃkara on the Question: Whose is Avidyā?" *Philosophy East and West* III 1 (April 1953), pp. 69-72.

———. See Vidyākara ; Brown, C. M.; and Singer (ed.), *Krishna: Myths, Rites, and Attitudes*.

Izutsu, Toshihiko. *Ethico-Religious Concepts in the Qur'ān*. Montreal: McGill University Press, 1966. McGill Islamic Studies I.

Johnston, E. H. *Early Sāmkhya*. London: Royal Asiatic Society, 1937.

———. "Some Sāṃkhya and Yoga Conceptions in the Śvetāśvatara Upaniṣad," *Journal of the Royal Asiatic Society* (Oct. 1930), pp. 855-878.

Kane, Pandurang Vaman. *History of Dharmaśāstra (Ancient and Medieval Religious and Civil Law)*. 5 vols. Poona: Bhandarkar Oriental Research Institute, 1930-62. Government Oriental Series Class B No. 6.

Kapadia, B. H. "Some Aspects of Vāmana Purāṇa," *Purāṇa* VII 1 (Jan. 1965), pp. 170-182.

Keith, Arthur Berriedale. *The Religion and Philosophy of the Veda*. 2 vols. Cambridge : Harvard University Press, 1925. HOS 31, 32.

Kinsley, David R. "The Portrait of the Goddess in the *Devī-Māhātmya*," *Journal of the American Academy of Religion* XLVI 4 (Dec. 1978), pp. 489-506.

———. *The Sword and the Flute: Kālī and Kṛṣṇa, Dark Visions of the Terrible and the Sublime in Hindu Mythology*. Berkeley, Los Angeles, London: University of California Press, 1975.

Kirfel, Willibald. *Der Hinduismus*, [in Hans Haas (ed.), *Bilderatlas zur Religionsgeschichte*. Leipzig: A. Deichert, 1934.]

———. "Introduction to The Purana Pancalaksana," Tr. from the German by P. V. Ramanujasvami, *Journal of Śri Veṅkateśvara Oriental Institute* VII 2 (July-Dec. 1946), pp. 81-101; VIII 1 (Jan.-June 1947), pp. 9-33.

———. *Das Purāṇa Pañcalakṣana, Versuch einer Text-geschichte*. Bonn: Kurt Schroeder, 1927.

———. *Symbolik des Hinduismus und des Jinismus*. Stuttgart: Anton Hiersemann, 1959. Symbolik der Religionen, Ferdinand Hermann (ed.), IV.

Kluckhohn, Clyde. "Myths and Rituals: A General Theory," *Harvard Theological Review* XXXV (1942), pp. 45-79. Reprinted in William A. Lessa and Evon Z. Vogt (edd.), *Reader in Comparative Religion: An Anthropological Approach*. 2nd ed. New York, Evanston, London: Harper and Row, 1965, pp. 145-158.

Kumar, Pushpendra. *Śakti Cult in Ancient India* (*With Special reference to the Purāṇic literature*). Varanasi: Bhartiya Publishing House, 1974.

Lanman, Charles R. "Sanskrit Diction as Affected by the Interests of Herdsman, Priest, and Gambler," JAOS XX 1 (1899), pp. 12-17.

Lévi, Sylvain. Book review of *The Mahā Bhārata*, for the first time critically edited by Vishnu S. Sukthankar. *Journal Asiatique* CCXV 2 (Oct.-Dec. 1929), pp. 345-348; CCXXV 2 (Oct.-Dec. 1934), pp. 281-283.

Lévi-Strauss, Claude. *The Raw and the Cooked: Introduction to a Science of Mythology: I*. Tr. by John and Doreen Weightman. New York and Evanston: Harper and Row, 1969.

———. "The Structural Study of Myth," *Journal of American Folklore* LXVII (1955), pp. 428-444. Reprinted in William A. Lessa and Evon Z. Vogt (edd.), *Reader in Comparative Religion: An Anthropological Approach*, 2nd ed. New York, Evanston, London: Harper and Row, 1965, pp. 562-574.

Levitt, Stephan Hillyer. "A Note on the Compound *Pañcalakṣaṇa* in Amarasiṇha's *Nāmalingānuśana*," *Purāṇa* XVIII 1 (Jan. 1976), pp. 5-38.

Lord, Albert B. *The Singer of Tales*. Cambridge: Harvard University Press, 1960.

Macdonell, Arthur Anthony. *A History of Sanskrit Literature*. New York, London: D. Appleton and Co., 1929.

———. *Vedic Mythology*. Strassburg: K. J. Trübner, 1897. Grundriss der indoarischen Philologie und Altertumskunde (Encyclopedia of Indo-Aryan research), hrsg. von G. Bühler III Bd., 1 Heft A.

Majumdar, R. C. "Ideas of History in Sanskrit Literature," in C. H. Phillips (ed.), *Historians of India, Pakistan, and Ceylon*. London: Oxford University Press, 1961, pp. 13-28.

———(ed.). *The History and Culture of the Indian People*. 11 vols. Bombay: Bharatiya Vidya Bhavan, 1951-69.

Marriott, McKim. "Little Communities in an Indigenous Civilization" in

McKim Marriott (ed.), *Village India: Studies in the Little Community*, pp. 171-222.

———(ed.). *Village India: Studies in the Little Community*. The American Anthropological Association Vol. 57, No. 3, Part 2, Memoir No. 83 (June 1955). Comparative Studies of Cultures and Civilizations, No. 6, Robert Redfield and Milton Singer (edd.). "This volume is also published in a trade edition by the University of Chicago Press."

Matsubara, Mitsunori. *The Early Pāñcarātra with Special Reference to the Ahirbudhnya Saṃhitā*. Ph.D. dissertation: Harvard, 1973.

Mazumdar, B. C. "Durga: Her Origin and History," *Journal of the Royal Asiatic Society* 1906, pp. 355-362.

———. "The Origin and Character of the Purāṇa Literature," in *Sir Asutosh Mookerjee Silver Jubilee Volumes*, Orientalia. Calcutta: Calcutta University Press, 1925. Vol. III, part 2, pp. 7-30.

Mirashi, V. V. "A Lower Limit for the Date of the Devī-Māhātmya," *Purāṇa* VI 1 (Jan. 1964), pp. 181-186.

Monier-Williams, Monier. *A Sanskrit-English Dictionary*. New enlarged edition, E. Leumann and C. Cappeller (collaborators). Oxford : Clarendon Press, 1899.

Morrison, Barrie M. "Sources, Methods, and Concepts in Early Indian History," *Pacific Affairs* XLI 1 (Spring 1968), pp. 71-85.

Northrop, F. S. C. *The Taming of the Nations: A Study of the Cultural Bases of International Policy*. New York: The Macmillan Co., 1952.

O'Flaherty, Wendy Doniger. *Asceticism and Eroticism in the Mythology of Śiva*. London: Oxford University Press, 1973.

———. *Sexuality and Asceticism in the Mythology of Śiva in the Sanskrit Purāṇas*. Ph.D. dissertation: Harvard, 1967.

Oldenberg, Hermann. *Die Religion des Veda*. Stuttgart: J. G. Cotta, 1917.

———. *Ṛgveda: Textkritische und exegetische Noten*. 2 vols. Berlin: Weidmannsche Buchhandlung, 1909-12.

———. "Vedische Untersuchungen 4," ZDMG 50, pp. 448-450.

Pargiter, F. E. *Ancient Indian Historical Tradition*. London: Oxford University Press, 1922.

———(ed.). *The Purāṇa Text of the Dynasties of the Kali Age*. With introduction and notes. London: Oxford University Press, 1913.

Pathak, V. S. "Ancient Historical Biographies and Reconstruction of History," in *Problems of Historical Writing in India*, Proceedings of the Seminar held at the India International Center, New Delhi, Jan. 21-25, 1963, pp. 11-21.

Payne, Ernest A. *The Śāktas: An Introductory and Comparative Study*. Calcutta: Y. M. C. A. Publishing House and London: Oxford University Press, 1933.

Pusalker, A. D. "Were the Purāṇas originally in Prakrit?" in his *Studies in the Epics and Purāṇas*. Bombay: Bharatiya Vidya Bhavan, 1963. Bhavan's Book University 36, pp. 63-67.

Quackenbos, George Payn. Cf. Mayūra.

Raghavan, V. "Methods of Popular Religious Instruction in South India," in Haridass Bhattacharyya (ed.), *The Cultural Heritage of India*. 4 vols. 2nd rev. ed. Calcutta: Ramakrishna Mission Institute of Culture, 1953-62. Vol. IV, pp. 503-514. Reprinted in Milton Singer (ed.), *Traditional India: Structure and Change*, pp. 130-138.

———. "Variety and Integration in the Pattern of Indian Culture," *Far Eastern Quarterly* XV 4 (Aug. 1956), pp. 497-505.

Rai, Ramkumar. *Vālmīki-Rāmāyaṇa Kosha* (*Descriptive Index of the Names and Subjects of Rāmāyaṇa*). [In Hindi.] Varanasi: Chowkhamba Sanskrit Series Office, 1965. The Kashi Sanskrit Series 168.

Ramchandra Dikshitar, V. R. "The Purāṇas: A Study," IHQ VIII 4 (Dec. 1932), pp. 747-767.

Rao, K. L. Seshagiri. *The Concept of śraddhā* (*in the Brāhmaṇas, the Upanishads and the Gītā*), Ph.D. dissertation: Harvard, 1966.

Rapson, E. J. "In What Degree was Sanskrit a Spoken Language?" *Journal of the Royal Asiatic Society* 1904, pp. 435-456, followed by "Notes of the Quarter" (pp. 457-487), an account of the discussion of the same topic by T. W. Rhys Davids, F. W. Thomas, G. A. Grierson, and J. F. Fleet.

Redfield, Robert. "Community Studies in Japan and China: A Symposium —Introduction," *Far Eastern Quarterly* XIV 1 (Nov. 1954), pp. 3-10.

———. *The Folk Culture of the Yucatan*. Chicago: University of Chicago Press, 1941.

———. "The Natural History of the Folk Society," *Social Forces* Vol. 31 3 (March 1953), pp. 224-228.

———. *Peasant Society and Culture: An Anthropological Approach to Civilization*. Chicago: University of Chicago Press, 1956.

———. *The Primitive World and Its Transformations*. Ithaca, N. Y.: Cornell University Press, 1953.

———. "The Social Organization of Tradition," *Far Eastern Quarterly* XV 1 (Nov. 1955), pp. 13-21.

———, and Singer, Milton. "The Cultural Role of Cities," *Economic Development and Cultural Change* 3 1 (Oct. 1954), pp. 53-73.

Renou, Louis. *The Destiny of the Veda in India*. Delhi: Motilal Banarsidass, 1965.

———. *Études Védiques et Pāṇinéennes*. 17 vols. Paris: de Boccard, 1955-67. Publications de l'Institut de Civilisation Indienne fasc. 1, 2, 4, 6, 9, 10, 12, 14, 16, 17, 18, 20, 22, 23, 26, 27, 30.

———. *Religions of Ancient India*. New York: Schocken Books, 1953, 1968.

Riviere, Juan Roger. "European Translations of Purāṇic Texts," *Purāṇa* V 2 (July 1963), pp. 243-250.

Rocher, Ludo. "The Meaning of *purāṇá* in the Ṛgveda," *Wiener Zeitschrift für die Kunde Südasiens* XXI (1977), pp. 5-24.

Sahai, Bhagwant. *Iconography of Minor Hindu and Buddhist Deities*. New Delhi: Abhinav Publications, 1975.

Sahni, Daya Ram. "Deogarh Rock Inscription of Svamibhata," *Epigraphia Indica* 18 (1925-26), pp. 125-127.

Sarma, D. S. *Hinduism through the Ages*. 4th ed. Bombay: Bharatiya Vidya Bhavan, 1973. Bhavan's Book University 37.

Sastri, G. "The Cult of Śakti," in D. C. Sircar (ed.), *The Śakti Cult and Tārā*, pp. 10-16.

Scheftelowitz, I. (J.). See *Ṛg Veda Khila.*

Shanmugan Pillai, M. "Code Switching in a Tamil Novel," in Harry M. Buck and Glenn E. Yocum (edd.), *Structural Approaches to South India Studies* pp. 81-95.

Sharma, Dasharatha. "Verbal Similarities between the Durgā-Sapta-Śatī and the Devī-Bhāgavata-Purāṇa and other Considerations bearing on their Date," *Purāṇa* V 1 (Jan. 1963), pp. 90-113.

Shulman, David D. *Tamil Temple Myths: Sacrifice and Divine Marriage in the South Indian Śaiva Tradition.* Princeton: Princeton University Press, 1980.

Singer, Milton. "Beyond Tradition and Modernity in Madras," *Comparative Studies in Society and History* Vol. 13 2 (April 1971), pp. 160-195. Reprinted in his *When A Great Tradition Modernizes*, pp. 383-414.

———. "The Cultural Pattern of Indian Civilization: A Preliminary Report of a Methodological Field Study," *Far Eastern Quarterly* XV 1 (Nov. 1955), pp. 23-36. Reprinted in his *When a Great Tradition Modernizes*, pp. 67-80.

———. "The Social Organization of Indian Civilization," *Diogenes* XLV (1964), pp. 84-119. Reprinted (without bibliography) in his *When a Great Tradition Modernizes*, pp. 250-271.

———. "Text and Context in the Study of Contemporary Hinduism," *The Adyar Library Bulletin* (Madras) XXV (1961), pp. 274ff. Reprinted in his *When a Great Tradition Modernizes*, pp. 39-52.

———. *When a Great Tradition Modernizes : An Anthropological Approach to Indian Civilization.* New York, Washington, London: Praeger Publishers, 1972.

———(ed.). *Krishna: Myths, Rites, and Attitudes.* With a Foreword by Daniel H. H. Ingalls. Honolulu: East-West Center Press, 1966.

———(ed.). *Traditional India: Structure and Change.* Philadelphia: The American Folklore Society, 1959. Bibliographical Series Vol. X.

Sinha, B. P. "Evolution of Śakti Worship in India," in D. C. Sircar (ed.) *The Śakti Cult and Tārā*, pp. 45-55.

Sinha, Jadunath. *Shakta Monism: The Cult of Shakti.* Calcutta: Sinha Publishing House Pvt. Ltd., 1966.

Sinha, Kanchan. *Karttikeya in Indian Art and Literature.* Delhi: Sundeep 1979.

Sinha, Surajit. "Vaiṣṇava Influence on a Tribal Culture," in Milton Singer (ed.), *Krishna: Myths, Rites, and Attitudes*, pp. 64-89.

Sircar, D. C. *Studies in the Religious Life of Ancient and Medieval India.* Delhi: Motilal Banarsidass, 1971.

———(ed.). *The Śakti Cult and Tārā.* Calcutta: University of Calcutta, 1971.

Smith, Wilfred Cantwell. *Faith and Belief.* Princeton: Princeton University Press, 1979.

———. "Mankind's Religiously Divided History Approaches Self-Consciousness," *Harvard Divinity Bulletin* Vol. 29 1 (Oct. 1964), pp. 1-17. Reprinted "in slightly abridged form" in his *Religious Diversity*, pp. 96-114.

Smith, Wilfred Cantwell. *The Meaning and End of Religion: A New Approach to the Religious Traditions of Mankind.* New York: Mentor Books, New American Library, 1964. First published New York: Macmillan, 1963.

———. "Methodology and the Study of Religion: Some Misgivings." Iowa University School of Religion, Symposium on Methodology and World Religions, April 15, 1974. Mimeograph copy. Published in Robert D. Baird (ed.), *Methodological Issues in Religious Studies.* Chico, Calif.: New Horizons Press, 1975, pp. 1-25.

———. *Religious Diversity: Essays by Wilfred Cantwell Smith.* Ed. by Willard G. Oxtoby. New York, Hagerstown, San Francisco, London: Harper and Row, 1976.

———. "The Study of Religion and the Study of the Bible," *Journal of the American Academy of Religion* XXXIX 2 (June 1971), pp. 131-140. Reprinted "with minor alterations" in his *Religious Diversity*, pp. 41-56.

———. "Traditional Religions and Modern Culture." Address presented at the XIth Congress, International Association for the History of Religions, Claremont, Calif., Sept. 9, 1965. Mimeograph copy. Reprinted "in slightly abridged form" in his *Religious Diversity*, pp. 59-76.

Sφrensen, Sφren. *An Index to the Names in the Mahābhārata, with short explanations and a concordance to the Bombay and Calcutta editions and P. C. Roy's translation.* Delhi: Motilal Banarsidass, 1963. Reprint of the 1904 ed.

Srinivas, M. N. "A Note on Sanskritization and Westernization," *Far Eastern Quarterly* XV 4 (Aug. 1956), pp. 481-496.

———. *Religion and Society among the Coorgs of South India.* Oxford: Clarendon Press, 1952.

———. *Social Change in Modern India.* Berkeley and Los Angeles: University of California Press, 1966.

———. "The Social System of a Mysore Village," in McKim Marriott (ed.), *Village India*, pp. 1-35.

Staal, J. F. *Nambudiri Veda Recitation.* 's-Gravenhage: Mouton and Co., 1961. Disputationes Rheno-Trajectinae V.

———. "Sanskrit and Sanskritization," *Journal of Asian Studies* Vol. 22 3 (1963), pp. 261-275.

Sukthankar, V. S. *On the Meaning of the Mahābhārata.* Bombay: The Asiatic Society of Bombay, 1957.

Tagore, Rabindranath. *A Vision of India's History.* Calcutta: Pulinbari Sen, 1951.

Thieme, Paul. "On the Identity of the Vārttikakāra," *Indian Culture* 4 (1937-38), pp. 189-209. Reprinted in J. F. Staal (ed.), *A Reader on the Sanskrit Grammarians.* Cambridge and London: The MIT Press, 1972, pp. 332-356.

Thompson, Stith. *The Folktale.* New York: The Dryden Press, 1946.

Tiwari, Jagdish Narain. *Goddess Cults in Ancient India.* Delhi: Agam Prakashan, forthcoming.

———. *Studies in the Goddess Cults in Northern India, with Special Reference to the First Seven Centuries A.D.* Ph.D. dissertation: The Australian National University, 1971.

Toynbee, Arnold J. *The World and the West.* New York and London: Oxford University Press, 1953.

Tucci, G. "Earth in India and Tibet," *Eranos Jahrbuch* XXII (1953), pp. 323-364.

*Vaidika-padānukrama-koṣa.* 5 vols. in 16 parts. Lahore: Viśveśvarānanda Vedic Research Institute, 1935-65.

van Buitenen, J. A. B. "On the Archaism of the *Bhāgavata Purāṇa*," in Milton Singer (ed.), *Krishna: Myths, Rites, and Attitudes,* pp. 23-40.

———. See Dimmitt, Cornelia and van Buitenen, J.A.B., and *Mahābhārata.*

van der Leeuw, G. *Religion in Essence and Manifestation.* Tr. by J. E. Turner with Appendices to the Torchbook edition incorporating the additions of the second German edition by Hans H. Penner. 2 Vols. New York and Evanston: Harper and Row, 1963.

Vaudeville, Charlotte. "Aspects du Mythe de *Kṛṣṇa-Gopāla* dans l'Inde Ancienne," in *Mélanges d'Indianisme à la Mémoire de Louis Renou.* Paris: Éditions E. de Boccard, 1968. Publications de l'Institut de Civilisation Indienne fasc. 28, pp. 737-761.

———. "Evolution of Love-Symbolism in Bhagavatism," JAOS Vol. 82 (1962), pp. 31-40.

Viennot, Odette. "The Goddess Mahiṣāsuramardinī in Kushāna Art," *Artibus Asiae* (Ascona) 19 (1956), pp. 368-373.

von Bradke, Peter. *Dyaus Asura, Ahura Mazdā und die Asuras.* Halle: M. Niemeyer, 1885.

von Fürer-Haimendorf, C. "The Historical Value of Indian Bardic Literature," in C. H. Phillips (ed.), *Historians of India, Pakistan, and Ceylon.* London: Oxford University Press, 1961, pp. 87-93.

Watters, Thomas. *On Yuan Chwang's Travels in India.* Ed. by T. W. Rhys Davids and S. W. Bushell. 2 vols. London: Royal Asiatic Society, 1904, 1905.

Wayman, Alex. "Climactic Times in Indian Mythology and Religion," *History of Religions* IV 2 (Winter 1965), pp. 295-318.

White, Charles S. J. "Kṛṣṇa as Divine Child," *History of Religions* 10 2 (Nov. 1970), pp. 156-177.

Whitney, William Dwight. *The Roots, Verb-forms, and Primary Derivatives of the Sanskrit Language.* Leipzig: Breitkopf and Härtel and London: Trübner and Co., 1885. Bibliothek Indogermanischer Grammatiken Band II, Anhang II. Reproduced New Haven: American Oriental Society, 1945. American Oriental Series Vol. 30.

Wilson, Horace Hayman. "Analysis of the Puránas," in Vol. III of his *Works.* Collected and ed. by Reinhold Rost. London: Trübner and Co., 1864, pp. 1-155.

———. "A Sketch of the Religious Sects of the Hindus," *Asiatick Researches* XVI (1828), pp. 1-136; XVII (1832), pp. 169-313. Also published in Vol. I of his *Works* (1862).

———. "Two Lectures on the Religious Practices and Opinions of the

Hindus," delivered at Oxford, Feb. 27-28, 1840. Published in Vol. I of his *Works*.

Winternitz, M. *A History of Indian Literature*. Tr. by Mrs. S. Ketkar. Vol. I: Introduction, Veda, National Epics, Purāṇas, and Tantras. New York: Russell and Russell, 1971. First published Calcutta: University of Calcutta, 1927.

Wright, Arthur F. (ed.). *Studies in Chinese Thought*. The American Anthropological Association Vol. 55, No. 5, Part 2, Memoir No. 75 (December 1953). Comparative Studies of Cultures and Civilizations, No. 1, Robert Redfield and Milton Singer (edd.). "This volume is also published in a trade edition by the University of Chicago Press."

Zimmer, Heinrich. *Philosophies of India*. Ed. by Joseph Campbell. Princeton: Princeton University Press, 1951, 1969. Bollingen Series XXVI.

## III. Other Material

Carman, John B. Personal Communication, Feb. 2, 1976.

Clark, Walter. Index of Purāṇic Proper Names. Unpublished.

Ingalls, Daniel H. H. Personal Communications, variously dated, and undated.

# Index